THE
GOOD
KINGS

THE
GOOD
KINGS

ABSOLUTE POWER
in ANCIENT EGYPT
and the MODERN WORLD

KARA COONEY

Washington, D.C.

Since 1888, the National Geographic Society has funded more than 14,000 research, conservation, education, and storytelling projects around the world. National Geographic Partners distributes a portion of the funds it receives from your purchase to National Geographic Society to support programs including the conservation of animals and their habitats.

Get closer to National Geographic Explorers and photographers, and connect with our global community. Join us today at nationalgeographic .com/join

For rights or permissions inquiries, please contact National Geographic Books Subsidiary Rights: bookrights@natgeo.com

ISBN 978-1-4262-2196-5 (hardcover)
ISBN 978-1-4262-2197-2 (ebook)

Printed in the United States of America

21/MP-PCML/1

For Remy—
who is not afraid (of me)

CONTENTS

ANCIENT EGYPTIAN CHRONOLOGY

(After Ian Shaw, ed., *The Oxford History of Ancient Egypt* [Oxford: Oxford University Press, 2000].)

PREDYNASTIC PERIOD .... CA 5300–3000 B.C
Upper Egypt
Naqada III/Dynasty 0 .... ca 3200–3000 B.C.

EARLY DYNASTIC PERIOD .... CA 3000–2686 B.C.
1st Dynasty .... ca 3000–2890 B.C.
2nd Dynasty .... ca 2890–2686 B.C.

OLD KINGDOM .... 2686–2160 B.C.
3rd Dynasty .... 2686–2613 B.C.
4th Dynasty .... 2613–2494 B.C.
KHUFU .... CA 2589–2566 B.C.
5th Dynasty .... 2494–2345 B.C.
6th Dynasty .... 2345–2181 B.C.
7th and 8th Dynasties .... 2181–2160 B.C.

FIRST INTERMEDIATE PERIOD .... 2160–2055 B.C.

MIDDLE KINGDOM .... 2055–1650 B.C.
11th Dynasty .... 2055–1985 B.C.
12th Dynasty .... 1985–1773 B.C.
SENWOSRET III .... CA 1870–1831 B.C.
13th Dynasty .... 1773–after 1650 B.C.
14th Dynasty .... 1773–1650 B.C.

SECOND INTERMEDIATE PERIOD ..... 1650–1550 B.C.
15th Dynasty (Hyksos) .... 1650–1550 B.C.
16th Dynasty .... 1650–1580 B.C.
17th Dynasty .... ca 1580–1550 B.C.

NEW KINGDOM .... 1550–1069 B.C.
18th Dynasty .... 1550–1295 B.C.
AMENHOTEP IV/AKHENATEN .... CA 1352–1336 B.C.
NEFERTITI .... CA 1338–1336 B.C.
RAMESSIDE PERIOD .... 1295–1069 B.C.
19th Dynasty .... 1295–1186 B.C.
RAMSES II .... CA 1279–1213 B.C.
20th Dynasty .... 1186–1069 B.C.

THIRD INTERMEDIATE PERIOD .... 1069–664 B.C.
21st Dynasty .... 1069–945 B.C.
22nd Dynasty .... 945–715 B.C.
23rd Dynasty .... 818–715 B.C.
24th Dynasty .... 727–715 B.C.
25th Dynasty .... 747–656 B.C.
TAHARQA .... CA 690–664 B.C.

LATE PERIOD .... 664–332 B.C.
26th Dynasty .... 664–525 B.C.
27th Dynasty .... 525–404 B.C.
28th Dynasty .... 404–399 B.C.
29th Dynasty .... 399–380 B.C.
30th Dynasty .... 380–343 B.C.
2nd Persian Period .... 343–332 B.C.

PTOLEMAIC PERIOD .... 332–30 B.C.
Macedonian Dynasty .... 332–305 B.C.
Ptolemaic Dynasty .... 305–285 B.C.
CLEOPATRA VII PHILOPATOR .... 51–30 B.C.

ROMAN PERIOD .... 30 B.C.–A.D. 395

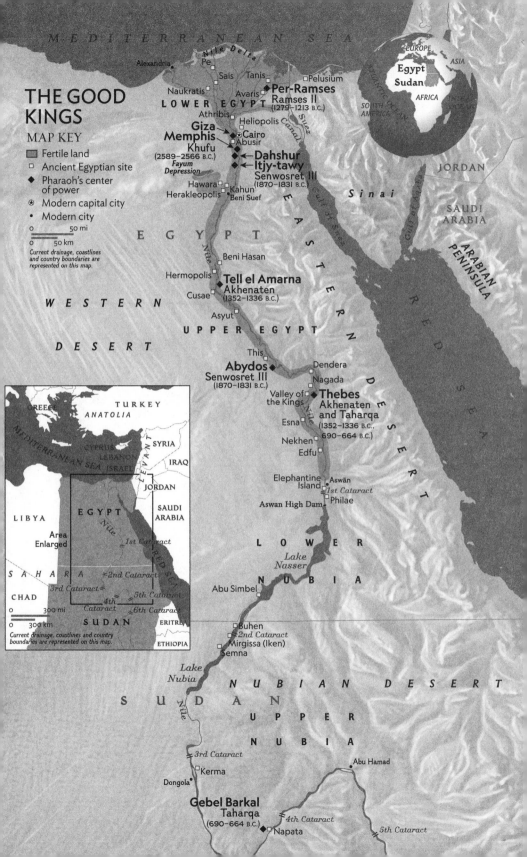

THE GOOD KINGS

MAP KEY

▨ Fertile land
□ Ancient Egyptian site
◆ Pharaoh's center
   of power
⊛ Modern capital city
● Modern city

0   50 mi
0   50 km

*Current drainage, coastlines
and country boundaries are
represented on this map.*

MEDITERRANEAN SEA

Alexandria

Nile Delta

Pe

Sais   Tanis   □ Pelusium

Per-Ramses
Ramses II
(1279–1213 B.C.)

Naukratis

Avaris

LOWER EGYPT

Athribis

Heliopolis

Giza
Memphis
Khufu
(2589–2566 B.C.)

◆ Cairo
Abusir

← **Dahshur**
← **Itjy-tawy**
Senwosret III
(1870–1831 B.C.)

*Fayum
Depression*

Hawara
Herakleopolis
Kahun
Beni Suef

E G Y P T

Suez Canal

Gulf of Suez

S i n a i

JORDAN

SAUDI
ARABIA

ARABIAN
PENINSULA

Beni Hasan

Hermopolis

Tell el Amarna
Akhenaten
(1352–1336 B.C.)

Cusae

Asyut

W E S T E R N

D E S E R T

UPPER EGYPT

This

Abydos
Senwosret III
(1870–1831 B.C.)

Dendera
Nagada

Thebes
Akhenaten
and Taharqa
(1352–1336 B.C.
690–664 B.C.)

Valley of
the Kings

Esna

Nekhen

Edfu

E A S T E R N   D E S E R T

R E D   S E A

Elephantine
Island

Aswān
□ 1st Cataract
Philae

Aswan High Dam

L O W E R

*Lake
Nasser*

N U B I A

Abu Simbel

□ Buhen
2nd Cataract
Mirgissa (Iken)
Semna

*Lake
Nubia*

S U D A N

N U B I A N   D E S E R T

U P P E R

N U B I A

3rd Cataract
Kerma

Dongola

Abu Hamad

Gebel Barkal
Taharqa
(690–664 B.C.)

4th Cataract
Napata

5th Cataract

Globe inset

Egypt
Sudan

EUROPE ASIA

ATLANTIC
OCEAN

SOUTH
AMERICA

AFRICA

INDIAN

Lower left inset map

GREECE

TURKEY
ANATOLIA

CYPRUS
LEBANON
SYRIA
ISRAEL
IRAQ
JORDAN
SAUDI
ARABIA

MEDITERRANEAN SEA

LEVANT

LIBYA

EGYPT
Area
Enlarged

Nile

1st Cataract

SAHARA

2nd Cataract

3rd Cataract

4th
Cataract

5th Cataract

6th Cataract

CHAD

SUDAN

ERITREA

ETHIOPIA

RED SEA

0   300 mi
0   300 km

*Current drainage, coastlines and country
boundaries are represented on this map.*

CHAPTER 1

WE ARE ALL PHARAOH'S GROUPIES

"*This is what the king who will reign over you will do: He will take your sons and make them serve with his chariots and horses, and they will run in front of his chariots . . . He will take your daughters to be perfumers and cooks and bakers. He will take the best of your fields and vineyards and olive groves and give them to his attendants. He will take a tenth of your grain and of your vintage and give it to his officials and attendants. Your menservants and maidservants and the best of your cattle and donkeys, he will take for his own use. He will take a tenth of your flocks, and you yourselves will become his slaves. When that day comes, you will cry out for relief from the king you have chosen, and the Lord will not answer you in that day.*"

But the people refused to listen to Samuel.

"No!" they said. "We want a king over us. Then we will be like all the other nations, with a king to lead us and to go out before us and fight our battles."

—1 Samuel 8:11-20

I am a recovering Egyptologist.

Like many of us in the field, I was initially attracted to the subject because of some unexplainable, irrational love for an ancient culture that lay millennia in the past. I felt I knew these ancient people somehow, and followed an indescribable urge to jump into the academic time machine to learn anything I could. I've now worked in Egyptology since entering graduate school in 1994, investing countless hours learning and teaching the ancient hieroglyphic language, committing kings' portraits to memory, traveling back and forth to Egypt, and waxing academically about what my research has uncovered.

The most common question asked of me as I stand at a podium for a lecture, or at a cocktail party with a drink in hand, is why I chose to become an Egyptologist. People want to know what a person like me is doing in a field like this. But other Egyptologists never demand my origin story; we all know in our bones that our urge to study that ancient place remains inexplicable, like the reasons we fell in love with someone. The heart wants what the heart wants. Maybe I just don't want to admit that I was drawn in by the dazzling gold, the massive statuary, the pyramids whose codes have yet to be cracked, the unabashed displays of power. Or maybe I fell for the idea of divine kingship that could reify miracles in stone and craft philosophical tales of complex religiosity.

But that unassailable strength of ancient rule, once so attractive to me, has now soured. The realization was like suddenly understanding that you're in an abusive relationship. Such sudden apprehension is not as stark as an addict hitting rock bottom; it's much more subtle. Your partner treats you real nice when he's in a good mood and buys you beautiful things. But everything seems stacked in his favor, and you begin to question your reality. Is he telling you the truth? And should you really be constantly submitting to his so-called better judgment? When what you thought were moral truths repeatedly turn into lies, it's time to admit you have a problem and find a way out.

Escaping from such an asymmetrical situation can be difficult, though. The cognitive shift is usually not a panicked run from a physical abuser in the dead of night. But it does demand unlearning what you have learned, or remembering what you forgot. Any victim of the more nuanced forms of psychological control knows that cognitive retraining is required to see what could not be recognized before, to understand that your cult leader does not truly have your best interests at heart, that you can indeed exist on your own.

Analogies to abusive partners and cult leaders may seem overblown. But suddenly I can't help but view my once beloved Egyptian kings—and their stunningly beautiful artistic and cerebral productions—in light of the testosterone-soaked power politics of the patriarchal system in which I live. I am quickly becoming antipatriarchal and anti-pharaoh, in whatever form the absolutism takes, ancient or modern. I now dwell in a strange in-between world in which the script has been flipped, where those gorgeous, chiseled kings have been revealed as bullies and narcissists.

I'm being naive, you might say. And, of course, you could be right. But how many of us have had deep obsessions with the ancient world—I just love Egyptian temples! I adore Greek mythology!—that are really symptoms of an ongoing addiction to male power that we just can't kick?

This book presents an analysis of how we make ourselves easy marks for the next charismatic authoritarian to come along. It's high time we see how fetishism of ancient cultures is used to prop up modern power grabs. And we need to admit—somewhere down deep—that we think the powerful patriarch, coolly in control, is superhot. Only then can we actually figure out how to smash him.

Antipatriarchal thinking doesn't mean being antimale; I have a son and a husband, and I love and support them both. Being antipatriarchal means refusing to support a "rule of the fathers," in which a few masculine elements of society pull most of the resources to themselves: a scenario in which fear, violence, threat, shame, and moralizing are used to keep everyone in line.

Patriarchy has been the go-to human social system since the dawn of the agricultural revolution, when farming and herding allowed a small percentage of men to monopolize most of society's material goods. This was also the era when marriage and law codes, organized religion, and kingship were born. The patriarchy was easily maintained during the hypercapitalism of the industrial revolution. And the benefactors of the patriarchy aren't just men. Women have helped enforce the patriarchy too, to survive or to benefit individually.

But some of us are starting to think that the patriarch who once seemed so sexy is now looking tired, paunchy, selfish, and cruel. The male-dominated religions that used to scare us into submission with the threat of ostracism from "good" society don't have the same hold over us anymore. The scales are suddenly falling from our eyes.

Nevertheless, we can't just destroy our golden calves or burn our icons, because those would be manipulative moves within the same patriarchal system; revolutions usually beget more strongmen, after all. Still, if we can't lean in and claim a bigger piece of the proverbial pie, then it's time to finally realize the pie doesn't exist for everyone in the way we think it does. If we want a more just future in which we all have equal opportunities—the same chance to pursue prosperity and happiness—then the patriarchy has to go.

Ancient Egypt can help us understand why we so easily bend toward authoritarianism, why it attracts and comforts us. This book is by no means a chronicle; it is not a history of Egyptian kings' reigns with careful accounting of the evidence of all that we do and don't know. It is, instead, a comparative impression of the impossible attractions of masculine rule, both yesterday and today.

And it's a story I need to tell. Indeed, who could be better prepared to explain how gaslighting personalities wielded their power than someone who was deep inside the cult as a willing believer?

When we stand before the pyramids, or the golden treasures of King Tutankhamun, or the soaring pylons of Karnak Temple, do we think of divine Egyptian kingship as something megalomaniacal and totalitarian? Probably not. We exult in the astounding beauty. But this is the key power of the patriarchy, and our continued glorification of its efforts only enables that power. I don't want anyone reading this book to think of it as a voyeuristic examination of primitive ancient kingship, a kind of institution in which they would never participate themselves. We are still participating in it.

THE AUTHORITARIAN SAVIOR

In the biblical Book of Genesis, an Egyptian king troubled by a dream called for a foreign man being held in prison to interpret it for him. That man was Joseph, the boy who had been thrown into a well by his many brothers when they became jealous of his coat of many colors. As he faced the king, Joseph was called upon for his skill in understanding the will of the heavens. He answered, "Seven years of great abundance are coming throughout the land of Egypt, but seven years of famine will follow them." A horrifying interpretation, to be sure, but Joseph knew the Egyptian kingship was well equipped for this challenge. "Let Pharaoh appoint commissioners over the land to take a fifth of the harvest of Egypt during the seven years of abundance," he advised. "They should collect all the food of these good years that are coming and store up the grain under the authority of Pharaoh, to be kept in the cities for food. This food should be held in reserve for the country, to be used during the seven years of famine that will come upon Egypt."[1]

As millions of the faithful can attest, Joseph's plan worked. The king held back grain, stored it, and redistributed it to his people during those seven lean years. It was extraordinarily simple, really. Because of his authoritarian power, this king was able to plan ahead and save his people. There was no squabbling or delay at court leading all to ruin. This Egyptian king, called "pharaoh"—a moniker that derives from the word for palace, *per-aa* in the ancient Egyptian language—won the day because there were no voices to counter him, no need to ingratiate himself to the will of the people, no pushback from elites upset at paying extra taxes. And because this king had the enlightened will to plan ahead for his country—not to mention access to the astute advice to put a plan into action—he was successful in countering the famine.

From the perspective of an American watching federal and local governments struggle to battle a pandemic that experts saw coming for decades (historians study much more deadly plagues, after all), such a strategic response seems unattainable. During the recent COVID-19 pandemic, we existed in a swirl of rumors, last-minute course changes, defunded and hamstrung institutions, bluster from our leaders, and the outright politicization of a crisis in which wearing a face mask, filling dorms with students, or lining up to get vaccinated became hot-button issues.

Perhaps there is some truth to the idea that a population can have too many freedoms; we may be shackled by liberty while we long for a mystical and apocryphal past. In such uncertain times, it's comforting to conjure up an era that we perceive as idyllic, in which strong kings were able to enforce the rules firmly, manage their country's finances with ease, step in with wisdom, and keep everyone safe. In the context of that reverie, we can't help but wonder why our leaders fail to act.

Did the biblical story of Egyptian famine have a kernel of truth in the historic record? Not directly. But we do have images of kings distributing wealth to their people. One of 18th-dynasty pharaoh Akhenaten's favorite images of himself, repeated by courtiers in the reliefs adorning their tomb chapels, shows the ruler and his wife Nefertiti leaning out of their window of appearances as they throw golden treasures down to tiny, cheerful elites below. It was a popular theme: the king's gracious handouts of abundant wealth from his palace storerooms.[2] The king was taking care of his people, much like the pharaoh in the Genesis story. We see the grateful elites bent at the waist, with arms uplifted to receive those golden trinkets from the god-king and his family—much like the guy in the corner office who's grateful for the stock option bestowed upon him to keep him from going elsewhere.

Some argue that Akhenaten was the world's first monotheist; some vehemently oppose this supposition. But no matter how we categorize his paradigm shift, Akhenaten went all-in with his new god, the Aten, building open-air temples that required no statue or sacred animal pen or other icon to represent it. This was the king who first foisted upon humanity the notion that god was single, omnipresent, omniscient—a round and perfect eminence far away in the sky, a mystery only the king could perceive, as if to say, "Only I can teach you the realities of your world." (I can't be the only one who discerns echoes of that philosophy within the structure of modern authoritarian fanaticism.)

If you visit ancient temples in Luxor today, you might notice many instances of a crudely fashioned figure of the god Amun next to a crisply cut image of a king, not realizing that such reliefs preserve the traces of an epic difference of opinion from long ago. Akhenaten ordered all the images of Amun carved away, but later kings had them roughly recut. The point here is that Akhenaten was so confident in his philosophy that he could remove any images that offended his thinking. And no matter how outlandish his demands were, no matter how wasteful his lavish offerings may have seemed—meat and bread heaped on hundreds of altars and left to rot—his aides carried them out. That was the power of ancient Egyptian kingship.

But what seemed at first glance to be devotion to the god now smacks of narcissistic, even psychopathic, behavior. In the end, kings have so much power that they can perform stunning cruelties while at the same time governing and behaving with apparent generosity. An authoritarian regime can carry out a national census as a tool to help create social equity, but it can use that same information to hunt down and remove undesirables.[3] Stalin, Mao, Kim, and Trump all demanded military parades and flyovers for the enjoyment of some of their people, while others went homeless and hungry.

If asked, most people who live in liberal democracies today would say that they would not want a king ruling over them because they don't want to be subject to one man's whims and selfish interests. Society is inherently unequal, but a society ruled by a king is perceived as grossly so. Kings can and do start wars with their neighbors over silly disagreements, leading to death, destruction, economic ruin, and political turmoil. (World War I, for example, was a massive conflagration sparked by the squabbling of royal Victorian first cousins that devastated ordinary families as a generation of sons was annihilated and homes and businesses destroyed.)

The list of downsides to having a king goes on. A ruler might be unstable and moody, with one dark turn setting circumstances ablaze. A king might be stupid, too inept to know that he is bumbling into a horrific mistake. A king might be mad, so mentally deficient that he cannot see reason in any counselor's advice. And no matter what his psychological state, a king generally surrounds himself with sycophants who tell him what he wants to hear, so he exists in his own echo chamber of propagandistic devotion to himself. Even at the moment when his people turn against him, the man most surprised at the ferocity of the populace's rancor is, in fact, the target of it.

A ruler is almost always a *he,* too. Rarely do women make it to this top spot, being usually relegated to wield their influence behind the throne. In Egypt, a few women were crowned king, but only when there was some kind of crisis. Those women who did manage to tear through the papyrus ceiling had to submit to a variety of compromises, from remaining unpartnered and accepting constant and unsolicited advice from men to having no legacy after they were erased from the history books. Then, as now, the patriarchy jealously guarded the halls of power, saying that only a man could do the job, that the people needed him, that they would be unsafe without him.

Authoritarian regimes do have some advantages, though. A king provides a balance of power. For both elites and average citizens, following a king is risk-averse behavior. People may not have as much freedom as they would like, but they don't have to fight constantly for their place. For those who have wealth, it allows them to maintain an edge, making sure that no one else can grab the brass ring of social mobility.

But without a king, there may be high levels of competition within society as everyone fights fiercely in a zero-sum game. Without a king, there is no one with an interest in strategizing 10 steps ahead—only a mass of strongmen grabbing what they can get in a moment of opportunity. Without a king, rich men can abuse and exploit the people with no oversight of their actions. Without a king doling out tiny slices of the pie as he sees fit, there is absolute chaos. Without a king to connect with divinity, there is religious discord. And without a king, there is nothing beautiful to consume with the eyes or stomach or ears—no one to commission stunning polychrome temples or monumental structures or breathtaking sonatas or button-popping banquets or hilarious stage performances.

The dangers of despotism aside, too many of us dealing with the exhausting absurdities and constant squabbling inherent in "rule by the people" would rather relax into the strong, fatherly embrace of a king telling us what to do. We long for safety. We desire order. In China, where the novel coronavirus began, the authoritarian regime pivoted quickly, completely locking down cities and protecting the health of its people. And, of course, even if people heard conspiracy theories, they could never do more than ponder them silently while they were following orders.

In contrast, during the coronavirus pandemic in the United States, democratically elected leaders argued constantly, degraded one another, and refused to authorize shutdowns, mandatory mask wearing, financial relief, or emergency social services. Every decision played out as a political battle royal, not a public health response.

Of course, it's a short hop from promoting law, order, and public safety to using authoritarianism for the self-aggrandizement of a few, or using the state's centralized, brute strength against one's enemies, or demanding association with the esteemed leader for social capital—like the Russian oligarch out hunting with Putin, or U.S. senators extolling when they last spent time with the president in a not-so-subtly conveyed threat to those not toeing the party line.[4] Maybe a king would bestow a kind of god-given grace to our messy human existence, empowering (some of) us in the process. But if this is the government some people crave, then all too often it becomes the government they deserve.

Much of the world's current population lives in democratic republics (or at least they are so named). Even Vladimir Putin is "elected" these days. Modern expectations dictate that elections be held for presidents and parliaments so that the International Monetary Fund, the United Nations, the World Trade Organization, and USAID can feel good about disbursing their funds. Today, monarchies, dictatorships, and police states are eschewed—or at least, not openly supported.

But some of us live in places that are becoming more authoritarian by the hour, our leaders more king-like with each manipulated election, as we surround ourselves with the fuzzy, warm mythology that we all enjoy life, liberty, and the pursuit of happiness, that "the people" make the decisions, that protests matter, that we have some say over our leaders. And yet, day by day, as our privileged perches in society are whittled down to powerless cogs in the corporate machine, we—like abused people who think their partners truly love them but are just going through a really hard time—choose denial, ignoring the true agendas of our overlords, cleaving closer to the bully, thinking the ends justify the means, play-acting at democracy.

In fact, we all live in the thrall of kings, real or imagined. We beat down the doors when King Tut comes to town, soaking up all that golden power, buying up T-shirts and trinkets, watching breathlessly as ancient coffins from his hometown are opened live on camera, participating in an arena of conspicuous consumption and monumentality through a glass case. We love and hate the pharaoh of the biblical Exodus, that man able to push an entire nation into slavery. We are obsessed with the creations of modern god-kings around the world—skyscrapers, Lamborghinis, multimillion-dollar yachts, sprawling estates, purchased presidencies. We consume information about our depraved leaders' sexual excesses, the harems of young girls pimped by confidants and enjoyed by the princes of business and society who are often beyond the reach of the law. But we never call these things by their true names.

The Egyptians didn't dissemble. They openly embraced their kingship, and we love them for it. Egyptian kings perfected conspicuous consumption in which their elites could also participate: pyramids and pillared tombs, sprawling temples and phallic obelisks. We continue to admire the wives of great Egyptian kings; we are gaga for Akhenaten's stunning Nefertiti, her bust abducted from her homeland to sit prisoner in a beautiful Berlin cage where guards exhort museum visitors to use only hushed voices in its ravishing presence. We continue to believe in ancient Egyptian kings' divinity to such a degree that the likes of Swiss author Erich von Däniken have enriched themselves touting the alien or Atlantean origins of antiquity. Every time someone asserts that the Giza Pyramids were the work of extraterrestrials, the Egyptian kings prove yet again their mastery of propagandistically proving their own superhuman natures to lesser minds.

A king is of spirit and body, immortal and mortal simultaneously. A king is sometimes believed to be made of everlasting materials—golden flesh and lapis lazuli bones for the ancient Egyptians—while nonetheless inhabiting a human shape of vulnerable skeleton, musculature, and skin. A king might find one part of his being in the heavens with the omniscient sight of a hawk, while his all-too-human feet are firmly planted on the ground in the royal palace. In Egypt, he could be depicted as a strong bull, impregnating all his harem women even though, in reality, he was an impotent product of incest.

A king can cross the confines between the human and natural world, uniting them. He was part lion and part man in Egypt, the only human who could coexist with such virulent animal power. In medieval France, he was the Sun King. In modern-day North Korea, he is the infallible Dear Leader. He can traverse the gates of the underworld, entering into the space of the dead ancestors, greeting them, feeding off of them, while still inhabiting the world of the living.

The king is a warrior, ordering young troops into battle, even though he exists in the body of an old man. As anthropologists of kingship contend, "Kings control nature itself. What usually passes for the divinization of human rulers is better described historically as the humanization of the god."[5]

And many among us want to believe. Not only are people attracted to the gold-encrusted absolutism of ancient kings (Egyptian or otherwise), but the perfection of brute strength also makes some crave that kind of leadership today. The institutional arm of a king is strong, and if punishment or any other kind of suppression is needed, a king can deliver it without mercy to keep all safe. "I will kill your friends and family—to remind you of my love," as King George says in Lin-Manuel Miranda's musical *Hamilton*. It should therefore come as no surprise that as the post-Confederacy Jim Crow South grasped for a pivot after its loss in the U.S. Civil War, it invested in revival Egyptian monuments such as obelisks and pyramids to terrorize Black Americans into submission. (If you couldn't use Jesus to sanction continued slavery by another name, then why not use the ghosts of Ramses or Thutmose?)

The irony of manipulating the Exodus story to cast a positivist light onto slavery is entirely lost on many people; they desperately need to believe in their leader's god-given grace. That's why tens of millions of Christian evangelicals and fundamentalist Jews thought Donald Trump was a kind of "King of Israel" mentioned in Isaiah 44:6, a latter-day Messiah, a strongman in the mold of King David to guide us back to a world in which women and minorities know their place, the unwanted unborn are guaranteed birth, Israel can bully Muslims with impunity, and the righteous are victorious at the last reckoning.

No one knew better than the ancient Egyptians how to draw on the perfection of god-given abilities in leadership, creating exactly the resilient and long-lived political system that elites prefer. Social mores are simplified when a good king rules over all; everyone else looks on in awe and is rewarded, both for their adoration and for knowing their place.

Today, we don't feel the need to get angry or be unsettled as long as we are provided with a velvet prison. Instead, we just need to aspire to rulers more like the stalwart ancient kings to keep us safe. We wish for politicians who can rule with such force of personality that we can view them as godlike; if such charismatic leaders aren't forthcoming, we manufacture them by creating effigies, including the disembodied faces of Mount Rushmore, a quartet of monstrosities blasted into the Native Lakota people's sacred ground in the Black Hills of South Dakota. Or we carefully tend former presidents' plantation homes that were once run by slaves, creating posthumous shrines of demagoguery to George Washington at Mount Vernon and Thomas Jefferson at Monticello. Such ancestors can work on American minds long after they have died, much in the same way that King Amenhotep III seems to have haunted Ramses II with his superior monuments (so many of which were standing in Egypt's temples that Ramses was driven to recarve his ancestor as himself dozens of times over).

Another reason to love kings? Kingship means continuity. Kings rule for life, allowing some royal subjects to live out their days under a single monarch. Kings have a longer runway to draft their plans, and a longer duration of time in which to implement them.

There is also a stability to kingship. Everyone knows what's coming, father followed by son according to tradition, forever and ever, so that there are no messy changes of power: none of the vulnerabilities that come with one ruler stepping down from office and another learning the ropes as he transitions in. Slavish elites can be assured that each king is trained to rule soberly and properly.

At its best, monarchy—like political family dynasties in democracies—avoids unprepared rulers as the heir learns from birth how to walk, talk, meet a gaze, command respect, strategize. Kings can avoid treacherous advisers by choosing counselors for their loyalty, rather than their skill—as Donald Trump did with his advisers. The demands of kingship keep the monarch himself in line, limiting frivolity and excess, forcing the king to bear the heavy mantle of so many royal responsibilities: as an interlocutor to the god(s), a military commander, a judge over right and wrong.

There is weight to such duty. A king has little free time to do as he pleases. He has to take care of his people. He must spend hours grooming and dressing for the part. There are expectations to uphold. Fashions to create. Sumptuous displays to prepare. All of that takes foresight and careful attention.

Kingships share other superiorities. Kings can unite diverse ethnic and religious groups within an empire under the aegis of loyalty to one ruler without divisive politics. Sometimes, love for an emperor and his fairness to diverse peoples can even keep sectarian warfare at bay. The institution of kingship allows people to invest in long-term emotional connections with politics; watching from afar as a boy grows from prince to heir to king can help citizens forge their national identity.

Kings are believed incorruptible. They don't need money, so they can't be bought or compromised. A man who is merely rich is not above such base motivations because he is not a king. He is incomplete. But a king is sated, content, unbribable; he owns the entire state. (*"L'état, c'est moi*—I am the state," as Louis XIV of France supposedly said.) According to Alexander Hamilton, a hereditary monarch has more incentive to be loyal to his nation-state, precisely because he is inherently less corruptible.[6]

Today, we quite openly equate having kingly sums of money with god-given abilities, as can be deduced from the many modern states that have elected seemingly wealthy men to lead them, including Italy, Ukraine, Chile, the Czech Republic, Taiwan, Lebanon, and the United States. The takeaway seems to be that if the fates bestow riches upon a man, he is obviously exceptional in our eyes, marked for power.

The same ideology that works for a king works for his elites: Those with money are doing what is right, good, and pure with that wealth, and those who are poor should look up gratefully without consternation. Many of today's wealthy believe they were predestined to be rich—not because they were given extraordinary opportunities, but because they are inherently better at making money, because they pulled themselves up by their own bootstraps, because they are better at creating jobs for other people. Indeed, many wealthy people believe that they are the proper recipients of their assets because the poor would misspend or misuse the same resources. Such ideology encourages lateral competition within class groups, leading people to compete only with their peers—which is certainly useful for those at the top.

Inside information is the currency of the elites, who use it in different ways depending on the society. The Roman aristocracy spread word of scandals, affairs, and conspiracy theories within their political arena. They reveled in spilling all the messy details, slanderous or not. Rumor-mongering haunted monarchs such as Catherine the Great of Russia and mad King George III of England, not to mention the pervasive accusations about Hillary Clinton's activities during the 2016 U.S. national election. The Egyptians, on the other hand, rarely whispered about the fallibilities of their ruler or the methods of their own compromise, and the elites leaked few state secrets. The Egyptians, in fact, were co-conspirators with their king, using their inside information to manufacture a reality that was meant to seem as if it had occurred naturally, having come from on high.

And under exactly such a system, elites had some measure of control over their god-king. Indeed, the more their ruler was divinized, the more burdened he was with pomp and ceremony, uncomfortable crowns, unwieldy rituals of grasping living ducks while running at a fast clip, suckling at the udders of a living divine cow, or marching for hours in the hot sun along a festival route in full regalia. As a result, elites eventually wielded extraordinary powers over their leader, who had to look to his expert priests and courtiers for the correct procedure, for what decisions needed to be made; the divinization of a king domesticated him. The Egyptian political arena was thus a constant, discreet, and unspoken competition between the elite bloc and their divine monarch as measured by the comparative sizes of pyramids and tombs, and the treasuries of the palace and temple.

As we see today, decentralized politics can be soul crushing, a long game driven by ratings and popularity, negotiation and consensus. But a king can be the dullest person there is. He doesn't need to be charismatic or interesting or cool. All of that will be veiled with the accoutrements of his station anyway—the crowns and robes, scepters and staves. He doesn't need to have something special about *him*. The circumstances of his birth and station are exceptional enough.

A king requires no game-show personality; that's not how he gets the job. God makes him monarch. A hereditary ruler is thought to have superior decision-making and moral character because of his connection to the god (or gods); he can thus counter human moral frailty.

A king also doesn't need laws. Such strictures were invented to control baser humans. The king can go above the law, make the law, is the law. And his royal position is all the proof of divine providence that his people need.

Even though we profess to abhor the abuses of monarchical power—the entitlement, the superstitions, the indignities, the loss of freedom—we respect the authoritarian impulse so much that we produce our own pseudokings every day. In our current decentralized states, we replace kingship with cults of personality, charisma, and executive order, with the divinization of Founding Fathers, the fetishization of wealth and the almighty dollar. Whether a leader is president, prime minister, premier, chancellor, strongman, dictator, or general, many people assume god helped him achieve his status. It's a political prosperity gospel of circumstance.

Those men understand they have signed a contract to broadcast their exceptionalism. Because we profess to eschew kingships while nonetheless longing for them, today's rulers have to fabricate a web of deceit. In dress and bearing, those men don't look very different from the rest of us; they try to blend in. Military uniforms used to be in vogue for the "everyman authoritarian ruler" of the 1950s and '60s, but now that look is too obviously associated with brutality and dictatorship. Today's pseudokings wear suits and ties, aping the upper-middle-class males of the human species even though everyone knows they are decidedly different.

We, "the people," choose these men, we tell ourselves, through the act of voting, through dynamic collaboration—or, if we don't vote, through silent acquiescence in our quest for order, harmony, safety, refuge, known paths, nostalgia for a certain kind of leadership, and a never ending hope that we might finally make ourselves great again through the divinely inspired goodness of these men. We search for just the right kind of magnetism, just the right degree of presidential "greatness." We twist ourselves into knots professing to hate the methods of overt authoritarian rule—and yet we choose it nonetheless, like junkies.

The truth is, we think modern societies, in which leaders are voted into power, are different from ancient kingships. We tell ourselves that we don't believe in such primitive, passé things, even though so many of us still search for a man marked by god as a divine leader, who reflects our will, who has insight into the workings of the universe, who represents cosmic powers, who displays respectable procreative abilities and power with a wife and children while having an obvious sexual appetite for multiple women (because what's wrong with that?), who has an everyman charm that makes us feel like we could happily have a beer with him, who reassures us that our interests are safe, who hates the same people that we do.

But deception is the most powerful of human abilities. A mythology of modern exceptionalism—We would never worship god-kings! We would never be so superstitious!—allows us to delude ourselves like the ancient Romans who screamed about the horrors of monarchy yet followed meekly behind their chosen First Citizen, the Princeps (named Caesar after a martyred dead uncle), in a divinized cipher of kingship that lasted for centuries. Perhaps it's time to investigate the object of our longing and call our modern methods of rule what they actually are, given that so many of us are selecting authoritarianism and police states anyway.

In a monarchy, the person who seemingly benefits the most is the leader. He gets the best house, car, money, stuff, power, women. It's good to be king! The elites are his foundation, and they must benefit too. Those aristocrats are the ones who prop up their leader, become mouthpieces for him, who create ideological systems that make him infallible.

Royal regimes work best when the elites are not slyly looking for ways to take down their top guy. In Egypt, the ideology that put the king into power seems to have been—usually—fervently believed by the elites who served under him. They swallowed the notion that their king was a god incarnate, fated to rule while still an undeveloped fetus in the womb. But in ancient Rome, the elites fiercely competed with one another to see which one of them could knock the emperor off the pedestal and take that position for themselves. Under such circumstances, the emperors generally lived very short lives, most dying from unnatural causes.[7] In this sense, Americans are quite Roman.

Today, we may hide our desire for a king from ourselves. But the ancient Egyptians were overt in their long-term love of monarchy, and they constructed its optics within an elegant philosophy of morality, goodness, beauty, and longevity. Biblical stories of pharaonic excess and

29

hardened hearts aside, we encapsulate that perceived god-given strength with one word—"pharaoh"—which instantly embodies all the wealth, military acumen, shameless bravado, sexual appetite, incest, religious weight, Technicolor costumes, and necessary cruelty. I don't generally use the word "pharaoh" in my work because of its imprecision and slanted biblical origins. But it does represent a mortal man turned into the ultimate taskmaster and protector, and the title certainly works for the subject at hand.

We are all willing collaborators of the pharaoh. We are those elites of Akhenaten, grateful to be thrown a few trinkets, if they are made of solid gold. Many of us would betray our values and morality if sanctioned by the forgiveness of a great leader. The ends usually justify the means— maneuvering to find a good position in Soviet Russia, naming names during Senator McCarthy's hunt for communists in the United States in the 1950s, reporting friends to the Stasi (Staatssicherheitsdienst— State Security Service) in East Germany, working with the Nazi government in Vichy France, cooperating with purity police in Islamic states, lobbying to gain lucrative government contracts, supporting a racist "War on Drugs" with mass incarcerations of Black Americans, or playing a stock market enriched by unsustainable consumption and the sale of weapons, pharmaceuticals, and petroleum.

Why do people bow to power so very easily? Because collaborators are well compensated for their loyalty. They are made comfortable. The grief and deprivation are not happening to them, not personally. Instead, it's happening to the steelworker addicted to some drug given to him by his doctor, to the Guatemalan child in a cage at the U.S.-Mexican border, to the college student who falls under DACA (Deferred Action for Childhood Arrivals) and can't qualify for a Federal Pell Grant, to the poor kid living in a Motel 6 by the interstate when her mother can afford it. We go all-in with authoritarianism, while calling it by another name—freedom, individualism, constitutional rights, exceptionalism, capitalism—because it will make us strong too.

In the end, many of us side with power. We even side with our oppressors. We wait for our leaders to bring the affluence, equality, and morality they promised—and until that beautiful day, at least some of us are prospering, turning into cultists awaiting a rapture that never comes. For most people, it's an easy exchange; they want to be enriched, empowered. They want to be in the room where it happens.[8] But most never have the opportunity to choose anything.

At the end of a regime's long game, when the jig is up and the emperor is revealed to have no clothes, the only thing keeping people in line with corrupt leadership is the desire that their families not suffer, and that their kids, too, can go to university and get a good job where they're hired for their loyalty, rather than their ability. Before the regime turns despotic, most deny any outright collaboration with something as dirty as authoritarianism, claiming that they are making decisions for other reasons: I am fiscally conservative! I am pro-life! My religious rights are being trampled! Immigrants are taking all the jobs!

For those who think they would never support such a regime, make no mistake: The kingship has been here for some time. Whether we live in a liberal democracy, a police state, a communist regime, or a strict theocracy, all of them share one thing: patriarchy—a moralistic rule by the fathers that relies on economic hoarding and authoritarianism, be it at the level of household or state.

Patriarchy has been the unifying political religion of every polity since the agricultural revolution. Even though some think the use of the word stems from a man-hating, foaming-at-the-mouth, feminist agenda, the principle is simply the manifestation of our standard system of agricultural and industrial rule. The patriarchy is a world dominated by fathers, brothers, and sons, kind and cruel, whose might is right, who are surrounded by fawning and obedient women who produce more such sons, brutally excluding those who must be rooted out—gay people, nonbinary people, atheists and nonbelievers, immigrants, and others—who control all the resources, and who bully some of the people with the necessary cruelties. Whether wielded by men or the occasional woman (whose fight on its behalf benefits her as an individual while leading to inequalities for others), the patriarchy is our current kingship.

But the patriarchy is showing its cracks, its once mighty dominance faltering before our eyes. This is why we can finally recognize our kings for what they are. Society is changing, and quickly, everywhere around the globe. Technology allows women to be just as capable as men, in both the virtual and real worlds. In fact, women are taking on combat roles in the military, and gender and sexuality are being accepted as fluid and nonbinary. Gay people are getting married. At the same time, marriage is suddenly no longer a necessity to enter respectable society. Inflexible religions are being abandoned. Even though the push to return to more conservative values is fierce, the debate itself is what allows us all to finally see that the king (or the patriarch) has been there behind that old way of life the whole time—and that he is wearing no clothes. Knowing that, some of us are strategizing our next move.

THE EGYPTIAN LESSON ON AUTHORITARIANISM

I work in a field of apologists who believe in an Egypt of truth, beauty, and power—and in many ways, I am still an adherent to my chosen faith. Scholars come to a field of study because they love it, and we Egyptologists find the proof of our love everywhere: in the thousands of hieroglyphic symbols taking the shape of sunrises and stems of flax; in the slightly off-center pouch in the upper lip of Amenhotep III; in the arcane rituals enacted by Egypt's kings, including jogging with rowing oars (cumbersome) and shooting an arrow in each of the four cardinal directions (risky). We don't want to write off these unique cultural elements as mere symbols that support authoritarianism; we can't simply cancel ancient Egyptian culture. There is much beauty in ancient Egypt, and I am not here to deride or belittle it.

Instead, I think the ancient Egyptians can help us recognize the king in our own system, show us how he behaves, and thereby teach us how we might neutralize him ourselves. We are all slaves to our short life-times, which makes seeing the long term difficult, but we can look back in history and watch the ancient Egyptian dynasties rise and fall.

For millennia, Egypt engaged in a push-and-pull relationship with the monarch. Sometimes he was strong; sometimes he was weak. Sometimes the country got out from under the heavy boot of absolute power, only to slip back under it. But throughout those ups and downs, Egypt main-tained a flourishing continuity of religious ritual, language and literature, artistic production, and cultural beauty. Egypt didn't need its kings; the kings needed Egypt. It's useful to remember that.

Perhaps you think ancient Egypt shouldn't be compared to any other regime—most especially, a modern state. If Egyptology were personified, it might actually agree with you, as it lives and breathes on particularism: all the dates and events and iconography and hieroglyphic signs exclusive to that place.

But particularism is itself a veil of another kind: a means of claiming those kinds of things could never happen here and now, or a way of hiding from our own apologist tendencies to laud ancient systems of masculine authority through positivist examinations of beautiful monuments and flowery hymns celebrating kings. Context is important, to be sure, to fit data into the proper social and historical rubrics. Without context, none of the ancient Egyptian texts can be read with any meaning.

Still, adherence to particularist blinders and descriptions for their own sake obstructs necessary comparative work. Particularism demonizes anything that smacks of universalism. How could the lives of people possess such similarities in different places and different times, we cry? Keeping ancient Egypt separate and vacuum-sealed allows us to fetishize it, to see the believers in these god-kings as primitive, silly people, nothing like us. Isolating any ancient culture to such a degree demands a belief that we would never fall for such manipulations by primeval demiurges.

With one state after another succumbing to authoritarianism while calling it democracy, though, we need to leave the safe confines of our modern exceptionalism behind. As we dissect our own cultural understandings of patriarchal power, ancient Egypt provides a useful lens.

Hotly contested debates in 2020 about Confederate monuments in the United States, as well as statues of those who benefitted from the slave trade or colonialism throughout the world, inspire the same defensiveness of cultural apologism. When people assert that a particular statue of Robert E. Lee must come down, defenders of the status quo retort that we should tear down the pyramids too, resulting in a common response from many an Egyptologist who rallies around the kings' tombs to say: "These monuments were not built by slaves, but by Egypt's people!"

It's worth noting, though, that both perspectives defend an authoritarian regime. Jim Crow—era statues and Egyptian pyramids represent the same masculine repressive powers; the only difference is the millennia separating one from the other—long years hiding the deep wounds carved into Egyptian flesh in the same ways that scarred U.S. society. And the distinction between slavery and draft labor is meaningless if participants were forced to take part.

Make no mistake: The Egyptian pyramids were built because the kings needed them. Just like statues of heroic Confederate Army generals on horseback, the Giza Pyramids are signs of a crackdown after a loss of power. However, neither kind of monument is evocative of absolute strength; Confederate monuments and pyramids alike embody a kind of political rally to an insecure toxic masculinity that must impose its will and constantly remind people of its god-given superiority, lest it be lost.

Don't get me wrong. I'm not advocating for the destruction of the pyramids any more than I am pushing to melt down statues that reify Black oppression in America. I am pushing for a reframing of every such monument, a paradigm shift that allows us to recognize how they cast a shadow over the power that abides there.

Conversations about that reframing are happening in every profession and institution as we recognize our lack of diversity, our inequity, and our exclusion, as if for the first time. Universities are discussing different names for buildings and institutes, removing problematic words like "Oriental," and reconfiguring department names. ("Near Eastern studies" are near to what, after all, if not the Eurocentric categorizers?) The last few years have encouraged Egyptologists to debate the skin color of the ancient Egyptians in a more nuanced way, finally seeing an African people of color where we had before imposed a rather tanned-White predecessor to our Greek cultural originators.

Today, as my colleagues in New Testament studies discuss adherence to a mythical White Jesus, it's also time to talk about a whitewashed Egypt in which people of European descent have claimed the monuments of the ancient Egyptians for themselves. They categorize these achievements as "Western," similar to the construction of the Parthenon in Athens and the Colosseum in Rome.

The modern-day Egyptians have themselves suffered millennia of colonial oppression, arguably dating to ancient Greek and Roman occupations. This gave the supposed Egyptian "Whiteness" that much more of a hold on the human psyche. The past 50 years, in fact, have seen the ascent of Afrocentrists claiming Egypt as Black, not White. But at the very moment the identity of ancient Egyptians is being redefined in the West, most modern Egyptians fiercely push back against any identity associated with Blackness.

No matter who claims it, though, ancient Egypt was still authoritarian, patriarchal, and colonially oppressive to the Levant in the north and Nubia in the south. We don't seem to care that the regime was brutal; we are still enthralled. In that regard, our collaboration with the patriarchy is definitely showing.

In Egyptian tales of wisdom, we marvel at the philosophy of the ancient kings. They seem to have been so wise, so able, so fair, so strong, so wonderfully arrogant. Massive tomes have been written about the concept of *ma'at*, the Egyptian word for "order" or "right" or "truth"[9]— but we generally approach the subject positivistically. Rarely do we put that concept under the microscope as an authoritarian tool of control.

The truth is, we Egyptologists have guzzled the ideological Kool-Aid, rarely examining ma'at in terms of its power to oppress. This scholarly blindness is proof that we are deeply embedded in our own patriarchal systems so similar to those of ancient Egypt that we don't recognize the ideological manipulation openly paraded in front of our eyes. Indeed, if punishment was shown being meted out for acting against ma'at in an ancient text or image, then, the scholar assumes, it was deserved in some way. A given person's captivity or poverty or otherness are all signs of immorality and weakness, just as the ancient Egyptians would have us believe. If wealth is god-given, the theory goes, then so is destitution.

Prosperity gospels are as old as complex civilization, as systems of patriarchy blind us all. Egyptian ma'at persists when we vote for law-and-order rulers, even if those same men incarcerate almost a third of the total Black male population in the United States while letting White men get away with shorter sentences for the same crimes.[10] Ma'at persists when women's exclusion from STEM fields (science, technology, engineering, and mathematics) is explained as a self-selection to do work that is more emotionally satisfying. Ma'at persists when the United States allocates another enormous load of resources to a military that engages in police wars and/or oil wars with no end. We love Egyptian-style order, understanding in our bones how to glorify those who stay in their lane, do what they're told, and follow the rules of the man in charge.

In a famous ancient Egyptian text called "The Eloquent Peasant,"[11] a poor man, through no fault of his own, is accused by a wealthy agricultural overseer of theft. Though the peasant did nothing wrong, he is imprisoned, beaten, and held for weeks, forced to plead his case constantly. He worries about his livelihood, his family, and their welfare. As his despair grows, he even contemplates suicide. Yet so impressed is everyone with the eloquence of this peasant that they draw out the proceedings. His case rises from the palace steward to the king himself.

It's a cruel tale of inequality and power, but Egyptological attention has been focused on the elegant turns of phrase and extraordinary aphorisms of the peasant, with little examination of the authoritarianism that put an innocent man into an impossible situation. When the peasant protested his unequal treatment, he was used as a source of entertainment by those in power. This peasant knew that to survive, he had to keep his head bowed and perform. He could not lose his temper—only the ruler is allowed such an emotion. He was thrust into the role of a performing monkey, forced to dance while hoping for a shred of justice.

As for the men in authority, they knew they could ignore the human trauma before their eyes and enjoy the spectacle of beautifully spun prose and brilliantly conveyed wisdom. Finally, when the peasant is at the end of his energy, they reveal that they had planned to set him free the whole time. This is ma'at in practice.

The comparisons to the Black American confronted by an armed police officer with gun drawn—he knows to keep his hands at ten and two o'clock, staying still until told to move—is chilling. James Baldwin is our modern American Eloquent Peasant, trying to tell us what we refuse to see: that we are not innocent, but complicit.

The poor of ancient Egypt had little choice but to comply with law and order. The peasant in the field who hated his cruel overlord had no recourse. He could stop farming, but that would only result in the starvation of his family and his inability to pay the landlord his rent in grain; resistance would harm him irrevocably.

Those rich in resources are well aware of that dynamic. Companies such as Uber and Amazon know that employees need the gig, that they will work for $15 an hour because they have little choice, and that someone else is always waiting to take that job. Resistance is futile. Such laborers are stuck, unable to stop working because their lives would be upended if they did. The weapons of the weak are few;[12] things have to be really bad for people to flee the farm and go on the move in search of a new patron, or to rise up against their overlord, putting themselves and their families at risk for generations to come.

Uprisings against kings and polities have occurred, of course. Historical texts preserve descriptions of revolutions, decapitated monarchs, executed royal families, guillotined elites. But every time a new uprising occurred, it always led to yet another regime, often more repressive than the one before.

Perhaps that is why the ancient Egyptian king was transformed into a god: You can't kill what's divine. Given the king's obviously human form, an Egyptian monarch was differentiated from the eternal gods of the heavens, river, sky, and sun. Those elemental gods were called *netjer a'a* or "great gods." Geb, god of the earth, was a netjer a'a. Horus, the remote, all-seeing one, was also a netjer a'a. The king, however, was called a *netjer nefer,* meaning "the perfect god" or "the good god," something that required a kind of "idealizing" intervention, given the frail human body in which the divinity was encased.

The Egyptian kings were not believed to be superheroes. They were not able to live forever; they couldn't fly or know all the secrets of the universe. It was only upon his death that a king became a "great god," having gone to the other side and mingled with the true essence of divinity, becoming one with a gilded pyramid and transforming into a being of light. Until that point, though, each king was considered *nefer,* or "good." The nefer was the veil, the ideological means of cloaking and beautifying the messy human reality.

But when you have to call something perfect, you inherently imply that there's also imperfection. A king is made of fallible human material that will break down and decay, just as any mortal will. It is the nefer element that got people to bow down to a king, to work for him, to believe that his interest was greater than theirs, to not compete with him, to believe him a perfected interlocutor with divinity.

This nefer element was the religious glue that bound the whole system together, and Egyptologists don't even really know how to translate it. The word seems somehow connected to morality or beauty, a transformation into what is right and pure. And yet this element is the reason so many Egyptians submitted to their king, because it domesticated an absolute power, demanding that anyone who occupied the post behave and act a certain way. The notion of "goodness" made authoritarianism safe.

The good god had to follow ma'at—the correct way that things should be done, a structured order. In other words, the king could not be a wild and crazy warlord, excessive in his cruelty or demands. Even the Eloquent Peasant got his justice in the end (or so the story goes).

In other words, ma'at is akin to the U.S. Constitution. A president can't do what is unconstitutional, can he? That would create a constitutional crisis, would it not? All the ideological controlling devices—an identity as "the good god," as a follower of ma'at—guaranteed that a king would not exceed the established boundaries, serve the gods by building their temple houses and acting as their chief priest, tax his people but not too much, serve in his own military but not use it against his own people, act as chief judge, but not for his own gain.

Every image of the Egyptian king shows him as the good god—a perfected human—doing what is right. Even smiting the enemy was not considered an atrocity, but a necessary cruelty against those who would harm the king's people. Similarly, a U.S. president will not openly discuss the atrocities committed during a particular deployment of police or soldiers. Rather, he will highlight how we need a tougher response to lawlessness at home and abroad.

Essentially ma'at is propaganda: a cleaned-up version of realpolitik, the ideology of rule, and certainly not the political truth. Indeed, this is the most insidious thing about the "perfected" god-king: No one can risk being cynical by rejecting the virtuous notion. Only when an Egyptian leader himself jettisoned morality to such a degree could elites also push back, maybe even ousting the leader, at that moment exposed as "bad" and "imperfect."

Ancient Egypt excelled at representing its kings as upright, pure, moral, and fatherly. Today we look at their creations, their pyramids and statues, as symbols of a kind of leadership to which we aspire. These positive optics are the chief focus of my investigation. How did one of the most controlling authoritarian regimes on the planet pull this off? How did they present one-man rule so magnanimously, to so many people, for so long—more than three millennia? Egyptian history never really shows us someone who exclaimed, "Wait, how is this fair?" Instead, we see generations of ancient Egyptians for thousands of years quietly uttering, "Yes, this power over me is god-given, the way it should be." And this is the authority many of us crave for our own circumstances, our own countries.

One of the first and most evocative images of kingship is the so-called Narmer Palette, named after one of Egypt's very first kings. This engraved ceremonial stone, dating from 3200 to 3000 B.C., contains all the ideological symbols connected to Narmer's god-given nature. Carved onto a flat stone two feet tall, the reliefs are full of images of the king controlling his enemies: a bull trampling a fallen foe; a parade in which the king walks toward a line of dispatched men whose heads and penises have been placed neatly between their lower legs; a scene in which the king holds a kneeling man by the hair as he lifts a stone mace above the enemy's head before bringing the weapon down on the skull. Divinity is invoked by cows' heads, and by a hawk holding the head of another enemy by means of a ring in the man's nose. The subject matter is horrific, and yet this object is celebrated and analyzed as an artistic masterpiece in which proportions and hieroglyphic bodily mannerisms are seen for the first time as the fully developed cultural expression of a mature Egyptian visual code.

Indeed, the very act of striking the enemy with a mace is so common that we Egyptologists call it a "smiting motif," not "murder." Kings who are about to smash in enemy brains are depicted all over Egypt—in the reliefs of 5th-dynasty Sahure's pyramid temple of 2500 B.C., on Thutmose III's seventh pylon at Karnak of 1450 B.C., on the front pylon at Edfu Temple of 50 B.C. We see dispatched enemy hands and penises heaped into great piles presented to the god Amun-Re by King Ramses III in his mortuary temple of Medinet Habu of 1150 B.C.

Enemy dispatch was such a typical Egyptian motif that we miss the cleverest part of the image: The artisans are only showing the moment *before* or *after* the violence, never the moment of the carnage itself.[13] The cruelty of the regime is thus sidestepped, the necessary brutality implied. We see a king who will do whatever needs to be done to maintain his state and his power, but who never actually shows himself getting his hands dirty.

The repeated images of smiting and post-smiting communicate that the good king could keep Egypt safe through the divinely sanctioned threat of violence alone. By showing what could happen if presented with rebellion, but by avoiding publication of the blow itself, the king got to maintain his purity, his innocence, his "goodness."

Other cultures were not able to avoid showing their bloody deeds. Regions in constant battle against one another didn't have the Egyptian luxury of glossing over the gory details, needing to display their will to maim and destroy with more specificity. Think of the ancient Assyrian regimes' willingness to depict war crimes, Maya and Aztec images of heart removal and self-sacrifice, and Roman atrocities shown on victory columns. Or pick up the Bible and read how it was considered right and good to stone people to death for certain transgressions. But continuous authoritarian regimes such as ancient Egypt seemed better at hiding how cruel they could be, masking the viciousness with a morality that communicated a necessity for pain in search of what was right.

The U.S. system of capital punishment presents a parallel case. We employ it to communicate to our population that some people deserve to die because their crimes were so heinous that only their utter removal from society will serve the greater good, and yet we veil the act of execution itself. We have invented some pretty weird contraptions—the electric chair that burns people to death internally, and now the injection of a cascade of poisons into a prisoner lying on a hospital gurney, ironically involving devices and procedures normally used to save lives—as we have tried to manufacture an execution with no bloodshed, no mess (and ostensibly, as far as an injection is concerned, no suffering—just a person falling to sleep, even though we know the reality is far from that).

In a way, U.S. capital punishment is exactly like the Egyptian smiting motif. It even gets a special moniker—"capital," an obscure Latin legal term meaning "first in importance"—lest we say with gory precision what we are actually doing to these prisoners. Showing an image of a man strapped to a gurney is a veiled enactment of violence meant to broadcast our piety and goodness in performing an act that must be done. And we feel ourselves good because we think we are avoiding undue suffering and an unseemly bloodthirsty glee.

In ancient Egypt the most violent rhetoric occurred in textual form, not in visual imagery. Thus, it was something to which only the educated elites had access. In Egyptian writings, there were myriad ways to express slaying, maiming, decapitating, and dehumanizing; a language reflects lived reality, like the stereotype of the Inuit people having hundreds of words for different kinds of snow. Some of this literature must have been spoken aloud at court, as laudatory hymns or dramatic reenactments of battles.

Although the ancient Egyptians deemed it appropriate to share the image of a violent king for the good of all, the elites were the ones actually tasked with creating the blood and gore. Military power is limited; you can't just keep invading until the end of time, and an army does not have an unbounded capacity to contain threats through force.[14] In the international sphere, most states rely more on the threat of violence than they do on actual brutality. The propaganda of violence is meant to instill fear and invoke reactions in people *before* one actually has to harm them in some way. It's a cost-effective strategy for those in charge.

Compared to its visual imagery, ancient Egyptian literature was more revelatory about the humanity of a given ruler, exposing crises he would not necessarily have revealed to the masses or doubts he may have expressed in a given situation. But because Egypt's elites fought and politicked and ate and worshipped alongside their god-king at court, they were exposed to a different side of him. Thus, the propaganda created by them and for them was necessarily different, filled with subtle threat rather than outright scare tactics or implausible super-humanity. In texts, Egyptians often communicated how the king could overcome his many challenges; even past failures of the court were obliquely admitted, broadcasting to every courtier the king's singular acumen and potential violent reaction to any who might try to break ranks and foment a coup. Even enriched elites required a mutually sustained and communal system of gaslighting to keep them all in line.

But the clever political operator knows that even when addressing insiders, direct truths are best avoided in text and in person. The clever leader is never straightforward about his intentions and actions; this is why successful politicians are so good at lying, obfuscating, fibbing, covering up, spinning. The untruth is better, even when it is obvious. Everyone who follows the news knows that *Washington Post* journalist Jamal Khashoggi was targeted for his anti-Saudi reporting and murdered in the Embassy of Saudi Arabia in Turkey, that bone saws were used to dismember him even before the moment of his actual death, and that his remains were mysteriously disposed of. Yet Saudi leaders have never taken responsibility for the crime. Instead, multiple Saudi men have been arrested and sentenced to long prison terms as expendable sacrifices for Crown Prince Mohammed bin Salman, who needed to retain his reputation of strict fatherly goodness.

The lie is everything for the man at the top; if his elites think he is untouchable, then they will also refuse to see it or talk about it, thus upholding the lie. Indeed, even though authoritarian leaders do all kinds of things that normal people cannot do, including torturing and killing and breaking taboos that others are compelled to respect, most leaders will demand that their courtiers avoid mentioning such mischief. Not only does the fear of retaliation silence them, but the ideology of divinely ordained rule makes speaking out that much more transgressive.

In the end, the yoke of responsibility cleanses the king. He has to make decisions you don't have to make. He has to serve the god(s) in ways you can't understand. He is chosen; he is different. And when it comes to responsibility for indiscreet bloodshed, his minions will always take the fall.

Ideology makes people feel that their leader is godlike, and thus someone they want to support. While the king is busy being king—issuing orders, acting as religious leader, and working with his advisers—it falls to the elite to construct propaganda campaigns. Because the king can pit those spin masters against one another, using the tactic of dividing and conquering, they will jump all over each other as they compete to out-sycophant each other.

In fact, all those images of the king as a god, all those texts written about the martial feats of the monarch, are made by men trying to show more loyalty than the other guy, men trying to accumulate more power, more money, more access. Many texts about royal power show how these wealthy men often make mistakes that the king has to fix, creating the opportunity for courtiers to doubt and accuse one another of not being loyal enough. Everyone is finger-pointing, while few point up the ladder at the king himself. The gaslighters become the gaslit.

The millennia that separate us from ancient Egypt's authoritarian regimes are a gift. Studying this archaic culture transports us to a world of pharaohs and harems and pyramids, all coated in a delicious golden shell. It allows us to investigate a political system with sobriety and distance, and even some patronizing judgment. The perspective we gain is especially useful now in a polarized world when tempers get hot and political cynicism runs high, when we disagree about the nature of the authoritarianism right in front of our eyes and yet cannot dissect our own system because we are so deeply embedded in it, rewarded by it, afraid of it, caught in its web, unable to see it for what it is.

For many of us, it's hard to figure out what, or whom, to believe. Our leaders cue up so many slogans on Social Security, the stock market, working mothers, men's rights, gun ownership, right to life, the radical Left, and the ultraconservative Right that it's hard to find an unmanipulated opinion. Their sales jobs include not only what we hear, but also what we see. Our leaders dress like we do, so—unlike the ancient Egyptians—we have a hard time even identifying the wizard behind the curtain. When a man appeared in ancient Luxor in a double crown—a white, Smurf-like tower nested into a red cap with a wiry protrusion—people immediately recognized him as differentiated from the rest of society by means of special regalia that showed his godlike nature. But if a leader in our world appeared in that kind of getup, we would laugh at him for his ridiculousness. For us, rule appears in the guise of a well-tailored everyman, a leader who is supposed to follow our system, appearing moral with the fiction of equality.

You may think you're different from an ancient Egyptian. You may think you don't have a king. You think you'd never fall for the absurdity of a god-king, or any of the other PR pitches made on behalf of the long-ago royals. Propaganda is for chumps, fools, people who live in repressive regimes in which they are constantly afraid for their lives and livelihoods. Right?

Wrong. Propaganda is absurdly quotidian. It is all around us, bombarding us. It is created not by Big Brother, but by our own peers, by ourselves. Political spin often just reinforces what people want to think anyway; the leader's transgressions are normalized, and we forget that the cover-ups are lies because his might is right. Instead of propaganda, we see public monuments as proof of resilience, of a people coming together under a series of strongmen who can commission beautiful things to grace our cities, who can accentuate problematic histories to show themselves as heroes overcoming evil.

And yet it is moral ideology that allows presidents and prime ministers to silence people who might criticize, expel minorities who are not a part of the whole, and delete problematic people. But maybe it's not propaganda if its benefits will eventually trickle down to you. Right? My own obsession with ancient Egypt first found root in the beauty that authoritarianism can create: the monuments, the riches, the gold, the animal-headed gods, the sprawling temples, the books about the underworld. I, myself, have bought into it for decades. I, myself, have been co-opted, unable to recognize the propaganda that the ancient Egyptians were creating, and drawing a hard line between Egypt's divine kingship and my own country's system of democratic government.

But how different is an Egyptian hymn to kingship from the current U.S. fetishization of our forefathers, our Constitution from sacred scripture, our flag from a totem, our mercenary soldiers from sacrificial victims for an imperial cult?[15] Our politicians rely on the will of "the people" as an explanatory cipher, rather than exposing the dirty scrum of how our realpolitik actually works. But we want to believe. We tell ourselves that we have freedoms and rights, and that our leaders must follow what the people want.

The philosopher Ian Hacking coined something called "linguistic idealism," in which you only see what is written about, only recognize what is represented, only process what has been monumentalized or recorded in some way. Everything else somehow becomes invisible.[16] In practice, this means that leaders get to maintain their stamp on history while everyone else is subsumed by their power, silenced and unseen.

Think of your favorite politician. Think of how he chooses to hit the same points again and again in speeches, tell the same stories over and over, creating an ideological truth just by hammering at the same topics, funneling his own curated reality into our history books. The truth is, propaganda is not some evil dude pulling the strings and manipulating all of us. It's a collection of created narratives that gaslight and divert attention, that reframe and perfect, that justify what might be considered bad or immoral behavior by turning it into policymaking, ideologizing it, cleaning it up.

It's fitting that most of today's authoritarian regimes—or countries ruled by authoritarian personalities—present themselves as "democratic," putting on elections, manufacturing the fiction that the people are choosing their leader when democracy itself has become the go-to means of political laundering. Democracy today works like the divine kingship of yesterday because it allows vast populations to deceive themselves communally, to think they are making a choice. What better ideology to support authoritarianism than that of fervently held individualism in which rights are granted and leaders chosen in free and fair elections? If an authoritarian leader is presented today as democratically chosen by the people, is that not the same as an ancient kingship presenting a royal regime as good and pure, convincing the elites that the gods chose a king and that only the king can lead the country out of the current haze and into the light? Whether you call it divine kingship or democracy, both demand moral ideologies.

Maybe you're still wondering if ancient Egypt can really teach us anything about our current systems of rule. After all, that civilization so removed in time seems very different from today; their kings were coddled and protected and dressed in splendor, while their ordinary people suffered pestilence and starvation and died young.

But modern exceptionalism has recently been laid bare by a simple virus. We are the same human mammals with the same DNA with (almost) the same social systems as the ancient Egyptians. Yes, there are almost eight billion people on the planet now. Yes, our systems are more complicated by necessity. But human beings still think very much in the short term, still use the same elite hegemony to maintain social inequality, still believe their self-serving stories.

Ancient Egypt gives us 3,000 years of history, showing us that things move slowly, that human societies don't pivot as quickly as we think they do, that when one exploitative ruler is overthrown, another is usually put in his place, that we are embedded in our geographies and climates. Egypt provides insights into ups and downs, booms and busts, prosperity and devastation, epidemics and plagues, and the human reactions to all those developments.

In the following five chapters, we will examine five different ancient Egyptian kings—Khufu of the 4th dynasty, Senwosret III of the 12th dynasty, Akhenaten of the 18th dynasty, Ramses II of the 19th dynasty, and Taharqa of the 25th dynasty. Each ruled with a different kind of authoritarianism. Each crafted different narratives of his rule. Each relied on a different balance between leader and elites. Each tweaked the ideology to maintain the king's authoritarian power. In their strategies, maybe we can more clearly see the political maneuverings of our own time and find parallels to their public images in the camera-ready posturing of modern leaders.

CHAPTER 2

KHUFU:

Size Matters

You may have heard the name Cheops—or perhaps the Egyptian version of the name, Khufu (r. ca 2589–2566 B.C.[1]). This, of course, was the king who built the Great Pyramid on the Giza Plateau, the only wonder of the ancient world still standing. Who better to start with in a book about authoritarian power than the man who constructed a veritable mountain of stone, irrevocably changing the landscape and creating a structure that still affects human minds to this day—so much so that some people still believe his pyramid to be the product of non-human extraterrestrials or a profoundly ancient human civilization with higher intelligence?

Khufu was the second king of the 4th dynasty, and he is essential to any discussion of kingship in ancient Egypt. He left us no diaries, no playbook of how he ruled. But the Great Pyramid is a testament to his authoritarian rule, a mathematical proof of success in stone. If he built it, that meant his reign was incomparable. His power was not only god-given, fated from the beginning, but so extensive and invasive that he could construct a behemoth with granite chambers and galleries floating in a massive limestone-capped expanse, oriented along exact cardinal points with such precision that we still cannot crack how the Egyptians actually did it.

This is power: unmistakable, obvious, massive, simple. And leaders around the world forever after have been scrambling for the kind of political clout that could manifest such monumentality.

But there is another way to look at this pyramid—not as a sign of a king's absolute power, but of his weakness. What if we see this structure as proof of an insecure king who now needed to visibly demonstrate his capabilities to his courtiers, who was obliged to build this massive tomb as a show of force? And instead of manufacturing more strength for the crown, the act of constructing this Great Pyramid would forever enfeeble the kingship, standing as a brutal reminder of royal excess and human exploitation. The act was an over-the-top extravagance demanded by kingship—and in the end, all the required investments in labor, engineering, and materials sowed the seeds of the 4th dynasty's destruction.

Fundamentally, the pyramid was meant to safeguard and transform the king's corpse after death. Though he didn't have any texts inscribed in the internal chambers, Khufu's prone mummy was certainly subject to days and nights of magical incantations pronounced by Egypt's highest priests, as well as his son and successor, Redjedef.

During those rites, Khufu was likely called "a spirit indestructible," with extraordinary powers outlined in these simple but powerful phrases: "If he wishes you to die, you will die. If he wishes you to live, you will live!"[2] The king was awakened ("Rise up! Take your head; collect your bones; gather your limbs; shake the earth from your flesh!"[3]), fed ("Take your bread that rots not, your beer that sours not!"[4]), purified ("cleansed is he who is cleansed in the Field of Rushes!"[5]), transported ("The sky's reed-floats are launched for [the king] that he may cross on them to light land, to Re."[6]), and divinized ("He comes forth and goes to heaven among his brothers, the gods."[7]). His destinations and manifestations in the afterlife were many—as the constellation Orion taking the form of Osiris; or with the "imperishable ones" among the circumpolar stars that never rise and never set; or on the heavenly boat of the sun god Re as he traveled through the sky; or within the embrace of his mother, the goddess Nut, as she concealed him from danger; or as Horus of lightland rising in the eastern sky; or as Sobek, fierce god of the Milky Way, which was the Nile of the heavens. None of these afterlife existences were mutually exclusive for the Egyptian god-king. He was everywhere and everything.

His place as god thus secured, Khufu was (probably) installed in his sarcophagus deep within Egypt's most unparalleled pyramid—the likes of which would never be built anywhere ever again—and sealed inside. Weeks of rituals had moved Khufu, body and soul, from the status of "good god" to that of "great god." But more important for those family and associates left on Earth, every chanted spell reified the current king within Egyptian society, and so Redjedef was installed as ruler with the empowerment of his father's funeral rituals.

THE CULTURAL MEMORY OF A DESPOT

After King Khufu's death, stories were written indicating not so subtly that he was a tyrant with little respect for his people. In one famous account written a few centuries later, Khufu sent one of his many sons, Hardjedef, to find a 110-year-old magician named Djedi—a man with a legendary daily diet of 500 loaves of bread and a side of beef—who possessed not only the ability to rejoin a severed head to its body, but also the knowledge to find his way into the secret chambers of Thoth's sanctuary, that is, the key to the workings of the universe and immortality itself.

After an arduous journey, the old wizard was brought to the Egyptian palace. Khufu wanted him to get to work right away, and he called for a prisoner to be beheaded so the magician could perform the miraculous head reattachment. Djedi was venerated enough that he could object to the king's command without censure: "But not to a human being, O king, my lord! Surely, it is not permitted to do such a thing to the noble cattle!"[8] A goose was brought instead, and Djedi performed his Frankenstein magic trick on the animal to the delight of the king.

All games aside, the king then got to the point and asked for the secret code to get into Thoth's sanctuary. At that point, Djedi demurred and launched instead into a prognostication that foresaw the birth of three new kings and the end of Khufu's dynasty.

Poor Khufu. Now he became depressed, knowing that his family line would soon run out. Even a god-king who was able to build the world's largest stone structure could be tamed by hubris.

Much later, the fifth-century B.C. Greek historian Herodotus tells us that it took Cheops—using the Greek form of his name—10 years to build the pyramid's causeway and another 20 to construct the pyramid itself, even with the aid of machines that supposedly lifted the blocks into place. The work was so overwhelming that the king gave in to his darker side and shut down Egypt's temples, to funnel all their wealth to his megalomaniacal pyramid project, burdening his subjects with the construction: "Cheops, who was the next king, brought the people to utter misery. For first he shut up all the temples, so that none could sacrifice there; and next, he compelled all the Egyptians to work for him, appointing some to drag stones from the quarries in the Arabian mountains to the Nile."

The details of Herodotus's story don't entirely fit the evidence. The pyramid stones did not come from the Arabian mountains, for one thing. Also, the years that he said were needed for the project were longer than Khufu's known reign. But nonetheless, we glimpse some historical analysis here, indicating that Khufu's short-term demonstration of power had real political costs. The pyramid's expense was so great, we are told, that Khufu even used his own daughter as a sex slave, charging men to sleep with her to pay for the blocks and their transport: ". . . so evil a man was Cheops that for lack of money he made his own daughter to sit in a chamber and exact payment (how much, I know not; for they did not tell me this)."[9]

Even though the sex-for-blocks scandal can likely be discarded as hyperbole, the traces of schadenfreude within Egypt's elite population are palpable. Khufu had reached for too much, and his dynasty paid the price. Both the Egyptian tale and Herodotus's account record disaffection with the great leader, though they were written long afterward.

This makes sense, of course, as one can only commit such things to writing when it is politically and socially expedient to do so. We can imagine that the Egyptians only whispered such treason among themselves, greedily preserving stories orally until some version could be committed to papyrus or some Greek dude came along and asked about the guy who had built the Great Pyramid.

However, this doesn't mean that Herodotus's story is true, only that some of its impressions are based on actual cultural memories of cruel kingship. Such tales—of kings who grabbed resources unchecked, who changed the landscape at their whim, who abused and misused people as they desired—were actively maintained by a literate elite bloc to remind the crown of its fragility.

Manetho's even later account of Khufu is equally conflicted. The third-century B.C. Egyptian historian writes: "Of these the third was Suphis, the builder of the Great Pyramid, which Herodotus says was built by Cheops. Suphis conceived a contempt for the gods, but repenting of this, he composed the Sacred Books, which the Egyptians hold in high esteem."[10] (The name Suphis likely was the result of a change of the "Kh" sound of the king's name to a sibilant.)

But no matter what we call the king, it seems that many thought he had pushed his divinity too far. That monstrosity of the pyramid was proof enough.

KHUFU THE GOD-KING

A massive pyramid instantly communicates might, just as the word "pharaoh" immediately evokes repressive leadership. In the time of Khufu, the king's administration was not referred to by the term *per-aʿa* or "great house" (the origin of the word "pharaoh"), but it is nonetheless true that as soon as kingship was born in ancient Egypt, it was associated with a palace surrounded by impenetrable walls. In fact, the first known kings' names—what we call the Horus names—show an image of a falcon sitting on top of or inside a residence enclosure. A palace evokes power, strength, vanity, stoicism. Ensconced in his fortress, the king is a hoarder of wealth, a war leader, a magician-priest, a ruler of his harem, a cruel taskmaster, an angry and unyielding man devoid of weak emotions. The king is the palace; the palace is the king.

In ancient Egypt, the royal residence had agency of its own. It institutionalized, separated, contained, doled out, ordered, extended, and allowed only so many individuals to participate in a king's power. And just like the United States' White House or Russia's Kremlin or China's Forbidden City, power was reified as more than just one man. The leader became a collective, intimately associated with the place from which he led, as if residence and ruler were one.

Of course, a tomb is no stand-in for details of political rule; for many kings, including Khufu, we have only the monumental evidence of their deaths. But we can assume Khufu lived in a grand palace close to the Nile. It was likely made of unbaked mud bricks, each about as long as a forearm, dried in the sun, stacked on top of one another, then plastered and painted a brilliant white. The ancient Egyptian word for these bricks was *dep*. The word "adobe" is the version that comes to us via the Moors who brought it to Spain; from there, the word moved to the New World to describe the construction of desert houses.

Adobe stays cool in the summer and warm in the winter; it was a type of architecture perfected in ancient Egypt. But simple adobe construction doesn't mean Khufu's home wasn't elaborate. It was probably radiant with inlays of precious things, painted inside with bright colors, and adorned with faience tiles and soft furnishings.

Khufu certainly had more than one such palace, all located on hills above the Nile floodplain, where the structures could last generation upon generation. He would also have owned river barges that were floating extravagances, and he would have taken portable tent palaces with him into the desert on military campaign or hunting trips.

The palaces must have been situated at various spots along the Nile and into the Delta.[11] All would have been surrounded by strong, well-guarded walls. Those walls made the palaces exclusionary structures by keeping out the unclean masses, maintaining a distance between those on the inside and those on the outside, and marking a leader who needed to be physically and psychologically separated from his people. The Egyptians used the symbol of the fortress enclosure, with its mud-brick crenellations and recesses, as a symbol for the entire Egyptian kingly institution—much in the same way that historians use the phrase "court life" to reference what happened in both a king's city palace and his country residence.[12]

The layout of the palace likely served to control all the senses. Corridor turns limited a clear line of sight. Passages created a veritable maze to confuse the uninitiated. Interior courtyards that allowed sunlight to stream into a space crowded with courtiers could make visitors feel trapped and contained. The aromas of incense, charcoal, and rich cooking could waft over the walls, enveloping those on the inside and intriguing those on the outside, while putrid smells were channeled out. Sound was enhanced within palace spaces for incantations or dampened with earth and textiles to allow for whispered conversations among scheming courtiers or lovers.

For the people allowed inside the royal residence, the structure collected and organized their bodies in every way possible. Everywhere, the hierarchy was architecturally reified; the palace classified everyone. Each person knew his or her rank by where they got to stand when all were assembled in a throne room or an open courtyard in front of a ritual space. The more important people were likely situated in exclusive rooms farther to the back, higher up, better ventilated, and with better views. Most elites saw Khufu only from afar, but some could get close and maybe even speak with him one-on-one.

The Egyptian language provides clues to this hierarchy. One preposition used exclusively for the king was *m-bah*, literally meaning "at penis level," indicating that every courtier stood before a king seated high on a dais.[13] Courtiers were expected to bow down, purposefully making themselves even lower in comparison to him.

During this period, the Egyptian kings put their advanced engineering attentions into their eternal stone pyramid tombs. For their quotidian needs of shelter, food, sleep, sex, eliminations, and cleanliness, they preferred to create practical but impermanent comforts. From Egyptian tales, we get only a tiny understanding of the daily lives of divinized monarchs. But we can imagine that all actions—from wiping the royal butt and cleaning his teeth to attending to his sexual desires and caring for his garments—were highly ritualized.[14]

In the 17th-century court of Louis XIV, the Sun King of France, all courtiers had their little jobs in a strictly hierarchical social system that demanded elite physical presence to ideologize and differentiate the king's divine person from the baser bodies of everyone else.[15] Even though a king created waste like other human beings, the ritualization of how he performed that act was the ultimate separator, and the person who had to clean the effluence was demeaned in the process.

We can imagine such court decorum in ancient Egypt, too—but all we have are the titles of men and women responsible for dressing, accoutrements, palace duties, dancing, grooming, sex, and so forth.[16] We have no letters with a discussion of the tasks to be completed, no complaints or comments. And because the Nile flooded its banks every year, we hardly have any royal palaces preserved in the archaeological record. Certainly, no residence remains from the reign of Khufu. And those few preserved from later times retain no beds or chairs, tables or toilets, or any of the other features that would help us reconstruct the bodily life of a god-king.

If the palace was the king and the king was the palace, necessary resources had to be funneled in and out of that place for the king to achieve his needs. Human resources were rounded up, including professionals with useful skills: doctors, engineers, administrators, tax collectors, bureaucrats, artisans, magicians, priests, even manicurists. If Khufu could collect such people, fund their ongoing training, and keep them within his walls, he could monopolize their abilities.

Young women were also accumulated, because the authoritarian leader needed access to unbounded and productive sex to create sons, to make sure he had many heirs in a world where death before the age of five was tragically common. Khufu's women would have been kept in a particular part of the palace, or within their own separate harem residence that he could visit. Women with the title of queen, and/or the king's blood relations, had the highest rank, but common women with nothing more than charm and beauty could probably have risen in the ranks—to the annoyance of many. We can imagine Khufu's mother keeping the harem system organized with the help of other older women, suppressing competition among the young women as well as hindering—and covering up—drama, bloodshed, and poisonings.[17]

The palace amassed wealth, too. What better place to control resources that could be siphoned away from their source—wheat, barley, flaxseed, metals, stones? What more secure location than inside palace walls to store precious resources—gold, silver, bronze, frankincense, myrrh, Lebanese cedar, soft woolen garments, gemstones, wines and olive oils from the Levant, and other special foodstuffs? (Egypt's naturally irrigated agriculture produced superior results for beer and flax oil, so no need to import those.[18])

In addition, a palace could serve as storage for weapons and war technology, to be improved constantly and disbursed when needed. The myriad treasury rooms were recorded and monitored, their contents distributed and restocked; each responsible official was armed with a title and a seal to determine who had last been in the room. Competitive systems of elite checks and balances ensured that one treasurer couldn't rob the place blind because everyone was constantly watching everyone, gossiping, slandering, suggesting.[19]

In short, Khufu's palace was more than just the king. It was an extension of the diversity of resources that he could collect, categorize, and control.

The king's daily life was certainly weighted down with accoutrements symbolizing his various responsibilities and dominion: the headgear representing different places and powers (including the red crown of Lower Egypt, the white crown of Upper Egypt, the double crown uniting both, and the striped nemes cloth), as well as the various linen kilts with special folds or starched extensions not allowed to normal people. All the adornments had carefully differentiated names that were categorized and believed to have their own divine essences. Each was considered to be alive, a divine protector and empowerer (much like Doctor Strange's red cloak in the Marvel comics or the sorting hat at Hogwarts in the Harry Potter novels.) Each crown or staff or crook was believed to be awakened, because each had been given its own opening of the mouth ceremony, which provided inanimate objects with a life force. Each was specifically associated with different divinities of protection.

Daily ceremonial dressing was akin to covering the king's body with otherworldly bodyguards—some female, some male. That process transformed the king from a frail human body into a perfected god within a force field of ferocious power, replete with goddesses upon his head who could spit fire at his enemies. In his hands, the king grasped scepter gods who could destroy and maim and corral. A fully dressed king was transformed into a superhuman, just in case any of his courtiers planned to work against him.

Indeed, we should not be surprised that none of these crowns, kilts, or other objects of formal dress have been found in (semi-)intact royal tombs—not in the later 18th-dynasty sepulchre of Tutankhamun in the Valley of the Kings, nor in the 21st-dynasty burial of Psusennes I at Tanis. Crowns were kept generation after generation, it seems, to be passed down to the next king, kept in (palace) shrines of their own. In a significant way, these embellishments of kingship were more powerful than the king himself. They didn't belong to him. He just borrowed them to perfect his human self for the short time he held the job.[20]

PYRAMID POWER

The king's tomb was not communally owned, though. His sepulchre was more like personal property, belonging to his lineage, and to him like his own body. Once the king's corpse was embalmed and placed in that pyramid, the whole structure was activated, transcending its origins as a massive vanity project and becoming a functional conduit to the heavens. Starting in the 1st dynasty, kings were buried just to the west of the capital city of Memphis so that ancestral rulers could watch over the current king—a simultaneous support and threat.

The first king to build a pyramid was the 3rd-dynasty king Netjerikhet Djoser. His final resting place was a stepped stone structure meant to evoke a staircase to the heavens. Khufu's slope-sided pyramid was constructed about a hundred years later, in the 4th dynasty. It stood more than 480 feet tall, was encased in dazzling limestone, and had vaulted granite chambers floating inside.[21]

Such gargantuan tombs were intended to stun viewers, and modern observers are not immune. If you visit the Giza Plateau as a tourist today, you can go right up to the edge of the Great Pyramid—something certainly not allowed for most people in ancient times. As you gaze skyward in awe, craning your neck to see up the steep 52-degree angle, you will barely be able to spy the top of the structure, and your peripheral vision will take in nothing but stone. The impact is overwhelming.

Now, imagine it in ancient times—before its entrance was pried open, the gilded pyramidion removed from its peak, and its casing stones quarried to build medieval Cairo. Perhaps you glimpsed the pyramid from the river's edge as a shimmering vision covered in smooth limestone, angled in straight surfaces evocative of the sun's rays. If you looked upon it when its limestone casing was freshly cut, it would have been so white that it blinded you in the noonday sun. Whether or not you were native to the place, you would have understood without anyone telling you that the person who ordered this wonder of stone construction could control endless labor and bottomless resources with political impunity. You would also have believed that he—and you knew it was a he without even asking—was a god among men.

But you are a modern person, you live with newfangled things like the internet and television, and you can watch a popular History Channel show called *Ancient Aliens,* in which "experts" claim that the Egyptians were not capable of building these pyramids themselves, and that some alien force or lost civilization, or both, were responsible for erecting those structures. Indeed, this question—Did aliens build the pyramids?—is a favorite during the Q&A sessions at public lectures. I used to roll my eyes at such queries and chalk them up to ignorance or racism, but I don't smack down those questioners the way I used to—even though, frankly, it *is* a racist question. I now understand that when people buy into such alternative facts they are simply buying into propaganda skillfully constructed by Egyptian kings such as Khufu.

In short, every time another (usually White) American asserts that the pyramids were built by aliens or were capable of producing electricity or exist in a state of constant levitation above Earth, they are falling into the trap so carefully set by Egyptian kings and their courtiers. The pyramids' raison d'être was to divinize authoritarianism, to moralize absolute power, to turn kings into inviolable superhumans. Pyramids reified political power as infallible and fated, like a Calvinist predestination that was set in motion before its existence. In other words, if the king could build such a fantastic structure, then his kingship was truly divinely conceived.

And that's why a pyramid had to be an extravagant construction that took decade upon decade to create. It was a lifelong endeavor of a leader, fabricated with generations of skill amassed from many human minds. No surprise, then, that we still don't know exactly how the pyramids were built.[22]

Of course the Egyptians would not have left us any blueprints for building pyramids. Why would they? It's certainly not the kind of knowledge they'd want to broadcast. The plans were state secrets, closely guarded weapons over the human mind meant to limit its ability to resist power.

Did the kings and elites responsible for the pyramids see so clearly behind the curtain of their own cynically created manipulations? Probably not. Think of the closely intertwined systems of religion and politics today. Militia members in the United States often believe in the imminent end times as prophesied in the biblical Book of Revelation; Taliban fighters are fundamentalist believers in the teachings of the Prophet Muhammad; hard-line Indian nationalists connect their politics to Hindu religious belief. Ideology is generally created by those inside a system—but they are at the receiving end of it too. Fervent beliefs are held and displayed to reinforce the high ground and to maintain positions of power vis-à-vis other stakeholders. Pushing beliefs onto people who aren't demonstrably benefitting from them, who might not believe, is much harder.

And this is where monumentalism comes in. Massive creations like pyramids work instantly to communicate a regime's potential for using repressive ideology on its people—even those people who are excluded from the intellectual specifics of a given regime. The intricacies of a religion are for the initiated insiders, while those on the outside are subject to basic shock and awe.

We will never know how much a king like Khufu believed his own propaganda—did he really think he was a god incarnate?—or if his elites truly bought into their monarch's ability to communicate with the heavens. But everything we do know about today's religious-political fervor suggests that the leaders had the most reason to believe the ideology that they, themselves, had constructed.

It should come as no surprise, then, that hundreds of years before Khufu, in the 1st dynasty, when kingship was new in Egypt, rulers would build grand death palaces in the desert expanse of Saqqara, near Memphis, and at their homeland of Abydos in Upper Egypt. Because each funerary palace commemorated the king's death, most were temporary, filled with short-lived structures that stood only as long as the rituals lasted. The dry environment has preserved traces of some of these death palaces in the form of massive mud-brick enclosure walls some 40 feet tall. The walls were crenellated, giving the structure a fortress-like look.[23]

There, inside that enclosure in the Western Desert, crowds of people were assembled, and many killed—in front of their own fathers and mothers, sisters and brothers, sons and daughters—to accompany the 1st-dynasty king in death.[24] The choice of the sacrificial victims was likely given to the reigning king, allowing a vulnerable young monarch to remove threats to his new kingship: brothers who would vie for the throne, young women whose fathers needed to be kept in check, difficult bureaucrats who knew too much. Perhaps the king made his selection then and there, in public—but we don't know any of the details.

Archaeologists also don't know the exact method of sacrifice. But whatever it was left little trace on the bodies deposited around the palaces and within the kings' tombs, ruling out violent stabbings or skull crushings.[25] Strangulation is possible; so is poison. However these people died, they did so in great numbers. Some kings of the 1st dynasty required as many as 600 people to enter the afterlife with them at multiple enclosed ritual sites.[26]

The reasons for the sacrifices were presumably associated with the precarious transfer of absolute power from a dead king to his successor. Nothing marked the next man for kingship better, it seems, than his ability to kill courtiers with impunity; nothing clarified his dominion better than the fact that so many agreed to die.[27]

The setting was important, too. These people were killed within organized hierarchies already reified within the palace walls that surrounded the king in life. After the rites were over, archaeologists believe, the palaces of death were carefully broken down, brick by brick, and the interior space covered with new clean sand, leaving little trace above-ground of the interred sacrifices. The sites of Abydos and Hierakonpolis preserve the last of these palaces: remnants of a kingship so unquestioned that it could dispense with some of a society's most valuable members.

Despotic abilities are inherently communicated through monumentalism, with size lending strength to a tomb or a palace—or a public persona. Being larger than life communicates a big personality, an overpowering charisma, and unquenchable demands, all of which we assume about ancient Egyptian rulers in our own popular media. Think of Yul Brynner in *The Ten Commandments:* a stunningly beautiful man whose only emotions were anger, desire, and spite, and for whom ambition was limitless and cruel. Such a terrifying and physically perfect man can do whatever he wants.

This Hollywood pharaoh is a merciless taskmaster whom we nonetheless admire and yearn for. His power evokes knowledge of secret goings-on about which we long to know. A snap of his fingers can mean someone's undoing. And yet we are attracted, wanting to spend time with our fearless leader at a rally, even on the fringes, or as a tourist at his pyramid site. Whether a millionaire, movie star, president, CEO, YouTube star, or just the most popular and powerful person we know, we love to name-drop and associate ourselves with that outsize source of influence. Social size matters, and the human mammal loves to organize its collective power pyramidically.

The King Is Dead—Long Live Khufu

Khufu would demonstrate his power pyramidically too. He ruled during the mature 4th dynasty of Egypt, long years after the horrors of human funerary sacrifices and just after his father, Snefru, had invented the first straight-sided pyramid. Khufu is the rich White CEO of our story who thinks he worked really hard for his spot in society—Nothing was handed to me!—when he actually inherited a foundation of an established divine kingship replete with myriad technological innovations. No surprise that Khufu forged the image of an unassailable king who was larger than life, disconnected, even heartless.

The length of Khufu's reign is uncertain, probably less than 30 years. Upon his ascension, he was granted his own unique set of royal names. The mechanisms of the conferral are veiled, but the monikers provide some insight into the practical creation of absolute power. How did Khufu choose to represent himself to his elites? What kinds of names did he and/or his priests choose? Assuming the names were selected in a dark, incense-filled room in perceived communication with the gods, they nonetheless provide an understanding of how Khufu wanted to be seen—or how his elites wanted to understand him.

Despite Khufu's fame for building one of the world's most evocative symbols at Giza, we hardly know what the man looked like. Images of his courtiers abound in the archaeological record, but representations of the king himself are few and far between. The Palermo Stone, a year-by-year chronicle of many kings' activities, tells us that Khufu had two statues created of copper and gold.[28] They must have been quite something to have made it into this formal record, but no trace of them remains.

The only statue inscribed with Khufu's name is a mere three inches tall: an ivory statuette with a squat, harsh visage that was found at Abydos, hundreds of miles south of the Great Pyramid. Another labeled image of Khufu appears in a carved stone relief in the Sinai Desert at Wadi Maghara, a place famous for its proximity to turquoise and copper mines.[29] Here we see Khufu holding an enemy by the hair, steadying himself to bring down his mace and splinter a West Asian man's skull. This smiting image symbolized Khufu's claim over the resources within that region, and marked one of the ways in and out of Egypt with a protective scene of violence.

Beyond this imagery, the pickings grow slimmer still. Fragments of reliefs from Khufu's pyramid temples at Giza show him being led into the company of gods. There's also the base of an alabaster statue in the Museum of Fine Arts in Boston, which shows just two lonely feet.[30] Two unattached and unnamed stone heads—one in Munich and the other in Brooklyn—may have belonged to Khufu.[31] If they did, we see again that he wasn't an attractive man, possessing a square head with grim, unkind features. Some Egyptologists suggest that the Great Sphinx's face was carved for Khufu, a point over which fierce debate continues to rage.[32] If the Sphinx belongs to him, then Khufu claimed the animal-like outcropping of stone as himself, transforming himself into a massive human-headed lion god.

What do we learn from these images? The potential Sphinx visage excluded, Khufu apparently ordered only intimate portraits of himself, preferring to keep his person restricted and allow only a few to glimpse him when they were inside an enclosure or abroad in a secure turquoise mine in the middle of nowhere. Also, when he created a statue, he demanded scarce materials such as metals or ivory to craft his human body.

One thing is for certain: Khufu was no Ramses II, who put up one colossal stone statue after another. Instead, Khufu was a monarch who kept himself inaccessible to the public, who didn't need to show off his physicality. This was likely a time when the person of the king was believed so sacred that only those properly initiated elites were permitted to glimpse the good god in all his glory. Perhaps it was thought that a "normal" person couldn't handle the awe-inspiring sight. But more likely, the king's person was restricted because he was thought to be simply too precious, too glorious, too much to share. In any case, Khufu kept his distance from the masses, monopolizing his own image just as he monopolized so many other resources. Probably only those people who had access to the king himself could see his statues.

As for that tiny inscribed ivory statuette of Khufu,[33] it's a problematic piece. The king is shown seated, indicating that he was meant to be served, rather than acting in service to gods. The fact that the statue was made of elephant ivory is evocative of the human power needed to bring down such a creature. The statuette shows Khufu holding a flail and wearing the red crown traditionally associated with Egypt's Nile Delta, the richest agricultural region in Egypt and a veritable breadbasket for the monarch. But what catches and holds the viewer's eye are the harsh features of the face—a formidable reminder, perhaps, of this king's power. Some argue that the figurine was made as much as a millennium after the lifetime of the king, a later version of a Khufu long deified.[34] Whatever the truth, it seems Egypt remembered him not as a jovial ruler, but as uncompromising and severe.

We automatically associate that sternness with his pyramid complex, even though we have absolutely no contemporary evidence of his personality. But pyramids are highly charged edifices. Pyramids are so evocative of repressive politics that many Egyptologists avoid the issue entirely and jump into other topics instead—documenting comparative pyramid sizes, building methods, architectural spaces, statuary, reliefs, texts, orientation, and religious meaning. Archaeologists investigate the areas surrounding a pyramid, uncovering sites such as Khufu's workmen's villages or the Tura limestone quarries, revealing information about how the pyramids were built, which stones came from which sites, and how far they traveled.[35] Researchers discuss the number of years of work such structures demanded, calculating the rate at which blocks needed to be placed to complete a given pyramid within a particular reign. (For Khufu, the calculation is about one block every two minutes.)[36] They examine the surrounding tombs, building family trees, figuring out who was related to whom by how many degrees, categorizing the titles, reconstituting a king's administration.[37] In short, we collect all the pyramid data to create a positivist reality of the structure—as a grand and miraculous human creation.

We are so busy collecting and processing the ample evidence that we often have no energy to bring a critical eye to the political system capable of building such a thing. This analysis is too often left to those who prefer to work unencumbered by archaeological data—conspiracy theorists, supernatural believers, White supremacists, even Keynesian economists.[38] These alternative thinkers discuss the king's power so imperfectly and so self-servingly that archaeology usually doesn't touch the larger political questions of pyramid building, except abstractly.[39] In other words, the monumentalizing has had a great effect upon us, turning all of us into Pharaoh's groupies, his apologists, who bring light to his burial ground as a means of aggrandizing his kingship and our own academic status. Even after thousands of years, the pyramid still cows us into submission.

Khufu didn't invent the straight-sided pyramid. He inherited the research and development from a line of ancestor kings. In the 1st and 2nd dynasties, the Egyptian kings' tombs were not surmounted by pyramids at all. They weren't even constructed out of stone; everything was still made of mud brick back then. Most tombs included two separate spaces: first, a subterranean burial containing the king's body and myriad tomb goods, covered with a mound of earth, and second, a death palace where the funerary rituals could take place, surrounded by a thick enclosure wall that was plastered and painted white.[40]

The sacrifices that took place there left an indelible mark on ancient Egypt. Indeed, when you visit the Pyramid of Khufu, you may hear the odd tourist saying, "Oh yes, the architect who built it was buried alive inside," or "His wives were sacrificed and put into the pyramids surrounding his." In fact, the practice of sacrificial burial was outmoded by the time Khufu chose the site of Giza for his tomb. But the cultural memory of it was only some 300 years in the past. The notion of employing a skilled architect, benefiting from his knowledge, and then sacrificing him within your tomb to serve you in the afterlife—well, it didn't happen in Khufu's Egypt, but it might have in the reigns of 1st-dynasty kings Djer, Djet, and Den. This is why we can't shake the idea that pyramid building was intimately associated with ruthlessness.

By the 3rd dynasty, Egypt developed tombs that were more public facing, with structures displayed to tens of thousands of people. On the one hand, this shift is evocative of the economic and political power to build such a giant edifice. On the other, though, it could mean that the king now had to show a physical power he hadn't been required to before. King Netjerikhet Djoser commissioned a complex that combined the death-palace enclosure walls of the 1st and 2nd dynasties with something completely new inside those walls: a massive, stepped pyramid covering the king's subterranean tomb, the world's first monumental building in stone. Djoser built this sepulchre at Saqqara, near the old killing fields of the 1st dynasty. Unlike those archaic mud-brick spaces, though, Djoser's entire complex was made of stone. The king ordered limestone hewn to mimic reed, wood, and mud brick; even the vast enclosure wall was constructed of stone. This was not a death palace to be dismantled after the requisite rituals, but a tomb-temple to be maintained in perpetuity. Ceremonial palace and tomb were now contained within the same complex for the very first time. And it still stands today.[41]

Djoser's mortuary complex had a northern focus, pointing to the circumpolar stars.[42] Indeed, a statue of King Djoser was discovered ensconced in a little stone hut peering out from two eyeholes canted at an angle precisely toward this constellation. The king's effigy was not meant to be seen by an audience but was placed to launch his spirit into the northern sky.[43]

We have no evidence of sacrificial burials from Djoser's complex. Instead, the evidence suggests that a number of elites entered this walled compound to participate in rituals, watch the king being laid to rest, and then reenter the space for further cult activity in the following years. Though the element of sacrifice was gone, the Egyptians retained those grisly reminders—first by choosing the location of Saqqara, where so much bloodshed had already taken place, and second, by placing the pyramid and its courtyards within high enclosure walls fencing in an elite populace.

We can't really know if these aspects were able to remind participants of the grisly sacrifices that had taken place some centuries before Djoser, but it might have been the reason that Egypt's kings would soon abandon the archaic architecture of high-walled death palaces so evocative of such bloodletting and move on to the radically new complex of the straight-sided pyramid.

LORDS OF LIGHT

At the beginning of the next dynasty—the 4th—a new king looked to differentiate himself from what had come before. As part of a family line used to being elite but not royal, perhaps he needed to impress courtiers with something completely different. Instead of high enclosure walls and death palaces, the new dynasty's kings styled themselves as solar gods, bringers of light, creators of even more public-facing tombs, now placing their temples front and center along an east-west solar axis. To reify this solar vision, the 4th-dynasty kings embarked on a technological quest to create a straight-sided pyramid that would place the monarch at the center of collected sunlight.

Without a palace enclosure to hem them in, the assembled elites probably used the ritual spaces in front of the pyramid in a different way, perhaps abandoning some of the strict hierarchies associated with the old ways. We could argue that instead of a differentiated assembly of people surrounding the king, we now see an elite community facing the monument in a linear temple space that replicated the sun's rising and setting. The pyramid complex was still surrounded by a wall, but its monumentality and claustrophobia were gone; this new wall was merely to control access, not obstruct sight lines. The massive tomb could now be seen easily over the walls, allowing a call-and-response with the new solar symbol for all Egyptians.

For their troubles, the 4th-dynasty elites received privileged burial places of their own around the new-style pyramid: row after row of mastaba (rectangular, bench-shaped) tombs for each official and his family. Instead of the trenches of human sacrifice, clearly demarcated individual tombs of courtiers in a modernized, planned city of death were organized in regularized grids.[44] Important queens were buried individually in their own pyramids, too;[45] it was as if these kings wanted to be super clear that their elites were being respected, that is, not dispatched before their time.

This 4th dynasty was a new beginning for Egypt's elites, offering a kind of Magna Carta of visible rights and privileges. Indeed, the very nature of kingship was changing. Instead of a bloodthirsty ruler who could order people to a willing sacrifice, this state-of-the-art kingship presented its spokesman as a human god capable of miracles and a physical emanation of the sun god himself. Before, a king's power had been very private, seen by few. Now, it had become something rather public, at least architecturally—seen by many, reified in a polished white pyramid that made the king's divine nature shine brighter than ever before

We can rationalize this growing ideological power by understanding royal divinization to be something imposed from below as a means of hobbling a megalomaniacal ruler. Divinization came with a cost—to the king, apparently. Gone was the swift judgment over life and death; in return, the court now had to bow down to their new human god. And yet, at the same time, the new pyramid arguably represents a king domesticated by his people, a once proud stallion broken by his rider.

The straight-sided pyramid was invented by Snefru, first king of the 4th dynasty, perhaps in an attempt to demonstrate that he did not in any way belong to the 3rd dynasty (not to mention the 2nd or 1st). Just as a new presidential administration might go out of its way to prove it has nothing to do with last one, Snefru would illustrate his new beginning with a monumental bang. Indeed, he considered it so vital to get his vision of kingship right that he didn't give up even in the face of massive failures. He started his pyramid experiments at the site of Meidum, where he created nothing less than a magnificent collapse. Building at too high an angle, he created a damaged and unsatisfactory pyramid. The structure was still activated through rituals, and the requisite temples added.[46] But the king moved on.

In search of better bedrock, Snefru shifted the quest for a perfect mortuary structure north to the site of Dahshur. This time he built what we call the Bent Pyramid, an inauspicious name that gives away the ending of the experiment. It seems his engineers tried to build the edifice with too high a gradient, almost 60 degrees; when they got two-thirds of the way up, the foundations started to crack. At that point, the angle was drastically changed to 40-some degrees, yielding a strange, stubby pyramid above the bend where the angle changes. The casing stones and east-facing temples were added nonetheless, apparently at great expense, despite the fact that Snefru had still not gotten it right.

Not one to be deterred, Snefru remained at Dahshur, where he knew the foundation rock was strong, and built what we now call the Red Pyramid: the first true straight-sided pyramid in human history. But it looks a bit squat, at a low 47-degree angle—certainly not the perfect triangular structure we see in our mind's eye. To the Egyptians, however, it must have seemed a revelation: a monumental edifice almost 40 stories tall, sided with gleaming white limestone and capped with a pyramidion incised with Snefru's names that was almost certainly gilded to catch the first and last of the sun's rays.[47]

The king ordered no less than three corbel-vaulted chambers to be constructed within the pyramid's massive bulk. And when his divine corpse was placed in its center, this structure not only became a resurrection device for one man, but also a divinity machine for Egypt's kingship. Egypt had turned the body of its great leader into nothing less than a miracle of white light: the sun god himself.

KHUFU THE BUILDER

Snefru's son Khufu would, of course, want to continue this ideological legacy. (Who wouldn't want to become the sun king?) We don't know how old Khufu was when he took the throne, but he was certainly no child, given the many years his father must have lived to have built so much monumental architecture. We do know that Khufu had the time and technology to build big; indeed, most of the research and development had already been done. And he followed his father's lead in choosing a new site for his burial.

The kings of the 1st, 2nd, and 3rd dynasties had clustered their tombs within the same royal burial grounds of Abydos and Saqqara; with these structures they physically reified their ancestral royal connections, not individual agency or narcissistic greatness. But the kings of the 4th dynasty would have none of the legacy tainted with blood. And so Khufu chose a new site, Giza, which was far from the superstitions of cruel nepotism, yet close enough to be visible from the capital city of Memphis.

The fact that Khufu chose not to be buried next to his father is an anomaly in the larger span of Egyptian history. Egyptian kings tended to congregate within marked royal burial grounds, finding power in numbers and lineage. Perhaps Khufu wanted to get out of the old man's shadow. Or maybe he wanted his miracle of stone to be viewed on its own merits, without advertising the previous work that had made it all possible. Whatever the reasons, choosing a separate burial site was a kind of slap in the face to past kings.

Over the following two decades, Khufu would build the biggest, grandest, most technologically proficient pyramid ever created on planet Earth; his Great Pyramid was some 50 stories tall. Some argue that the height was first passed when the central spire of the Lincoln Cathedral in Britain was finished in the 14th century. That spire collapsed in the 16th century, though, and it was not until the Eiffel Tower was erected in Paris in 1889 that Khufu's pyramid was finally eclipsed by a modern creation—some 4,400 years later. It was during the early 20th century when humans were really able to flex their architectural muscles with structures that touched the sky, and such constructions are patriarchal power visualized. We haven't yet stopped building higher still.

Khufu's pyramid tomb was an extraordinary achievement. He proved the divinity of Egypt's kings, and of himself. In a sense, Egypt was now ruled by protomodernists, impressed with their own novel achievements in architecture and industry. Anyone who was 50 years old at the beginning of Khufu's reign had seen the state move from building a stepped structure to smooth-sided stone peaks.

And yet, by the time Khufu's reign was at an end, the downward slide had already begun. No later generation of kings would replicate Khufu's wonders. If monuments are evocative of political power, then how are we to understand this? Why did these 4th-dynasty kings invest so much research, experimentation, wealth, and labor into these structures, only to abandon all they had learned? Why would a people work so hard to manufacture a massive straight-sided pyramid, only to content themselves ever after with inferior replacements? Let's try to decode this conundrum.

The inside of Khufu's pyramid is a wonder to behold. The technology is confounding, breathtaking, mind-bending. It is also very difficult to get inside and see. The inclined tunnels are too low to walk through even bent at the waist. Short of crawling on your hands and knees, the best method is to crouch and chicken-walk your way up.

After some meters of indignity and more than a few strained muscles, you come to the Grand Gallery, a corbel-vaulted expanse multiple stories tall. From there, you walk upright to the burial chamber, a perfectly right-angled space of 10 by 20 cubits that amplifies the sounds of visitors with sharp precision. Elsewhere inside this granite mountain are relieving chambers meant to stop the massive weight from crushing the empty spaces. We still do not know the technological mechanisms used to create these interiors, except that the Egyptians built them as they moved up, adding more with each stone course.

Here, Khufu hid monumentality within monumentality. He displayed a wondrous interior to only a few dozen people at a time: social exclusivity reified architecturally. Only his most favored elites would have been allowed to consume the interior with their eyes and express their astonishment to each other, distinguishing them from all those who would never have had a shot in hell of getting inside.

Those elites probably only talked about this privileged sighting obliquely. It was not seemly to advertise one's own greatness to those below them, later Egyptian instructions tell us.[48] The privileged court insiders knew that the secrets of how this pyramid had been built were not to be divulged, but strictly maintained to demonstrate their king's godlike abilities to the select set of powerful courtiers who really mattered. At the same time, Khufu was displaying a heretofore unseen architectural grandeur to the masses—simultaneously creating interior exclusivity alongside an exterior public broadcast of his power.

A cross section of the Great Pyramid shows two narrow tunnels shooting out from the burial chamber through the mass of stone, exiting high on two sides of the pyramid and pointing toward the eastern and northern horizons. (You may remember that a robot explored one of those tunnels in a 2002 television documentary featuring celebrated Egyptian archaeologist Dr. Zahi Hawass.)

For Khufu, the tunnels were like projection devices for his soul, meant to move him along to specific parts of the sky, launching him to the constellation Orion in the east and to the circumpolar stars in the north. On the outside, Khufu's pyramid complex was all about the sun and its bright light, built as it was to catch the rays of the rising sun. But hidden inside were the telescopic channels oriented to more distant stars, and to true north. How Khufu's engineers worked with such precision is another of the pyramid's mysteries.[49]

A few years ago, on a visit to the Great Pyramid, I arrived in the burial chamber to find a group of people meditating to channel whatever energy they felt could be sourced there. Some were sitting in a circle with crystals around them, chanting. Another was actually lying in the sarcophagus, arms crossed over his chest. (Yes, I peeked in, not expecting to see anyone or anything inside, and almost screamed in terror.)

A part of me wanted to groan in the face of this fervent belief in Pyramid Power. But it was truly something to hear the sounds reverberating around me, to hear the incantations carried with an unimaginable clarity, as if the room itself had been designed for chanting voices. I realized that the stone had not been chosen just to show the geographic reach of the king (it came from Aswan far to the south) or the monarch's ability to cut it (dolerite pounders were used, because the normal bronze chisels were too soft) or his wealth of resources (it required thousands of men laboring long months to shape the blocks).[50] It was also believed to awaken the dead with its auditory power, allowing the king to rise up and find his place in the heavens. I have those true believers in supernatural kingship to thank for their enthusiastic experimental archaeology that allowed me to understand the acoustic functionality of this space.[51]

The miracle of the Great Pyramid was never repeated. One and done, you could say. Some readers might be thinking, But wait, there's another huge pyramid right next to it. What about that one? Well, Khufu's son Khafre, another king of the 4th dynasty, literally chose the high ground next to his father's pyramid, giving his structure only the appearance of being taller. Yes, the second Giza pyramid needed a mass of stone and took decades to build—but Khafre had inherited the crackerjack pyramid-building system invented by his father, and the workers were by then practiced in moving blocks along river and canal and setting each block in place efficiently and economically. In addition, Khafre dispensed with the engineering it took to float granite chambers within the limestone bulk, contenting himself with simple rooms cut into the stable bedrock; no need for relieving chambers or complex mathematical calculations for right angles and load-bearing capabilities. Khafre also abandoned the tiny telescopic tunnels and corbeled vaulting. Installing a red-granite corridor into an underground chamber was a relatively simple feat in comparison to executing his father's design. Just put the chamber in place while planning out the pyramid foundation and then build on top of it.

Only a few meters' difference separate the pyramids of Khufu and Khafre, of course. But . . . size matters. People use monuments to understand the scale of power every day. Cheating matters too, and Khafre targeted a higher part of the plateau to make his pyramid seem bigger while skimping on the interior design. He should come up short when we consider ancient constructions and the technological abilities of their builders. Compare, for instance, the Pantheon (concrete dome!) with the Great Wall of China (4,000 miles long!) and Göbekli Tepe (30-foot megaliths!) and the Roman Colosseum (elevators!)—the contest is like an architectural Godzilla-versus-Alien monster-truck rally.

In the same way, researchers examine the sizes of all the different Egyptian pyramids, comparing area, height, angle, cubic blocks of stone, estimations of the labor force, number of years needed, length of time allotted to place each block. And it seems to have been a real thing for the Egyptian kings as well, as they compared their structures with those of their predecessors and tried to beat them. Even at the risk of making a simplistic argument, we can say that pyramid size does seem to have evoked a certain kind of strength. Khufu was at the apex of that pyramid power. After his feat was completed, there was nowhere to go but down.

STATE SECRETS

So much more can be said about the 4th-dynasty pyramids, and countless volumes have already detailed the various elements: the mortuary temple on the eastern side, the valley temple at a special quay that connected directly to the Nile and allowed the king's body to be offloaded from his bark, the covered causeway that connected valley and mortuary temples, the outer wall, and so on. In Khufu's case, only the hard basalt foundation of his mortuary temple is left. The valley temple, completely destroyed, was probably located under the Kentucky Fried Chicken franchise that arose as the behemoth outskirts of Cairo crept in.

But the pyramid grounds did safeguard multiple cedar boat burials. The lumber had been shipped from Lebanon as mighty tree trunks so that Khufu could have riverboats magically transport him into the afterlife.[52] If the king couldn't sacrifice people as in the 1st dynasty, then at least he could sacrifice objects such as priceless boats—an act, we must assume, that was keenly appreciated by the elites who had worked so hard to get that cedar and craft those vessels.

For Khufu, waste was the point. The king's conspicuous consumption proved to his elite society just how much he, himself, was worth. This was a narcissistic kingship, all about flattery, and being the biggest and the best. One of Khufu's boats is still perfectly preserved, ropes and all. (Cedar contains its own insecticide, which is why we use the wood to protect wool sweaters.) Archaeologists are currently reinstalling the vessel in the new Grand Egyptian Museum on the Giza Plateau.

Let's put a critical face on all this data and ask why a king would spend such a massive amount of resources, technology, training, and time to build a pyramid of this magnitude at all. The short answer is: You build a pyramid because you have to. Khufu's power needed to be publicized. He and his father felt they had to build bigger and better from one generation to the next. That stated, it didn't take long to realize that the whole game had built-in diminishing returns. A 2nd-dynasty king couldn't commit human sacrifice like the 1st-dynasty monarchs did. It was too expensive socially, too harmful a means of showing power. Likewise, Khafre couldn't expend the same resources as his father on his pyramid; it was too costly. At the beginning of their lineage, the 4th-dynasty kings needed to differentiate themselves from those leaders who had come before them, creating a new burial ground and a new architectural layout in their quest for something new new new, something that would shock and stun, something that would make their elites believe in the divinity of kingship again.

But just because Khufu's pyramid was a technological wonder, let's not overlook the fact that the king's pyramid scheme was actually a sign of royal weakness. As Egyptologist John Baines first suggested, the mere existence of a pyramid implies that the kingship was somehow doubted.[53] It was a sign of deep insecurity, not unlike the young, beautiful, new wife of an old, fat, jowly politician with a comb-over. Each new generation of Egyptian kingship had to reinvent itself to continue to hold ideological sway over the elites. The king could not keep doing the same old tired—or cruel—things his father had. In ancient Egypt, with each new family lineage, there was the expectation of a new miracle to prove that the king really was a god.

How did the Egyptians implement their pyramid scheme? Well, we are never going to find a document entitled, "How to build a pyramid in 20 years or less." Those were state secrets, after all, with only a handful of confidants read into the program. If the tricks were not revealed, the power would seem greater than it was. Apparently, Snefru and Khufu felt that kingship had lost some of its mystery, particularly because they were the first kings of a new dynasty that inherited the downward slide of the last one. They needed to present themselves as modern.

Thus, Snefru and his elites hit upon the straight-sided pyramid, in a new burial ground. It may have taken them three tries, but they succeeded in the end. Even given the scale of Khufu's or Khafre's pyramid, Snefru's three pyramids put together would easily dwarf each of them.

The frail human mind seems wired to fall for such physical demonstrations of power. Egyptologists still argue with one another about methods of pyramid building and sources of labor. But there's no need for supernatural explanations, because the evidence that pyramids were built by human hands is scattered all over the Western Desert. For instance, some blocks in the Great Pyramid bear cursive texts with the name of the work crew that hauled them—one crew was cheekily named "The Friends of Khufu."[54] We also have the archaeological remains of the pertinent stone sources, including the Aswan granite quarries far to the south, as well as the Tura limestone and Hatnub alabaster quarries closer to Giza, the latter replete with ramps for moving blocks.[55]

We know that boats were essential to transporting the stone from these quarries to the work site. Indeed, if you're going to move a block into place every two minutes, then you had better be using water as much as possible. Dragging blocks over sand is beyond laborious and was kept to a minimum. Egypt's oldest surviving papyrus, from Wadi el-Jarf on the Red Sea, is one particular guy's shipping log that offers information about how the stones were transported from Tura via barges.[56]

But even though we have more than enough evidence to demonstrate that the Great Pyramid was not built by aliens (or slaves), we still don't have enough information to say, exactly, how those blocks were moved into place many feet up. This is where things get tricky, and scholarly debates often feed the conspiracy theorists.

The pyramid was built to manufacture two different kinds of inextricably intertwined power. There was the ideological power to make someone believe a supernatural thing: that the king was a god. And then there was the messy political power to convince someone to raise taxes or follow a decree or build an army, which they might have been more inclined to do knowing that the king ordering them to do so had the ability to build a massive pyramid. In the short term, the existence of the pyramid got men to jump to task, because they knew what the king was capable of. In the long term, however, that same pyramid would actually end up empowering the very men who had built it for the king.

This is how a similar scenario played out in modern U.S. politics: To beat a weakened Jimmy Carter, whose administration was suffering from failing social programs and foreign policy, Ronald Reagan latched onto a new ideology. Reaganism was based on rugged individualism, low taxes, small government, and "winning" in the form of unabashed self-interest. Reagan, the man, was divinized in the process, becoming a kind of god of the Republican Party.

Politically, the divinization of Reagan was of extraordinary short-term benefit to the presidency. It meant the creation of a new American founding father who could rally his politicians, judges, cabinet members, and business leaders around him: a 20th-century George Washington. When that divinization occurred, the pyramid was complete, so to speak.

But Reagan's ideological power is still very much with us today, our own Great Pyramid whose shadow still falls across the landscape. It has ended up empowering the very men who created that prosperity gospel of narcissistic individualism, weakening government itself over time and creating political polarization so great that it resulted in a semi-authoritarian corporate regime unwilling to fight a global pandemic for the common good. In the longer term, it has been those Reagan supporters who have benefited as they gutted the middle class, deregulated businesses such as banks, dismantled social services, and became the nation's top 2 percent.[57]

Turning back to ancient Egypt, how could a pyramid end up destroying the kingship that built it? Monumental engineering often has unintended consequences. On one level, it seems that Khufu was able to monopolize everything during the construction of his own tomb and those of relatives and nobles. He pulled resources from everywhere, marshaled man power in the tens of thousands, trained genius engineers, created loads of jobs. From an ideological point of view, the pyramid proved that Khufu was a divinity among baser men, thus putting the elites in their place. His queens, nonthreatening extensions of him physically, were placed next to the king in their own mini-pyramids. His elites had their squat mastaba tombs built in linear adjacent graveyards. The surrounding necropolis literally organized all of Egypt's great families as the deceased members were clustered in death around the body of the king—some in big tombs, most in smaller ones.[58]

But to implement all this construction, Khufu had to delegate massive amounts of power. He needed engineers, bureaucrats, administrators, and viziers. By the end, after all they had developed and learned and created, they only needed the king as a figurehead. In the same way that Reagan's ideological empowerment allowed the rise of an oligarchic corporate America based on smash-and-grab patriarchal capitalism that would destroy government itself, Khufu's godhead castrated the monarch, demoting him from the scrappy, feared warlord that the Egyptian king once was, and transforming him into a remote divinity: idealized, packaged, regularized, covered in the expected crowns and royal gear (much like today's ready-for-TV, airbrushed politician wearing makeup and false hair).

THE MORTUARY INDUSTRIAL COMPLEX

When we remove our leaders from their baser tasks, fabricating god-kings and shielding them from what is really happening in the trenches, they become emasculated. In the modern world, Reagan almost certainly didn't know about the secret sale of weapons to Iran to fund the right-wing Contra rebels in Nicaragua. Bush Jr. was good-old-boy clueless compared with Dick Cheney, his Darth Vader lieutenant who gloried in his machinations to monetize war and legitimize Blackwater mercenaries. Bill Clinton was apparently underworked, having the leisure time to hunt down sexual liaisons while America's prisons were privatized amid law-and-order crackdowns. Obama was helpless to enact any social change amid ever louder White supremacist cries against the so-called demonic agenda of socialism. Trump was the racist, fat-cat boomer playing golf while White CEOs engaged in self-help to shut down any regulations that might inhibit their own astronomical economic growth.

Some of those figureheads rarely engaged in actual heavy lifting or spreadsheet perusal. They were all too busy living in Reagan's Shining

City on a Hill, acting the role of eminent leader and rallying supporters and troops while their empowered elites were busy doing the real work, and grifting the whole time.

In the ancient world, Egyptian pyramid construction irrevocably empowered the elites. To build such monuments, both Snefru and Khufu created an elite bloc of construction experts who could pass on their knowledge, wealth, and power to their own lineages, engendering a whole series of mini-dynasties and broadening society's power beyond the king. In essence, rulers created a Mortuary Industrial Complex by authorizing men to do the research, testing, and building, which in turn enabled the men to develop skill sets so vital that the king could not dispose of them. As a result, they became so politically empowered that they could easily run circles around their monarch.

The mortuary industrial complex demanded the king show his men some respect. Sure, those courtiers had to display loyalty to their liege— maybe even obsequious, over-the-top, slavish loyalty—but the king could no longer be cruel and dismissive to the top guys, because they could now walk away and take their precious pyramid-building genius with them.

In the 1st dynasty, the royal tombs had been relatively easier to build, but the power of the mortuary industrial complex was likely in its infancy then. Perhaps it was the skilled shamanistic practitioners— empowered by their magical indispensability—who could demand that the king drop the mass sacrifices by the 2nd dynasty, and who created novel ersatz rituals instead (bring a statuette of a servant into the tomb instead of a servant).

The dynamic between the king and elites can be tracked through time by relative tomb size. As the king's tomb got bigger and more techno-logically advanced, most elite tombs were rather small, simple, and placed in clusters around the king's burial. But as the pyramid of the king became smaller, those same elites' children and grandchildren built larger tombs that included complicated, accessible, and flamboyant architecture for their own complex funerary rituals, as well as inscribed funerary texts that were once the prerogative of the king.

Here we see another dynamic in the divinization (read: weakening) of the Egyptian king: It necessitated the release of state secrets. The 1st and 2nd dynasties had maintained the secrecy of magical incantations to reanimate their king for his existence in the afterlife, or sacred fetish objects to open his mouth for that same purpose. Massive engineering developments, however, demanded that more people be briefed about the Pyramid-building Program. Even if Snefru had been able to keep the technological details classified, Khufu's project was so ambitious that it demanded increased communication and transparency among the many people needed to move the stones on pace to meet the deadline.

We don't know exactly how the Great Pyramid was built with precision and without collapse. Most ancient Egyptians had no idea, either, even if they served as skilled stonemasons on-site (and certainly not if they were unskilled, drafted labor). Most men would have been familiar with only their department, so to speak, their own specialization. But a small selection of engineers and administrators overseeing the full project needed to share information with one another if they were going to get the beast built.

Thus, state technology secrets, from engineering to magic, must have been revealed with increasing intensity during the 4th dynasty—from Snefru to Khufu to Khafre to Menkaure. The high officials who served those kings had the authority to pass on classified knowledge to their trusted repositories, their own apprentices and sons. And with each generation, more and more people came to learn the tricks. With this process, the pyramid itself quickly lost its mystique, becoming less impressive in the minds of the elites—so much so that kings soon stopped putting so much effort into building them and started casting about for something new that would again elicit some awe.

While they were busy reaching for technological breakthroughs to master pyramid technology, the elites must have competed with one another too, creating a kind of meritocracy within their aristocracy. But once the pyramid code was cracked, those same elites didn't need to outdo each other anymore to please their king. Now indispensable, they could act together and even compete—subtly though directly—with the king himself.

The mortuary industrial complex took on a life of its own as the Egyptians empowered a middle class of skilled craftsmen. The settlement at Heit el-Ghurab[59] on the Giza Plateau provides evidence for the enrichment of craftsmen trained in architecture and sculpture in the 4th dynasty. These men were no high elites, but they seem to have been afforded some of the finer things in life: homes provided by the government, for instance, and decent tombs with limestone-slab gravestones. They were also given nice cuts of meat, countless loaves of bread, and lots of beer to keep them as happy as possible so that pyramid construction could stay on schedule. These artisans forged ties to officials from the highest levels of society by making themselves essential workers as those officials competed with one another to create the next fabulous tomb.

The grand shift in power away from the king and toward the elites had arguably begun already with the reign of Snefru, when we see officials starting to commission statues and tombs in greater numbers and of greater quality. That process ramped up with Khufu, then went further still with Djedefre and Khafre. If we examine some of the elites of the 4th dynasty, the excavated data demonstrate that their social power was aggrandized throughout the process of pyramid building.

Those men with the best statues and the best tombs were either kings'
sons and/or were associated with the engineering of the pyramid in
some way.

Rahotep—likely one of Snefru's sons—was interred at Meidum, the
first burial site of that king. He was high priest at Heliopolis, overseer
of royal constructions, and a general. The statue depicting him and his
wife Nefret is so lifelike—he with his pencil-thin mustache, she with
her plump face, double chin, and thick, bobbed hair—that the modern
workmen who found the pair reportedly fled in terror.[60]

Ankhhaf, another son of Snefru, was overseer of the pyramid construction and vizier. He helped engineer the Great Pyramid of Khufu—
who was likely his own brother—and maybe even the carving of the
Great Sphinx. His statue now in the Boston Museum of Fine Arts is a
tour de force of human portraiture, a craggy face set in a bald head,
etched with lines of knowledge and responsibility.[61]

A man named Hemiunu was chief overseer of royal works. He was a
grandson of Snefru, likely a cousin of Khufu, and the probable intellect
behind the greatest of constructions on the Giza Plateau. A statue of
him, now in Hildesheim, Germany,[62] shows a lifelike portrait of a cor-
pulent and happy official with man breasts.

It's no surprise that all these men got massive tombs for themselves
and their families, complete with fancy decorations that included statues
and reliefs. After all, they magnified their own power alongside that of
the king.

How closely a given portrait may have matched the actual physiognomy of a man can never be answered, but the individualized faces of
these statues are particularly evocative of the period. For most of pharaonic history, only the king got his own special portrait: a kind of personal branding that was a royal privilege. Nonroyal people generally got
bland, idealized faces that could have belonged to anyone. Portraiture

moved with the fashion of the times, each official copying the monarch's style of eyes, nose, mouth, and facial shape the way we might follow fashions from the runways of Paris. But during the 4th dynasty, some high elites were so mighty that they managed to get a face of their own carved in stone.[63] Ankhhaf and Hemiunu were essential to the court of Khufu, and thus men to be placated and kept happy. We can imagine that as each official's tomb construction was under way, the king might have granted them special favors: a block of red granite for a sarcophagus, access to a royal craftsman to commission their own portrait statue, a prime spot in the necropolis. In the short term, Khufu gained the undying loyalty of his officials. In the long term, elite power only kept growing.

A KINGSHIP IN DECLINE

Why did such a powerful monarchy give away so much? Essentially, because the king had tied his agenda inextricably to that of his elites. He had to appease them with favors. He needed them, and they knew it.

We can assume that their indispensability was reaffirmed with court activity—among the elites assembled for the sumptuous banquets and the temple rituals, among the boys of the harem nursery, on hunting expeditions, and in combat training. The king could still scapegoat and ridicule certain officials as he liked, but probably only those with whom he could dispense, and for whom there was already collective ill will. He could not be cruel to his most important men—not if he wanted his pyramid built, his temples serviced, his army maintained, his trade routes continued.

The king was thus required to give the elites a share of his monopolies. (They were the ones running things for him, after all.) He doled out luxury items such as cedarwood from Lebanon, granite from Aswan, and gold from Nubia much in the way U.S. presidents have doled out plum regulatory positions to corporate insiders with obvious conflicts of interest—giving the position of secretary of the treasury to an investment banker, for example, or postmaster general to a man with an interest in the for-profit corporation UPS. Just as the U.S. president's power has been diminished little by little in favor of an oligarchic corporate world, the Egyptian kings' exclusive control was similarly chipped away.

In the 1st dynasty, kings' sons may have been slaughtered en masse as an honor guard of death so as not to compete with their newly crowned brother-king. By the 4th dynasty, the king empowered his sons by steering as many high-income jobs as possible to them, rather than to their cousins or distant relatives. If his own boys became Egypt's administrators, viziers, high priests, and building overseers, they would form a loyal inner circle he could trust.

Nepotism, however, was a short-term solution. After just one generation, those same sons would be in competition with one another as well as the next king—likely, their own brother. Indeed, after Khufu's death, two of the king's sons—Djedefre and Khafre—were enthroned in succession, suggesting infighting within the royal family and a lack of power that would have enabled Djedefre to secure the kingship for his own son after his death.

The aristocracy was running the show, apparently. It was at this time that we start to see evidence for mummification among the high elites, a practice previously reserved only for the king and his close family. Once the method had been researched and developed, the secret formula was released as more embalmers were trained to treat more bodies in grander royal tombs.

And then the elites wanted in on the game. Having a corpse embalmed was a social separator par excellence, as powerful as today's plastic surgery, personal chefs, and private jets. It manufactured the perfection of a human ancestor, making individual families appear inherently more long-standing—not just in life, but also forever after. As the technology was declassified, all the top men would have been displayed with embalmed bodies; the lower elites would have scrimped and saved to get access to some version of the process.

It's at this time that the whole house of royal cards starts to tumble. After only three generations of kings, Khufu's family was pushed aside for another lineage. Why? There's a clue in the Westcar Papyrus, probably from the 13th dynasty, in which Khufu is depicted as the prototypical out-of-touch leader willing to have one of his prisoners beheaded for sport. When the magician Djedi admonishes the king, essentially putting him in his place, Khufu accepts the criticism without taking any sort of revenge against the old man. Instead, he hands over an extravagant payment for the magician's services. This was a king dependent upon learned intellectuals for his entertainment, health, building projects, knowledge, afterlife transformation, and everything else. If this story preserves something of how literate Egyptians perceived their king in the 4th dynasty, is it corroborated in the archaeological record?

In a way, it is. When Khufu died, it seems Egyptian kingship enjoyed a short-term bump in the polls. But not for long. Khufu's heir, Djedefre, tried to replicate his father's success. Like Khufu and Snefru before him, Djedefre stayed away from the old burial grounds so reminiscent of cruel sacrifice. Choosing a new place in which to build his mortuary complex, the site of Abu Roash to the north, he commissioned another straight-sided pyramid. He ruled about 10 years,[64] created Egypt's first freestanding sphinx statues, and invented a new cartouche name that we call the Son of Re.

Yet no matter what Djedefre created, he could not pivot his kingship. He just did not have enough time, and there is some evidence that his pyramid was even purposefully destroyed after his death. How could a people move so quickly from the apex of pyramid power to the political and ideological fall of a hated ruler, attacked and scorned? Perhaps Djedefre had inherited all the problems created by his father's excess and over-the-top divinity.

The next man to take the throne wasn't Djedefre's son, but his brother. Brother-to-brother transfers smacked of family infighting and were frowned upon in ancient Egypt. Through their mythologies of Horus, Osiris, and Seth, the Egyptians were very clear in that the son must follow the father to avoid discord; this was the legal manner of transferring power.[65] The details were never disclosed, so we don't know whether Djedefre's sons were unready or unliked. But Khafre, the second son of Khufu, took the kingship before it could be transferred to one of his nephews. And then he did something remarkable. He returned to the Giza Plateau to erect his own pyramid.

Khafre, too, was looking for a short-term bump in popularity, and he was riding in the wake of his divinized father to get it. Khafre had to shore up his power, and fast, so he went for public grandeur at a discount. By claiming the plateau's high ground, he made his pyramid look larger than his father's when viewed from the city of Memphis, even though it wasn't. He also claimed the Great Sphinx itself, putting his pyramid right behind the leonine-shaped mass of stone and thus creating that elegant Giza composition replicated in countless postcards and coffee-table books today.

A closer look at the interior of Khafre's pyramid reveals more money- and time-saving strategies—no floating granite chambers, no grand gallery, no granite burial chamber, no telescopic tunnels, no relieving chambers.[66] But his mortuary temples were larger than anything we have evidence for during the time of Khufu, allowing more of Egypt's wealthy to collect inside for rituals and offerings to their king. Khafre also included dozens of statues of his person, including multiple attestations of himself in anorthosite gneiss, a stone that gives off an eerie blue glow by lamplight.[67]

These clues are revealing. Khafre was not only trying to impress his highest elites, those few men who would have had access to the inside of his pyramid. No, the long-term repercussions of empowering an administrative corps were coming to bite him. Khafre needed to impress the middle and lower elites too. Thus, the king showed his royal might to more people in a more open social context by creating larger gathering spaces than ever before, as we see at his mortuary temples. Building a grand gallery inside his pyramid would have gotten him very little return on his investment, it seems; better to build a stunning set of statues that would get more people talking.

In other words, what a tricked-out pyramid interior was invented to do—prove divinity to a select and exclusive set of men—no longer paid dividends. The kingship itself had already been divinized and thereby domesticated. It is even possible that Khafre's own brothers were pushing back, demanding that fewer resources be spent on the king's pyramid chambers and thus free up more wealth for their own use. If kingship itself was a game of trying to get the most intellectual and educated men around you to continually believe that you were a god on earth with special powers, then Khafre had already won.

And lost. On the one hand, the kingship had a real monopoly on wealth, resources, knowledge, and violence. But on the other, the king didn't administer any of it personally anymore. Khafre had all the trappings of kingship, but none of its real powers. The more officials became entitled, the more the pyramid complex itself became their playground of misappropriation and payoffs. The mortuary industrial complex was lovingly maintained, but it was elementally changed to serve elite needs.

Khafre was able to hand the kingship off to his own son—a win for the divine kingship column, to be sure. But his heir, Menkaure, would be the 4th dynasty's second to last king. Menkaure felt the need to stay in his father's shadow, adding an unprecedented third pyramid and thus completing the Giza tableau. His pyramid would be the smallest of the three.

But what seems like a sad little structure in comparison to the monstrosities next door might, indeed, have been part of a clever ploy. Situated as it was, it may have linked the king to the constellation Orion and its belt of three stars—two bright and one dim—placing the king in a triumvirate of ancestral divine power.[68] Menkaure even began to use rows of red granite as his pyramid casing stone, apparently having decided that if he must go with a smaller model, it would at least be impeccably finished.

Building in granite was so laborious and expensive that it was akin to dipping a building in molten gold. We don't know whether Menkaure envisioned doing all the casing in this hard stone, because only the bottom courses had been finished at the time of his death. The rest of the casing was completed posthumously in plain white limestone. Like Khafre, Menkaure also spent comparatively more to build grand temples in front of his pyramid—and to commission breathtaking statues of his divine self in the company of his queens and divinities using Egypt's most archaic stone—the same greenish graywacke that King Narmer had used to fashion his engraved palette of enemy destruction some 500 years before.[69]

From the perspective of the Giza necropolis, Egypt's 4th dynasty looks strong and stable. But in truth, much of it was a facade. The last in the dynastic line was a little-known king, Shepseskaf, who was probably not related to Menkaure. His reign was short, some five years at best. The new king spent more time completing the unfinished tomb of Menkaure than creating his own non-pyramidal mastaba[70]—a strange thing for a god-king to do, and certainly suggestive of a vulnerable man unrelated to the divinity of Khufu's line. Shepseskaf seems to have been looking to shore up elite loyalty with pious displays meant for a family greater than his own. With his death, the 4th dynasty was over—but the dynastic line had arguably drawn to a close already with Menkaure.

The end of a royal line is often perceived as a decadent event involving a fall into despotism, a lack of honor, and a dearth of honest dealing. Time for something completely different, most new kings think. And indeed, the new 5th-dynasty rulers appear to have been brothers born of a priest of Re, styling themselves more like elites than kings. They seem to have realized that divinization came with its own baggage. Better to toss it out and become real men again, because if you served god as priest-king, then you were back in the fight.

These new kings didn't focus all their attention on their own tombs, but built temples to the sun god as well—a devout and virtuous signal to their court.[71] Their pyramids were purposeful, modest affairs: rubble cores with simple limestone casing, complete with comparatively large temples that practically screamed their ostentatious piety.[72] In some ways, the chief commodity now was religious knowledge, and these kings tried to corner the market on solar spells, incantations, and public rituals, thus making themselves indispensable to an elite who fervently believed in their divinities and desired better interlocutors to connect with the secrets of heaven.[73]

The accompanying de-skilling process is palpable, and it's arguable that by the 5th dynasty, hardly anyone knew how to build a monumental stone pyramid anymore.[74] Instead of being the god at the center of the wheel of power, these kings put the sun god into that spot, serving more as his priest-kings. The pivot had happened. Kings were no longer the focus of religious fervor, but of service to a religion almost wholly separate from them. The 4th-dynasty pyramid bill had finally come due.

THE ENDGAME

If size matters so very much, then that is why political entities with unquestioned control are responsible for the latest record-breaking skyscrapers: the Burj Khalifa in Dubai, the Shanghai Tower in the People's Republic of China, and the Abraj al Bait in Mecca, Saudi Arabia. A skyscraper is not about steel or stone. It is a manifestation of ideology, just as a pyramid was. Its very existence broadcasts the deeply held reasons that social inequality needs to be maintained and grown, driving a wedge ever farther between rich and poor, ideologizing that separation as something divinely sanctioned and moral. The stock market is no different. Built on a premise of endless growth, too much is truly never enough.

For the elites of the world, growth is an arms race that the powerful need to maintain lest they lose everything. In the corporate world, that has led to monopolies growing unimpeded by regulation or even taxation, thus becoming the new monarchs of our planet. Think of today's megaconstructions—monster corporations such as Amazon, Apple, JPMorgan Chase, Wells Fargo, Microsoft, and Boeing, whose giant empires are behemoths Too Big to Fail, and whose machinations drive local businesses into extinction. What seems to be a charming microbrewery may actually be owned by Anheuser-Busch InBev.

The United States has never had a king, of course—but we now have oligarchs in abundance. Think Jeff Bezos and Mark Zuckerberg. Some of those men engage in overt government patronage. Some, like the Koch brothers, are on the Right. Others, like Bill Gates, are on the Left. Some own private islands that boast all the markers of economic glory, as the disgraced, deceased financier and sex offender Jeffrey Epstein once did. Others, like Warren Buffett, are lauded for parsimonious living and manage to keep rather apolitical.

But as the state is eaten from the inside out by the very elites who claim to have built it, social inequality rises. As a result, much of the world's population not only has no way of acquiring such wealth, but also lack even the basics of food and shelter. Why? Because to be poor—in the eyes of the higher-ups—somehow means being immoral and undeserving.

What is the endgame of all these megaconstructions? Well, in ancient Egypt, the late 6th-dynasty state had not only become so large that it was nonfunctional (think of the giant cable company that never answers the phone), it had also become a mass of intercompeting elites who used the government to serve no one but themselves. (Think of today's relentless multimillion-dollar bonuses, payoffs, bribes, insider trading, and fraud, all happening openly with no one going to prison.) As the competition ramped up, and as the Egyptian state became more impoverished from mismanagement, the end result was nothing less than war.

Competing elites left the capital, returned to their estates, and took up arms against each other, using a once common ideology to take down the other side, demonizing and othering one another. As they engaged in ever more violent competition of family against family, the rest of the Egyptian population fell in behind their patrons. Heracleopolis in the north fought against Thebes in the south; monuments honoring past kings were desecrated by those who hated the overt claims of hegemony. It was the bloodiest civil war Egypt had ever experienced.

Why would our culture be any different? In the United States, regionality is everything; North versus South is a trope, as is urban versus rural. Each side has its beliefs, nostalgia, heroes, particular understandings of history. And people on both sides are now armed with semi-automatic weapons.

The current political climate in the United States is primed for civil conflict. The year 2020 is the new 1855. What fuels it? When we build too big, we mythologize too much, manufacturing greed and disaffection, careering toward a mighty fall, separated into factions, distrusting the other side, and weaponizing the same ideology we had once been united behind. In other words, the mythologies of the Founding Fathers and the American flag and the heroic veteran are too big to fail. People don't kill their countrymen because of mere social inequality or unfairness. But they do fight and kill for ideals that they think are divinely inspired, believing in their righteousness and the other side's wickedness.

The Egyptian pyramid is a cautionary example. It was used as an ideological weapon to transform some people into gods—but it also tore society apart from the inside out.

CHAPTER 3

SENWOSRET III:
THE KING STRIKES BACK

You may not be familiar with Egypt's king Senwosret III (r. ca 1870–1831 B.C.), let alone the fact that there were three kings of that name. But if you see one of the monarch's statues in a museum, his face will stop you cold.

Senwosret III invented the ancient world's most arresting image of kingship: a dour, careworn leader who seems profoundly grief-stricken yet simultaneously exasperated. This was a king ably signaling his martyrdom, weighed down as he was by the dual responsibility of caring for and punishing his grabby and entitled aristocrats. His lined face seems to be saying that we should not covet the unspeakable burden of a power we cannot understand, that this king will work for our better interests in spite of our petty desires, that we should shut up and do as we are told.

But Senwosret III was more than just an arresting face. He was an absolutist ruler who understood the political game in his bones—a man who could move the pieces on the board at will, strategizing multiple moves ahead of time and outmaneuvering his opponents. Like Henry VIII of England, Louis XIV of France, Vladimir Lenin of Russia, and

Mohammed bin Salman of Saudi Arabia, to name a few other absolut-
ists, Senwosret III centralized control of multiple branches of government, applying ruthless pressure and bending strongmen to his will.

Senwosret III inherited a dynasty that was on the defensive, content to take whatever aristocratic loyalty it could get. This Egyptian
ruler would end up transforming diminished royal power into an
ironclad kingship that required Egypt's elites to come crawling to
their master in his capital city for favors that only he could dole out.
The pinnacle of his achievements rests on groundwork laid by his
predecessors, particularly the dynasty's founder, the double-crossing
Amenemhat I, and Senwosret I, who used tactical patronage to
reestablish supremacy over quasi-sovereign elites.

Senwosret III was the fifth king of Egypt's 12th dynasty. He is known
for his two burial spots—one, a pyramid at Dahshur next to the pyramids
of Snefru of the 4th dynasty, and the other at Abydos, just next to the
burials of the archaic kings of dynasty 1.

Senwosret didn't lack for confidence in associating himself with some
of Egypt's most well-known rulers. He would place his funerary installations at the sites most associated with divine kingship. He would erect
his expressive and commandeering statues everywhere, marking his
territory with an unyielding visage. He would wrest control back from
recalcitrant elites who had previously allowed a king to exist only as a
figurehead. Senwosret was not content to be a domesticated monarch.
He wanted more.

Some 700 years after Khufu's reign, we glimpse a more vulnerable
and weathered Egyptian kingship. The rulers were still viewed as god-
kings, of course—but now they were men openly revealing themselves
as priests dependent on their divinities.[1] The civil wars after the fall of
Egypt's Old Kingdom had revealed a ruthless savagery for all to see.
Now, for the first time, Egyptians were openly discussing—in their

literature and song—the place of a king in their world. This liminal leader was seen as a balancing power, but also a potential source of weakness that could send the entire land into confusion and chaos.

Egypt's 11th dynasty had expanded northward from its base in Waset, the Egyptian name for what we call Thebes, modern-day Karnak and Luxor, and made attempts to reunify the strife-torn country. The 12th dynasty's royal line would close the circle, but it was hobbled by a regicide that cut the ruling family to the quick. Amenemhat I was murdered while he slept.[2] It was an inside job by a trusted courtier—a betrayal so cold-blooded that the family spent the following century on hyperalert, launching emergency powers over Egypt's aristocracy, a bellicose series of foreign campaigns that enslaved generations of Nubians to mine gold for Egypt, and a new propaganda machine that churned out royal panegyrics.

By the time Senwosret III ascended the throne, the cold war between the king and his elites was heating up again. Whether the king broke the aristocracy with military might or paid them off is fiercely debated to this day.[3] But in any case, the landed gentry of Upper Egypt seem to have disappeared quite suddenly and were replaced by faceless direct reports to the king.

Senwosret had confronted his elites—with their private armies, independent sources of wealth, and inherited power—and won. It may have been Khufu's dynasty that originally empowered such men, but it was Senwosret who would strike back, probably using a combination of court bribery, military threat, and political strategy to make them kneel again at their god-king's feet.

Senwosret's face impressed all who looked upon it. His propaganda machine was rolling, and his elites were falling all over themselves to compose the next big hymn to celebrate their king. Egypt's treasuries were flush. And the landed gentry had been made to take up residence at their king's new capital city—a center of power to which all had to report, a purpose-built city that was the Egyptian version of St. Petersburg in Russia, Brasilia in Brazil, and Abuja in Nigeria.

With the reign of Senwosret III, the dynasty seemed victorious against any and all challenges. But within just two generations of the death of this great king, his line would suddenly die out, subjecting Egypt to poverty and the cage fights of warlords. The country would not witness another elegant and monumentalized kingship for another 300 years.

A Royal Ancestor's Capital

Before we get to Senwosret III and his strong-arm rule, let's take a look at the forces that shaped the country he inherited when he took the throne.

Senwosret's 12th dynasty arose in Thebes, located at the southern end of an east-west bow in the otherwise south-to-north-flowing Nile. Called the Qena Bend, that stretch of the river was particularly difficult to pilot, given the currents and wind directions.[4] In antiquity, the Qena Bend was a protected part of the Nile Valley. It was hard to monitor, tax, or invade via the river there, which enabled political consolidation within the bend itself as well as resistance to control from the outside. From there, it was relatively easy for warlords to launch ships to the north or south, thus dominating expansive regions beyond.

And the Qena Bend had another advantage: easy access to Eastern Desert wadis that were rich in gold and copper, and that provided passage to the Red Sea for other scarce resources. The Wadi Hammamat area was the best source of gold within the traditional boundaries of Egypt, a massive concentration of a coveted raw material that was otherwise obtainable only by journeying south of the first Nile cataract (the first of six rocky outcroppings in the river as one travels south) at Aswan.

The Qena Bend had nurtured Egypt's 1st dynasty, and now, after debilitating civil wars had torn the country apart, it became a bastion of the emerging 11th dynasty. That line of kings was composed of a series of warriors named Intef and Mentuhotep, men whose capital was Thebes, but who were slowly extending their power northward.

Their long-term plans would be thwarted. A man named Amenem-hat, who served as vizier and general under the last of the 11th-dynasty kings, claimed the throne and started a new lineage, the 12th dynasty.[5] Amenemhat I would extend his newly established royal power, finally bringing the Two Lands—Upper and Lower Egypt—together again under one king.

Amenemhat I needed a capital from which he could launch his armies of soldiers and bureaucrats. He could not maintain a power base in Thebes; that may have been a good place from which to federate and instigate aggressive power grabs, but it was a provincial backwater, far from the action in the rest of the country. He also chose not to rule from Memphis, Heliopolis, or any of the other well-known urban sites at the apex of the Delta.

The 11th-dynasty kings had been trying to reunify Upper and Lower Egypt for some time. To succeed where those rulers had failed, Amen-emhat I knew he would have to conquer enemy territory. Perhaps that made him especially leery of the old strongholds of power with their complex marketplaces ruled by interconnected mercantile families—power blocs that could overwhelm a new kingship. Amenemhat I decided he would have Egypt's elites come to him.

And so the new, self-appointed king chose a site near the entrance to the Fayum, about 350 miles north of Thebes.[6] There, a Nile offshoot dumped freshwater into the Western Desert, creating a large lake and a mass of marshy land. Untouched by urbanization, the area was a rich place to live a hunter-gatherer's life but was not good for farming in its waterlogged state. Amenemhat I drafted legions of laborers to drain it with hydraulic systems and create new agricultural lands—a reification of a new authoritarian statist vision that tamed nature and swept the past away with one stroke.

If the 12th dynasty had started with a coup—we have to guess, because Amenemhat I doesn't tell us the manner of his ascension—then the choice of the capital was offensive and defensive simultaneously. It satisfied the demand for new land to reward soldiers, bureaucrats, and officials without having to take it from anyone else. Also, the income from the Fayum would presumably funnel directly to the crown, filling its granaries for more payoffs and more military campaigns.[7]

In the newly transformed Fayum, the king built a state-of-the-art capital city. Archaeologists still haven't located the ruins, either because they lie buried under millennia of Nile silt or modern urban expanses, or both. But they know traces of the city are there somewhere.[8] (In several ways the modern U.S. capital of Washington, D.C., resembles the city that Amenemhat founded. It too was built in a kind of no-man's-land beyond the established cities, between north and south, on marshy land belonging to no one, and became an avant-garde center of power.)

The new capital, Amenemhat-Itjy-tawy, was specifically named after its subjugator. Translated as "Amenemhat Who Seized the Two Lands," it was a nod to the king's accomplishment of reunifying the country by force. (The verb *itjy* means "to conquer," or "to seize.") The shortened version of the name, Itjy-tawy—"The One Who Seized the Two Lands"—puts the emphasis on the smiting action that brought together north and south.

This new city became the power base for a new Egyptian family of warlords. The regime, along with the entire 12th dynasty, had a rather militaristic quality; its founder did not obfuscate the military power that had gotten him to the top. Everyone had better be silent and follow his every instruction, was his message.[9]

The military conquest was pretty much complete. The economic front was now open. The choice of location had avoided political problems from established families, and they were now invited to come to the new capital. It was time for the new dynasty to set about creating some serious ideological power.

Something similar is happening in today's Egypt as the government of President Abdel Fattah al-Sisi, in power since 2014, moves massive amounts of earth and steel to build a new administrative capital in the Eastern Desert. The city will be home to all the government buildings, including the parliament, presidential palaces, and ministry offices. Propelled by a new wave of nationalism and authoritarianism, Egypt's current leaders have turned their backs on the crowded old capital of Cairo as well as on the city of Alexandria in the north. Those places have already been claimed by various competing interests and are confusing, organic sprawls, difficult to control.

Sisi's regime wants something new, untouched, legible, and disconnected from patrician families (not to mention the hordes of people demanding so many social services). After all, if you build in a new place, the unclean masses will be kept out, while the wealthy elites will have to come to you, bringing their money and connections with them. Foreign governments are already building their new embassies in the new capital at enormous expense, abandoning their old compounds in Cairo. In addition, new shopping centers are going up left and right, inserting the globalized economy too, but on Egypt's terms.

Purpose-built capitals physically destabilize old systems of power.[10] We have already mentioned some, but there are many more: Ankara in Turkey, Canberra in Australia, Mandalay in Myanmar, and New

Delhi in India, among others. It's a good methodology, and one that ancient Egypt perfected with Itjy-tawy.

Another strategy of Amenemhat's new dynasty was a return to pyramid building. There had been a break in that funerary practice during the time of the Thebes-based 11th-dynasty kings, whose tombs and temples were tiered structures blending into the desert cliffs rather than the stark, white limestone pyramids of the earlier rulers in the north.[11]

Amenemhat I was Theban, to be sure, named after the Theban god Amun. But building a tomb in Thebes had become problematic. It's not that he didn't try; there is evidence that he started his tomb on the Theban west bank of the Nile, only to abandon it.[12] Perhaps there was pushback by 11th-dynasty loyalists, with feelings still running hot because Amenemhat had taken the throne from their lineage. Or maybe building in Thebes was just a waste of advertisement money. The ideology and cult of the king's tomb were now needed up north, where the dynasty's power was only just now being established.

Building in the north had its own problems, of course. Amenemhat I was likely looked down upon by the old families of Memphis and Heliopolis, who may have viewed him as merely a provincial warlord valuable only for his gold, army, and brutal strategy.[13] The new king cast about for something that would give him the patina he craved and instantly link his upstart regime to the dynasties of old. He looked to the massive edifices of the 4th-dynasty kings for inspiration.

Reproducing the kind of grand structure that Khufu and Khafre created was out of the question; it was far too expensive and time-consuming. But the smaller pyramids of the 5th- and 6th-dynasty monarchs were cost-effective and had the added advantage of being relatively formulaic. No research and development was needed to build the valley temple, pyramid temple, causeway, burial chamber, pyramid, and so on, with great efficiency.[14]

And so Amenemhat I constructed an old-fashioned pyramid on the empty ground to the west of his brand-new capital city, which was under construction at the same time. He even had blocks shipped in from Khufu's pyramids, literally building his tomb out of stuff from one of the revered god-kings of old.[15] Not only did that mean he didn't have to quarry all the stones, but if he could include Khufu's name and image within his new structures, even as unseen building material, the association was clear. Amenemhat would take any ideological foundation he could get.

This was only one of many clever strategies of Egypt's new conqueror. His next policy was to keep power within the family. Connections of blood and marriage are among the best tools for political entities who distrust advisers and ambitious newcomers; the family is as dependent on the leader as the leader is on the family. Think of John F. Kennedy appointing his brother Robert as U.S. attorney general. Or Bill Clinton choosing his wife, Hillary, to run his health care campaign. Or Donald Trump choosing his son-in-law, Jared Kushner, to work on projects such as brokering peace in the Middle East, whether or not Kushner had the background to implement them. Also, loyalty is often favored over education or ability. A top man's most stable relationships are with family, while lieutenants may easily be thrown under the chariot.

Rulers of the 12th dynasty seem to have had a habit of creating co-kingships—or co-regencies, as Egyptologists tend to call them. Joint rule is, inherently, a defensive plan of action, implying a lack of trust in the sons and courtiers who will install the next king after the death of the last one. A king might choose his heir, but no dead monarch can crown his successor or make sure his rule continues unmolested. No ruler, no matter how divinized, has any political control after he is placed in his tomb. If a king was worried about maintaining certain plans of action, or avoiding pesky power plays, then it would be useful to lock in future plans by choosing the strongest, canniest, cleverest son and elevating him to the throne before the king's death.

This is what historians believe Amenemhat I did with his son Senwosret I.[16] This co-kingship would have split power between the wise old king and the young whippersnapper who was ready to fight. For Amenemhat, who had been through so much already, it would create a double threat—the king's ability, in essence, to be in two places at once.

The utility of a co-regent is clear, but it still implies a certain weakness, a distrust of courtiers, an anxiety about the infighting of many sons.[17] Egyptologists seem quite convinced that such co-kingships were standard for most of the 12th dynasty.[18] But perhaps Egyptian monarchs were claiming an idealized non-reality. There are a few double-dated monuments, such as one from Abydos that records Amenemhat I's year 30 and his son Senwosret I's year 10, suggesting that the elder king appointed his son as co-ruler in his 20th year. But those are all formal images meant to be placed in temple structures. We have no trace of side-by-side leadership from the archaeological record, no preserved kingly decrees from both men. Perhaps such co-kingships were actually manufactured by the son and heir to prop up his own insecure rule by claiming that his dead father had really and truly wanted him the whole time.[19]

Whatever the truth of the co-kingship—and Egyptologists will continue to debate it—it was a useful political strategy in appearance, something that made the king look established, valued, ensconced in his power. Such co-rule—real or imagined—conveyed the father's blessing from the past and provided the current king with a stronger family foundation than he may have actually held. Such partnerships of power were thus not formalized, but ideologically implied as support from the previous generation.

We Egyptologists seem to willfully misinterpret co-kingships according to our own historical bias, though. Take the cases of Neferusobek and Hatshepsut, for instance. Those two female kings, of the 12th and 18th dynasties, respectively, used their father's names in association with theirs, promoting stories of co-rule to prove their legitimacy. When presented with these narratives, many historians see only manufactured histories, not real occurrences[20]—because women were not chosen as heirs but only stepped in during a crisis. Historians automatically treat a female's rule shared with her father as propaganda, or lies, or worse.

But Senwosret I did the exact same thing, presenting his kingship in close step with his father's, implying a co-rule with the elder king—and we Egyptologists believe him without question. There is more than a bit of academic sexism at work here as we take these good (male) kings at their word, rarely trying to deconstruct any monumental documents as idealizing fabrication.

Make no mistake: These 12th-dynasty kings were masters of ideological spin. They could take an established narrative, apparently known by all in the palace, and twist it to their liking, repeating the new story so many times that their own people probably didn't even know what was true anymore.

Authoritarianism is all about the lie that is repeated to gauge loyalty and construct a foundation of power.[21] Operatives who push the lie, who help manufacture alternate realities, who fall into conspiracy creation, feel like they are insiders, like they know something exclusive. If the U.S. president says his inauguration was the biggest yet, it doesn't matter that actual documentation proves otherwise. The lie is the point, and when his press secretary repeats the lie again and again, even when he knows it not to be true, the authoritarianism has taken hold. If the Egyptian king claimed rule alongside his father before him, even though it never actually happened, elites could mark themselves as loyal with its faithful repetition.

Egyptologists argue incessantly about co-regencies, poring over the evidence, including inscribed reign years on this stela or that inscription, rarely questioning why its manufacture might have been useful propaganda for the current king and his entourage. Did Amenemhat I really institute such a co-kingship when he was feeling quite fit and able, with 10 years still left on his clock? Did the two kings really rule side by side? The fact that we are still so confused by the possible functionality of these co-kingships is part of their ideological power. They destabilize courtiers' (or historians') ability to pinpoint and target authority, to the detriment of those professional scrutinizers of signals. The king is dead, long live the king—same difference.

Shared rule—formalized or not—was often used by Egyptian kings whose dynasties had taken the throne by force, creating a partnership between the father and his lieutenant son: a picture of two strongmen establishing god-given power over their grateful people. Examples include Amenemhat I and his son Senwosret I at the beginning of dynasty 12; the two brothers Kamose and Ahmose, who established the 18th dynasty; Ramses I and his son, Seti I, who created the 19th dynasty; Setnakht and his son, Ramses III, who occupied the 20th dynasty. We could go on. None of these pairs needed to have instituted a formal co-kingship, but all of them nonetheless presented their rule as an unassailable family bloc of continuous, unbreakable might.

As for the co-kingship of Amenemhat I and his son Senwosret I, we should at least entertain the possibility that it might all have been a fiction to cow competitive brothers and cousins—and to weaponize the emotionality of family connection. Does this claim of co-regency make Senwosret a liar? Maybe. But isn't that the foundation of authoritarian rule? A king makes his own truth. It's up to the Egyptologist to find the untruths rather than believe royal narratives without question.

EMPOWERED ELITES

The next thing on Amenemhat I's to-do list was a spree of elite co-option.

We can assume that a new king would need the support of the aristocracy. Those old families had owned large parcels of land up and down the Nile for generations; if you, as king, had just claimed all of Egypt with your big Theban army, and dozens of elites who would rather work with you than fight you had capitulated, then you would want to reward them with nice stuff. Also, you could test their loyalty by sending out some of your lieutenants to take a look. Or you could encourage a nearby aristocrat, and pay him well, to watch over your newly domesticated gentry.

If, however, some of the more recalcitrant elites just would not cooperate, you could send in your army, kill the head of the family, and put your own guy in his place. But this would be an expensive course of action—much more costly than bribery or salaries for officers—and it would certainly create bitter resentments for years to come. It would be the risky choice, too, because after you went to all that trouble, what if the new man was just as untrustworthy as the old one?

Every new king of Egypt would have had to use such a commingled strategy of elite co-option and replacement. As for the aristocrats themselves, most were likely positioning themselves for enrichment at the king's expense, knowing that he would need their support. Few would take the risk of raising arms against him, but they would advertise their power through a variety of means: building grandiose tomb chapels along the Nile, showing their piety to their gods, and funding their own armed forces. Egypt's elites were not buried around the tomb of their king anymore, as they had been in the 4th dynasty. Those aristocrats acted as sovereigns in their own towns and were instead buried there. The towns included Beni Hasan, Deir el Bersha, Meir, Asyut, Thebes (before kings arose there), and Elephantine.[22] There must have been elites who ruled in the Delta, too, though we have much less archaeological evidence from that part of Egypt.[23]

The kind of power those men held alongside a newly centralized kingship is worth considering. They could bequeath the power from father to son, cooperate with kings when it suited them, and were more than happy to exist without any overlords. And they could outlast kings, acting as lords of their land and protectors of their people when Egypt fell into decentralized factions, as it so often did. Strong kingship only accounts for about half of Egypt's long history, after all.

In short, provincial strongmen did not depend on a king for their power, but they were smart enough to work with such overlords when required. Their decorated tombs show access to all kinds of wealth independent of any centralized government. Such men likely had connections with the western oases and the Eastern Desert, and controlled and taxed trade. They were enriched in the process, and invested profits into private armies of paid soldiers.[24]

A new king would have needed those elites more than they needed him, which may be why we see evidence that Amenemhat allowed his aristocrats to keep most of their taxes and to trade, to maintain their armed men, to pass on their power and wealth to their chosen heir. The king just demanded a bit of their time and energy for his new regime, and a great deal of their loyalty. After all, he wouldn't want to be betrayed as he himself may have done to his own lord and master.

For most of the early 12th dynasty, Egypt's wealth remained among the provincial governors scattered throughout Egypt; the king was impoverished in comparison to their collective might. This was no court of Louis XIV in 18th-century France, but more of a 13th-century

Louis IX who spent his reign battling recalcitrant vassals who didn't share any of their proceeds with the crown.

Egypt had been living with empowered elites since the fall of the god-kings of the 4th dynasty. That was 500 years of no king telling the landed gentry what to do, of decentralized ownership when "what was ruled by one was in the hands of ten."[25] For the first part of those long years, the kingship had maintained itself, to be sure—but the monarch had served more as a priest-king, interlocutor, judge, arbiter, harem organizer, and figurehead. For some 250 years of that half millennium, the kingship had been an unqualified disaster, contributing nothing but civil war and devastation.

Just because Amenemhat I had reconsolidated the crown and planned an extravagant new capital didn't mean that the landed aristocracy would just hop to and let him boss them around, though. All the archaeological evidence indicates they were waiting to see what this new dynasty was made of, still thinking themselves quite grand, none of them feeling the need to move their tombs to the royal burial grounds and cozy up to a god-king's pyramid. These men showed no interest in allowing their power to be regimented or homogenized, their final resting places tamed like the tombs of 4th-dynasty yes-men, their mortal remains plopped into a network of similarly sized sepulchres in nice, straight, neat rows, ready to serve their monarch in the afterlife. No, these men were warlords who followed their own regional styles within the larger cultural unification of Egyptian language and religion. They protected their own territory from incursion. They engaged in trade deals with foreigners. They matched their daughters with other rich men's sons. And their tombs demonstrate a presumption of authority.[26]

Their tomb chapels depict lives of leisure—the kind that rich, entitled, connected people usually enjoy. Scenes show elite Egyptians fishing and fowling or lounging about, just as the powerful of today do when they take out their multimillion-dollar yachts with family and friends. Egyptian desert-hunting scenes reveal the prowess that an aristocrat might have with his bow, akin to today's wealthy heading off to Gstaad or Vail for a week of helicopter skiing.

Yes, these Egyptian scenes had religious meaning—vanquishing disorder and finding a path in the afterlife—but they also had a base social currency. This is most obvious in the tomb scenes that depict private armies. Entire walls were devoted to various wrestling holds, assemblies of armed men holding different kinds of weapons, engagements with non-Egyptian enemies:[27] all visual demonstrations of how strong and technologically equipped each aristocrat's personal forces were, like a right-wing U.S. businessman showing off his private collection of semi-automatic AR-15s in his living room. This is oligarchy.

But monarchs want to monopolize violence. King Narmer showed himself doing exactly that on his monumental palette, smiting a foreigner of the marshlands. King Khufu did it when he was depicted holding an enemy by the hair in his Wadi Maghara rock inscription in the Sinai. The provincial governors were maintaining their own ability to wreak violence, holding the very power that the king wanted to dominate.

In the United States today, that scenario is akin to the overblown understanding of the Second Amendment of the U.S. Constitution, by which provincial landholders and urban homeowners feel the right to arm themselves not just with rifles, but with actual weapons of war that compete with the national military power. These patriarchs often demand that their women and children revere their masculine leadership, prep for end times, and hold to fundamentalist ideologies that subsume people to their violent will. Such are the fractured loyalties when the monopolization of power has broken down and decentralized into multiple competing factions.

This is not to say that the owners of the Beni Hasan or Deir el Bersha tombs were fundamentalists. But they were not exactly politically amenable to a new kingship trying to consolidate territorial power, and they had their own ideologies to back them up. They used the means at their disposal—their tombs, their coffins, their funerary goods, their women, their dress, their homes, their Osirian religion—to advertise their positions. Tomb scenes from Beni Hasan, for example, show the local, presumably well-paid soldiers all in a line, organized and controlled, equipped and ready to fight: a clear statement to fellow elites or to the king, if he deigned to visit this provincial place.[28] It is also a statement to the historian of what those men could get away with. These were powerful warlords with whom—not against whom—the new kingship of Amenemhat I was willing to work.

The elite tombs also displayed the gentry's hereditary connections, advertising the unbreakable lineages of old families: A father is seated on a chair while his son stands before him giving him bread and beer[29]—reminiscent of a "humanizing" *Vanity Fair* photo of a billionaire and his family that evokes vast wealth held in the stock market, shell companies, offshore bank accounts, and trusts exempt from estate taxes when the patriarch passes down his billions, untouchable by the centralized government. In Egypt, the handoffs of power were visible in provincial elite cemeteries, in which the son's tomb was placed next to his father's, advertising a dynastic line all their own.

The coffins of those men bear religious texts that provide a bit more insight into social place and power. Inside, they are covered with the magical incantations used to awaken and transform the dead for their eternal existence in the next life.[30] In the days of the 4th-, 5th-, and 6th-dynasty kings, such spells—which we call Pyramid Texts—were restricted to the royal family—monarch and ranked queens—with the understanding that only those personages would be given the privilege of an afterlife as Osiris.

As the power of kingship waned during the 6th dynasty, however, and the royal pyramids became smaller while the elite tombs got bigger, those funerary texts found their way onto the burial chamber walls and coffins of a few resourceful elites.[31] A few hundred years later, the landed gentry had appropriated those same texts that had once been exclusive to kings. Not only that, but they were adapting them, adding to them, making them work for themselves and their loved ones, because every elite could now hope for an afterlife as Osiris.

The old texts had been invented by priests for their god-kings, and as such, they expressed the godlike authority of the dead. Elements of superhumanity were retained in the 12th-dynasty texts, and we now see coffins with incantations in which nonroyal men and women were called to find Osiris by following the map encoded in the Book of Two Ways.[32] The king had once guarded such secret rites, but the elites now claimed divine transformational power for themselves, too, so that they could also become like Osiris in the afterlife. The previously restricted spells were now inscribed for a fee by professional funerary priests. Did the elites want to include the spell that transformed the deceased into a bird so he could fly to the northern sky's circumpolar stars that never rise and never set? Or did they want the spell in which they could locate their loved ones amid the afterlife confusion? They got to choose whatever they liked, it seems.

For the elites, the funeral was a potlatch of excess in which one competed fiercely with other rich people and even the king—essentially saying to the latter, "Yes, you used to be powerful, but no more, as we have appropriated all the secret spells that were yours." The king had become a mere symbol, an echo of the true glory of former kings. Such elite tombs—and all the treasures they contained—extended all the way from Cairo to Elephantine. They were almost certainly scattered throughout the Delta too, demonstrating just how much power was now held in the hands of aristocrats.

Large audiences were a must at the funerals of powerful provincial lords. If attendance at the actual interment wasn't possible, no matter; the painted and accessible funerary chapel would always be there to receive visitors and their ooh's and aah's as they inspected the colorful scenes.

King Amenemhat I was trying to coexist with and simultaneously co-opt the elites who held so much of Egypt's collective wealth and power. He knew they didn't need him; in fact, he realized that they actively worked to thwart him. And this is why he built his new capital city outside their areas of control. Amenemhat-Itjy-tawy was meant to create an independent stream of revenue for new men: direct reports providing the king with a mechanism to subvert the landed elite who wouldn't submit to the king's rule.

The threat to the king was eventually fulfilled when Amenemhat I was murdered; the culprit remains unnamed. In one preserved literary account, a harem administrator named Sinuhe tells us that Amenemhat I "ascended to his horizon" and "united with the sun disk"—a high-minded way of saying he had died. But the circumstances were not good. "The residence was hushed; hearts grieved; the great portals were shut; the courtiers were head-on-knee; the people moaned."[33]

The king's son and heir, Senwosret, was away in Libya on campaign, and messengers were dispatched to let him know what had occurred. As for Sinuhe, who was an official in the service of the king's daughter, he fled Egypt entirely, as he "believed there would be turmoil and did not expect to survive it."[34] How was Sinuhe connected to the plot? Did the murder originate within the harem palaces? We are not told any of those details.

A more direct version of the story is told in Amenemhat's own words, in a text called the Instruction of Amenemhat for His Son, crafted as if his ghost could whisper to Senwosret from the grave:

> It was after supper; night had come. I was taking an hour of rest, lying on my bed, for I was weary. As my heart began to follow sleep, weapons for my protection were turned against me, and I was like a snake of the desert. I awoke at the fighting alert and found it was a combat of the guard. Had I quickly seized weapons in my hand, I would have made the cowards retreat in haste. But no one is strong at night; no one can fight alone; no success is achieved without a helper. Thus, bloodshed occurred while I was without you; before the courtiers had heard I would hand over to you; before I had sat with you so as to advise you. For I had not prepared for it, had not expected it, had not foreseen the failing of the servants.[35]

Amenemhat I was murdered in his palace by a trusted courtier, we are obliquely told. The man who had seized the two lands, who had created his new capital city from nothing, who had consolidated a national kingship, had been killed. And, we are also told, Amenemhat had not prepared for such an eventuality. Maybe karma had caught up with the king. If he had actually stolen the 11th-dynasty throne from another family of Theban kings in a coup of his own, he had embittered a generation of southern courtiers who lay in wait for their opportunity to exact their revenge. Perhaps the remnants of the Mentuhotep family had risen up, with a candidate of their own for the throne. Or maybe there was a prince behind the scheme to kill his father, a blood relation to what was left of the 11th-dynasty lineage on his mother's side.

We have to give up on the hypothesizing. We don't have the words of the plotters in our histories, only the perfected accounts of the men who put down the revolt and claimed power afterward. We can't expect any outright explanation of the assassination or the agendas behind it.

But wait. Haven't we been told that Amenemhat I and Senwosret I had a co-kingship lasting 10 years? Seems odd to attempt a coup when another empowered party was already on the throne. If Senwosret I had already been crowned, the plotters didn't have to kill just one king, but two. But the instruction text implies that the king had not yet picked out his heir by the time of the murder, that the courtiers had not yet been informed about the king's plans, and that it was even before the king could give his son any advice and brief him on the more problematic issues coming his way. In this literary instruction, the murdered king Amenemhat talks of his anxiety about a succession crisis as if various strongmen were going to jockey for the top spot.

How could anything like that even be remotely possible if Senwosret I was already occupying that throne as co-king? If he had actually served for a decade, we have to imagine such a co-regent would have had a supporting entourage back at the palace when he was out of the country. We should also surmise that anyone engaging in a palace assassination plot would make sure to have some political buy-in and support for the coup beforehand; no one foments regicide without a plan for moving their candidate into place after the dispatch. It seems more likely that the instruction text is talking about a prince who had to rush back to the palace to claim his throne among multiple competitors, not a co-ruler already on it. As Amenemhat says in the instruction: "Bloodshed occurred while I was without you."[36]

In short, the co-kingship seems to have been fabricated by Senwosret I to cement his power after the fact. The evidence for a double-dated reign was a method of implying, or even proving, that he had truly been his father's choice as king all along.

The existence of this co-kingship smacks much more of weakness than it does of strength—and in terms of realpolitik, it feels much more like a fabrication than reality. Even though the story of Sinuhe mentioned a King Senwosret I, it was likely written during that king's reign. As for the stela from Abydos with the double-reign lengths, a new king with so much competition and struggle—campaigns in foreign lands, a murdered father, a still vulnerable dynasty—may have chosen to predate his own reign, claiming a fictional beginning to his kingship: one linked to founding the new residence of Itjy-tawy. And even this may present too rosy a picture, rather than the potential messy reality in which multiple sons of the king may have competed fiercely with one another for the throne. Hence, the backdating of a king's reign was thus the implied predestination of the next kingship.

But what about the rest of the 12th dynasty, which seems to have many of the same co-kingships, or at least co-dated reigns? Maybe many of these reigns were constructed just like Senwosret I's—made to seem as if all the kings overlapped, as if there were no power vacuums, as if the dynasty had been planned from the beginning as impenetrable and invulnerable. Perhaps Senwosret I's manufacture of a co-kingship started a trend of the heir connecting his new reign with the last years of his father, tying his rule so closely to his father's that they were virtually indistinguishable.

Of course, we will never know the actual circumstances of Senwosret's dating. The murder of a king was not something that an Egyptian openly admitted or discussed. Like the mythological murder of the god Osiris by his brother Seth, such disastrous encounters were only referenced in a roundabout way. For example, the first king of the 6th dynasty, Teti, may have been killed as the result of a conspiracy in his own harem, but the pertinent documents are so inexplicit that we don't really know if the king was even killed at all—exactly how the Egyptians wanted to keep it.

Here, at the beginning of the 12th dynasty, Senwosret I did recognize the assassination, which is extraordinary in and of itself. But the regicide was so unexpected, so brutal, that the new king decided to manipulate it to gain emergency powers and moral propaganda. Senwosret constructed mythological guilt trips and moralizing tales of right and wrong. He turned a necessary defense into a brilliant offense, constructing a patriotic ideology that marshaled his loyal men around him and frightened intransigent or noncooperative elites. His father's kingship had been based on military power and a new capital; Senwosret now had to get all of his aristocracy to toe the party line.

To achieve this, he went on a propaganda blitz, commissioning multiple texts about the assassination of his father, including the Instruction of Amenemhat for His Son, written in the voice of the dead king himself. The tale of Sinuhe was probably written during his reign too. These new literary works included not-so-veiled threats to any who would betray their lord, manufacturing a new moral code for how the Egyptian elites should behave and what bad things would come to pass if they did not.

These texts stressed how the king would give sympathy and riches to loyal men. Much of the new literature centered on a time of profound disorder and chaos when Egypt was without its monarch, each narrative closing with the glorious arrival of a strongman able to put everything to right again. Only I can fix this, Senwosret I was telling his people. He was invoking big themes such as right and wrong, and disfavor of the gods, but also more quotidian fears such as ostracism and comparative poverty.

In one text, Senwosret told his men that the sun god Horakhty had set him on earth as a kind of cosmic balance before all his courtiers: "He appointed me shepherd of this land, knowing him who would herd it for him . . . he who does all as he desires and conveys to me what he wants known."[37] Here, he presented his power as divinely sanctioned, predestined, unchallengeable. But how powerful was Senwosret, really, if he had to commission such texts?

Patronage of the King

It seems safe to observe that the kingship needed the power of the gods on its side again. But 12th-dynasty Egyptians knew that ideological systems had irrevocably shifted, that the crown could no longer demand what Khufu and Khafre had of their men. The authority of kingship had been sorely challenged. The 6th dynasty had died out in a whimper of royal ineffectuality, leaving a decentralized Egypt in the hands of a comfortable, if not monumentally realized, group of linked aristocrats. Egypt's various landholders donated to and built all kinds of temples (in mud brick) to their divinities and maintained the temple rites—just as today's wealthy donate to churches, build hospitals in their local cities, get their names on educational buildings, and create charitable foundations. In all cases, these contributions help donors establish ideological power and position themselves as the foundations of a good society.

As king, Senwosret I would jump into this game of piety and patronage with the energy of a progressive U.S. president of the 1930s, spending on temples throughout the land, creating jobs in dozens of localities throughout Egypt, proving in stone that Egypt was, indeed, great again. In so doing, he would not spend as much on the new capital of Itjy-tawy, instead spreading the wealth around the centers of his landed gentry.[38]

It was a canny decision, offering a means of creating new social capital while forging a new entourage of men loyal to him. His father, Amen-emhat, had obviously been resented; maybe it had been the old king's method of taking power. Or perhaps it was the amount of energy he had lavished on his new capital city, demanding that people live in a construction zone with few amenities. The details of the irritation are not known, but we can see that Senwosret I took a different tack, bringing hard-earned tax money out to the gentry, placing new stone chapels and statuary in the sanctuaries of their provincial temples, plastering his face and name everywhere in Egypt, and driving a wedge between the landed gentry and the people.

We are discussing monuments quite a bit these days in the United States and Europe—in particular, those statues dedicated to former great men, warriors, or other powerful protectors of a past status quo. We ask what place a statue of Christopher Columbus has in a modern Italian American neighborhood, or who erected the thousands of Confederate monuments in the South and why.

When something is created in stone, it is empowered, all the ideas behind that image reified. Those images can be public—like a statue in a square, or a pylon in front of a temple. Or they can be private—like a bust of Robert E. Lee in a Whites-only country club, or an Osirian-style statue of Senwosret I set in front of the sanctuary entrance at Amun's temple. No matter where, such embellishments change a landscape. Mountainsides must be blasted, ancient mud-brick pylons dismantled to make room. The old folk objects of before are deemed embarrassing as a new cosmopolitan style dominates.

This is the campaign on which Senwosret I embarked: a stone-temple beautification project meant to empower him with elite interests, not just at his capital but also throughout Egypt. Each donation was likely accompanied by a personal visit from the court—either the king himself or one of his entourage. Local elites were called to receive the gift in a kind of ancient ribbon-cutting ceremony, to publicly show their acceptance of this monarch whose father had been assassinated. Each donation was supported by an endowment of lands, providing the priests who worked in each temple with a new income. The king's largesse had a shiny glow of generosity and piety. Senwosret had the money, it seems, to buy his way out of this political problem.

And those elites who had been maintaining their provincial temples? Well, now their donations looked shabby and self-serving, causing local men to look askance at the stinginess of their longtime aristocratic patrons. Senwosret was claiming clever bureaucrats and priests as his own loyal foot soldiers, cutting off the aristocracy from their traditional systems of patronage. He was not reaching those people at the very bottom of society, perhaps (because who needs the loyalty of peasants?). But he got to those mid-ranking guys, those men who would benefit the most from shifting their hard work toward a good king rather than waiting for their manor lord to throw them some crumbs.

Senwosret I presumably made an appearance at many a provincial temple, suffering the ritual indignities demanded of him. In one pre-served relief from the temple of Min at Coptos, now housed at University College London, the monarch is shown engaged in a complex series of rituals.[39] He runs full speed holding an oar in one hand and a builder's square in the other before the god himself, who is pictured with a fully erect penis sticking out of his mummy wrappings. This relief was part of a grand set of constructions that the king had added to Min's temple, apparently in preparation for his 30-year Sed festival. Senwosret was using the festival not just to aggrandize himself, but also to make his kingship indispensable to his people by creating jobs and launching construction all over Egypt.

This was not the first time an Egyptian king had claimed that he alone could build the correct structures that called the divinities to earth, that he alone was the proper ritualist to intercede with the gods. But it was the first time a monarch had done it with such systematic fervor, all over Egypt. Mentuhotep II of the 11th dynasty had made a good run, adding stone elements to temples throughout Upper Egypt[40]—but without political unification, he couldn't go any farther. Given Senwosret's successful military campaigns in the Levant, Libya, and Nubia, ample resources were available for a massive, statewide, temple infrastructure program. Given the scale of his working mines in the Wadi Hammamat for graywacke and gold, in the Sinai for turquoise and copper, in Kom el Ahmar for quartzite, in Wadi el Hudi for amethyst, and in Aswan for granite, Senwosret had the raw materials.[41] His building program would be a political-ideological tour de force.

In the Nile Valley and Delta, the king's power was now monetarily inserted—in the form of land endowments—into local places once dominated by the aristocracy. And it would last as long as those endowments were protected. But endowments are tricky things. Just ask any development office at a prestigious university how they vet the donors, how long it takes to lock down a gift, and they will talk freely. Then ask how endowments run their policy, and they will go silent—because money always gives patrons the right to tell recipients what to do. Thus, within Egypt—or Harvard—endowments add another layer of leadership that can last for generations.

This doesn't mean the local elites couldn't subvert endowments. Money can always be diverted to interests not supported by the donor. In Egypt, endowments could apparently be skimmed and exploited by those same local aristocrats, because the king and his lieutenants couldn't be everywhere at once to watch how the income was spent. The endowments were the injection of a king's power into a place—but also, in the long run, they represented a means of dominion by a power bloc of priests and administrators now dependent on the income. One could argue that the Egyptian kingship had just set in motion the creation of self-endowed temple institutions that would eventually rival the crown: Egypt's deep state.

Senwosret I rebuilt the temple of the god Atum-Re at Iunu, which Egyptologists call Heliopolis, the city of the sun, just north of Cairo. He included two monolithic granite obelisks, each about eight stories tall— the earliest such obelisks preserved.[42] Each would have been tipped in gold and visible even to those who couldn't enter the sacred grounds. Instead of trying to shock and awe with one pyramid of massive proportions, the king found it better to diversify his portfolio by putting up mini-miracles like this all over Egypt, stunning his viewers inside and outside the temple without as much expense.

Adding statues and reliefs to private temples brought a veneer of piety to the attempts at control—akin to the U.S. president saying, "I'm giving up my paycheck for you." Thus, Senwosret I added stone elements to mud brick, or ripped out the old mud brick altogether and started afresh in stone.

But make no mistake: Senwosret was not giving equally to each of the 42 localities. He was focusing on the gods around whom all his people could rally—Atum of Heliopolis, Ptah of Memphis, Min of Coptos, Osiris of Abydos, Amun of Thebes, Khnum of Elephantine—and creating a new national religion with the king at the center.

At Thebes, Senwosret I set up statues of himself as the god Osiris at Amun-Re's Karnak Temple.[43] There he also commissioned his so-called White Chapel, a place for his kingly person to rest in communion with the god Amun during his Sed festival rituals.[44] On this chapel, along the bottom, the king named the 42 different provinces of Egypt, each listed with their local gods, and each of them, presumably, touched by Senwosret's largesse as he made pious donations at temple after temple. He was saying to all his assembled aristocrats: "I haven't forgotten any of you; I'm giving each of you something." He enumerated his generosity in a spreadsheet of economic piety.

At that chapel, the give-and-take between king and god is clear. Senwosret I calls the god Amun "my father," who in turn praises the king for his strong rule, without which Egypt would be lost. It is an exchange: The king gives the god all kinds of things, including a place in which to dwell, endowed by ample lands; his own ritual knowledge and activity; and, when he is not present, a phalanx of priests to do those rituals for him. In return, the god grants the king unmitigated power.

It is this reciprocity that Senwosret I memorialized again and again on temple stones throughout Egypt. The crassness of the exchange is visible and invisible at the same time because religion erases pay to play, turning the two sides into devout offering and fervent belief. What we see, instead, are beautifully carved forms and faces, an embrace between king and god, a connection between heaven and earth, divine favor, perfectly executed rituals, sacred incantations. It's difficult to see the politics lurking behind such religious imagery, especially if we aren't embedded in that world. But this is why our own modern leaders—our own authoritarian god-kings—so often use symbols of patriotism, memorialized military heroics, pious tax breaks, veteran outreach, and jet flyovers to veil their own political machinations. The strategy works.

Senwosret I's main wife was his own sister—a certain Neferu—we think. And it seems that the next king—Amenemhat II—was a product of that incestuous union.[45] Not an auspicious move, genetically, but it avoided an aggressive father-in-law and the interference of outside family influences.

The choice of Amenemhat II as the next king hints at a continued vulnerability of the royal office, as perceived by everyone in the royal residence. Why? Because the kingship—and all its offices—were kept as the status quo. The daughters of powerful aristocrats could easily have brought competition into the palace, fostering the same kind of infighting that had killed Amenemhat I—and so the (genetically superior) offspring of such women were avoided. The co-kingship ideology also continued into the reign of Amenemhat II, and we have double-dated monuments suggesting that Senwosret I appointed his son in his 43rd year.[46] This gave the new king a bit of a head start—and, apparently, protection from any aggressive brothers. Or at least, that is what Amenemhat II wanted his people to believe during his reign.

This is the Egypt that Senwosret III would inherit—overseen by a kingship constantly trying to assert dominance over competing elements in the royal family, with the twin goals of overpowering a loose confederation of competing aristocracies and influencing foreign lands too. God-king or not, the Egyptian monarch of the mid-12th dynasty was a leader of a conglomeration of local powers. What Senwosret III wanted, however, was absolute power.

The acute crisis of assassination was over, assuaged during the long reign of Senwosret I. Amenemhat II and Senwosret II were both rather short-lived monarchs, but they kept the caravans running on time, adding to the established script. Senwosret III realized he would need to bring in a different kind of power, something more politically canny and simultaneously brutal. He would marshal a combination of money, ideology, and threat to bring Egypt's aristocrats to heel—and by the end of his reign, no landed gentry would build grand tombs in their own homelands.

By the time Senwosret III was finally laid to rest, those provincial governors had been cowed. They were being brought to the capital of Amenemhat Who Seized the Two Lands to be buried near their great god-king in neat little rows—just as such officials had been hundreds of years before during the reign of Khufu. Even their faces were no longer their own; their visages would soon resemble the careworn features of Senwosret III himself.[47] His officials were tripping over themselves, trying to keep up with the fashion of the king's personal image, virtue signaling to one another and to their royal patron just how loyal they had become.

Senwosret III walked many routes to this end. On the whole, he used a carrot-and-stick approach—rewards if you leaned in, ostracism if you tried to retain your independence. The third Senwosret was especially good at using the threat of end times to maintain an ironclad order. His paeans always ended with his own narcissistic person coming to the rescue to save Egypt from its baser inclinations.[48]

In the same way that the threats of socialism, communism, terrorism, anarchy, and unlawful assembly have hung over modern societies (leading today's leaders to curtail personal freedoms), the murder of Senwosret III's dynastic progenitor was still palpable within his own political arena. Senwosret carefully tended the stories of that king's murder, even commissioning new literature about how the crown had saved Egyptian society. Only 90-some years had passed from the assassination of Amenemhat I to the ascension of Senwosret III (or perhaps a bit more if some of those co-rules of fathers and sons were mere political concoction). Egypt's literate elite maintained a communal memory of the regicide, and Senwosret personalized it, stroked it, scratching through the scab to keep the pain alive.

If Khufu had empowered his elites to make his kingship stronger by getting that damn pyramid built, then Senwosret III was on a mission to take power from his elites to make his monarchy great again. Endowments and gifts served to make Egypt's aristocracy addicted to the king's patronage, showing the landed gentry who was actually in charge, weakening them all until slowly but surely they would move their own wealth and graves to Itjy-tawy, tails between their legs. Like in the banquet scene of *The Untouchables*, when Al Capone is surrounded by his mob bosses at a round table, all happily chomping on proffered cigars and with brandies in hand, their continued enrichment was conditioned on their abasement to him—a point proved with vicious and unexpected blows to the head of the disloyal man at the table.

PORTRAIT OF A KING

What has survived best for our astonished examination is a new and bold visual representation of Egypt's king. In literature, statuary, and relief, we see overt depictions of Senwosret III's wisdom and piety, exhaustion and pain: a god-given counterweight to confront potential evils. Given the number of newly concocted loyalist poems, hymns, songs, and stories of kingship fighting the forces of darkness, we can imagine that courtiers were well rewarded for composing their praises of the king (and perhaps openly punished for whispering anything against their lord). The tragic early days of the dynasty were hammered into the Egyptian psyche—an ever reapplied message that Senwosret fostered.

This king would invest not only in the obedience of his subjects, but also in a bold new image for himself and his family. He commissioned avant-garde statuary that masterfully depicted a weary elder statesman coupled with the chest and pectoral muscles of an energetic young man who was still ready to strike at a moment's notice—a ruler who still retained the paraphernalia of crowns and a bull's tail, those old symbols of kingship projecting outright masculinity.[49]

It was a complicated image of kingship—not flawed necessarily, but not idealized either: a king with a tired, crumpled visage, yet still somehow ready to face any storm. In the texts likely read aloud at court for the assembled aristocracy to hear, the king was praised as a crusher of enemy skulls, an invader of outside lands, the keeper of truth, and the only one who could save Egypt from itself.

The king's new portraiture packs a punch. A face that was at once drawn, sad, angry, fierce, protective, and formidable represented a shocking new look. The founders of the dynasty had gazed upon their people with smiling faces, always showing the appearance of goodwill, if not political favor: a king who says, "Let's all work together!" Senwosret III was done with such games. He seemed to be saying, "I'm pissed off, tired, and beyond done with you all." It's the most effective guilt trip ever carved into stone—the face of a disheartened parent, exhausted because of his rebellious children. It's the image of performative authoritarianism straight out of the Vladimir Putin playbook, a no-nonsense, non-smiling dictator.

No documentation tells us why Senwosret III rendered himself in this way, no royal diary pages revealing what it all might mean. There are many potential reasons for the new look. His great-grandfather, Senwosret I, had inserted his physical form into dozens of Egyptian temples. Now Senwosret III wanted to follow that political strategy but put a finer point on the oppression inherent in the act. There is no reason to see Senwosret III's stone visage as realistic in any way. This was ideological.[50] Check out the size of Senwosret's ears, which are in no way naturalistic. They're exaggerated beyond human, massive and pushed out like a lion's. One message was that the king could hear every whisper of every elite at court and beyond, like an ancient Egyptian magical Santa Claus—able to see you when you're sleeping and awake, knowing if you've been bad or good, but just not happy about what he's hearing.

This was a kingship materialized as something greater than one man. Senwosret III checks and raises; each of his statues had to be treated as an individual divinity worthy of its own offerings. And at many temples, he tripled or quadrupled his presence, adding multiple statues—each with the same stature yet none exactly the same, clearly communicating that he was not just one person. He was 10, he was 20, he was legion.

For the elites who paid homage to their fearless leader, the king seemed everywhere at once, his statues terrifying in their mastery of stone. Like a pyramid, like an obelisk, the lifelike features of forbidding emotionality, with human feelings emanating from such hard stone, were miracles of empowered kingship. Senwosret III's statues transformed the king's vulnerable, feeble, even murder-able person into strength. In other words, this king knows that you know that he knows—giving you the impression of a reluctant leader, while crushing you if you dare to oppose him.

Senwosret III's elites followed his lead in their own statues. Not one of these men would have a face of his own; relying on the features of the king, they have the same downturned, drained look. They had to ape him, it seems, to demonstrate their loyalty. And by extension, Senwosret was able to communicate that his courtiers—even the most powerful among them—were mere extensions of his person, watching on his behalf, listening for any whisper of rebellion, all of them made haggard in the process, just like him. These elites didn't, or couldn't, copy the king's superhero body, and most of their chests are cloaked. These men were followers of their lord, not meant to be warriors in their own right. The king had finally monopolized all the violent power in Egypt.

The quantity and quality of his statuary also broadcast a good economy—and if the economy was good, the gods were pacified. The statues and new buildings were physical proof of the king's god-given right to rule (not to mention his ability to buy the loyalty of his elites). Senwosret had mastered political predestination as proved by economic excess. Money is morality.

At Thebes, where Mentuhotep II's mortuary complex still received offerings, Senwosret III set up a dozen of his royal statues, essentially claiming the ousted 11th dynasty's popularity for himself. (This would be like the current U.S. president putting up a dozen statues of himself in front of the Lincoln Memorial in Washington, D.C., so that he could claim to be exactly like Abraham Lincoln, but updated and better somehow.)

With his statue series at Deir el Bahri, Senwosret III simultaneously mocked and honored the hurt feelings of Thebans still loyal to the

Mentuhotep royal lineage. This was a throw-down in his family's hometown, stirring up bitterness that had been fermenting for generations. The statues he set up were of a dark granodiorite, the bodies taut and fresh, the faces brutally drawn, verging on vengeful. Each figure was carved with both hands outstretched over his kilt, piously praying[51]—an image not unlike that of Donald Trump holding a Bible in front of a church on a street that had just been cleared of protestors through the use of tear gas. Every Theban present when the old temple was invested with these new statues had the clear impression that Senwosret had just claimed the origins of Theban kingship for himself. Everyone knew to sit up and listen.

ENRICHING THE KING, FORGING UNITY

Like his namesake, Senwosret III was able to perform a Sed festival of kingly renewal.[52] His extensive building program was in preparation for that very year of jubilation. Walking behind Senwosret I's happy visage, Senwosret III put his grim face into the same temples and festival courtyards, constantly trying to one-up his ancestor—and presumably also repurposing the dead king's endowments for his own celebration. Thus, the statuary campaign was probably kept cost-effective even while it awed hearts and minds.

Sed is an Egyptian word that means "tail," and *Heb-Sed* means "festival of the tail." Presumably, this jubilee associated the king with a newfound patriarchal power, perhaps connected to that first moment when the king tied a bull's tail around his waist, transforming himself into a dominating animal force.

In many of the images commissioned to celebrate this kingly renewal, Senwosret III called himself *neb iret khet*, which means "lord of doing ritual." This appellation indicated that he was the chosen one who went into every temple to make sure the rituals were happening as they should, on time, with the correct offerings. Only he could do it right, Senwosret III was telling his people. Only he could make sure that the god's favor was bought and paid for. His Sed festival of renewal was essential to appeasing the invisible and visible divine worlds.

How did the king pay for all those media appearances? Senwosret III started wars—against the Bedouin of the Eastern Desert, in the land of Canaan in the Levant, but most especially in Nubia, that expanse of territory south of Aswan that the Egyptians had named specifically for its gold (*nub* is the word for that metal in Egyptian).[53] In the eighth year of his reign, Senwosret renewed a canal around the first Nile cataract, making the transport of armed men and goods into Nubia a relative breeze. (No more marching overland to the second cataract!) Once this was accomplished, he constructed a series of eight massive mud-brick fortifications along a 40-mile stretch of the Nile at the second cataract—essentially building a network of structures to tax goods, and to use as a base from which to control the local people and their valuable resources.[54]

Now, Senwosret III had everything he needed to systematically terrorize Nubia, which we know he did in his eighth, 10th, 16th, and 19th years, brutalizing its people and turning the land into a hellscape of exploited workers mining gold and precious stones. The Semna Stela,[55] now in Berlin, reads, "I carried off their women; I carried off their subjects; I went to their wells; I slaughtered their bulls; I cut their grain and set fire to it."[56]

Senwosret III created new wealth at a fast clip, professionalizing his army in the process. So many men were stationed long term in Nubia that they would marry local women and lead bicultural lives,[57] creating the kind of international relationships so common in today's U.S. border towns. The king boasted about how easily he could pay off his army: "Enrich the young men who follow you; provide with goods; endow with fields; reward them with herds."[58] He professionalized his bureaucracy in Nubia too, establishing a direct report to the crown so that wealth couldn't be siphoned off by enterprising officers, but was deposited directly into palace treasuries.[59]

Senwosret was not shy about aggrandizing his accomplishments: "I have made my boundary farther south than my fathers. I have added to what was bequeathed me. I am a king who speaks and acts. What my heart plans is done by my arm."[60]

Not surprisingly, during Senwosret III's reign the Egyptians invented execration texts, a kind of dehumanizing voodoo doll manipulated against foreign enemies.[61] Hymns to the king focused on these Nubian campaigns, not only making the war effort patriotic, but also implementing fearmongering and law-and-order logic to justify obvious war crimes.

There is absolutely no trace of remorse in those texts. Indeed, such violence was meted out for Egypt's greater good according to these pledges of allegiance to the Egyptian king. Here's a passage from one of them:

> Salutations to you Khakaure [Senwosret III], our Horus
>   Godlike of Transformations,
> Who has protected the land, and has extended its
>   borders,
> Overwhelming the foreign lands with your crown,
> Enclosing the Two Lands with the deeds of your hands,
> [Encompassing] the foreign lands with the strength of
>   your arms,
> Slaying the bowmen, without striking a blow,
> Shooting an arrow, without drawing a bow.
> Terror of whom strikes the cave dwellers in their land.[62]

Manufacturing hate and fear for foreigners can be a very effective political strategy. For Senwosret III, it defined Egypt by determining and demonizing what was not Egyptian. To "other" is to identify a people as so uncontrollable, so base, so evil, that they need to be utterly vanquished. In Senwosret III's rhetoric, he positioned himself as the good king who was constructing a foundation for order in the backward land of Nubia.

Such rhetoric today emboldens hate crimes, police brutality, disenfranchisement, and systematic incarceration of those considered foreign. The people who buy in believe that the "others" *need* order imposed upon them. Think of the old adage that enslaved people in the U.S. South never had it so good, or the common dog whistle that Mexicans are rapists and criminals. Fearmongering can make the incarceration of children at the U.S. border seem necessary. And it can allow Greek leaders to turn away migrant families from resort beaches lest their land be overrun.

If xenophobia is a first step toward nationalism, then Senwosret III was the world's first such authoritarian nationalist. Under his reign, hate speech became popularized—when songs of war crimes were sung at court parties, when vile words were written on stereotypical enemy figurines or bowls of clay to be smashed, destroyed, burned, and cursed. These embodiments of Egyptian supremacy created an us-versus-them mentality shared by an entire population of bureaucrats, soldiers, priests, and aristocrats; their nationalistic zeal might even have been reified with public sacrifices and/or executions to demonstrate the Egyptian power over the "other." One excavated area at a Nubian fort revealed an upside-down human skull placed on a saucer accompanied by curse texts, a flint knife, and burnt wax;[63] the exact meaning eludes us, but it smacks of effective nationalistic witchcraft.

Examining Senwosret III's Egypt clarifies how hate rhetoric broadcast within a society created political cohesion. Emasculating an enemy through dehumanizing ideas and acts forged a nation.

CRACKDOWN ON THE ELITE

Senwosret III had a fierce look. He had wealth. He had nationalism. But he needed a better hold on his aristocrats. Today, Egyptologists continue to debate what really happened to his landed gentry.[64] The evidence is extensive—so far-flung and numerous that it's hard to piece together a clear picture. Generally, though, it seems that the provincial elite had great power of patronage in their own lands until it vanished, suddenly, in the reign of Senwosret III. The king apparently created his own Cosa Nostra and squelched any power plays within the mob family.

Egypt's aristocrats had accumulated a great deal of wealth and power by the early 12th dynasty. As we see on Senwosret I's White Chapel at Karnak, there were 42 different districts, or nomes (*sepat* in Egyptian): 20 in the Delta and 22 in the Nile Valley. Each was headed up by a nomarch, a *hery-tep;* up and down the Nile there are tombs naming such men and depicting their assets.[65] But by the reign of Senwosret III, those painted tombs and the title of hery-tep were no more, replaced with the title of *haty-a*—mayor—apparently given to men who had been specifically appointed by the king to oversee a district.

What happened? Senwosret III was no longer interested in dealing with an empowered aristocracy. The archaeological record doesn't preserve a violent series of events, and some Egyptologists argue that there was actually no crackdown—just our misunderstanding of what those titles meant.[66]

But perhaps we are looking for something a little too violent, too overt, when we should instead be seeking evidence for a series of co-options and veiled threats that ended up taking down the elites. Let's start with a comparison with the modern United States. Before the 2016 election, numerous politicians spoke openly about their disdain for Donald Trump—Lindsey Graham, Mike Pompeo, Marco Rubio,

Rand Paul, even Kellyanne Conway. But after his win, all of them had to bow down to his authority, openly lying for him when necessary. None of those political operators was openly threatened—at least we have no evidence of suppression in our historical record. But all were compelled, ultimately, to submit to their president's power.[67] Perhaps we should expect a similar scenario as we look at the domestication of Egypt's aristocracy.

The king would only need to oppose one or two elites openly; only one guy had to have his head bashed in if everyone was in attendance watching the spectacle. After that, word would spread quickly, creating an organically driven mechanism of capitulation. The king could then send out his bureaucrats to make sure taxes were paid to his treasuries. He could take their trade routes in the western oases and Eastern Desert for the state. He could recommission their private militaries. He could demand that the aristocrats personally move their main residences to Itjy-tawy, and that they build their family tombs right next to his own pyramid; indeed, he would even throw some money their way to help them do it.

At that point, the king would make sure the elites knew that if they wanted any of the resources he controlled so tightly, they would have to serve him to get access. And if they gave in, those men would be rewarded with the best of everything: the finest linens, the nicest wigs, amazing statuary made by skilled royal stonecutters that looked just like the king's, and extraordinary tombs the size of which they could never have had back home. Elites would be encouraged to compete with one other by showing off their fine, subsidized possessions at the capital, rather than being cut off from view in their own provincial estates.[68]

Senwosret III wanted to keep his aristocrats where he could see them, essentially making them an offer they couldn't refuse. Moreover, very little of this process of co-option, if any, would have been written down in the formal documentation; instead we have to piece the story together by examining elite objects, tomb inscriptions, and the changing locations of tombs over time.

Senwosret III couldn't have subdued his elites as easily if he had been dependent on their bureaucracy to keep his government working. Khufu and the rest of the 4th-dynasty kings had found themselves unable to say no to their aristocrats' ever growing power because the latter had their fingers in all the pots of government workings. Senwosret III, on the other hand, had created a clever mechanism to subvert the power of those men—in essence, a bureaucratized system of lower elites. In texts dating to this time, we read about something called a *djadjat*—a staff of men in charge of each district—reporting directly to the vizier, the king's man. There is new evidence that many of the districts now had mayors unrelated to the landed gentry running them. Senwosret III had created a shadow government, a state within a state: a group of professional bureaucrats to replace the nomarch dynasties, a set of lower elites to report directly to the king and his lieutenants.[69]

The word "crackdown" seems imprecise for what was, essentially, a clever combination of bribery, threat, and bureaucracy. Senwosret III created administrative divisions run by multiple men, complicating the established patronage system of the landed gentry. One official could always skim off the top and tell no one. But a council of senior staff, all of them well paid, could watch one another like hawks, scrutinizing each man's honesty while benefiting the centralized kingship that had pitted them against each other. The king effectively stopped the provincial governors from skirting taxes, hiring their own militaries, and trading on their own, while the central government stepped in to monopolize and professionalize it all: tax intake, trade, military institutions, political communications, even temple workings. All of it was being centralized, and Egypt would never be the same again.

The best comparison to what Senwosret III was able to do can be seen in more glorious detail in the 17th-century court of Louis XIV—also known as Louis le Grand, le Roi Soleil—King of France and inventor of the European age of absolutism.[70] His reign was considered god-given, and Louis himself was called Dieudonné—a miracle to his royal parents who had experienced nothing but stillbirths for two decades.

Even though many of Louis's elites had taken part in the rebellion against his kingship, known as The Fronde, when he was just a boy, he nevertheless succeeded in dominating those elites over an astonishing 72-year reign. He took away their private armies and security forces, making armed competition against each other impossible and safety on their own lands problematic. He left Paris—too organic, too messy, too territorialized to claim as his own—and moved many miles down the road to a purpose-built capital, Versailles. He then invited the elites to move to his elaborate residence there.

Creating a new bureaucratic nobility that answered only to him, Louis chipped away at the economic power of his landed aristocracy, only exchanging funds for service and fealty. He had their letters read, and spies reported everything from treason to gossip. Once his elites had proven their loyalty to his own deep state, he granted them bits of economic and political power, but at his discretion. He pitted them against one another effectively, homogenizing them. He overturned an edict that had granted religious lenience to France's Protestants, and though ostensibly a Roman Catholic himself, openly competed with the Pope's power over the Church's bishops and administration. Warfare abroad was a regular feature of his reign, and it brought income to his court.

Louis XIV created absolute power for himself, but the social systems of the French provinces would be forever weakened in the process. And when a disenfranchised peasantry arose in revolution in the late 18th century, it was largely the result of a system of cruel patronage constructed to funnel resources directly to Versailles. With trust between the landed gentry and their peasants so broken, it became an easy thing to lop off all the highborn heads—even that of his grandson, King Louis XVI. This is what happens when an emasculated aristocracy can't or won't administer their lands with sustainability according to long-established social contracts. Good for the king in the short run, maybe. But bad for the kingship in the end.

Archaeological clues from Senwosret III's Egypt tell us about the elites who came to live in the purpose-built capital of Itjy-tawy. Take the case of Khnumhotep III, for example. He was the grandson of a provincial elite named Khnumhotep I, whose tomb at Beni Hasan displayed paintings of his private army, economic wealth, and religious independence. But Khnumhotep III now owned a grand, decorated tomb in the shadow of his lord's pyramid. Hundreds of fragments have been discovered in the desert sands of Lisht, and the tomb has been reconstructed on-site by a team from New York's Metropolitan Museum of Art.[71] Judging from this final resting place, we have to wonder what other wealth the owner held in his nearby villa, now lost under alluvial silt. Khnumhotep III was amply rewarded for moving to the capital, surely. But how was he politically disempowered?

We have some clues about Egyptian court life that could provide an answer—particularly the practice of fostering the sons of foreign kings at the court and funding their upbringing and education. Such a system was likely imposed on a defeated enemy such as the king of a city-state in the southern Levant, whose son could be taken to ensure the foreign ruler's loyalty to Egypt. Educated at the court with the king's sons and other elite boys, that Levantine royal heir would become Egyptianized and devoted to his foster king's cause.[72]

Perhaps the same was now being done with the sons of Egypt's aristocrats. Maybe the nomarch Khnumhotep II—like other elites—was compelled to dispatch his heir to Amenemhat Who Seized the Two Lands for (re)education.[73] Having his beloved heir at the capital would make the aristocrat amenable, even docile. And the enculturation would have domesticated the boy Khnumhotep III, having taken him away from his family and homeland where he would otherwise have learned about the local patterns of the yearly flood, the canals that needed to be dredged, which sharecroppers were the natural leaders of a village, how to perform the rituals at the local temple, and how to manage the books.

Dependent on their king and spoiled with the great riches pouring in from Nubia, Libya, and the Levant, such boys grew up to be yes-men, young aristocrats now kneeling at the feet of their lord, the good king. To flip the analogy of teaching a man to fish so he will never go hungry, Senwosret III took away all the fishing poles and redistributed them to his direct reports, who gave the king all the fish, which the king, in turn, then doled out only to those who pleased him best. It didn't take long before the elites had forgotten how to fish at all. Senwosret III seems to have created a situation in which the best men of his country had lost the will to resist. They were too fat and happy in their fine cages.

Now the contest was under way to see who could best please the king. Egyptologists see a new literature of royal adulation. This was a court doing whatever it could to prove obsequious service. For instance, in the Loyalist Instructions, we read:

The king is the Ka [soul].
His utterance is Abundance.
The one whom he brought up is one who will be
    somebody.
He is Khnum for all limbs,
The Begetter of the begotten.
He is Bastet, who protects the Two Lands.

The one who praises him will be protected by his arm.
He is Sakhmet against those who disobey his orders, and
  the one with whom he disagrees will be laden with
  sorrows.
Fight on behalf of his name; be obeisant to his life.
Be free and clear of any instance of negligence.[74]

Embedded in such hymns is more than a hint of threat. If you did a good thing, you would be rewarded; if you did a bad thing, you would suffer. To soften that harsh rhetoric, we see a great deal of xenophobic talk about foreigners who were set up as targets of the king's ire.[75] Manufacturing a set of common enemies is in the playbook of many authoritarians, and Senwosret III was no different. Also popular were tales of woe, which focused on a barbaric past when governments collapsed, gangs roamed the countryside, and people went so hungry that they turned to cannibalism—all before the strong king's presence had put everything back in order.

If our current zeal for apocalyptic films and television series captures the zeitgeist, it is accompanied by support for that great man (White, usually) who will save us. The Egyptians of Senwosret III's time had the same end times obsessions, hitting all the big talking points: starvation, civil war, unrestrained migrants, criminals ravaging the land, poor people claiming rich people's goods, neglected temples empty of worshippers, women raped with impunity—pretty much everything on any modern-day authoritarian's political platform. Cultural memories of dark times are useful in manufacturing loyalty.

RETURN TO PYRAMID BUILDING

At the same time that Senwosret III was building statues and temples for his Sed festival, he was also constructing massive tombs for himself.

And like the 1st-dynasty kings of old, he actually built more than one, kindling generations of debate among Egyptologists about which was used for his actual interment. The first burial site followed the traditions of the 12th-dynasty family, with the construction of a modest pyramid up north. In this endeavor, Senwosret went to Dahshur, ground zero of pyramid power, where Snefru had invented the first straight-sided pyramid hundreds of years before.[76] In the same way that Senwosret had claimed the power of the 11th-dynasty Mentuhotep II at Thebes, he now assumed the god-king abilities of the 4th-dynasty progenitor of monumental kingship in stone. (Let's face it: He did not lack for hubris.)

The king's pyramid site at Dahshur has an enormous hole in the middle, created when French archaeologist Jacques de Morgan thought it was a good idea to use explosives to get to the juicy pyramid center in the late 1800s. De Morgan didn't find any fabulous treasures in the king's burial chamber through his big bang, but his explorations nonetheless uncovered a jewelry hoard belonging to the king's wives among the many thousands of limestone temple fragments and tomb goods.[77]

As for the pyramid itself, the core was built of mud brick, not of stone or even rubble. Compared to the structures of Snefru, Khufu, and Khafre, it was a total cheat. But Senwosret III had learned that it really did not matter what a pyramid looked like on the inside. The mud brick allowed him to build a pyramid of respectable size with speed so he could set up an ornate mortuary temple out front and—*ta-da!*—gain instant connection with the kingship of Snefru.

Senwosret III picked a prime location on the plateau, siting his pyramid in the area closest to the capital of Itjy-tawy (about 20 miles away), from which his people would be able to see it, and using Snefru's Bent and Red Pyramids as his backdrop. With this, he constructed a brilliant mise-en-scène for an infallible kingship.[78]

His second tomb was more remote, but by far more audacious. It was a monumental structure at Abydos, a place of much older ghosts, because it had been the burial ground of Egypt's very first kings.[79] Senwosret III was returning to a site of those elite sacrifices of a millennium past, claiming connection to an archaic kingship of grisly power that extended even into death. Whether anyone in his court—himself included—knew the details of those long-ago human sacrifices remains unclear. But like the rest of Egypt, Senwosret would have believed this site to hold profound powers within the burial place of Osiris himself, the god mythically capable of rebirth even after betrayal and murder.

How overt was Senwosret III in these associations, we might ask ourselves. Perhaps he was actively comparing the murder of his great-great-grandfather, Amenemhat I, to the murder of the god-king Osiris by his brother Seth. If we can see the comparison millennia into the future, then I'm sure for contemporary Egyptian elites—much better versed in Egypt's history and mythology—the king's meaning was clear. Senwosret was styling himself as the heir of the wrongfully assassinated king, the Horus incarnate, the savior of Egypt from Seth's disorder and ruin.

Where Senwosret III was actually buried—Dahshur or Abydos—has not been determined. What we can say is that the pyramid at Dahshur shows little evidence of a king's burial, if any. Abydos, by contrast, contains a burial chamber built on the defensive, full of deep wells and even boasting a kind of hidden red-granite sarcophagus. If the Dahshur pyramid was a traditional place of homage for his elites to collect and give cult offerings, then the Abydos tomb was a secretive bastion of primeval power. Without any royal body as evidence, let us content ourselves with the notion that Senwosret was the first king since the 1st-dynasty rulers of old to have multiple burial sites—the first king to again say: I am legion; my burials are too.[80]

After 39 years of rule, Senwosret III flew to heaven, mingling with the gods from whence he came. His son Amenemhat III would reign for an astounding 45 years.[81]

Senwosret III had been a tough father, it seems, not sparing any sentimentality for his sons. One text includes the chilling line, "The true son is he who champions his father, who guards the border of his begetter. But he [who] abandons it, who fails to fight for it, he is not my son, he was not born to me."[82] Perhaps this was a veiled message to his plentiful offspring, each probably vying for the top spot of crown prince through martial savagery. One can imagine the old king training his sons in ruthlessness, positioning the heir to maintain his regime through ridiculing and shaming courtiers and enemies alike.

The heir of Senwosret III was well chosen. Amenemhat III would continue his father's policies in war, temple management, and aristocratic control, taking the short-term gains but not heeding the long-term repercussions. The third Amenemhat would pass his kingship on to his supposed son Amenemhat IV, a man who somehow died without an heir and left the 12th dynasty to sputter out under the royal daughter Neferusobek, Egypt's first documented female king. She was only allowed to rule because there was no man to do it, and she left no heir.[83]

The collapse of the 12th dynasty was followed by the strange 13th dynasty, a series of kings so short-lived that they seemed to rule in rotating fashion.[84] This allowed the empowered deep state to tamp down competition as best it could, everyone cleaving to temple institutions and notions of religious purity. Nubia and the Levant were left to their own devices until warlords took hold of Egypt again. There would be no strong king to lead Egypt for another 300 years.

It all fell apart so quickly, and Senwosret III's absolutism is largely to blame for this sudden disintegration. The regime centered continued prosperity on the lone person of the king—and when there was no more king (potentially because of all the incestuous pairings practiced at court), the whole construct collapsed.

Initially, it was useful to disempower the aristocracy. But over time, the lack of decentralized power irrevocably broke established patronage systems, putting peasants at the mercy of an empowered bureaucratic class, tearing up social contracts, and enfeebling the entire country. Senwosret III, the 12th-dynasty's strongest king—the grim taskmaster, the conqueror of Nubia, the one who had wrested back control from his elites—had hastened the end of his own dynasty, which came after just two generations.

The parallels with Louis XIV, as we have observed, are extraordinary. If we can compare Itjy-tawy to Versailles, then why not take it one step further? Let's include such private presidential compounds as the Kennedys' spread in Hyannis Port, the Reagans' Rancho del Cielo (the "Western White House"), and Trump's lavish retreat at Mar-a-Lago. Those estates provided an easier means of controlling the president's court, making his elites come to him to beg for favors and economic intercession, allowing him to note presence or absence, allowing lobbyists and/or CEOs to run the show. In the process, such dealmaking has empowered the corporate lobbyist and hamstrung the old Washington, D.C., system of lawmakers, taking down many of its cherished institutions with it.[85] We are only now seeing the long-term repercussions of such actions. Perhaps our own fall is soon to come.

CHAPTER 4

AKHENATEN:
Drinking the Kool-Aid

Every state has its heretic leader: that man remembered for fun-neling all the ideology of rule to his own person, warping and manipulating ideals that had been built so assiduously, constructing a pyramid of the mind. Egypt's apostate king was Akhenaten (r. ca 1352–1336 B.C.)—the 10th king of the 18th dynasty, who reigned at a peak of Egypt's power and prosperity. He was the son of the magnificent Amenhotep III, the globe's first sun king.

Akhenaten would bear the same moniker as his father until he rejected it with a flourish, becoming a strange, beautiful, grotesque leader who wanted nothing to do with Dad. His reign lasted just 17 years, but the man still had more than enough time to implement a political-religious agenda that consumed Egypt from the inside out. He would promote a little-worshipped divinity, the Aten, the physical manifestation of the sun in the sky. This was a god he could twist to his own machinations, allowing him to suppress other gods, elevate his own kingly cult, and take Egypt down a path it had never walked before.

This was a kingship of relentless norm breaking, during which the elites were continuously stunned by the next royal proclamation during a series of never ending and destabilizing changes. It was a time of untold wealth, which allowed Akhenaten to implement that upheaval, no matter how chaotic, to pay off and elevate his loyalists, to drive deep wedges into Egyptian society. It was a regime of winning, when loyalists got unbelievably rich by following their king in all things, selling their souls for power, and getting caught up in a fervor of their own absolutist investment. It was a time when religion was weaponized to display one's power, belonging, and righteousness, enabling a loyal few to ram through a new agenda with impunity. It was an era when people no longer knew what the truth was, or didn't even want to see it, because a distortion field was created around reality again and again to keep loyalists in power.

Today, the same specter is afloat in the United States, Russia, Britain, Poland, Hungary, Brazil, India, Egypt, Nigeria, and other places too numerous to list. Leaders are using new interpretations of religion and state ideology to pull more and more to themselves, consistently breaking established norms, enabling their oligarchs with more money and custom-made deregulation. Ancient Egypt has been down that road before. Akhenaten is our harbinger of the days to come.

Let's imagine a scene from that reign. Just after dawn, officials, courtiers, and priests assembled in the Great Aten Temple, where hundreds of altars were heaped with freshly slaughtered animals, thousands of freshly baked loaves of bread, and bushels of vegetables—already a feast for the hordes of flies that always seemed to be the most honored guests on such great festival days. The sun's rays slant into the open-air space as the Aten's physical presence begins to consume its bounty.

The participants stood in the rapidly increasing heat, in the humidity of the inundation season, in a capital city under construction far from the luxuries of Memphis and Thebes. They suffered the added indignity of bending over at the waist if ever within 10 feet of the king—may he have life, prosperity, and health! Many furtive glances may have shot between them as their king performed his rituals to the sun in the sky. The king stood upon his dais, speaking his prayers exactly as he had composed them, offering up the different foodstuffs to his god—first some milk, then beer, then bloody haunches of meat, after which he would move on to the next altar to make offerings to more solar rays.

The ceremonies were interminable. I doubt that most of the attendees ever thought they would end up *there*—amid rotting flesh, with insects crawling in the corners of their eyes and up their noses, immersed in the constant clang of hammers and cries from construction crews. Each of them bowed, with nerves taut, awaiting the next order from their god-king, or one of his lieutenants.

But this was the bargain each had made to become rich, to advance at court, to become a friend of the king. Each had become a true believer and a loyal henchman for an off-the-rails, entitled monarch who had gleefully pushed conservative and superstitious old men aside, removing what he thought were their false idols, reallocating funds from Egypt's old centers, and channeling it all to this new, sun-drenched place and the coffers of his loyalists. They had all been rewarded—but now, perhaps some were wondering about the bargain they had struck.

The king's name at birth was Amenhotep, the same that his father had borne, meaning "Amun Is at Peace." But he would change it to Akhenaten, approximately "The One Who Is Beneficial for the Aten."[1] This king didn't invent the god Aten,[2] but he elevated the divinity to heights not seen before. He created new art forms, new architectural styles, new temple forms, and new ways of worshipping. In place of the state cults of Amun-Re (the Theban god of hiddenness), Atum (the solar creator at Heliopolis), and Ptah (the craft god of Memphis), he chose just one to support his kingship: the Aten sun,[3] which ended up being the most useful god to simultaneously diminish divinity and aggrandize Egyptian kingship.[4]

Akhenaten achieved all this in a country that trusted its good and divine kings so much that it gave them a latitude never granted to leaders in other parts of the world. In other, more competitive places—in western Asia or southern Europe, for instance—such a king would likely have been dead before the first year was out. But because of his divine status, this Egyptian king was sanctioned to exhaust the Egyptian priests and courtiers day after day, as yet another unprecedented change was openly announced or furtively communicated throughout the court.

Akhenaten's zealotry was so extreme that his entire community would become dependent upon him as their only channel to the god. Religion was made terrifyingly simple, cleansed of its statuary and icons, made so logically binary that everyone was forced into black-and-white thinking—you are with me, or you are against me; this god is true, and that god is false. Was this king crazy, schizophrenic, experiencing delusions of grandeur, or sociopathically using religion to bring about political ends? We will never know, and it doesn't really matter. What matters is the human system that nurtured and supported a leader like Akhenaten.

THE 18TH-DYNASTY FOUNDATION

We left our story of Egyptian kings at the end of the 12th dynasty, when Senwosret III's absolutist policies had weakened a nation. Now we will jump ahead, past a period of mass migration and warfare, past the consolidation of Egypt by the early 18th-dynasty Theban warrior kings—Ahmose, Thutmose I, and Thutmose III—and on to the end of the 18th dynasty and its many overindulgences.[5]

The 18th dynasty presented itself as a southern law-and-order kingship. Like the United States in the mid-1800s, Egypt had been enmeshed in an ongoing north-versus-south war—sometimes cold, sometimes hot—rooted in different economies, competing political styles, contrasting political machinery, and a load of distrust between the two. The border between the Delta and the Nile Valley had always been Egypt's breaking point, and when centralized power was lacking, the country split into two factions along that line. People in the north were more urban, more diverse, more tribal, richer in agricultural production, less centralized, more competitive. People in the south were more conservative, more provincial, more unequal, poorer in agricultural production, more militaristic, and more prone to unification under one man.[6] We can assume that Egypt's northerners often felt distrust for those southern kings who seemed to rise with such regularity to force their rule upon regions not their own.

Those southern kings played a canny ideological game with their northern compatriots, using religion, and kingly divinity, to play down their own ambitions. Kings such as Hatshepsut and Thutmose III manufactured oracles claiming that they only served as king at the god Amun's pleasure.[7] They were chosen in a public spectacle for all to see, an ancient version of "Let Amun Take the Wheel." Such temple rituals evoked extraordinary power, inextricably intertwining politics and religion, like the U.S. South's reliance on evangelical Christianity and its vengeful God.

But a closer look reveals the weakness connoted by such a construct. The king was now playing down his own personal ability to take power, relying on a god—not himself—to make important decisions. It was a necessary choice. Openly expressed ambition elicits pushback. People don't like it when someone brags that they have all the power, all the money, and they can do whatever they want. The Theban kings knew that, and they created a kind of ideological buffer, constantly repeating something like, "I'm only doing this because my father, Amun-Re, told me to." Such ideological justification was extraordinarily powerful in the minds of the Egyptian people.

Those southern kings had founded their rule on a god-given militarism, linking warfare with moral goodness, fighting the good fight not to hurt and destroy, they tell us, but to protect and maintain the Egyptian people. Piety to a vengeful god could justify anything, even atrocities such as the severed human hands displayed on a Theban warrior's spear to show his kill count.[8] The 18th dynasty's propaganda machine was founded on stories of their king's violent incursions into the Delta, where he swept vile foreign invaders—the Hyksos—out of the country, taking Egypt back for Egyptians.[9]

The repeated royal military campaigns created a hegemony of cruel power in the neighboring southern Levant and northern Nubia that enforced ongoing payments in goods, labor, and natural resources. The purveyors of such cruelty became rich, and ostentatiously showed themselves giving it all back to god, offering Amun-Re the ultimate credit.

As the 18th dynasty continued, however, its kings inflicted less overt militarism as the need and appetite for warfare lessened and polities settled into a system of professionalized militaries, tribute payments, and work camps.[10] As we see in the 20th-century arc of the United States—in which a booming military-industrial complex was created during World War II, leading to ongoing military activity in places such as Korea, Vietnam, and the Middle East—such military hegemonies, once established, enrich a people while the act of war itself becomes socially exhausting. Egypt, too, would move from a militarism in which everyone was actively participating to one that just wanted to maintain budgets and jobs.

At the end of Egypt's 18th dynasty, the elite no longer wanted to go to war; they were rich already. No need to risk their own or their sons' lives for anything—certainly not to gain the king's favor. Let the paid soldiers go out and keep the territories in line. At this point, the raison d'être of the military was to procure funds for an institution, not to make actual war. The infrastructure had taken over. This was Amenhotep III's Egypt, when elite entitlement and royal monumentalism reached their apex.

Amenhotep III was not a king of the battlefield, but a monarch of never ending palace fetes for which everyone bent over backward to get an invitation. The king called himself "the Dazzling Sun."[11] He probably came to the throne when very young, maybe even around the age of 10. He must have been told his whole life that he was not just special, but divine.

Throughout his almost 40-year reign, he would reify his presumed sacredness in stone, placing his fabulous creations throughout Egypt—north, south, east, and west. He commissioned statues of himself three stories high along with sprawling temples populated with strange sculptures in stone—images of himself in the company of crocodile and hawk divinities, for instance, which might have been expected in relief but had never been made as three-dimensional statuary.[12]

All of it was breathtakingly beautiful and extraordinarily expensive. The quality of Amenhotep III's production was unparalleled, with its strong lines chiseled by the practiced hands of master artists who were funded to produce more than ever before. The king constantly one-upped himself with new, miraculous technologies of glassblowing, faience crafting, and metalsmithing.[13] Quartzite, red granite, and calcite were favored stones because they seemed to glow in the sun's light or had a luminosity in lamplight. Objects were embellished with gold or electrum; inlaid with ivory, cedar, and ebony; or encrusted with precious stones such as lapis lazuli, carnelian, and turquoise.

A famous stela[14] explains exactly what Amenhotep III built, where, and what materials he used. It reads like a narcissistic Instagram page filled with Prada handbags, Givenchy pantsuits, country estates in the

Hamptons, and weekends at Mar-a-Lago. When describing the ceremonial bark he had constructed for the god Amun, the stela says: "It is
very wide and great; the like has never been made. Its interior is made
pure with silver; it is worked with gold throughout. A great shrine of
fine gold fills the entire surface."[15]

Essentially, the king used all the best materials—tremendous materials, the best ever. Whereas previous kings presented an Egypt grappling
against military foes with pious leadership, Amenhotep III created a
colossal temple text to document his conspicuous consumption of massive quantities of wealth: the solid gold toilet of the ancient world.

The construction of the extraordinarily ambitious Temple of Millions
of Years in Thebes was meant to celebrate the king's divine cult after
his death, but also to display his ostentatious power to his elites. It was
a temple bigger than anything any ruler had ever constructed in one
lifetime, 30 acres in area. And it was sited not on the high ground, as
had been the norm, but in a part of western Thebes that received yearly
floodwaters. The temple was specially built to be inundated part of the
year, in fact, so that it could represent the mound of the first earth
emerging from the receding waters of pre-creation.[16]

In complexity and scale, the project was like a Roman emperor commissioning a giant water battle in the Colosseum. For three months of
the year, the temple and all its contents were bathed in Nile waters that
cleansed and regenerated it, and likely allowed sacred boat processions
and other extravagant novelties. We can imagine all the priests having
to move treasures and ritual implements from the ground floor to higher
areas for safekeeping during this time. When the waters receded, the
religious logic went, everything would have been reenergized with creativity and new life.

Because the Nile River was the source of Egypt's massive irrigated grain
production—money in Egypt really did grow on trees—Amenhotep III

was linking his predestined riches with the seasonal life cycle of Egypt itself. Indeed, he used the temple to conceive a stellar and lunar sky chart in stone,[17] including two life-size statues of Sakhmet the lion goddess for each day of the year—730 of them at least.[18] All were stationed around the square perimeter of this temple; each day was represented by a Sakhmet of good fortune and a Sakhmet of bad fortune, both of which needed extensive propitiation. The current archaeological site, called Kom el Hetan, reveals dozens of new statues every season—the ubiquitous lionesses, and wild and crazy creatures such as lion-crocodile sphinxes, jackals, and giant scarab beetles, as well as colossal images of the king himself.

Because the site was flooded in antiquity, and because the king himself redid his own statue program more than once, archaeologists seem to find new colossal pieces every time they put a spade in the ground. This was a king who put up extraordinary monuments to elicit everyone's ooh's and aah's—but when those things got old, he buried them to start again, like a colossal ancient Roman vomitorium, but full of stone to consume rather than food.

In Amenhotep III's reign, it seems that the Sakhmet of good fortune kept coming up on the roulette wheel. Wealth was increasing for Egypt's elites. The king was long lived. There was no regicide or elite competition. Egypt had no hot military campaigns, and all its territories were contained and producing dividends at full tilt. There was no reason not to believe that the king had cracked some sort of divine code; everyone believed the king's press, especially the king himself.

This kind of prosperity gospel is alive and well today—particularly in evangelical Christian centers of the United States, where wealth is linked to being marked by God for special duties. The Gospel reaches a baroque political apex as superchurches move into old sports stadiums and leaders are appreciated more for their number of practitioners, private jets, and estates than for religious philosophies. In other words, if God favors you, you are rich, and those riches translate into political power.

As for Amenhotep III's elites, their circumstances were enhanced beyond anything we have yet seen, comparable to the lifestyles enjoyed today by the Zuckerberg, Mercer, Koch, Bezos, Soros, and Gates families (and before them, the Rockefellers, the Gettys, and the Hearsts). In Egypt's one-party royal system, all showed obeisance to their king, but their own personal wealth and influence must have been enormous. With titles such as chief priest, general, and chief treasurer, they dipped their fingers into the different pots of government, skimming as much as they could off the top. They competed with one another through their tomb chapels, sarcophagi, golden coffins, temple statuary, and—although we don't have them preserved—very likely their villas, chariots, weapons, wigs, and clothing. It was a time of broadcasting one's excess, like a 1980s Gordon Gekko greed-is-good zeitgeist: a human instinct that would ramp up unsustainably.

AMENHOTEP III'S LEGACY OF EXCESS

As Amenhotep III's reign continued in languorous splendor, the king prepared his magnificent Sed festival, a ceremonial renewal of kingship.[19]

In a way, the festival acted as a kind of release valve, with the king using the festivities to distribute even more wealth to all his elites. He handed out celebratory inscriptions that they could display in their homes like collectors' items: big, glazed scarabs carved with texts about how the king had once gone on a hunt and killed a whole bunch of lions, or how he had once dredged a massive and super-fabulous lake at the palace of Malkata for the private enjoyment of his Great Royal Wife Tiy.[20] (Stars! They're just like us!) Once embellished in precious metals, these hand-held scarabs would have been as good as the contents of any Oscar party swag bag. The king communicated excessive wealth like a headline in *Us Weekly,* ostentatiously bequeathing gold and riches to the elites, jobs to their sons, and promotions to everyone.

That's what the Sed festival had become. What was once a method of showing inviolable absolute power had now morphed into a blowout like New York's Met Gala. Amenhotep III didn't just celebrate one Sed festival. He had (we think) three of them—one after the traditional 30 years of rule and two more in later years.[21]

But there were shadows on the horizon. Amenhotep's sons had already started dying. People must have been worried, the pettiness among them increasing. The Sed festival excess may have taken off the edge, allowing them to forget or ignore the realpolitik around them.

Similar trends are seen in modern oligarchic societies such as Saudi Arabia and the United Arab Emirates, where rulers give party favors of extraordinary extravagance—cars, houses, domestic workers, Apple stock shares—in exchange for continued loyalty.[22] This is a key feature of many authoritarian regimes: shiny entertainment for high elites—like a stunning Oprah moment—You get a car! And you get a car! And you get a car!—meant to co-opt, distract, and hide reality.

At the same time, as the king claimed solarism with his own person, the last part of Amenhotep III's reign was associated with an uptick in the display of religious extremism. His officials vied with one another to display their own solar hymns, their own pious connections with sunlight. Amenhotep III would marry two of his daughters as he got older, just like the sun god Re. He even had an image of himself worshipping himself in divinity form carved into the Soleb temple in Nubia, the king having become an otherworldly being, deserving of cult offerings. [23]

Perhaps his elites did not quite know how to wrap their heads around this norm breaking. But maybe it matched the zeitgeist, like the suggestion of adding one more divinized presidential head to Mount Rushmore's lineup. Nubia was the source of the king's gold, after all, with the ore coming out of the earth in such excess that it was like the grains of desert sand, as King Tushratta of Mitanni wrote in a beseeching dispatch to the Egyptian rulers.[24]

The royal succession was probably that one niggling anxiety on everyone's mind as they partied and prayed away those last years of Amenhotep III's reign. The various candidates would have been compared and sorted according to seniority, family lineage, personality, entourage, abilities—but verbally, never in writing, never formally, just communicated slyly among many interested people with little to do but gossip and scheme about a horde of princes.

Throughout most of the 18th dynasty, a younger son had usually been chosen to rule as the next king.[25] How that heir was selected is as shrouded in mystery as anything else a divine king might do. But the patterns are clear: The court preferred younger candidates who could be more easily molded to the duties and responsibilities of the office—perhaps because someone less mature could potentially be more amenable to the suggestions of the elites around him, or more ruthless depending on the needs of the day. (This brings to mind the modern selection of Mohammed bin Salman as the Saudi ruler instead of one of many older established royal sons and grandsons.) Even when an 18th-dynasty Egyptian king had ruled long enough to have older sons, those were often skipped over in favor of the younger ones. Amenhotep II, Thutmose IV, and Amenhotep III were all young when they took the throne. But this was about to change.

Amenhotep III had been on the throne for almost four decades, almost certainly having sired sons who had reached their 30s or at least late 20s. Indeed, the king had already named his crown prince, Thutmose, who was given the positions of High Priest of Ptah at Memphis and Overseer of (all!) the Priests of Upper and Lower Egypt.[26]

But Thutmose died before his father. The kingship then passed to another son who was never included in his father's temples or inscriptions—one who was probably never meant, or groomed, to be king. He would be called Neferkheperure Amenhotep, the fourth king in the dynasty to include the name of the Theban god, Amun.

Still, this was no moldable, uninformed boy to be brought up in the push and pull of pleasing and antagonizing his advisers, allowing himself to be instructed in the way things normally work and what his new weighty responsibilities would be. This was a man who already knew his own mind, who had been competing with brothers and elites—and who, evidently, had some clear ideas about the way things should go under his watch. He had been observing the excesses of his father, Egypt's aristocrats, and priests for some time, and it seems he felt that royal executive power had been sorely diminished. This was, potentially, an embittered king in the making—or, at the very least, a monarch with baggage. This Amenhotep IV had a unique view of Egypt's kingship, formed by years paying homage to the Dazzling Sun.

THE TRANSFORMATION OF AMENHOTEP IV

Let us never forget the nature of a perfected kingship in Egypt. The monarchs would leave us no political treatises, no diaries, no letters— just ideological faultlessness. And it is by sifting through that perfection that we can parse the reign of Amenhotep IV, using his temple reliefs, statue production, and monumentalized royal decrees to learn just a bit of what was really happening.

Not every regime produces documentation of its inner workings, though some do eventually. The Watergate trials caused the release of Richard Nixon's list of enemies. The fall of East Germany opened millions of files from the Stasi (Staatssicherheitsdienst—State Security

Service). Such records split open the realpolitik, showing complicated strategies that the leaders would prefer to remain invisible.

But the Egyptians didn't keep such intricate documents—certainly not in a way that we would like. Thus, we must bring to bear the same methodologies historians use for the propaganda of Kim Il-Sung's North Korea or the Fox News of Donald Trump's America. Amenhotep IV's story, as we read it, is one written through the lens of positivity and perfection as it appears on temple walls, punctuated by a rare note of open complaint in a diplomatic letter, and censured by the skeletal remains of workmen.[27]

Amenhotep IV opened his kingship with a game-changing structure that must have left the mouths of his courtiers agape. He built a new temple at Thebes, his royal dynasty's homeland, choosing a place where the state god Amun-Re dwelled: Ipet-Sut, the most select of locations, what we now call Karnak. The Temple of Amun-Re there had become a bastion of elite power for high priests, treasurers, and architects.[28] Since the days of Senwosret III, it had grown into a self-supporting system of its own, largely independent of a king's direct control. Egyptian elites used such temples as a means of procuring income without having to ask the king; they could also evade taxes by running endowments through it. Egypt's kings had created this problem for themselves some 300 years before, and by the 18th dynasty it had only gotten more out of control.

In Egypt, a building was never just a building; it was a front organization for a hidden political economy.[29] Military powerhouse kings such as Thutmose I and Thutmose III had used the Temple of Amun-Re to religiously launder their ambitions, issuing statements that amounted to, "I would never grab power; Amun gave it to me; I only serve my father and god." Elites learned to do the same, whitewashing their intentions, using the temple as a shield to bypass any micromanagement from the king. More powerful elite positions than ever before were based on temple money. Amenhotep IV, it seems, had a sense of how this conflicted with his executive interests; indeed, his first temple constructions may have been overt attempts to take on this giant institution and claim its rich economy for himself, diverting funds into something new over which he would have direct oversight.

Amenhotep IV also finished many of the construction projects his father had begun, adding his own image to them in the process. Egyptologists have uncovered only scattered fragments of these first structures at Karnak,[30] but the new king seems to have appeared in a traditional guise, in the company of gods in human-animal form such as the sun god Re-Horakhty, the hawk-headed divinity of the rising and setting sun.[31]

Amenhotep IV was already obsessed with solarism, like his father before him. In his first temples, his portrait was crafted to resemble Dad's: full body, chubby cheeks, a short, broad nose, even a double chin—the picture of an overfed, entitled monarch. But he would soon abandon this strategy. Building in Karnak meant working by the temple's rules, conferencing with its high priests, adding to its coffers, compromising his vision. Amenhotep IV realized at some point that he had to avoid all of it to effectively subvert the temple institution. So he created a work-around, a strange new monumental temple completely outside the walls of Amun-Re's sacred house.

His Karnak 2.0 was dedicated not to the god Amun-Re but to the Aten, the actual sun in the sky, and included not just one new temple but many. The main holy place was called Gem-Pa-Aten, or "the One Who Discovered the the Aten"[32]—a strange name evocative of the king as a prophet who could find the source of god's light. The name screams, "Look everyone, I found god!"

Amenhotep IV was already pulling Egypt's religiosity directly toward himself. He dedicated his temple to the sun—not as Re-Horakhty, or

Khepri, or Re-Atum, or any of the other solar manifestations, but as the physical solar emanation itself: that bright yellow-orange disk in the blue sky. We only have reliefs preserved—the ancient Egyptians made no statues of the sun in the round—but those two-dimensional images preserve the Aten's convex surface, as if the Egyptians did indeed understand the sun's spherical nature.

In Amenhotep IV's depictions of the Aten, he stripped out the humanizing elements. His sun god had no face, no eyes, no body—just the round shape, the source of long, incised lines of solar rays terminating in tiny, schematic human hands. This divinity had no discernible gender in its physical depiction. The written hymns to this god refer to it as he, but usually it's referred to as "the Aten" or "you," and hymns associate it with a birth mother capable of nurturing, as well as with a father whose sperm produces the next generation. On the disk, or "head," of the Aten was an unfurled cobra—the female protector-divinity ready to spit fire at enemies, and the same emblem depicted on the forehead of the king.

As the focus of his political-religious machinations, Amenhotep IV had chosen a god that was smaller than himself, at least as viewed from Earth—more remote, and yet somehow also a king in its own right. There was a simplicity to this divinity. Gone were the gods' imaginative headdresses and colorful garments, the animal heads and hybrid manifestations. This new philosophical system was one of abstraction, directness, a kind of strict rationality, a denial of spiritual complexity, a rejection of substitutions in favor of what was clearly visible in the world. The sun was what Amenhotep IV saw in the sky—not a bird or a lion or a beetle—and that was what he worshipped. It was simple.

To draw even more attention to himself and the object of his new piety, Amenhotep IV announced a Sed festival in his second year—an unparalleled early date. But he had a work-around for that too: The festival would be for the god Aten, not for him, he implied. He would be the god's stand-in.[33] The festival was, thus, a mechanism for announcing his pious kingship, ushering in a new monarchic, almost messianic, faith that would set Egypt on the correct divine path.

The festival construction frenzy began, and to build as quickly as possible, the king instituted a fabrication method that he would never abandon: erecting the core of a given structure in mud brick with thin layers of stone facing inside and out—a Disneyland kind of assembly that concerned itself with the visible surfaces, not the quality of architecture. Thus, archaeologists have uncovered tens of thousands of the facing stones, called *talatat* blocks, which are much smaller than the traditional large blocks that spanned the thickness of a wall.[34] Whatever Amenhotep IV wanted to build—and he wanted to build a lot—his architects had figured out a method of cheating, so to speak. It was the only way to fulfill the extensive royal orders—starting with the construction of a massive temple in less than a year, timed for this noncanonical Sed festival.

Amenhotep IV was not only diverting temple funds to a different agenda (the better to control it) and building something unprecedented; he was also beginning to represent himself in a strange new manner.[35] His portraits display an elongated face, spindly upper body with narrow shoulders and protruding clavicles, attenuated wrists and ankles, a tight waist with a pendulous belly, and broad feminine hips. His belly button is pushed down flat, misshapen by the preponderance of flesh.

But it was his face that must have stopped Egypt's elites cold. It was an inhuman visage dominated by oblique eyes and a wide mouth pulled down in the center to a pursed expression. An extended line ran from each eyebrow along the bridge of the long nose, past the full lips, down to a narrow chin jutting far below the jaw and ending in a royal false beard. Viewed from the side, these colossal faces look animalistic, prognathic, like a lion's snout. It was an image of Egyptian kingship no one had ever seen before, and it would be repeated hundreds of times, as Senwosret III's image had been, in multitudes that lined the new temple's procession way and interior courtyard. We can imagine the Amun priests of Thebes walking the grounds of the Gem-Pa-Aten as the colossi were set up, each statue three to four stories tall, looking from side to side in consternation and confusion, knowing at a glance where all their temple's money was going. Most of the sandstone statues depicted a kilted and crowned king—but at least one showed him seemingly naked but with no trace of genitalia: a strange, hybrid, nonsexed human.

Some Egyptologists have explained the king's unparalleled depictions of himself as his attempt to show his true physicality, a body mangled by some sort of deformation or congenital birth defect. With the discovery of Amenhotep IV's imagery at Karnak, a new kind of medical Egyptology was born as everyone tried to figure out the malady that could shape a person thusly. Some argued he was part male and female, and hence a hermaphrodite, while others found evidence that men with drooping breasts, full belly, and big thighs share certain genetic disorders—Marfan or Fröhlich's syndromes, among others.[36] Most Egyptologists have since veered toward the scholarship of Dorothea Arnold, who argued that the king had filled a vacuum of his own making, manifesting himself as male and female, animal and human.[37] He had, in effect, become all those things that the god once was, with the king's body now serving as the new embodiment of divinity: the only cult object, and the focus of worship by every man, woman, and child in the land.

Amenhotep IV loved commissioning images that showed him in his window of appearances—an elevated opening from which his people could see him. If we imagine the full pageantry and spectacle of this king revealing his entire body within such a frame in his new Karnak Temple, accentuated by the first or last light of day, then perhaps we can understand his strange hybrid shape as a human manifestation of solar power. In the same way that the kings of the 4th dynasty used pyramidal constructions to turn the interred royal body into solar light, Amenhotep IV's statues were meant to show the optical deformation of a human body caused by light.

This symbolism was evoked as Egypt's monarch stood on a dais, at the window, before an assembled audience when the sun was right behind him. As the light suffused the king's figure from the back, the eyes of the audience would have been blinded. The royal body would have appeared transformed by that light, disfigured and stretched in the head, neck, arms, wrists, legs, and ankles, while the mid-body became confused, somehow both male and female. The whole figure was topped by an impossibly long and narrow crown.[38]

Photographs taken at the moment when archaeologists discovered Amenhotep's statuary show how sunlight created shadows to carve out unnatural cheekbones, accentuate the clavicles, reveal a rotund belly, and produce a squashed navel.[39] When we look at these same statues in a museum under electric lights, we lose not only architectural context but also the natural surroundings. We need to understand these figures in the outdoor spaces in which they were meant to be seen and felt. With sunlight slanting down upon them, these statues evoked the king's intent—because in the daylight, the statue's belly suddenly looks pregnant with new life, and the body itself seems commingled with luminescence.

We can see Amenhotep IV trying to communicate the same ideas in his temple reliefs. One image now at the Fitzwilliam Museum in Cambridge, for example, shows the king as a chief officiant. He offers nothing—just stands there bathed in solar rays, his body stretched and transformed by this infusion of light.[40] The king's later hymns to the Aten lay out his solar intention: "Your rays are on your son, your beloved. Your hands hold millions of jubilees for the king Nefer-kheperure, sole one of Re, your child who came from your rays." In other words, the king's body was formed out of the Aten's streaming light, shaped into the god's representative because "You build him in your image like the Aten."[41]

In his early Karnak reliefs, Amenhotep IV showed Re-Horakhty with the same pulled, hybrid body that he himself had, the same physicality suffused with light. The message implied—though it was never explicitly captioned as such—that the royal body was the same as Re-Horakhty's form. The king was Re-Horakhty's manifestation, a human-solar entity.

As the new religion continued to evolve, there would come a point in Amenhotep IV's machinations when Re-Horakhty would only appear in the text and would not be visualized. Eventually the hawk-headed god would be removed entirely from the king's oeuvre, as only the royal body was allowed to take on that role of light-filled flesh.

In short, the way the king's body was depicted was a demonstration of his new theology. In the same way that a pyramid's monumentality still makes some modern people assume that aliens created it, Amenhotep IV used his body's depiction to make his people think him beyond human. He became his own, personal pyramid. All his statuary and reliefs were meant to evoke the king as he wanted to be seen in temple revelations and within his larger philosophy; his body itself was the miracle.

The choice of such an unmanly representation seems a problematic move for a god-king. For most of Egyptian history, and certainly during the 18th dynasty, the monarch was shown as hypermasculine, bare-chested, warriorlike. He was Putin on horseback, Qaddafi in full military kit and sunglasses, Mohammed bin Salman in the flowing robe of a Bedouin warlord. Many leaders feel the need to show themselves as young and brawny. Or if that's too much of a stretch, as a wise leader—

the sickly but brilliant Roman emperor Claudius, the philosopher-emperor Marcus Aurelius, or bookish, gangling Abraham Lincoln, who led the United States toward what was right against all odds.

No authoritarian leader ever looked like Amenhotep IV, though, at least none I can think of. And maybe that's because he was more of a cultural icon, a kind of Iggy Pop or Andy Warhol, whose images were suffused with unprecedented and shocking power.

It seems the strangeness of the king's image was the point—so much so that it was replicated thousands of times in his new temples in the form of colossal statues and human-headed sphinxes, and in the complex scenes showing him entering the sacred space on his chariot, being carried in his palanquin, or holding up offerings of wine to the bright Aten in the sky. His was the divine figure to which everyone looked. And he reran it endlessly, as if he were on television.

THE EVOLUTION OF ATENISM

How in Aten's name did Amenhotep IV come up with all this new religious thought? Did he have previous religious training, perhaps as high priest of a sun god? Had his father requested such religious rumination on the nature of divinity before his own death? Had he engaged in deeper thoughts, writing the solar hymns and philosophy so in vogue during the last decade of his father's reign? We will never know. The man before he became king was always shielded from view in Egypt. But this fourth Amenhotep seems to have ascended the throne with a set of fully formed notions of what divinity was meant to be, and we can see the remnants of his ideas reified in stone almost immediately after his coronation.

Archaeologists have found Amenhotep IV's new Aten temple in pieces, because it was deconstructed and used as fill in later temple pylon gateways, and as foundation stones for new buildings. Later kings, horrified by the bizarre imagery, didn't waste time or money smashing the blocks to dust. They just removed the stones from sight as quickly as possible. In the end, the imagery was so aberrant, and the size of the blocks so different from what was traditionally used in building, that everything had to be hidden—fortunately allowing us to find much of it millennia later. In fact, talatat blocks have been found in profusion not only in Thebes, but also beyond.[42]

One of the king's favorite scenes—found at the Gem-Pa-Aten, as well as his temples and monuments throughout Egypt—shows the king, alone or with his wife and daughters, offering to the Aten high above. The Aten's light slants down, each ray ending in a human hand holding an ankh, a symbol of life.[43] One ray always moves toward the king's nose to provide him with god-given breath.

The way the light emanates from the sun—starting at the convex edge and shooting down obliquely—echoes the 4th-dynasty pyramid with its angled straight lines. But Amenhotep IV's angle is steeper, about 60 to 70 degrees instead of the 50-some degrees of Khufu's tomb, creating a pyramid of light that bathes the king as if he were standing inside such a shape.

The king became obsessed with how light made its entrance to the earthly world—and he may even have been intrigued by 4th-dynasty solarism, as he would include a diorite bowl inscribed for Khafre of the 4th dynasty in his tomb.[44] The Gem-Pa-Aten and other new temples were open-air, the pylons always unspanned, so that sunlight could pierce through to the floor. Ceilings became anathema. In sacred spaces, light itself was the only cult statue allowed besides the king's own body.[45]

The king had hit upon a new *thing*, and he had the money and access to reify it in stone. Egypt was still wealthy. The stock market, so to speak, was still on the upswing. Everyone was happy—confused, perhaps, but content—with all the activity, jobs, celebrations, and especially, the baubles that courtiers were depicted receiving from the king's hands. Just like his father, Amenhotep IV was demonstrating that he had the full favor of divinity.

Amenhotep IV made elemental changes to Egypt's traditional temple scenes. What had been the norm—the give-and-take between king and god, shown on the same scale—disappeared. Now the king and god appeared radically different in measure: the king large, the god small. Filling the void were scenes of the king in procession, the king offering, the king with his Great Royal Wife, the king as a sphinx, and the king in festival, all bathed in the light of Aten depicted above repeatedly. It was all king, all the time.

The Aten provided the perfect device for a monarch who wanted to be the center of everyone's attention. Without the god's body to show, Amenhotep IV himself could revel in the sun god's bounty. We see complex scenes of stockyards and fowl yards, butchering, cereal reaping, bread and beer preparation, grape harvesting, and wine production—all shown carefully spreadsheeted by bureaucrats, pen in hand, writing down quotas, constantly counting what was to go into the king's new temples in a kind of ritualization of massive fund diversion.

The scenes of bounty showed the king's own piety as well as great wealth.[46] Money and religion were one. Even human beings were shown as commodities. Servants were everywhere, bent at the waist, still intent upon their work, if the king was in sight. We also see Nubians and Libyans trussed up as enslaved peoples, or as richly dressed diplomats kissing the earth[47]—apparently another tick in the spreadsheet of the king.

Amenhotep IV was showing his economic foundation to all his elites, priests, courtiers, military, and treasurers. He combined wealth and religiosity in temple reliefs—and presumably in real life too, heaping food onto altars in his new temples. Images of the avant-garde Aten rituals show him before altar after altar, hundreds of them, piled high with expensive commodities such as cows cut into ribs and heads and legs, ducks with wrung necks, loads of vegetables, breads of different shapes, jars full of beer, and imported wines. All the goods anyone could imagine were collected in the king's temples to be eaten by the sun's rays, before the eyes of the elites. This was the authoritarian's statement—taking all this wealth and showing off his ability to waste it, seemingly saying, "If you want it, you go through me."[48]

Amenhotep IV's religious changes rolled out gradually, with the king including solar manifestations like Re-Horakhty alongside the Aten at first but then simplifying his solar divinity to its barest physical manifestations: the Aten, Shu (its light), and the king (its mouthpiece). The first temple scenes don't show outright monotheism, but they do have an outright economic intent—meaning economics led the cultural change as much as anything else. Nothing is ever purely religious, least of all religion.

To fully encode his wealth into his temple's religious detail, Amenhotep IV ordered his sculptors to cut scenes at a much smaller scale than ever before. The traditional Egyptian temple would have had mostly life-size reliefs and statues of king and god repeated on columns, punctuated with some small-scale scenes of economic and ritual activity. But Amenhotep IV's Karnak temples included the king's image both on a massive scale in statuary and relief and on a tiny scale, all of it repeated ad nauseam.[49]

When Egyptologists pieced the blocks together, they revealed strange, busy tableaux full of tiny elements depicting temple installations—parts of the arcane ritual—all stemming from the overactive mind of a prophet-king who had many new inventions and much to teach his elites. We see a repetition of particular tropes—the regimented offering rituals to the sun, every detail of the king's Sed festival procession, every step of the butchering and food preparation—like a Marvel comic book moving in slow motion.

Missing from this imagery is most of the customary captioning that would have explained the temple scenes and named the ritual or action. The hieroglyphic inscriptions are mainly names, titles, and epithets of king, queen, and god. Few, if any, religious explanations were given, nor coding for the new (or old) rituals.[50] It was almost like the stereotypical product of an obsessive mind whose one-room studio apartment is covered in pictures and sticky notes with terse names and identifications of places, connected with red string, with no explanation of the larger purpose.

The germ of Akhenaten's upcoming iconoclasm was quickly being formed, diverting attention from the traditional temples with new structures—a new look, new rituals, all of it modern but resting on old foundations and ciphers that everyone knew and understood. Amenhotep IV, in all his alien-like glory, still had himself shown wearing the *shendyt* kilt and white crown, and holding crook and flail, thus maintaining most of the expected imagery of kingship in his mind-blowing statuary and relief. He did this at Thebes as well as at other traditional capitals such as Memphis and Heliopolis, and at sites far to the south and outside of Egypt's traditional borders, such as Jebel Barkal in Sudan.[51]

With these acts, Amenhotep IV was constructing, and adding to and communicating with, Egypt's many sacred spaces—not destroying them. Not yet. But historians can look ahead and see that this was the origin point of a kingship that would soon veer toward fanaticism, exclusionary zealotry, and idolatry. In this brave new world, you were either with the Aten or you were against it, understanding that this new binary religion was a choice between light and dark.

The culmination of Amenhotep IV's traditional kingship occurred when he celebrated his Sed festival sometime between years two and five of his reign. Yes, previous monarchs had fudged the dates a bit—the

12th dynasty's Senwosret I, for example, if he predated his reign with his father's, and the 18th dynasty's Hatshepsut, who had combined all the collected years of her Thutmoside family's rule to allow a celebration in her 16th year. But Amenhotep IV's extraordinarily early Sed was beyond any of those contortions.[52]

Not only that, Amenhotep IV's explanations for this date were even more unorthodox: He seemed to be celebrating the jubilee of kingship for the Aten sun, not for himself personally as king. He had already put the name of his preferred deity into a cartouche ring replete with epithets, including one that called him *netjer nefer,* "the good god," a moniker previously used by kings as living gods.[53] He now made his own physical person the human representative of his god, a recipient of the honors as he was paraded around beneath the sun.

Amenhotep IV elevated the Aten as king over all the other gods in the Egyptian pantheon, while he, the monarch, was the Aten's only spokesman. It was likely a kind of unspoken test—as all the norm breaking of such leaders ultimately is—determining which men would fall in line and which men would raise objections. This festival was the king's public way of communicating to elites everywhere: Make your choice, and do it now.

The king's Great Royal Wife, Nefertiti, whose name means "the Beautiful One Has Come," made her appearance in the midst of the Sed festival—and was shown in her own carrying chair as a part of the rituals. She was the essential female accompaniment; Amenhotep IV even built her a new temple that showed her ritual activities for the Aten at Thebes.

Nefertiti was an extension of her husband's religious power, the feminine part of himself. Sculptors were ordered to depict her with the same body shape as the king—the same full hips, thighs, and belly, the same spindly upper body, arms, and lower legs, the same animal-human face and slit-like eyes, all presumably suffused with bright sunlight. Her figure also breathed in the same ankh signs held to her nose, a privilege limited to the royal couple. And in temple scenes, Nefertiti is also shown on repeat, in front of different offering tables, under the Aten's gaze.[54]

Even the most untutored tourist to Egypt can identify the shift in art styles, from normally proportioned, idealized human faces and bodies to something very different: a new artistic system for a new king. Egyptian craftsmen of the 18th dynasty used a grid system to create art as a group. If you had a workshop of five guys—draftsmen, stonecutters, painters—and you wanted to lay out a big scene on the wall of a temple or tomb, you used a grid. You dipped string into red paint and then snapped it on the wall at hand's-width intervals, vertically and horizontally, creating regular right angles in which to apply your drawing. The lead artisan would sketch the scenes, using 18 squares for a standing human figure, knowing on which grid line to put the forehead, the eye, the top of the neck, the shoulder, the belly, and so on. Amenhotep IV's new royal image effectively demanded two extra grid squares: one for the neck to account for his elongated, animal-like look, and the other for his hip-thigh-stomach area that was now so pronounced. His wife Nefertiti received the same extra squares in her grid.[55]

It's astounding how much of Amenhotep IV's artistic vision seemed fully formed right from the start. No Egyptian king had created anything like it before. It was something profoundly new, and that was what the king wanted—much in the same way that short skirts and rolled-down stockings must have been perceived as deviant in the 1920s, or sparkly white eye shadow, Technicolor shades, and go-go boots seemed so radical in the 1960s.

You might think of all this visual change as the plan of a madman. But if Amenhotep IV was so unhinged, why do all his modifications come off as so systematically clever? What we are seeing in the Theban evidence is a cascade: the manipulation of temple monuments to craft a radically new religious ideology that, in turn, created a different economic methodology that, in turn, formed a new political reality.

Boom! Amenhotep IV had moved his vision from the abstract to the physical and back to the abstract. There is no need for cynicism on our part when we see such masterful social engineering, because we can be sure that he believed wholeheartedly in the truth of his schemes. We can even be sure that some of his loyal lieutenants had a profound belief in them as well. Never forget that the most successful ideologies are those in which people trust most fervently. Faith is not mutually exclusive with power. Faith is power.[56]

We have a bit of insight into the king's micromanagement of his new artistic style in a depiction of his chief sculptor, a man named Bak, who claimed to have learned how to draw human figures from the king himself.[57] The artisan set up a stela down south at Aswan, on which he depicted himself on a very small scale, impeccably dressed, replete with waxen cones containing sweet-smelling resins upon his head (the visible perfume of the ancient world). Bak is in the presence of the king beneath the solar disk. Only the king was shown bathed in the sun's life-giving rays; Bak remained outside of the solar embrace. Simple humans, it seems, could not understand the nature of the sun, and thus could not be touched by its true power. Bak showed himself with arms upraised in worship of his king nonetheless. No one in Egypt, especially the craftsmen, had the opportunity for any kind of real pushback, let alone sharing deeper thoughts on the complicated matters of the day.

At Thebes, we can see a step-by-step progression toward Amenhotep IV's radical revision. The southern vizier, Ramose, who had served under Amenhotep III and now worked for Amenhotep IV, left an unfinished tomb[58] in the most fashionable part of the Theban elite necropolis. The tomb's images, cut from a fine-grained white limestone, bear artistry so beautiful that the place packs in the tourists. But both styles of art are visible there: the traditional style of Amenhotep III and the new style associated with Aten worship.

A scene in the new style, using the new artistic grid, displays a novel pyramidal sun tableau. Under the Aten's rays, we see Amenhotep IV standing in his palace's window of appearances, leaning forward with his hand outstretched, offering some sort of reward to Ramose below. The face of Ramose did not have the old idealized look to it. It was elongated—not to the extreme of the king's, but somehow different. More ominously, Ramose was now bent at the waist in slavish service to his king, whereas before he had stood straight and tall.

Such scenes help us see how Egypt's elites were given a stark choice by their king: to be pulled in as useful lieutenants or to lose everything for themselves and their offspring. The tomb is the evidence we need to see that Ramose decided to go all-in with his god-king, successfully pivoting to please the unusual ruler. But tombs of other elites—such as the tomb of the king's steward Parennefer,[59] also situated in the Theban west bank—suggest that some officials fell out of favor. Parennefer's names and figures have been chiseled away, even though the new artistic style was used. However it happened, Parennefer was erased from the world of the elites. Apparently, even if your family had been working for the king for generations, one step out of line and you were excised.

These tombs offer a snapshot in stone of the state of Egyptian politics. At a similar moment in American politics, Republican never-Trumpers either ended up pivoting their views to align with the new president's or were publicly ridiculed on Twitter and left behind. In Hungary, people keep their lucrative government positions if they're loyal to the presidency, or submit to the purge already under way if they are not. A willingly co-opted elite looks to the top man, his policy writers, religious leaders, and new cronies rewarded for their piety and loyalty—even for their hate and exclusion—though not necessarily for their age or abilities. These were the stakes in the Egypt of Amenhotep IV; all were forced to decide which side of the line they would stand on. There was no way to be neutral.

These changes must have been deeply upsetting to the Egyptian people. There is evidence that elites felt betrayed, sold out, and bitter toward this new king; they were probably also resentful of the new minders who were ready to report or slander any one of them.

It was a story of profound change that featured all the destruction that accompanies such upheaval, including, but not limited to, torn-down temples, purposefully buried objects, smashed statuary, erased names, and hacked-out figures. Everywhere chisel marks reflect a king's orders for removal, or an official fallen from grace, or the brutal physical reactions to the whole political-religious experiment.

Collectively, this ancient material still carries a sense of foreboding; although the actions in question took place some 3,000 years ago, we can still sense the coming fall of a dynasty. The world's first ideological regime would last fewer than two decades, a blip on the human time line. And yet its political philosophies would burrow deep into the human psyche, lying dormant like a willfully forgotten memory, waiting until political actors from outside Egypt—among them a little-known tribe of Israel in the highlands of the southern Levant—marshaled the monotheistic ideology in support of a very different kind of kingship.[60] We can wonder if the Israelites had any idea that they were taking a page from a reviled Egyptian playbook.

Unlike the Levantine highlands, though, the religious change in Egypt came from the very top. Amenhotep IV would even alter his name to show his newfound piety. His birth name, Amenhotep, was discarded, abhorred, never to be used again—so repellent that he would eventually send men out to destroy the name of the god Amun wherever it was found. By going after Amun-Re, king of the gods, namesake of his father and his dynasty, Akhenaten publicized a rejection of Egypt's divine father. Akhenaten was going to create a new father—a better father.

The comparisons between Akhenaten and modern dictators such as Kim Il-Sung of North Korea are many. Indeed, Kim Il-Sung's name means "Kim Becomes the Sun," and we see strikingly similar imagery to Akhenaten's in the Korean propaganda posters: a face embedded within the sun's round disk, his people looking up at him from either side in a pyramid tableau.

But how do you get people to go along with such transformative change? How do you get them to drink the Kool-Aid, in the manner of the cult in Jonestown, Guyana, where Jim Jones got 900 people to consume poisoned punch? The answer is simple: You sweep aside their old gods. You tell people to forget their families. You remove them from their parents, their homes, their original realities, their tribes. You tell them that what had been there before was evil and wrong, and that you—only you—know the correct path, and they must follow you. You isolate them. You take a new name, and you give them new names too.

Indeed, all of Akhenaten's new ideological realities—new names, new temples, new body, new gods—seem like a first-edition modern cultist strategy. If you pull away old associations, destabilize their futures, and remove all escape routes, people will follow you—even if they have to stand bent over in the sun all day long; even if they see all of Egypt's precious resources being wasted; even if they witness cruelties and injustices; even if they have to move everything to a new capital city not yet built; even if they have to listen to prophecy after prophecy, each one more off the rails than the last; even if they must relinquish afterlife ideologies allowing them rebirth as Osiris. Why? Because they believe they have little choice. This is how fanaticism works on people.

Like the Star Wars mythology of the Sith, we are dealing in this scenario with absolutes. And if we take the analogy further, one could even
venture that when Amenhotep IV hunted down and murdered the god
Amun-Re, Darth Akhenaten was born.

A New Capital

Akhenaten's new religion was so simplified that it allowed his followers
to speak with one voice—the same way that those who follow today's
law-and-order parties of nascent authoritarians find they have clearer
messaging compared with diverse liberal agendas in which no one can
agree on a platform. In Akhenaten's Egypt, you either chose the king
and his new ways and were amply rewarded, or you got left behind in
the dark with nothing. Knowingly or unknowingly, Akhenaten had hit
upon a brilliant scheme of religiously proving who was with him and
who was against him.

And the more outlandish the new ritual, new statues, or new temple,
the better. The craziness is the point, because such a test allows a leader
to see who is truly loyal. Most cultlike leaders package themselves as the
new father of their people, basing their ideology on family duties and
connections to their homeland. Akhenaten would now ask his loyal
followers to leave everything behind and follow him to someplace completely new.

Akhenaten wanted a pure capital city for himself and his god.[61] He
could not build his vision in Memphis, Thebes, or Heliopolis, where the
elites were already deeply intertwined in the social fabric; he had already
started to erect temples to the Aten in those centers, but it wasn't working to his satisfaction. Founding a new city that could be more easily
controlled and administered, with temples, palaces, administrative
buildings, and residential areas built from the ground up, was the gateway to the innovative new reign he imagined.

Akhenaten had already severed ties with the name of his dead father. In his fifth regnal year he would leave every physical manifestation of his old life behind. He was on a new path that demanded a total rejection of his past. He refused to play the traditional kingly game any longer. But instead of just walking away, he flipped the game board into the air.

First on the agenda was choosing the perfect spot for his state-of-the-art capital, so Akhenaten traveled to Middle Egypt to find territory along the Nile unassociated with a god or goddess. Presumably camping in a plush tent decked out with amenities, he inspected the domain for his sacred city in style "mounted on a great chariot of gold, like Aten when he dawns in the horizon and fills the Two Lands with his love."[62]

The king did not hold back; he wanted to play the role of a shining hero on a brilliant quest. So he called his city Akhetaten, or "the Horizon of the Aten"—only one consonant different from his own new name, as if place and king were one and the same. He identified it thusly: "It belongs to my father [Re-Horakhty], who rejoices in the horizon in his name of light (Shu) that is the Aten, who gives life forever, with mountains, deserts, meadows, new lands, highlands, fresh lands, fields, water, settlements, shorelands, people, cattle, trees, and all other things that the Aten my father shall let be forever."[63]

In fewer than 10 years Akhenaten would construct his utopian vision without compromise. As was the case with the 12th dynasty and its city of Itjy-tawy, he knew he would unbalance the regime's elite stakeholders, who would no longer have their villas and lands, factories, metalsmiths, political connections, or temple networks. Instead, they would have to look to their philosopher-king to provide those benefits.

Akhenaten had inherited a rich country from his father, but Egypt was being eaten alive by all its grifting elite. The king wanted to seize true power again, and the elites would need to show their "faith" at a new court. Thus, the king moved the army, archives, economic taxation system, treasuries, justice department, diplomatic corps, building programs, and temple hierarchy. He established new faience workshops, glassblowing kilns, pottery workshops, chariot-construction factories, horse-breeding facilities, and flax-weaving installations, bringing all the skilled practitioners from other cities.

Were these craftsmen and women moved to the new city against their will? Or did they come happily? They likely had no choice in the matter, having been told one day, "We're shutting this down and moving it all to the king's new city." With this call, Akhenaten had potentially lost generations of know-how and regional networks. But for him, industry was about controlling production, not about making the best objects or improving its quality.[64] Of course, some craftwork requires certain geographic conditions of aridity or marshland or access to particular natural resources—but that wasn't the point. Akhenaten wanted it all in his city.

If this was how he treated craft installations that were once regionally organized, we can only imagine the same philosophy was applied to his men, in that control was valued over quality and ability. Loyalty and maintenance of the regime were the primary goals; functionality was secondary. This is how it works with modern authoritarian regimes as well: A quick look at modern-day Venezuela tells us that although markets, imports, and health care are not fully functional, that matters little because the regime is intact.[65]

Moving to a new capital arguably allowed the king to appoint a slate of new officials: trustworthy lieutenants dependent on no one but him.[66] Historians call such appointments elite replacement.[67] In modern U.S. terms, elite replacement happens every time there is an election—for the White House, or a governor's office, or officials in city hall. Within democratic systems, elite replacement is baked in, or at least it should be. But within authoritarian regimes (or democratic systems that veer toward authoritarianism), we see a more brutal understanding of it through purges and violence that drive out long-established aristocrats in favor of loyal up-and-comers.

Egypt of the 18th dynasty had delegated great power to its aristocratic families, who thereby enjoyed a certain status quo that kept competition to a minimum. Officials often handed the reigns of a particular official post to a son, thus maintaining continuity and institutional memory. There had occasionally been some mini-purges, but overall, during the reigns of eight kings from Amenhotep I to Amenhotep III, Egypt was characterized by an empowered and continuous elite.[68]

No longer. Akhenaten had created a mechanism for easily shoving established officials to the side.

Across many civilizations, some of the world's most ruthless dictators have displayed cruel elite replacement to stakeholders and reveled in the horror. Hitler exposed traitors by hanging them from meat hooks, for instance. And Vlad the Impaler did to recalcitrant aristocrats what his nickname suggests, leaving their bodies all around his castle to rot.

But such spectacles only kept elites in line over the short term. The Egyptians did not put on such performances openly, preferring to hide their brutality while making every new change seem driven by religious intent and piety.

Akhenaten left little trace of messy human contests, even while he reveled in monuments to his religiosity. According to the surviving record, he simply took his vast wealth and military power and moved away from the old centers—no mass firings necessary, just the name changes, the turnover of officials on the basis of loyalty, and an uptick in military presence. We can imagine many of these new officials did not necessarily know what they were doing, guided solely by their own short-term, survivalist thinking. Nevertheless, we don't see institutional failures in the idealized monuments of Akhenaten, only the small clues that survive in the archaeological record. They're minor tells really, suggesting that many mistakes had been woven into the fabric of this new governmental system.

Now, try to imagine a bunch of spoiled, wealthy Egyptians accustomed to having servants for every little thing who were suddenly expected to move to a backwater and, it seems, live in tents and temporary shelters to lay out the king's future city. We can envision these men riding about on their chariots as Akhenaten did, drawing up when the king earnestly insisted on another impromptu worship session of his solar father— "Having proceeded southward, his majesty halted upon his great chariot before his father . . . at the southeastern mountain of Akhetaten, the rays of the Aten being upon him with life and health for the renewal of his body every day."[69]

It seems that everyone was essentially expected to rough it while they figured out how to build a city isolated from all their known social networks, institutions, temples, and trade connections. They had their great leader on his golden chariot; and they had each other, one supposes. But the competition must have been fierce as all were vying for the favor of the man at the top. Deprivation must have been a key element to Akhenaten's self-sufficiency. It proved who could handle it all, who could handle him.

The king brought the royal family too, including his highest-ranking wife, Nefertiti. He bestowed upon her a new name: Neferneferuaten, "the Beauty of the Beautiful Ones of the Aten." Presumably his other wives came along with his young daughters and—although they were never openly named during his reign—his young sons too. His mother, the venerable Queen Tiy, also relocated to the new court. Everyone who was dragged to the new unbuilt capital was wholly dependent upon him—his money, his vision, his way.

Akhenaten was quite careful to communicate that he was only commanding people to this rustic place because the Aten had told him to:

"Now, it is the Aten, my father, who advised me concerning it . . ."[70] The king thus addressed the worries of his people openly, telling them essentially, that hey, this wasn't politically based decision-making. No, no, this was heavy, divine stuff that the king would never have done out of his own ambition.

Shifting responsibility is a key feature of authoritarian rulers, and nothing new for Egypt's kings. (The female King Hatshepsut had similar things to say about her divine father, Amun, asserting that she was only claiming the kingship as her father had asked of her.)

But Akhenaten was responsible for more drastic changes than Hatshepsut was, including an elemental reform to the Egyptian written language. He discarded the old Middle Egyptian—which for the Egyptians of his time must have been on par with *Beowulf* for English speakers today—and updated the current grammar, word order, prepositions, and vocabulary. He thus simplified and standardized written Egyptian, probably removing the privilege of literacy from the old aristocracy and making it easier for new men to participate in his government.

Never underestimate the power that the written language holds over humans when controlled by leaders. The French first established the Académie française in the 17th century to implement language standardization from above. Atatürk reformed Turkish in the 1920s, changing grammatical forms and establishing a new writing system in Latin-based script; this simplified the written language for a rising class of nationalist bureaucrats and helped push out the old Ottoman imperial ways. The People's Republic of China created a simplified script in the 1950s, rejecting thousands of archaic characters and dialectal remnants and paving the way for a communist state in which everyone could participate. Or consider the language shift instituted by the Viet Minh, who eschewed French in favor of Vietnamese written in their own new script.

In Akhenaten's case, the language changes allowed more people from a broader swath of society into his court—and for most of them, such changes must have been perceived positively.[71]

But Akhenaten felt unsafe somehow, apparently challenged by discord or slander. One of the markers on the borders of his city reads:

> As for the . . . in Akhetaten—it was worse than those things I heard in regnal year 4; it was worse than [those things] I heard in regnal year 3; it was worse than those things I heard in regnal year 2; it was worse than those things I heard in regnal year 1; it was worse [than] those things [Nebmaat]-re [Amenhotep] heard; it was worse than those things which . . . heard; it was worse than those things which Menkheperre [Thutmosis] heard; and it was worse than those things heard by any kings who had ever assumed the White Crown [that is, controlled the south]![72]

We don't know what horrors Akhenaten perceived, but perhaps they were related to the drama associated with moving to this new place, and the unease of many of the dug-in patrician families. We can't know for sure, because Egyptian elites did not keep diaries, nor did they write any letters saying how much this new king was destabilizing their livelihoods and peace of mind. Any upheaval was only referenced obliquely.

But we do see clues of the storm raging in Egypt. A man named Amenmose, for instance, who was associated with the Temple of Amun in Thebes, changed his name to Ramose to work for the Aten Temple.[73] We also see a proliferation of new men connected to the armed forces and police, many of them with an "Aten" element added to their personal names—a change likely made to please their king. There had been no such Aten names in the reign of Amenhotep III; they had now become the norm.

Akhenaten's increased use of his army is telling. He displays officers, police chiefs, and generals more prominently in his parades and festivals. Their tombs are large, illustrative of a social status they hadn't previously enjoyed. Indeed, more police and army men seem to serve the king in higher official positions than ever before in the 18th dynasty.[74] It seems that to implement his vision, Akhenaten pulled wealth from Egypt's treasurers and priests and redistributed it to a nouveau riche, up-and-coming military class of men happy to take on new names and enter the king's court. The army and police were Akhenaten's means of speeding up operations and compelling his people to go along with each new change; if some of his most powerful and rewarded supporters were connected to the armed forces, then it follows that the king's regime was probably based on violence and coercion.

All the king's closest followers, family, and hangers-on were now isolated in the same bubble as Akhenaten—cut off, surrounded by men empowered with sanctioned violence, and all looking toward a king who used religion as his last, best offense and defense. The experiment had begun in earnest. Everyone was listening to state-sanctioned press, and we see no real outside word from anybody else in this new city. Like Fox News watchers communicating only among themselves on Facebook, or L. Ron Hubbard isolated with his followers on his private yacht, or Louis XVI and Marie Antoinette far removed from poverty and despair in a gilded Versailles, Akhenaten had manufactured his own forced happiness.

Although we don't have any evidence that Akhenaten's people were not allowed to leave his new city, he does claim that he himself would never abandon his new home. Trusted people must have gone in and out, but those on the inside were certainly caught there.

Amarna is the name of the archaeological site of Akhetaten, the new capital city located along the east side of the Nile, in the land of the rising sun. The king was making a statement about where he did choose to build as much as where he did not, picking a point along the river north of Thebes and south of Memphis. He stayed clear of the Delta, although the roads to the eastern Levant originated there and the grain grew like weeds. The likely reason was that he was from Upper Egypt, and the Delta was an uncontrollable unknown for him. Neither did he choose Elephantine in the south, the entrance to gold mines and quarries, perhaps because it was too removed, too associated with Nubian culture, less amenable to agricultural growth. Instead, the city of Akhetaten was positioned in the center of its king's known universe.

He organized his main city around two temples: first, a massive structure larger than 30 football fields in an area that archaeologists call the Great Aten Temple, and second, a smaller sanctuary to his god, now called the Small Aten Temple, which was perhaps exclusive to the royal circle and possibly functioned as his Temple of Millions of Years. Nearby, villas were built for his elites and palaces for himself.

Surrounding the whole city were boundary markers—about a dozen on the east riverbank and a few more on the west bank to delineate where the capital city began and ended. It seemed vital for Akhenaten to communicate the limits of his new urban expanse to his loyal followers—clearly indicating that when they left it, they had somehow entered a land of darkness, nonexistence, and threat.

The king's temples, open to the air, were architectural symbols of his vision. As in the old temples, Akhenaten maintained a separation of space by means of pylon gateways that one moved through. Abandoning an enclosed sanctuary, in which the statue of the god would have previously been hidden in a veiled shrine, Akhenaten insisted on a temple configured so that as the initiated walked into the space, the floor rose to the sky, to the Aten. The uncovered rear of the temple held no effigy of the god; the only idol was the sun.

Akhenaten was a literalist. His god was felt and seen, touching the skin with its warmth. The king built his temples for that effect, filling their spaces with hundreds of altars upon which he placed countless offerings of food and drink for the sun to consume with its solar rays. Akhenaten's rituals would have happened systematically—like clockwork, we can imagine—at certain times of day until the orb of the Aten set in the west. Equinox and solstice days must have meant special feasts.

We can only guess that Akhenaten demanded his people watch Egypt's bounty being consumed as they stood in worship within the Great Aten Temple. No matter your social place, everyone was meant to see the solar rays absorbing the plenty all around them. Maybe some lower elites could only get into the first court, while the more important men and women found their way into the second or third courts. Only the royal family and highest priests must have been allowed access into that last, most exclusive area of the temple.

Withholding wealth and displaying excess are still associated with behemoth religions, authoritarian regimes, dictatorships, and cults. The Pantheon in Rome, St. Peter's Basilica at the Vatican, the Blue Mosque in Istanbul, and Salt Lake Temple in Utah all represent massive displays of wealth, because money implicitly means the blessings of God. Indeed, the true sign of the fall of communism for those who had suffered its economic consequences was the supermarket full of out-of-season fruits and vegetables, along with cheap, fast food. Capitalism was proven the winner ideologically by its ability to produce excess for its participants— and so, an ideological leader uses wealth to keep his lieutenants in line.

Akhenaten's stratified rituals must have solidified social place in the world—but at the same time, they would have also created a real anxiety as people watched good food rotting in the sun. Traditionally, many people had been fed from temple offerings. Food placed upon the altar was taken down and given to those who worked in the religious sphere.

This represented millennia of social reallocation—pulling wealth into the institution and then redistributing it.

But now the system seems to have broken. Putting that food into the open sun must have compromised collection and redistribution. Taxes were demanded, apparently, so they could be claimed by the king for his god, but then what? The details of Akhenaten's solar offerings remain unclear, but Egypt's elites must have been questioning the entire game in stark terms: Where was the wealth going? What would be their cut?

Akhenaten's temples were akin to a televangelist demanding cash from his followers, only to set it on fire with great fanfare and make everyone watch it burn because God can and will make more for his chosen people. In Akhenaten's case, we can imagine him displaying the fanciest, best produce and then keeping some of it for himself and his family to eat and enjoy. Make no mistake: The act of display is essential to an authoritarian's power.

The sheer size of the Great Aten Temple is mind-boggling. It included associated installations such as animal pens, bakeries, breweries, and butcheries. Its high-walled presence within the city must have been oppressive, like a freeway or a city block that is too long, not functional for its citizenry, but mandatory for the displays of the ruler. And inside those walls were row upon row of altars upon which Akhenaten demanded offerings of food in his temples, all of it played endlessly.[75] His architectural utopia was one of uniformity and reprise.

In addition to his own statues populating his Aten temples on repeat, Akhenaten also focused on his female companions in the form of statues of brownish red and purple stone, the color of the sunset or sunrise. Sexualized women and girls were depicted as, though not overtly stated to be, the mothers and daughters of the sun god, and thus those who consorted with and reproduced his own self. Nefertiti was depicted with a full belly and lower body, implying that she was the bride of the solar orb whose sexual congress created the god's own rebirth. Daughters, too, were shown with full hips and thighs, full bellies, all ready to be fertile for their lord.[76]

Akhenaten wanted to showcase his own sexual abilities to produce and reproduce like the Aten, so he commissioned dozens of intimate family reliefs in which he and Nefertiti sat next to each other in charming palace scenes, cavorting with their daughters, cuddling, kissing, and relaxing. The scenes were so unusual and private that they wouldn't have just raised Egyptian eyebrows; they would have stunned everyone with their explicitness. In one famous image, Akhenaten lifts his eldest daughter to his lips, kissing her on the mouth, his hand and arm resting between her thighs—an obvious sexual allusion between father and daughter. Such things were not forbidden for the son of Aten, and he would elevate at least two of his girls to royal wives and produce offspring with them (perhaps even Tutankhamun himself).[77] As is often the case, the taboo of sex between adult and child was and is broken by a religious practitioner claiming special license from God.

THE DARK SIDE OF THE SUN KING

Akhenaten had been using all kinds of solar ideas pulled from millennia of theological examination of that most powerful element in the Egyptian world—sunlight. His father, Amenhotep III, had called himself Aten-Tjehen, "the Dazzling Sun," associating his person with the entity that moved through the sky. Now, Akhenaten took this notion and ran with it, becoming light incarnate, a kind of human pyramid.

These are abstract notions, to be sure, but there is real political and economic intent behind all the philosophizing about sunlight. Kings desire association with an element that can see all, touch all, allow all to grow, and always rise again. The sun also represents riches. Its yellow color is associated with gold, that malleable, portable, displayable medium of wealth: something a leader could use to pay or co-opt or placate people. A sun king is automatically assumed to be wealthy, a kind of golden god, and such a solar association avoids direct, crass statements about money. The sun king moniker was code that would have been clearly understood physically and monetarily by all the elites who clustered around their king knowing that some of the sunlight would trickle down to them.

Connections between patriarchal authoritarian rule and the sun have appeared all over the world. There have been many "sun kings" throughout history, including Roman emperors who called themselves Sol Invictus and wore the radiating crown; the Chinese emperor called the Son of Heaven, which included the sun, moon, and constellations; the Japanese Emperor of the Land Where the Sun Rises; and the Inca rulers who celebrated Inti Raymi sun ceremonies while riding in a golden chariot.

The sun is an inherent sign of power, usually associated with masculinity. It is farseeing, always on the move, cyclical in its strength and weakness, permeating everywhere as its warmth gets into every crevice. Without the sun, we are lost, unable to see, with no ability to function, literally stumbling in the dark. Our radiant leader provides that ability to perceive; he is our guide. But we must be careful. The all-powerful sun can burn us, too.

Akhenaten's officials were fond of depicting the king's largesse in their tomb chapels. In one such scene we see Akhenaten at his second-floor palace window, with his elites shown as tiny, clustered figures, bent at the waist, at ground level below him. The king lounges in a relaxed fashion as he looks down, his arm resting upon a brocade-covered cushion. He is accompanied by his wife and girls, a happy family scene. The sun's ever present rays float down from the orb above his head, turning him into that now familiar body of light.[78]

And the elites below are not just kowtowing. They're stretching out their hands, like people do when a New Orleans' Mardi Gras float passes in the hope of catching beads and coins. The king often threw precious baubles from his window of appearances—necklaces, collars, insignia of honor made of solid gold, and other precious things. It is the most evocative image of a co-opted elite ever produced in ancient Egypt and, I dare say, anywhere in the world.

If the Egyptians normally shied away from showing coercion, political pressure, or military force, they didn't have a problem revealing overt rewards for services rendered. The quid pro quo was depicted in loving, colorful detail. You scratch my back, and I'll scratch yours. The king got to proclaim his wealth and power, and the elites broadcast to other elites their elevated connections.

Money and power are rather obvious bedfellows—and are even more overtly so in the United States, now that the Supreme Court has ruled that corporations can buy their way into political decisions without any of the normal subterfuge.[79] It has come to a point where we don't even try to hide the hold that economic interests have over our politics anymore. Everyone knows that leaders in coal, oil, technology, and other industries act as lobbyists and raise money for campaign donations as they blatantly support self-serving policies such as low tax rates and favorable trade deals that will enrich them as well as the legislators who pass the policies into law.

Under Akhenaten's rule, we may assume there were dozens of elite families willing to do anything for the right reward. Those same people would be more likely to use unfair practices, even outright brutality, to keep the king happy and to maintain the flow of wealth and power in their direction. As for the king, well—he had god on his side. He could do no wrong.

We should not be surprised that bioarchaeologists have found damning evidence of forced labor camps at Akhetaten, proving that people worked too hard and too long. Skeletons show disproportionate evidence of malnutrition, acute injuries such as broken limbs that healed badly, repetitive stress injuries to backs and joints, and increased markers of infectious diseases—perhaps tuberculosis and intestinal maladies—all of which must have caused great suffering until the workers died an early death and were deposited in their graves. Some of the laborers were children, removed from any adult presence if the burial conditions are in any way representative of their lives. Some Egyptologists insist these mass burials are the result of plague, but that doesn't explain the other maladies. The bodies seem to represent systemic oppression and undernourishment.[80]

How could people inflict such cruelty just to build a city? Why would such a wealthy Egyptian king need to work people to death? Such abhorrent labor practices could easily have come about organically without any direct orders being given. If we assume that the king ordered his officials to build quickly and extensively, richly rewarding those who were on schedule and under budget, that could pave the way for such problematic treatment. Or if the king only paid a set amount per contract, with the expectation that leftover monies could be pocketed by the responsible contractors, then the effort to come in under budget would fall on the backs of the workers; there would have been no oversight of means if the deliverables appeared. Such methods of rule—particularly if wrested from established social contracts and the oversight of respected elders in this remote city—could easily have turned into the systematic abuse of a working population.

Akhenaten could have claimed plausible deniability, because he had merely ordered his elites to build this or that with a giant reward if it was done quickly and to spec; no one ordered anyone to abuse anyone. A leader makes his followers commit the atrocities, keeping his own hands and conscience clean.

We might also consider the possibility that Akhenaten ordered such work camps as a direct means of generating power over certain groups of recalcitrant people. It would have been a useful message for this king and his faithful lieutenants to force Egypt's former aristocrats, disrobed and disrespected, to pick up rubble and bricks and do other menial labor under the blazing sun until they died. Such things have certainly happened elsewhere in the world, and they could have happened in Egypt, too.

Using reeducation or labor camps is often supported by ideological systems—think of the Spanish *reducciones* where missionaries worked Native Americans to death, WWII concentration camps where inmates labored under the slogan *Arbeit macht frei* ("Work sets you free"), and China's Laogai prisons during Mao Zedong's Cultural Revolution. Forced labor camps are associated with just about every authoritarian system on Earth, and constructing them is often considered pious work, like building a church or some other sacred space.

The discovery of mass graves filled with mistreated people at Amarna has started to change the way Egyptologists see Akhenaten's Egypt. Until that point, without any evidence for such misdeeds, we relegated Akhenaten's reforms to a rather harmless religious experiment that may have cut into the Egyptian psyche on the nature of god: a philosophical test but not a police state in which people were rounded up, forced to name names, or pushed into inhumane situations. Those things seem so un-Egyptian, so out of character for the good kings we admire so much. Egyptologists often assign the phrase "religious revolution" to Akhenaten's changes, as if it were a grassroots movement of collective fervor—an ideological cover for all the economic and political agendas fomented from the top down.

But the evidence is there. Any examination of the bioarchaeological reports shows striking parallels with skeletons found at modern labor camps uncovered by forensic work.[81] The interesting point is not that such mistreatment occurred, but rather our lack of interest in recognizing it as such because it would remove the pageantry and force us to see Akhenaten's system for what it was: officials driving people brutally, not properly feeding and clothing them, and benefiting from other people's suffering—all condoned by their leader, who could say he was only doing what his god told him. This is not the Egypt we want to claim.

We can only speculate how the systematic abuse in Akhetaten affected city residents such as a sculptor named Thutmose, whose grand villa was discovered with sculptures still inside (including the famous limestone bust of Nefertiti, now in Berlin). Thutmose was a wealthy man—certainly unusual for an 18th-dynasty artisan, and not a status for which we have earlier evidence. Craftsmen were generally not wealthy in any premodern society; even famous artists like Michelangelo or da Vinci were hardscrabble guys working for one patron after another, always on the move, always looking to the next gig.

Akhenaten, it seems, was elevating people who would not normally have risen so high. Thutmose created extraordinary sculptures that graced buildings, and now we suspect they were constructed by forced labor. His main job was to make the king and his women look good, to idealize them in stone. Did Thutmose witness the violence inflicted by this king? Did he, himself, mete out any of that pain to the men working in his atelier? After all, he was rich—a damning characteristic in this city, perhaps proof enough of unscrupulousness.

Violent power may have been prevalent in all sectors of Akhetaten—among the military, priests, diplomats, stewards and butlers, harem officials. It was an element of society that no lieutenant of Akhenaten wanted to show openly, but it was discovered some 3,000 years later nonetheless.

THE ROLE OF NEFERTITI

Nefertiti's role in this whole scheme is problematic, too. We all want to know: What did she know, and when did she know it? Was she watching, waiting, biding her time, comfortable in her position as the second most important person in the known universe, but uncomfortably recognizing the horrors of it all? She had always been an essential piece in Akhenaten's new religious puzzle, and his ideology included her almost as much as it did him.

Akhenaten surrounded himself with the protection of his female family members. He never explicitly mentioned a male member of his royal family during all his time in Akhetaten—not a son, certainly not a brother.[82] He was like a guy whose friends are all women. He only allowed us to see his many daughters, his chief wife, Nefertiti, and other women such as a secondary wife named Kiya.

At the same time that Akhenaten's elites were commissioning altars showing their king in happy family life with his daughters—to display a family portrait of the religious patriarch in the home as a sign of loyalty and respect—Akhenaten began his campaign of iconoclasm. He sent his chisel bearers to enter into temples and remove the names of Amun and other gods from wall reliefs and statues. Nowhere does he record these actions or the reasoning behind them in his many texts that explain his god. We must piece the story together from the traces of the damage itself.

As the king's religious experiment hardened into exclusionary beliefs, Nefertiti became essential to his political-ideological machinations, even made equal to him. She was the beauty beside him on the throne, the element that softened his hard edges for his people, the apologist. Images already showed Nefertiti with an unusual flat-topped crown never seen on a queen before, at the same height and stature as the king, and with the same weird body shape. Nefertiti already had her own grand temple space in the new capital. She had already been shown smiting enemies[83]—something we have never seen a Great Royal Wife do in ancient Egyptian ideological scenes—or trampling them under her feet in her guise as a female-headed sphinx.[84]

As Akhenaten locked down his regime, he felt the need to share power with his queen, formally elevating Nefertiti to co-king status alongside him.[85] The veiled manner in which this was done has elicited endless debate from Egyptologists who are unclear about whether the new co-king appearing in the king's monuments—named Ankhkheperure-Nefer-Neferu-Aten—was originally Nefertiti or someone else. However, because of the retention of the name Nefer-Neferu-Aten, most now agree that Nefertiti had been renamed and morphed into a co-ruler, a politically defensive and unprecedented move in terms of feminine power. (The only other female co-king to take her place beside a male already enthroned was Hatshepsut, more than a hundred years before—and only because there had been a child-king on the throne apparently in need of support.)

Akhenaten was no child unable to make his own decisions, but a grown man. Why would he have needed equal help with rule and decision-making? Maybe he required another, trusted set of eyes, another brain with which to mull over strategy. Perhaps he desired somebody else to watch over his vulnerable new regime, but someone completely loyal to him, utterly dependent upon all that he had already built. Maybe Akhenaten was ill or something had gone wrong in his entourage, weakening him within his political circles. Whatever the circumstances, the elevation of a wife to co-king suggests that Akhenaten did not trust other royal family members, priests, or officials and that his regime was in need of urgent help. He chose Nefertiti and renamed her Ankhkheperure, "the Manifestations of the Sun God are Alive," a throne name so similar to his own Neferkheperure, meaning "The Manifestations of the Sun

God are Perfect," that it seems a purposeful twinned kingship. He was the Good Sun King; she was his living accompaniment.

Akhenaten didn't want to be the bad guy; he wanted to cast himself as the savior-hero of his people. And so he used his new philosophy to create his own revisionist history, cloaking his darker intentions and actions behind a narrative of family values: a doting husband and father, a co-king willing to share his power with a woman. He played these stories on repeat to a captive population that couldn't get much alternative entertainment from anywhere else.

After stripping away the folklore and drama of the former divine pantheon, Akhenaten created a human fantasy of kingly innovation overcoming adversity. The images—of the king and queen on their chariots, leaning out of the window of appearances, giving offerings to the Aten, kissing and canoodling like characters in a Harlequin romance novel—were hammered into his people's hearts and minds: Here is your good king, the son of god, whose elongated male-female body is an image of the sun, with his gorgeous female counterpart.

His people viewed the tableau in temples, on their home altars, even in their tombs, which now eschewed Osiris and any other afterlife divinities, as well as the traditional invocations for transforming the dead. Akhenaten played the same song on a loop—his song—and new people born into the regime would have had no memory of the way things had been before. Children of nine or 10 years old only remembered this place, these rituals, this king, this way.

The outside world must have been confused too. The Egypt they had known for so long was going through some strange upheavals of internal cultural confusion, feeding on itself, smashing its own gods. Fortunately, we have the extraordinary opportunity of looking at Akhenaten's Egypt through diplomatic texts to the Egyptian court called the Amarna Letters, most written by outside rulers. The clay-tablet missives contain baroque greetings and generally ask after the king's condition. But there are also scattered complaints about not having received the expected amount of gifts or trade from Egypt. The Babylonian king Kadashman-Enlil, for instance, wrote to Akhenaten about one of his diplomats: "But now when I sent a messenger to you, you have detained him for six years, and you have sent me as my greeting-gift—the only thing in six years— 30 minas of gold that look like silver."[86]

But the most eyebrow-raising complaint for the discussion at hand hits upon the perceived strangeness of Akhenaten's rituals, which we see in a letter from the Assyrian king Ashur-uballit: "As for the ambassadors, why are they continually standing outside so that they will die outside? If their standing outside is profitable to the king, then let them stand outside. Outside, let them die! Profit for the king or not, why should they die outside?"[87]

THE RELIGION BEHIND IT ALL

Egypt's highest elites at Akhenaten's court were now expected to reject traditional gods such as Amun-Re (the sun god of Thebes), Re-Atum (the solar creator god of Heliopolis), Sobek (the crocodile god of the Nile flood), Ptah (the craftsman-creator god of Memphis), Sakhmet (the fierce lion goddess of fate), and Khnum (the potter god of Elephantine). Only the Aten was available for prayers and appeals. But there was a problem; no one but the king could actually worship the sun directly. Even though the light touched everyone and warmed everyone's skin, only the king could truly understand the god's nature. Thus, when the Aten was pictured, only the ruler and his wife were bathed in its rays. Everyone else stood in the cold shadows beyond the sun's reach.

There was more. On their tomb walls, elites needed to display their piety—not to the sun god, but to Akhenaten as their lord and personal savior. Tombs included long Aten hymns said to have been personally composed by Akhenaten, which read like catechism notes on the nature of divinity. Here's a passage from one of them:

> You rise, beautiful from the horizon on heaven, living disk, origin of life. You are arisen from the horizon. You have filled every land with your beauty, you are fine, great, radiant, and lofty over and above every land. You are raised by the lands, the limit of all you have made. You are the sun. You have reached their limits. You bind them for their beloved son. You are distant, your rays are on earth. You are in their sight, but your movements are hidden. [88]

The sun was various and mysterious, unknowable by all but their king. Night, he told them, was the rational absence of the sun's light: "You rest in the western horizon and the land is in darkness in the manner of death. Sleepers in chambers, heads covered, no eye can see its other. Anything of theirs can be taken from under their heads and they wouldn't know it."

Without the sun's light, the king tells them, everyone is rudderless, evoking the need for a king's leadership. These hymns were a coded ideological threat that seemed to say when the sun is not there, you will weep in terror—and if you do not want to weep, I will make you.

But Akhenaten imparted good news too, that the sun would always return at daybreak: ". . . arisen from the horizon, shining as the disk in day, you remove the darkness, you grant your rays and the Two Lands are in festival, awake and standing on their feet, you have raised them up." In this new city, every morning was a time to rejoice again. The ideology was meant to be emancipatory, freeing people from irrational mythologies.[89]

Parts of the hymn to the Aten contained in the passages offered found their way—modified, but phrase for phrase it seems—into Psalm 104 of the Hebrew Bible.[90] For example, a phrase from the Great Hymn to the Aten—"Every lion comes from its den"—is uncannily represented in the Hebrew Bible as, "The young lions roar for their prey; when the sun rises, they withdraw and lie down in their dens." Or the phrase in Akhenaten's hymn "When you have dawned they live; when you set, they die" becomes in the Psalms for Yahweh "When you hide your face, they are dismayed; when you take away their breath, they die."

Akhenaten's religious thought somehow crept out of Egypt and into the Levant, taking form in the nascent Yahweh cult. The philosophies of a defensive king formed through entitlement and excess would find a home with a people who held a cultural memory of bondage under exactly such rulers. If historians must assign the Exodus story to a particular Egyptian time period, though, it would be hundreds of years after Akhenaten's reign, around the time of Merneptah, son of Ramses II.

But at this point in his reign, Akhenaten was just coming up with these ideas. He shared what his god had revealed to him and to him alone—that the Aten caused sperm to grow in women, that (like the yolk in the human egg) the sun allowed new life to live in the womb of the mother, and that the Aten was both father and mother, the ultimate creator. Behind all of these beautiful philosophies, though, the political intent still lingers.

Akhenaten was the first religious leader to develop an idea of divine exclusivity. He invented the notion of one god—one creator who has millions of forms and manifestations—before anyone else, and he asserts this point explicitly. His religion had already been fanatical, abandoning long-worshipped divinities, but now it was overtly so. In his great hymn, Akhenaten called the Aten "the one god, the unique god, besides whom there was no other," seemingly making the initial steps toward monotheism.[91]

Many scholars maintain that because Akhenaten retained the gods Re-Horakhty, Shu, Maat, Hapy, and Khepri, his new religion was never true monotheism.[92] But we can see evidence that Akhenaten himself had been mulling over these dissonances too, purifying his philosophy as he went along. For instance, early in his reign Akhenaten had given his Aten god a complicated cartouche name that implied a polytheistic system of many solar gods existing within the solar orb: "The living Re-Horakhty, Rejoicing in the horizon, in his name as Shu who is in the Aten." But at one point he removed Horakhty, which means "Horus of the Two Horizons." That left "Re," which in this case probably referred to the sun rather than the god. One could argue that when Akhenaten retained other "gods," he did so only as abstract meanings. In the Egyptian language, Shu means "light," Kheper means "come into being." We also see the retention of Maat as truth, and of Hapy, but probably only with the meaning of the Nile inundation. Akhenaten was combing through every retained element of his religious creation, removing tangles, and inventing new expressions. But he couldn't throw out the entire Egyptian language. If a word had a broad enough meaning, he seems to have deemed it noncompetitive to his beloved Aten.

Akhenaten narrowed his focus on the Aten, making sure no one could mistake his meaning: "O sole god beside whom there is none! You made the earth as you wished, you alone, all peoples, herds, and flocks. All upon earth that walk on legs, all on high that fly on wings, the lands of Khor and Kush, the land of Egypt. You set every man in his place. You supply their needs. Everyone has his food, his lifetime is counted. Their tongues differ in speech, their characters likewise, their skins are distinct, for you distinguished the peoples."[93]

The king formulated a rational philosophy in which everything started from this one power source, this one light, and then refracted into millions of parts to make plant, animal, and human, Egyptian and foreigner.

He wanted to present the world as he saw it, removing fantastical stand-ins of hybrid human-animal divinities for elements like the sun, the moon, and Earth, eschewing idol worship, and concentrating only on what could be seen and touched. Akhenaten was a literalist, a fundamentalist, an absolutist. In his mind, the supernatural world did not exist at all; only the Aten and his creation were true.

But now we come to the main political element and the reason such a beautiful philosophy is so tainted. The king told his god: "You are in my heart. There is no other who knows you, only your son, Neferkheperure, Sole one of Re, whom you have taught your ways and your might."[94] Therefore, it followed that if Akhenaten was the only one capable of knowing the mysteries of this god, if no other human being could understand them, then this was no grassroots religion whose secrets were revealed to the initiated; it was an exclusive one-man show. Aten was the only god, but Akhenaten was the only son of that one god and his only true representative on Earth.

Akhenaten demanded his people worship him as the true manifestation of divinity, a messiah. He wanted altars, images, statues, reliefs made of him. He instituted new processions of himself on his chariot traveling between palace and temple like the sun's circuit, an imposed daily ceremony to display his person to his people.

But behind the refracted light was a megalomaniacal and narcissistic ideology. Thus, we split hairs to avoid calling it the first monotheism, finding the names of other divinities within the Aten hymns and referring to it as henotheism instead. Most scholars prefer to see Israelite Yahwehism or Iranian Zoroastrianism as the moments when humanity truly made their first leaps toward a belief in one god, not the half-baked egomania of a North African god-king.

Most Egyptologists sidestep the monotheist discussion entirely, preferring to see Akhenaten as an eccentric ruler who got wrapped up in his obsessions about the nature of the universe and his place in it. To them, he was a monarch who fomented a hippie-like commune experiment—a kind of excessive festival of sun and drunken love—whose only real harm was to create an existential crisis about the meaning of divinity. But we can clearly see how this belief system arose within the context of an authoritarian, absolutist kingship that didn't just ask for followers but demanded them, imposing changes from the very top instead of making them based on faith, solace, or salvation.

Perhaps we have conflated our expectations of what we think monotheism should be with what monotheism actually does. Monotheism—though certainly not a term Akhenaten himself would ever have used—was politically useful to a king because it inherently created black-and-white thinking among his population. He created an ideological bubble; inside, all were good and bathed in sunlight, but outside, there was only darkness, evil, and threat. Like a fundamentalist Christian refusing to vaccinate her children or participate in Halloween celebrations because of their demonic nature, such binary thinkers recognize victimization and oppression everywhere. Indeed, exclusionary philosophy enables modern U.S. society's most enfranchised participants—White Christians—to claim they are the persecuted ones.

Dichotomies foment crusade. Akhenaten was the first leader to perfect such binary thinking to defend and expand his power from the top echelon of society. Armed with this ideology, he set himself up as a king so oppressed that the situation demanded sweeping action, emergency powers. We can never know how many actually believed in Akhenaten's new faith—but that probably wasn't his purpose to begin with. Although there are many beautiful and moral elements within monotheistic faiths, they too often serve as ideological tools of social control—just as we see visualized in Tommaso Laureti's 16th-century painting "Triumph of the Christian Religion" in the Vatican Museums,[95] which alludes to Emperor Constantine's imposition of his new religion across his entire realm.

Akhenaten didn't use the one-god belief to get his people to love him; indeed, most Egyptians did not love him, destroying all trace of him as soon as he was dead. Akhenaten utilized exclusionary thinking to over-turn perceived enemies and to create the political reality he wanted.

On the face of it, his religious experiment may seem an egocentric but earnest drive to find his truth, causing him to tumble down a rabbit hole of conspiracy theories in which everyone had been colluding to keep that truth from him. But in so doing, Akhenaten hit upon an unparalleled political strategy, providing an invisible power that even reason and com-mon sense could not combat, that gave him leave to take swift and brutal action. A belief in one god swept away all the nuance and imposed a clarified system of loyalty to the Aten, and thus to the king. This particular interpretation also fabricated threats that had to be quashed at all costs, causing the king to send out his men on earnest missions to destroy other gods in other temples in other towns. The humans clustered around those other divinities became collateral damage in a cosmic crusade. Such binary thinking allows people to be erased simply for an idea.

Monotheism allowed the king to become outraged, victimized, sub-jugated by nothing more than a threat created in his own mind. The reason that we refuse to call Akhenaten's religion monotheistic is the same reason that monotheism remains so politically powerful in our world today: because we are so deeply embedded in its black-or-white manipulations that we cannot even see our way out. We believe so fer-vently in the threats—hellfire, witchcraft, pedophile cabals, socialism—that we simplify anything that falls outside our realm of belief as wrong, something to reject, to hate, to destroy.

Exclusionary thinking—from Abrahamic faiths to iconoclastic Marx-ist observations like "religion is the opiate of the masses" to the MAGA

Found at Abydos, this three-inch-tall ivory statuette is the only complete surviving representation naming 4th-dynasty King Khufu.

ABOVE: Perhaps designed by architect Imhotep, the Step Pyramid of 3rd-dynasty king Netjerikhet Djoser at Saqqara was the world's first such monument in stone.

BELOW: In a stereograph of Giza from about 1908, the Sphinx—perhaps carved with Khufu's face—stands near the 4th-dynasty king's pyramid.

OPPOSITE: An engraved illustration from *Views in Egypt,* published in 1801, shows the arduous climb to the burial chamber inside Khufu's pyramid.

ABOVE: Unearthed at Giza, King Khufu's 143-foot-long funerary boat of Lebanese cedar was reconstructed from about 1,200 parts.

OPPOSITE: A granite statue of 12th-dynasty king Senwosret III shows a careworn face and large ears listening for any whispers against his rule.

ABOVE: Senwosret III's daughter Mereret was buried at Dahshur with this necklace of gold, carnelian, turquoise, and lapis lazuli.

BELOW: About 16 inches tall, a sphinx of stone quarried in Nubia couples the dour face of Senwosret III with a lion's powerful body.

OPPOSITE: Wrestlers in a Beni Hasan tomb illustrate a local ruler's power to raise a private army during the First Intermediate Period.

OPPOSITE: As in many of his strange portraits, Akhenaten appears here with an elongated, animal-like face and feminine features such as breasts.

ABOVE: A glazed steatite scarab from Amarna with Akhenaten's name may have been meant to guarantee royal patronage for the owner.

BELOW: In a relief from Amarna, the Aten sun disk's rays deliver symbols of life to Akhenaten and Nefertiti as they cuddle their daughters.

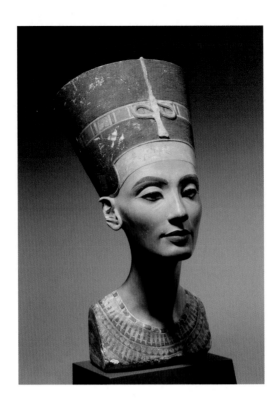

ABOVE: This stunning portrait of Queen Nefertiti was uncovered at Amarna in the workshop of a court sculptor named Thutmose.

BELOW: The coffin from tomb KV 55 in the Valley of the Kings may have belonged to Akhenaten. The face and names were destroyed in antiquity.

OPPOSITE: A colossal statute of Ramses II with his tiny daughter Bint-anat has been restored and reerected at Karnak's Great Temple.

ABOVE: In Nefertari's beautifully restored tomb in the Valley of the Queens, the wings of the goddess Maat frame the queen's name.

BELOW: Known as the Ramesseum, Ramses II's mortuary temple at Thebes included a palace, two temples, and various administrative buildings.

OPPOSITE: Dispelling night's darkness, floodlights gild the statues of Ramses II at the entrance to the main temple at Abu Simbel in Nubia.

OPPOSITE: Taharqa is often depicted wearing this typical 25th-dynasty cap-like crown with a pair of cobras rising from the brow.

ABOVE: A ram representing Amun-Re, the powerful god of sun and air, protects King Taharqa in this statue from a shrine at Jebel Barkal.

BELOW: Offering wine in two round vases, Taharqa thanks the god Hemen for the annual Nile flood after a period of drought and famine.

Jebel Barkal's pinnacle rises like a cobra above rattle-shaped columns
meant to calm the goddess Mut as she emerged from her temple.

cult—channels and manipulates human energies into action. Akhenaten is the king who allows us to see the invention of one-god worship for what it really was: a patriarchal cult leader's tactic, the modern manifestation of which many of us still deludedly follow. I'm not saying that every practicing monotheist is an authoritarian. I am saying that monotheism was specifically invented to support authoritarianism.

ATENISM'S ENDGAME

Even god-fearing kings may live to see their ideas come crashing down around them. In Akhenaten's unfinished tomb, carved into the rock of his capital's eastern necropolis, we see reliefs presumably taken from real life. One shows the king and the royal family grieving, a hand on each head as a sign of mourning. They seem to have been devastated by a great loss—possibly the untimely death of a young princess. Akhenaten's new religion would offer nothing much to heal their pain; that part of the ideology hadn't been developed yet. Thus, they had no incantations, no spells, no Osirian intercession: only the positivism of food offerings and grief. Akhenaten had stripped away too much. The only solace was mourning and money.

When Akhenaten himself died, he was placed in a gilded coffin set in a red-granite sarcophagus carved with an Aten sun disk upon it.[96] But archaeologists found that stone container smashed into tiny bits—an indication of the true feelings of his subjects and a testament to how reviled the king had become as a heretic among his own people. His capital city was abandoned; it had been overplanned with single-minded vision and was not sustainable for the organic use of its citizenry. Its statues and reliefs would be left in place, to be obliterated or buried in the ensuing years.[97] Seventeen years of such ideology had been enough, his people tell us in their actions. And so the court quickly moved back to the old ways, worshipping many gods, returning to their former towns and villages, and busily populating courtyards in front of sprawling and disorganized temple spaces.

After his death, Egypt may even have lived under the short rule of Akhenaten's erstwhile co-king, Nefertiti, who possibly ruled alone under the name Ankhkheperure Smenkhkare. The nine-year-old Tutankhaten, possibly Akhenaten's son, would be crowned as the next king.[98] He and his entourage would feel compelled to remove the Aten element from his name and declare his allegiance to the Amun cult of his Theban family by renaming him: Tutankhamun. Everything the child had grown up with had now been rejected—a confusing reality for a boy god-king, to be sure.

Although Egypt rejected Akhenaten's Aten religion, the profound political and ideological changes would have long-term repercussions. Akhenaten—not to mention his Great Royal Wife and the later kings associated with this regime, Tutankhamun and Ay—would be forever reviled in Egyptian history. He would not be included in the monumental king lists, because he was considered an aberrant blip in a long line of good kings. He had held all the power of divine kingship, only to use it to tighten the noose around the necks of his people and paint himself a victim—awakening an insight among Egypt's elites of the potential fallibility of their king.

Akhenaten started out with ideologies that seemed, at first light, to be beautiful and equalizing, only to use those same belief systems to cruelly control those who did not follow along. In the end, there is not much difference between hieroglyphic Aten hymns and Bible passages when they are all treated literally and without nuance by those who wield them. Ideas are humanity's most potent weapons—for better or for worse.

CHAPTER 5

RAMSES II:
THE GRAND ILLUSION

The next player in our authoritarian tale needs no introduction: Ramses the Great, one of the most famous kings not only in ancient Egypt, but also in the sweep of human history. The reign of the country's second pharaoh of this name was long—some 67 years (r. ca 1279–1213 B.C.). And he left such a deep mark that his fame still resonates in our cultural memory.

As a leader, Ramses II was larger than life; he excelled in the art of the spin. He faced the Hittites at Kadesh and won spectacularly (or so he tells us in a brilliant piece of propaganda in which he drives a chariot through the melee to win the day). He maintained the pretense of Egypt's fabulous wealth even though his palace income couldn't touch what Amenhotep III had amassed in his treasuries. He positioned himself as Egypt's greatest campaigner with the Levantine and Nubian territories wedged firmly under his chariot wheels, even as foreign empires chipped away at Egypt's erstwhile dominance. Throughout it all, Ramses excelled at hyperbole. And he had the resources to spin a good yarn. His military campaigns continued to bring in live captives and booty, and his mines and trade networks still managed to churn out riches. He sired hundreds of children, apparently with hundreds of wives—the most famous of which was the breathtaking, rosy-cheeked Nefertari, whose tomb remains the great masterpiece of Egyptian tomb painting.

And his tale continues to be told: Millennia after his death, in 1976, Ramses' mummy received its own modern Egyptian passport in advance of a journey to Paris for a blockbuster exhibition that included his coffin and funerary creations. Newspapers ate up the story. This famous pharaoh was still a celebrity, and his trip resembled the farewell tour of an iconic rock musician.

Like the star of any successful tour, Ramses II excelled in the very modern arts of branding and packaging. He may have been the first leader in history to spin his own personal mix of demagoguery and political entertainment, playing not just to an exclusive court, but also to the crowd, becoming the showman who could connect with Egypt's rising populism.

Ironically, Ramses II mastered the optics of power while losing authentic clout to a system out of his control. If, as we have seen, a pyramid can be read two ways—as a sign of preeminence or of deep vulnerability—then Ramses' endless series of colossal buildings and statues either made him an untouchable god-king or hinted at a profound lack of something.

This king perfected quantity, not quality. He invented the practice of spreading his own image over a temple landscape built by another king. On the surface, it speaks to extraordinary power, the ability to build anything, everywhere. But those same images should make us stop and ask: What kinds of insecurities was this king hiding?

As you enter the Egyptian galleries of the British Museum in London, a prodigious statue greets you. It's called the Younger Memnon, the romantic moniker given to the smiling visage before the decipherment of hieroglyphs allowed anyone to identify its owner as Ramses.[1] First sighted by Europeans as it lay on its side at the king's funerary temple, it was brought to London in the early 19th century by Giovanni Battista Belzoni, an Italian treasure hunter working for a collector named Henry Salt. For some time, this nine-foot-tall head and upper torso has been one of the leading symbols of English Egyptology; it also embodies the European need to transport colossal statues and obelisks to cities back home in a desire to appropriate and exceed the monumentality of others.

In the days of Ramses II, the Younger Memnon was one of a pair of statues at the king's Temple of Millions of Years at Thebes, what we now call the Ramesseum. The matching statue still lies on-site, broken at the neck, its disembodied head atilt on the temple pavement as if judging the feet of all the visiting tourists. The two statues, displaying the king in double colossal form, once stood on either side of a great gateway as guardians of the temple.

The Younger Memnon itself is an intriguing mix of red and gray granite—a stone sculpted so that the head was red while the body was of the darker granodiorite: a clever way to create the impression of sunshine on the face of this great king. This statue was just one of hundreds of images of Ramses II at the Ramesseum, thousands in Thebes, and tens of thousands in his cities of Per-Ramses, Memphis, and Heliopolis, as well as other locations throughout Egypt. For modern-day tourists, the country often seems like the Ramses the Great Show. This king seems to have been able to insert images of himself everywhere, sinking his name deep into Egypt's stones and subconscious.

Many people see statue and temple production as reflections of real power: that ability to control labor and resources, to work and tax people, to maintain and hire the best craftsmen. But in fact, the Younger

Memnon is not reflective of any such tangible power; that was a fantasy. Closer examination reveals the statue was not cut for Ramses II at all, but ordered by Amenhotep III. Indeed, the marks of Ramses' reappropriation are everywhere. The face was recarved in the eye area, with a rim added around each eye's almond shape. The lip area, too, has traces of reworked stone, giving it a lighter red hue compared to the rest of the head. The cloth "nemes" headdress has been cut back and is missing its original striping, which is strange for a large, finished colossal piece; Ramses' craftsmen probably painted it with blue and yellow stripes to cover the usurpation. The chest was redone as well, with an awkward line around the pectoral muscles clearly appearing in the stone.

The artisans working for Ramses II modified this masterful object and its companion just enough so that the king could claim it for himself and add it to his own growing statue collection. The distinctive features of Amenhotep III—anime-large eyes, overly full lips with an off-center pouch under the top lip, full cheeks, fleshy chest, and paunchy belly—were recarved with the features of Ramses II—smaller eyes, lips cut back and drill holes added at the corners to create a more pursed and smiling mouth, cheeks and nemes both reduced for a narrower face, torso scraped down to sculpt the strong pectoral muscles and taut belly Ramses obviously preferred.

The Younger Memnon proves that Ramses II was engaging in an economic subterfuge: a contrivance of power that he did not necessarily have. He could not, apparently, just send the required men to the quarries at Aswan to mine all the stone he desired, as Amenhotep III had done; it seems he was not able to pay his craftsmen the required amount to create all his statues from scratch. In fact, Ramses II reused so many statues of Amenhotep III that his artisans had to invent a new portrait to better match the face they were reusing—broader, squarer than the way earlier images show him.

Ramses was clever at hiding this mass repurposing, just as we are good at not acknowledging it. The British Museum website doesn't mention Amenhotep III in its description of the Younger Memnon, nor do most museum labels of other such pieces around the world. It seems we are quite happy to go along with the intended rebranding. We want Ramses to be great too.

During his lifetime, Ramses' physical person provided the metaphysical evidence of divine support, because he was given an extraordinarily long life and rule. But physicality needed to be matched with materiality, and Ramses II looked to fabricate his greatness. This necessitated a building program to show himself as strong, handsome, and perfect: a king who was able to vanquish foes and create new streams of income and was also the chief priest in the temple and a lord of his throne room. The ancient Egyptian prosperity gospel demanded new storytelling. Material production would prove the gods' blessing of this king.

We have now left the dark and confusing days of Akhenaten behind, but Egypt was still suffering the wounds inflicted by that king. By the beginning of the 19th dynasty, Akhenaten's reign—now four decades in the past—was still within people's cultural and personal memories. Fathers and mothers, grandfathers and grandmothers likely whispered about those times of upheaval, how that heretic had created horrific changes, and how so many had gone along with his decisions.

Until Akhenaten, the 18th dynasty had been a period of extraordinary imperial strength. The country was wealthy, resilient, steady, growing. If it hadn't been for that apostate king and his harebrained schemes to reorganize social power, Egypt would be on firm footing still (or so the thinking may have gone). But then again, only in Egypt could a king like Akhenaten have gotten away with so much. Only in Egypt—where stakeholders had such interest in the status quo, where there was so much wealth to pay people off, where the recurring Nile flood cycle ensured abundant grain most years, where deserts and seas protected the land from invasion—did a divine kingship develop that could do no wrong.

But the damage had been done. After Smenkhkare, the throne moved to Tutankhamun, who would be the last member of his family to rule. Although the kingship could have been given to Tutankhamun's Great Royal Wife, Ankhesenamun, as had been done in similar scenarios, Egypt was having none of it now. Instead, Ankhesenamun was used as a token of power, likely married to the next man to take the throne: a former vizier named Ay.

Why did this royal wife and daughter not become a female king at dynasty's end like Nefertiti? It would have been in the interest of Egypt's aristocracy, allowing them to keep their positions and maintain their social place. But that same patrician class had been irreparably weakened by Akhenaten's relentless policy changes. New men were in charge now—members of the military and procedural bureaucrats. We can imagine that when the vizier Ay claimed the king's widow as nothing more than his wife, norm breaking or not, Egypt's new elites were quite happy to go along with it.

After Ay, the next man to claim the kingship was General Horemheb, a strongman with no intention or need to connect himself with the royal family of Akhenaten in any way. Horemheb's relationship to Ay remains problematic for historians. Was he handpicked by Ay? Did he take the throne by force? There is evidence of internal hypercompetition among all the new elites. Statues of high officials such as Nakhtmin, a general under Tutankhamun and perhaps Ay's son, show brutal destruction of the face and other scars that must be traces of battles for power.[2] However it happened, Horemheb made the claim in his Saqqara tomb that he had been marked for kingship long before the death of Tutankhamun. Perhaps Ay had died naturally with no son to whom he could bequeath

his kingship. Or maybe Horemheb killed Ay's son. Either way, Horemheb would present his kingship as divinely ordained, its legitimization
even predating actuality. But, more to the point, with Horemheb we see
a military man take the reins of Egypt.

There had not been a military shake-up of Egypt's kingship since the
end of the 11th dynasty, around 2000 B.C., when Vizier-general Amenemhat I took the throne from the last Mentuhotep, started a new royal
lineage, and established his purpose-built capital. Horemheb didn't
build a new city named after himself, but he did have the military in his
pocket. He had been Egypt's head general during the reigns of Tutankhamun and Ay, and he may even have served as such under Akhenaten
himself (though under a different name, Paatenemheb,[3] connecting him
to that king's favored god).

Horemheb actually came from a village south of Amenemhat's city of
Itjy-tawy—today about 50 miles southwest of Cairo—and had no obvious patrician roots.[4] After winning the throne, he started reusing statuary en masse. He was a mature monarch, and he obviously needed to
make a big splash quickly. He took any statue that Tutankhamun had
prepared for himself, ordered the old name removed, and inserted his
own in its place. He also went after Akhenaten's constructions with a
vengeance; his military background added a systematic edge to the
destruction. What Tutankhamun and Ay had allowed to stand would
now come down. Horemheb jammed Akhenaten's old talatat blocks
into the fill of his two new pylons at Karnak and undoubtedly dismantled
and repurposed more old structures elsewhere. As for Tutankhamun's
and Ay's monuments, Horemheb had those reinscribed for himself too.[5]

If Akhenaten could have looked down from some solar perch in the
afterlife to see all his beautiful temples being taken apart, he may have
realized that he only had himself to blame. Not only had he imposed an
absolutist ideology on Egypt, but he had also empowered a new military

elite to such an extent that it had weakened the traditional aristocracy, which was then unable or unwilling to support his dynasty.

How the next king, Ramses I, came to power, is as much a mystery as most dynastic upheavals in ancient Egypt. We don't know if he had Horemheb's blessing or if he stole the throne from one of Horemheb's sons. At this period of court infighting, anything was possible. But as we should expect, Ramses I styled himself the legitimate successor to the previous king.[6]

When a father-to-son dynastic transfer had taken place before Akhenaten, most new kings ascended to the throne as adolescents or young men. As those rulers matured, they were expected to fit themselves to the institution of kingship. Now, Egypt's kings were taking the top spot as grown men, cynical and battle weary, in no way malleable to the kingship and perhaps even expecting the institution to cleave itself to them.

At the same time, we see an inability to start a dynasty. Neither Ay nor Horemheb was able to pass the throne on to his own son.[7] We do not know the reasons for this. Was it because they did not have living sons? Or was it perhaps because the Egyptian militarized elites were not interested in seeing the kingship pass from father to son at all? Maybe they were averse to such a dynastic system starting up again, instead desiring to see the throne pass from strongman to strongman, with those loyal to the winner carried along with him. That was potentially the case in the transfer from Ay to Horemheb at the end of the 18th dynasty, and in the handover from Horemheb to Ramses I at the start of the 19th dynasty.

Egypt perceived its own history as a series of royal family lineages, which are preserved in the quotations of a third-century B.C. Egyptian priest named Manetho. Still, transitions of family power remain imprecisely understood some 2,000 years after they were written down.

Manetho placed Horemheb in the 18th dynasty, choosing to view Ramses I as Egypt's fresh new start for the 19th dynasty. Perhaps this demarcation is telling, indicating that Ramses I engaged in shadier undertakings to wrest the throne from Horemheb's family. The possibility shouldn't surprise us; when competition is rife in human institutions, we often see men unable or unwilling to name a successor, spending most of their energy on maintaining their position.

If the transition from Horemheb to the first Ramses was as smooth as history would have us believe, it would make sense that Horemheb, a former military general, would hand off his power to another such man—his vizier Paramessu—at which point all the other generals and officials agreed among themselves that this was the right choice. It's possible. Once on the throne, Paramessu removed the "Pa" element of his name—meaning "the Man Who"—and became Ra-mes-su, "The Sun God Has Born Him."

In an inscription on what is known as the Four Hundred Year Stela, in which multiple generations of Ramses I's eastern Delta family were named, we learn that his father was called Seti, after the storm god Seth, and that Ramses I had a son, also Seti, and a grandson named Ramses—a ready-made line of rulers.[8]

It's hard to explain just how aberrant this inscription actually is. In the 18th dynasty, kingly origin stories were never provided; texts only say the man's elevation to the top spot was the will of the gods. The monarch's life before kingship was largely unknowable and undiscussed, and certainly did not lead to a collection of family details committed to stone. A new king could not openly bring his family with him into the palace, and any older connections were trumped by new, divinely inspired relationships (including all those new wives in the harem he received as king). The preferred sons were only those produced while a man was king, and not before—likely the very reason that so many

18th-dynasty kings were so very young when they were named monarch. The family of Ramses would upend all those long-cherished norms.

The times, they were a-changin'.

A New Northern Dynasty

This was a new cultural moment for Egypt, as a paradigm-breaking 19th dynasty decided that the breadth and depth of their family was integral to taking power. That family was shaping and forming the kingship to fit its members, setting aside many of the old protocols as the dynasty's long-term succession plans were openly declared on the Four Hundred Year Stela. Ramses I was essentially saying, Look, I know I'm old, but I am an effective warlord with a plan: I have a son who's strong and able to rule, and a grandson to take power after him. In the end, Egypt's many kingmakers collectively considered Ramses I appropriate. The aged monarch would mark his successor at his ascension—a key signal to everyone who had dealt with the repeated false starts after Akhenaten's demise that Egypt would now return to the former glory of continuity.

But there was more. The most shocking thing was the fact that Ramses I's new dynasty was not Theban. Nor was it southern. This was more than unusual; it was practically deviant. The kings of Egypt had almost always found their consolidation of power in the south of the Nile Valley—in Thebes, Abydos, Hierakonpolis, and Nekhen. The south was the place where a warlord could easily unify his people, working with vassals up and down the river.

Egypt's Delta, on the other hand, was a wilder place in which regional leaders tended to neutralize one another before they could consolidate meaningful power. For millennia, southern Egyptians had knocked the Delta about, taking it into their hegemony and taxing its more prolific grain production with impunity. When Egypt reconstituted after the civil wars at the end of the pyramid age, the southern kings of the 11th and 12th dynasties were the ones to move their power north, to the apex of the Delta. When warlord kings rose again in the 17th and 18th dynasties, southern kings settled in the cities of Memphis and Heliopolis and again used the Delta as their breadbasket.

We can almost feel the resentments building among Egypt's northerners, bitter at always being taken advantage of, seeing their resources seized and redistributed. Thus, we should not be surprised that when a strong, military-based kingship finally rose in the north, it would be intent on changing the system to rebalance the scale. Not only were these new Ramesside kings northern, but they were also from the northeastern Delta, on the road to West Asia, just a short journey through the Sinai from the southern Levant and the Canaanites.[9] These kingly upstarts were practically foreigners, nothing more than a bunch of Egyptianized descendants of the Levantine kings known as Hyksos, the "Rulers of Foreign Lands," who had taken power about a century and a half ago. It was as if the second-generation Cuban American Marco Rubio had finally become president of the United States. A man whose family had so long been looking in from the outside was now on top of the heap.

West Asia was part of a much more cutthroat social system compared to Egypt, and it was much harder to unify. There were fewer geographic boundaries to separate the overlapping territories of each city-state, and less wealth to go around in a hardscrabble land reliant on rain-fed agriculture and sheep and goat herding. In West Asia rivalry, invasion and siege were the orders of the day. If Egypt was the planet's first regional state, West Asia was its fractured cousin, fighting ongoing wars of religion, ethnicity, and identity and refusing to cooperate with anyone.[10]

That sounds like a disadvantage, but for those men who grew up on the border of such merciless conflict—men such as Ramses I and his relatives—ceaseless warlording was what they knew. These men were socially embedded in military systems that needed to be honed and battle-ready, constantly innovating new weapons and technology, always politicking and building coalitions. Compare that readiness to Egypt, spoiled and drunk on ample grain, physically protected from invasions by desert and sea, united into a political status quo replete with cushy jobs men could hand off to their sons.

The family of Ramses I would make the eastern Delta its base of operations, eventually situating its capital city there—at Per-Ramses, "the House of Ramses." Ramses II was its official founder. In some ways, this new headquarters allowed the Ramesside kings to follow in the footsteps of Amenemhat I, who had founded Itjy-tawy, and Akhenaten, who had founded Akhetaten, and create a clean slate. Also, a new capital city would work well to nationalize resources and consolidate military power. But these battle-worn men were drawing upon a much older foundation of eastern Delta heritage, too, because there had always been a hybrid Levantine-Egyptian social foundation there.

How did the rest of Egypt feel about this tribal band taking over their kingship? It's unclear, but these northern kings felt brazen enough to keep the given name of Seti—even if it did reference Seth, a northern god. I see a bit of my own family in this dynasty as I think of my second-generation Italian American mother naming her daughter, my sister, Elena in the Italian fashion in 1969, refusing to use the Anglicized name Eleanor that her own mother had imposed on her in 1920s Chicago. The second generation of immigrants often uses the third to reclaim its roots. In the case of the Ramessides, they must have felt Egyptianized enough to fly the flag of their ethnic origins.

Seth was beyond frightening. He was a storm god associated with the dry red lands, the Sinai, foreigners, anger, and force, those on the other side of the wall. He was thought to have a strange, mythical, animal look with a long snout and ears, forked tail, red hair, and red eyes. Whether or not the Egyptians said it outright—and how could they criticize the king openly?—much of the population likely perceived these Delta kings as semi-foreign interlopers.[11]

The Thebans must have looked on this emerging kingship in quiet horror. They had enjoyed generations of power; now it had been wrested from them. Once in control of the entire show, they bitterly, though discreetly, denounced the new power in the north. But the establishment needed to fall in line and bow to their new masters.

To be clear, none of this human emotionality made it directly into our formal documentation. But it makes sense to infer that not everything was rosy between Egypt's north and south—especially since Akhenaten had just torn Egypt asunder with his radical schemes and religious ideologies. This was a big moment: a massive shift in power from south to north that we cannot overlook, and the south's resentment at having lost their great influence cannot be underestimated. Although the old Theban aristocrats had almost certainly hated Akhenaten, that didn't mean the new northern kings were their allies, either. Southern conservative families must have now looked northward with distrust and anxiety toward a newly cosmopolitan, competitive world they did not truly understand—one in which new imperial powers of West Asia were rising.

Meanwhile, from their new capital city, the Ramessides harped about the atrocities Egypt had suffered at the hands of Theban kings (echoed in the modern cries that it was all Hillary's fault, all Obama's fault, all Trump's fault, depending on whose side you are on). They had plenty of evidence, given all the turmoil that the Egyptian people had faced from the late 18th dynasty into the early 19th.

The Ramesside kings were not without their own insecurities. One tell was their decision to site their final resting places in the Valley of the Kings to link their power to the 18th-dynasty monarchs buried there. This, more than anything else, was akin to Khafre's return to the Giza Plateau to be buried near Dad. If these Ramessides really wanted to present a perfected kingship, they had to become a little bit Theban, whether or not they wanted to. They had to appeal to their most pious base.

That said, at this juncture it is worth addressing the distribution of evidence. Even though the source of Ramesside power was northern, most of our data come from the south—Thebes in particular—for the simple reason that modern development has swallowed up the Delta with housing, heaps of waste, and generations of agriculture (not to mention the rising water table from inefficient irrigation and dammed waters). Also, the capital city of Cairo is an extraordinary expanse of humanity, holding an estimated 20 million people; its vast urbanity has destroyed countless archaeological sites. Thus, even though our 19th-dynasty story revolves around northern kings, we are relegated to spinning that narrative with information from the south, because that's where material has been preserved. Our data set is skewed, despite ongoing excavations at Qantir, the site of Per-Ramses.[12]

Egypt's weakest point was always that stretch of river below the Nile Delta, the region most likely to break asunder when warlords fought for dominance. But the Ramesside kings would hold the state together and keep most of its elites prosperous. Even if its kings lacked the extraordinary wealth of the late 18th dynasty, Egypt was still strong and rich, there were plenty of resources to go around, and the economy was still on the upswing. War meant money: perhaps the reason the Ramesside period seems defined by constant fighting, real or imagined (much like the post–World War II United States, with its series of conflicts in Korea, Vietnam, Kuwait, and Afghanistan). In the end, Egypt's wars generated revenue with which to reward the country's elites: the generals, lieutenants, and cavalry soldiers who needed to be paid off.

As crown prince, Seti campaigned for his father, Ramses I, in Syria. After his ascension to the throne, he started his own offensives right away (as quickly as George W. picked up on the military agendas of George Herbert Walker Bush). These were not easy battles. Seti had to face the rising Hittite empire of Anatolia, which was horning in on Egypt's territory. But he was able to win back the essential stronghold of Kadesh in Syria, riding into the city, we are told, with his son Ramses by his side. Seti also wreaked havoc in West Asia and Nubia, with the proceeds consolidating his power among his men. In the same way that some American elites made money hand over fist through connections with companies such as Lockheed Martin, Halliburton, and Blackwater, as U.S. forces invaded Iraq and Syria, the Ramesside royal family acted similarly, placing family members and loyal lieutenants into elevated positions of authority and thus enriching the clan.

But just like the pyramid of the 4th dynasty, the constant military campaigning of the Ramesside family was itself a sign of a weakened kingship: a need to show power, maintain what was lost, and find new streams of income to feed the political beast. Those wars would create income, but Egypt had now empowered more people to compete for it in an endless cycle of industrial complexes: wars to create jobs, weapons to use in war, wars to maintain jobs.

Both Ramses I and Seti I had to find novel methods to reward their men, because their kingship owed its existence to them. Instead of thinking themselves entitled and divine, they would have tried to prove themselves real and good kings to a class of enabled, empowered, and militarized elites. [13] How much southern Egyptians were excluded from this system of risk and reward is debatable. But Theban tombs indicate that southern elite families played a part in these wars and their spoils too, gaining positions within the priesthood and bureaucracy that such wealth afforded.

A Newly Opened Society

Compared to the 18th dynasty, society now showed a much broader economic, political, and military entitlement; there were simply more power players now. And because this was no longer a society bound by the whims of a wealthy aristocrat or king, Ramesside Egypt also produced more texts than Egypt had ever seen—especially legal texts. Now every actor, elite or king, had to show evidence for the best course of action: oracles obtained, armies supported, bureaucracy checked, with documents in hand. In triplicate.

Egypt had shifted from a culture run by a closed set of landowners and court officials with personal connections to the king to a new, open society, based on sprawling institutions with power of their own: the temple, army, treasury, and bureaucracy, in addition to the royal court. People may have owned less individually, and there were fewer great families. But the wealth was more broadly distributed, and everyone looked to Egypt's institutions, which now owned vast tracts of land and had thousands on the payroll.[14]

As we see in today's large corporations—Apple, Boeing, Amazon, Walmart, JP Morgan Chase Bank—such human organizations have their own collective will to dominate, their own agency to shape and mold people. If the 2010 Citizens United decision of the U.S. Supreme Court continues to stand—extending the free speech clause of the First Amendment to corporations and nonprofits, which are now allowed to spend money on political communications without restriction—we are meant to understand that corporations are not just people, but more than people, with an enormous ability to influence politics. The institutions of Ramesside Egypt were similarly empowered.

Within those institutions, the bulk of elite society was now more competitive than ever before. Instead of the 18th-dynasty elite son following his father, inheriting the family's land, sending one of his daughters to the harem, and meeting fellow elites at court, we see more people jockeying for position. Thus, job training—military, priestly, or scribal—became a requirement for elite sons to succeed. Loyalty and connections were still essential, but in a broader society, everyone now looked for that extra edge.

As a result, elites moved from job to job with an alacrity never seen in the previous dynasty, switching from the temple to the military to the scribal service and back again. There was upward mobility, too, now that mercenary military men could become kings. As we will see later, a man named Bakenkhonsu could rise in the temple hierarchy in much the same way that a janitor's assistant named Sidney Weinberg moved up at Goldman Sachs when he became a clerk, then a trader, and finally, in 1930, CEO of the whole company.

In this newly corporate society, even an Egyptian king would have trouble throwing his weight around within institutions such as the great Temple of Ptah in Memphis or the vizierate office in Per-Ramses. The Egyptian monarch was now dealing with thousands of people who had their fingers in all of Egypt's various pies. High priests and army commanders were replaceable, but the institutions were not; this was the new Ramesside conundrum. The king had to work with—not against—these actors, whether or not he wanted to.

But probably because of this broader buy-in by society, the king nonetheless had to present himself as more powerful than ever before, proving his worth to his people with monumentality (striving for the highest ratings, so to speak). Ramses II created statue after statue and acres of temple relief more colorful than the last as he tried to convince the populace that he was truly what he said he was. The quantity of colossal statues Ramses II produced betrays the king's need to connect with a ruthless mass of people who were much more powerful as a bloc than he was individually.

You might think that a more broadly entitled society would demand a different kind of kingship, one that presented itself as less divine than what had come before. And in some ways, you would be right. Ramesside kings such as Seti I and Ramses II presented their military power in community with their men; their ritual activity showed grander festivals with more participants and public access than ever before. This was not a perfected solo kingship whose actions were restricted to a few courtiers. Elites and institutions now craved more of the heroic optics of kingship than ever before, even if the screws may have been tightened on the privileges of the crown. Thus, a Ramesside king would show his figure prominently at the head of a grand festival procession or aboard a chariot larger than any other as he led an army of thousands, manufacturing the appearance of a great godhood now embedded in a writhing collection of humanity.

From this perspective, Ramses II was just the tool that Egypt's institutions now needed, rather than the other way around. The rules were being rewritten. If every potential scribe now had to prove his writing ability and every army commander his logistical planning skills to compete for the next promotion, then every king now had to display his monarchical credentials. He had to advertise his own abilities, his connection to the gods, and exactly how he fit into the royal succession.

There was so much sudden change that the family of Ramses I became skilled at manufacturing nostalgia—that ability of looking back to the past and connecting with what had previously rewarded people. That type of sentimental, good-old-days ideology is almost inviolable. In the United States, for instance, even though new insights reveal institutions upholding White supremacy, people fiercely defend those same systems because they themselves have benefited from systemic racism. Thus many Americans demonize those who would dare to criticize their statues of Confederate war patriots or tell them to take down their flags.

A famous example of such political nostalgia is preserved at Abydos, where the mythical first king of the universe had appeared some 2,000 years before. The place had since been transformed in Egyptians' minds as the burial place of Osiris. In Seti I's temple to Osiris there, the king and his son, Ramses, appear in front of a list of monarchs going all the way back to Menes, the first mythical king of the 1st dynasty.[15] Father and son stand in worship of these kings, but also in receipt of the weight of Egypt's largely southern crown. Having created the king list, cleaned it up, removed any aberrant rulers such as the female king Hatshepsut and the heretic Akhenaten and his immediate successors—Smenkhkare, Tutankhamun, and Ay—Seti I and his son could claim intimate association with good kingship and its birthplace at Abydos in the south.[16]

That statement in stone is similar to the way in which today's politicians appropriate the past by speaking in front of the colossal statue at the Lincoln Memorial to visibly associate themselves with the president who won the Civil War, or by using phrases from the speeches of Ronald Reagan to signal an association with his celebrated tax cuts. With such backward-looking ideology, the bad and immoral things of the past are nullified; only the elements with which we want to connect are retained.

Seti I's images at Abydos are arresting, beautifully carved by master artisans who manipulated the high-quality limestone by cutting crisp lines of relief.[17] The art was originally brightened by colors, whose traces are still visible on the temple walls. Indeed, the temple of Seti I at Abydos remains one of the most stunning works of art I've ever seen, and I imagine its effect must have been similar across the ancient world. Egypt's elites would have easily perceived the unspoken intent of Seti I, this man from an upstart family who was nonetheless able to insert his person into this hallowed place, showing his deference to what had come before and reifying in stone his right to be king.

If the son of a Delta warlord could build such a wonder at Abydos, the very birthplace of Egypt's kingly power, then he could also prove his royal predestination in the eyes of his elites. Seti I journeyed to this southern place, bowed down to its southern kings, and publicly humbled himself before them, openly offering gifts. This, it seems, assuaged many of Egypt's stakeholders—just as flag-wrapped patriotism, deference to the troops, and anticommunist rhetoric averts our eyes from the corporate oligarchic policies of U.S. presidents today. It is useful for leaders to focus on ideology because its moral weight, to the exclusion of everything else, transforms even self-dealing billionaires into pious men who create jobs and protect what is deemed honorable and right.

But the Ramesside family was not overconfident—not yet, at least. Seti I put in the effort to prove himself to his people, and his temple at Abydos stands as proof that he was trying to show he could create miracles in stone. As only the second king of a new dynasty, he would have remembered a time when his father was not Egypt's monarch, when such aspirations were not even entertained. Seti I was an outsider on a throne that went back thousands of years. Upon his ascension, he knew to focus on quality—of military campaigns, of temples built, and presumably, of political connections established.

Seti I was largely responsible for the Great Hypostyle Hall at Karnak, filling in the open courtyard between the second and third pylons with hundreds of grand columns that were pierced with clerestory lighting.[18] His innovative monumental reliefs of war violence are still visible on the outer walls of this great hall.

Everywhere he sought to romanticize the past, either long gone or recent. He ordered chapels to piously memorialize his father, Ramses I, at his Abydos temple and at his own memorial temple at Thebes—

a dutiful son always looking back to his ancestors, always giving credit where it was due. His tomb (KV 17) in the Valley of the Kings was the most extensively and painstakingly decorated of the entire royal necropolis at that time—the longest of its kind at 446 feet, with passages extending even beyond the burial chamber holding his sarcophagus.[19] His tomb's corridor walls were carved with unprecedented displays of Books of the Underworld such as the Book of Gates, Book of Earth, Books of Day and Night, Book of the Heavenly Cow. He ordered the best mummification money could buy, and his embalmed corpse remains a wonder of preservation, providing insight into what we assume to have been a strategic and measured personality.[20]

Seti I had even greater ambitions for Egypt's embellishment. According to a stela at Aswan, he ordered obelisks and monumental statuary,[21] though none that bear his name survive. The reason we don't see them is because so much of what he built was appropriated by his son and successor, the second Ramses, who seems to have had very different sensibilities from his father.

Ramses II had grown up in the royal court with the expectation of becoming king. This was a man who believed his own press, who displayed none of the insecurities of his father or grandfather, and who used bombast to make an impression. Seti I ruled only 10 or 11 years, so it is not surprising that the obelisks and colossal statues he commissioned would be taken over by Ramses II and set up in front of Luxor Temple within the first few years of the latter king's reign. Quick work, easily done, an impression made. Indeed, many of Seti's other artistic works—such as the Hypostyle Hall itself—are believed to have been taken over by his son, who carved his name and images so deeply that there could be no doubt of his achievement.[22]

Not only that, Ramses II largely abandoned the quality of his father, no longer requiring most images to be carefully and beautifully carved.

Who cared anyway? Ramses II would effortlessly move from quality to quantity, ordering mass production of colossal statues and monumental temples throughout Egypt. To put up that much stone in so short a time, the king needed a work-around. Avoiding Akhenaten's method of building with mud brick and stone facing, Ramses II instead reused statues and carved blocks with impunity. We can imagine the old aristocrats, particularly the Thebans, rolling their eyes as yet another image of a southern king fell to Ramses' re-carvers. But the great monarch didn't seem to care. He was the best, the biggest, the greatest ever, and he would prove it by chiseling the claim in stone until it became reality.

Ramses II also took credit for establishing the new capital at Per-Ramses—not exactly a purpose-built capital, but certainly situated within the family homeland. The city's location had a dark history for some Egyptians, tainted by those who had claimed it before. This had been a strategic location where the so-called Hyksos kings—*heka-hasut,* or "Rulers of Foreign Lands"—had put their capital of Avaris some centuries before at the end of the Middle Kingdom.

The Hyksos kings (the 15th and 16th dynasties) had lost power to a Theban royal family (the 17th and 18th dynasties), who would never let anyone forget it. They crowed about their great victory over Asiatic interlopers who had used decentralized and tribal tactics to get and maintain power. In the early New Kingdom, the notion of "tribalism" seems to have worked upon people's minds like the word "socialism" today. The Hyksos became a synonym for evil in a massive propaganda campaign against vile enemies that claimed Egypt for Egyptians.[23]

But now Egypt was ruled by the Ramesside kings, who openly built their new capital just a few miles from the old Hyksos stronghold, reifying a connection not only with the eastern Delta but also with Levantine kings. To their credit, the Hyksos had given Egypt the world's greatest war machine, the chariot, along with horses, weapons such as scimitars, and even new metal technologies, all of which the Ramesside kings were now using. The new city served as a strategic launching point for countless campaigns and became a military-industrial complex of chariot making, horse breeding, and metalsmithing.[24] These kings were the Kennedys, once reviled as dirty Irish papists, now proudly connecting with their White House Camelot and their Bostonian roots.

These Ramessides had mastered the Egyptian game of ideology, and Ramses II would play it expertly. His favorite image of himself would be his upright figure standing alone in his horse-drawn chariot with the reins wrapped around his waist, shooting volley after volley of arrows at the overwhelmed enemies who would soon fall under the wheels of his war machine.

Ramses II nonetheless had to cloak some of his family's baser origins from the conservative Egyptians by using the guise of old kingship. Because he knew he was still considered a little bit alien, he stepped up his game and showed himself as the real Egyptian in the way that a Catholic entering the Protestant world of American power would whitewash his religion, remove any ethnic speech or tropes, become a political hawk unafraid to take on the communists, advertise his patriotism, and marry a highborn, drop-dead woman to stand by his side. We see the Ramesside ruler with the same kind of cultural chip on his shoulder, which pushed him to do things he would not have done otherwise—such as taking on a growing empire.

Ramses II was not hiding his connection to West Asia but repackaging it, making it Egyptian. Remaking an image needs more than talk, though; action is required too, and to that end, Ramses II continued the military activities of his father. Seti I had depended upon a sprawling extended family, as well as ranks of soldiers and bureaucrats who needed to be rewarded with wealth, and Ramses II inherited the same. Seti I had campaigned in Nubia and the Levant, and Ramses II would go on military campaigns there as well.

But Ramses II had a problem that his father did not: Seti I had been able to confront regional city-states with a strong Egyptian army; Ramses II had to take on the Hittites, who were rising in the Anatolian peninsula as a fully operational, expansionist force.[25] The Hittites had their origins in modern-day Turkey, and their empire had been forged through repeated invasions and colonization from Mesopotamia to their southeast. Egypt would have to improve its military game.

A KING AT WAR

The entire Mediterranean was entering a phase that modern historians call the Bronze Age collapse, a calamitous time of climate change, drought, state disintegration, and war.[26] Trying to stem the tide, the Ramesside kings engaged in all the normal human reactions: increasing warfare, building walls, hiring mercenaries, and establishing massive refugee camps while dealing with a surge in human trafficking and the inclusion of immigrants in a booming service economy. But the economy was growing in Ramses II's Egypt, which allowed the elites to ignore the coming calamities for some time.

In Ramses II's second year, he beat off an invasion of foreigners called the Sherden. They were one of the ethnic groups making up what historians generally call the Sea Peoples, who were now on the move around the Mediterranean. The Sherden may have come from Sardinia or even farther afield; they saw Egypt as a place of prosperity and new starts, of established rules and safety. Ramses II tells us that he repelled them easily (though some of the men became his paid fighters, as we will see later). In his fourth year, he sent an income-generating campaign into Syria, which he recorded as a success. This was all practice for what was to come.

Ramses' fifth year of rule saw the culmination of his military activity, when he engaged the Hittite Empire in a battle over the mastery of Syria. In 1274 B.C., when Ramses II was in his early 20s or even younger, he met the Hittite king, Muwatalli II, in a massive showdown. Ramses put the battle in the win column, but historians still dispute the outcome.[27]

Ramses plastered images of his heroic role in the battle all over Egypt, providing us with a play-by-play narrative. We are told that four Egyptian divisions massed against their Hittite enemies at the city of Kadesh. Both sides employed mercenary soldiers, the Egyptians using many Sherden warriors to fight on their behalf. The Hittites had almost 20 allied states and cities fighting alongside them, a coalition of epic proportions. At least 5,000 chariots were involved in the battle.

The texts accompanying the painted reliefs of the melee tell us of two Hittite spies who leaked the false intel that the Hittite king and his forces were far away. After two other Hittite spies were interrogated, the Egyptians learned that the Hittite king was actually waiting nearby to ambush them. The Hittite army was more numerous than the grains of sand on a beach, the spies revealed, ready to fight and lying in wait behind the city.

While Ramses was absorbing this information, a division of Hittite chariots attacked the Egyptian forces head-on. The Hittites broke through one division and then another, threatening the life of the king with each advance. Ramses tells us: "No officer was with me, no charioteer, no soldier of the army, no shield-bearer."[28] Completely defenseless, he fought his way out on his own. The survivors of two divisions then rallied to his aid, leading multiple chariot charges as the king called to the god Amun for divine assistance.

The narrative tells us that the Hittites fell victim to an old temptation: They stopped to plunder the Egyptian camp. Ramses saw his chance and pounced, ordering a counterattack and overtaking the slow Hittite chariots with his faster Egyptian ones.

When the Hittites counterattacked, a surprise force of foreign mercenaries fighting for the Egyptians—the Ne'arin—saved the day. They pinned the Hittites against the Orontes River and forced many of them to abandon their chariots and swim across the water. Many of the fleeing soldiers drowned; the rest of the Hittite army retreated. Ramses II, apparently unable to inflict a long siege upon Kadesh, returned to Egypt, where he spent his long life broadcasting his tremendous victory in full color.

Ramses made sure that he narrated the heroic story in the royal first person: "My majesty caused the forces of the foes from Khatti to fall on their faces, one upon the other, as crocodiles fall, into the water of the Orontes. I was after them like a griffin; I attacked all of the countries, I alone. For my infantry and my chariotry had deserted me; not one of them stood looking back."[29] Given the hyperbole of the dramatic events, Ramses apparently needed to stress the truth of his statements: "As I live, as Re loves me, as my father Atum favors me, everything that my majesty has told, I did it in truth, in the presence of my infantry and my chariotry."[30]

Clearly, we are to understand that if it weren't for Ramses II's heroics and the god Amun's blessing, Egypt would have lost the battle. At the same time that he claimed all the credit for the win, he used his soldiers as witnesses to his glory. Ramses would play his Kadesh battle on repeat, creating his own celebrity as the hero of the battlefield, the savior of Egypt. He tells us he was: "...A bowman without his equal, / Who prevails over vast numbers. / Head-on, he charges a multitude, / his heart trusting his strength; / Stout-hearted in the hour of combat, like the flame when it consumes. / Firm-hearted like a bull ready for battle, / He heeds not all the lands combined; / A thousand men cannot withstand him. / A hundred thousand fail at his sight. / Lord of fear, great of fame, / In the hearts of all the lands; / Great of awe, rich in glory, / As is Seth upon his mountain."[31] Ramses compared himself to Seth, the god of violence who the Egyptians believed could vanquish Apophis every night in the seventh hour, the only one who could conquer disorder.

Akhenaten had said that he alone could understand his god Aten. Now Ramses II would present himself as the only one who could compete in military battle when it mattered. To prove his point, each monarch used his buildings to duplicate the trope again and again. It didn't even matter whether or not the narratives—the Aten religion or the Kadesh heroics—were true. What was important was the repetition of the desired truth. Ramses II put his victory on all his temples painted in bright polychrome, accompanied by an epic poem and a bulletin of the battle details, highlighting the king's winning tactics.[32]

What was presented as a mission accomplished, historians actually believe to have been a loss, not just of the city of Kadesh, but also of all the tribute payments associated with its territory.[33] The so-called Egyptian Empire was shrinking. In year seven of his reign, Ramses led another Syrian campaign, and then again in years eight and nine, when he captured the cities of Dapur and Tunip. In his 10th year, he lost and regained some of those same territories.

We can be sure that some of his military knew the complicated truth, particularly the ones who were there at the battles. But if the ongoing campaigns made them and their sons richer, then who was to complain? Control over Nubia and all its minerals was secure. Tribute was still paid from many places in the Levant. Ramses II and his men continued to use the region to source live captives and other valuables, which was reason enough to continue the ongoing skirmishes with the Hittites and their allies. Finally, in year 21, Ramses II signed a nonaggression treaty with the Hittite king, Hattushili III.

The treaty itself is presented as an agreement among brothers: "But in the name of Muwattalli, the great chief of Hatti, my brother, he fought with [Ramses], the great ruler of Egypt. But hereafter, beginning from this day, behold [Hattushili, the great chief of Hatti, is [in?] a treaty for making permanent the policy which Pre made and Seth made for the land of Egypt with the land of Hatti, so as not to permit hostilities to be made between them forever."[34] Things had gotten so bad, and so expensive, that the kings actually sat down with each other, as peers, and discussed terms. They agreed to borders, mutual promises of aid and military support, and even the extradition of political dissenters.

Ramses II sealed the deal by marrying a few Hittite princesses some years later. We have the remnants of a stela—not well preserved—in which the pairing was presented with all the pomp, garments, and gifts one would expect from the spectacle of a royal wedding.

The Hittites and the Egyptians seem to have agreed that they should calm down a bit—like a nuclear arms treaty between Russia and the United States when enough money had been spent, enough labor wasted, and enough fear fomented in both populations that the political climate on both sides was simply done with it all. Ramses II walked away from his campaigning so he could enjoy his Hittite princesses and relax into a kind of Pax Aegyptiaca in which the main thrust of his martial might was sent to Nubia. The Hittites were just too strong, and Ramses knew it.

RAMSES THE POPULIST

In the 18th dynasty, kings displayed their military prowess on temple walls. Amenhotep II, for example, displayed his ability to shoot arrows through a metal ingot, which we can imagine happened in front of a select, appropriately admiring crowd. Other 18th-dynasty kings publicized their hunting prowess. Thutmose III, for example, documented his dispatch of a slew of elephants in Syria—quite the patrician thing to do in front of other patricians. Amenhotep III bragged about killing a mass of lions in the desert (almost certainly corralled there for his massacring pleasure)[35]—much in the way some wealthy Americans post photos of themselves on Instagram with the latest semi-endangered species they have killed on safari.

Ramses II knew that such dainty heroics would now be perceived as meaningless at best, ridiculous at worst. He chose to display his authentic battle exploits with him driving his chariot and shooting simultaneously in the heart of danger. This would appeal to the more open 19th-dynasty society that craved spectacle.

We have not seen an Egyptian king like this before—in the company of his men, driving his horses into the maelstrom of battle, even getting off the chariot and fighting hand-to-hand with his sword. Thutmose III, the sixth ruler of the 18th dynasty, had presented himself as a brilliant strategic thinker in story form, but he didn't show his battles in pictures. Ramses II wanted to be a character like Maximus Decimus Meridius in *Gladiator*—that good general who went around to check on his men, greeting each of them as they were getting ready for battle, showing them he was one of the fellas who fought alongside them, unafraid. That was the ideology that Ramses II was going for—one of the guys, but divinely empowered.

The 18th-dynasty kings had to ingratiate themselves to a small, clubby set of patrician families who sent their sons to court, where the young men all hung out, hunted, and fished together. In contrast, Ramses II's family now needed to prove itself to a whole set of military and temple institutions that kept it in power. Ramesside kings needed to key into popularity cults like never before.

That meant appealing to the hopes and fears of lower elites to counter the power of the ever difficult aristocrats. In this way, we see Ramses II draining Egypt's swamp, energizing his base of support because he had less sway over—or trust in—Egypt's highest elites and intellectuals. Within such nascent populism, Ramses positioned himself as the direct patron of Egypt's mercenaries, record keepers, artisans, and accountants, weakening the old families and allowing massive corporations to take their place.

This new strategy set up a king who had little patience for elite interference, but would gladly empower great institutions such as temples or armies. One could argue this was exactly what Akhenaten had started some 60 years before—and indeed, Ramses II had inherited that foundation of power based on military corporations, social upheaval, and radicalism.

There are many patriarchal comparisons with today. Consider Egypt from 2011 to 2020, when a people's revolution overthrew Hosni Mubarak's dynastic regime, followed by the democratic election of Mohamed Morsi, the Muslim Brotherhood's representative, who instituted religious reforms reviled by most. When the military overthrew Morsi, the coup enjoyed the overwhelming backing of most of the Egyptian people.

The new military regime, led by General Abdel Fattah al-Sisi, started out with great support as a pure populist movement. But year by year, Sisi has instituted more executive control of the legislature, more crackdowns on political dissent, more unfree and unfair elections, more propagandistic posters of Egypt's leader that are visible from the freeways and city squares, more fear within society. Egypt now finds itself under the thumb not of one person, but of massive institutions. The Egyptian Army and police employ millions of people throughout the country, with a variety of country and sports clubs available to everyone from army officers to police commanders to enlisted men. And more prisons are filled with political dissenters than ever before. Populism and prisons, it seems, go hand in hand.

Ramses II's Egypt now found itself facing an imposing new wave of migrations. It was suddenly fashionable to commission stelae that showed Ramses executing enemies with maces and scimitars, a way of celebrating his insider status.[36] The king reassured his risk-averse population that any cruelty was only employed to keep them safe. He built new walls and massive fortification systems, upgraded the manned barriers in the Delta's northeast, and constructed a new deterrent system in the Delta's northwest against a new stream of peoples entering from regions in Libya.[37] Watchtowers were built within visible distance of each other so that signals could be sent quickly, creating a border between what was Egyptian and what was not, what was good and what was evil.

Even if an ordinary Egyptian never had the chance to glimpse those great fortification systems himself, word would have spread that they existed to keep the country safe from incursion by lawless hordes bent on its destruction. Ramses II utilized these barriers as a means of ideologically defining his people and his kingship: building walls, not tearing them down, separating real Egyptians from imposters rather than creating an inclusive and cosmopolitan connection. These were populist strategies of fearmongering—creating an "other," a demonized entity against which all had to fight.

Just as we see in the United States today, the growth of racist attitudes occurred in conjunction with an increase in immigration and an intensification of mercenary service within Egypt's own professional army, which included foreign migrants. Make no mistake—Ramesside Egypt was arguably the most diverse it had ever been,[38] and perhaps that was exactly what created the tipping point. Those newly immigrated on the Egyptian side of the wall may have been the best foot soldiers to keep newcomers out. Even though the Ramesside family itself likely had foreign origins—or at least origins in the eastern Delta, which would have been much the same thing in the eyes of many Egyptians—they now fought to define who belonged as real Egyptians and who did not.

Diversity of identity can feed internal competition, fueling the demonization of foreigners, attempts to keep them out by manned borders and other means, and increasingly vociferous demands for cultural assimilation. Systematic othering goes hand in hand with increased pressure that people act and look the same and speak the dominant language. A variety of diverse people were now understanding that if they were to enter Ramses' army, they would have to become more Egyptian than Egyptian.[39]

In the United States, immigrants from places such as Ireland, Poland, Italy, and Cuba were once thought of as not "real" Americans. Many of their descendants now find themselves the key base of support in efforts to exclude new immigrants from the country, in calling for people to speak English, in using patriotism, gun displays, and flag-waving to mark their ownership of place. Now on this side of the divide, many Mexican American families on the southern Texas border find themselves happy to see a wall go up. Those who assimilated most recently are often a state's fiercest defenders.

This was the political attitude that Ramses II nurtured and fed. As a result, an Egyptian patriotism arose that had never appeared before. Patriotism demands the buy-in of a larger populace. Egypt was now selling tickets to its bully train—in the temple, in the army, in the treasuries—and xenophobia factored heavily in getting people to participate. As more foreigners had been "Egyptianized," they could now attack the same people they once were—those reviled stereotypical Nubians, Libyans, Asians, and now Sea Peoples.[40] The Egyptian caste system still stood, but an illusion of inclusion that could justify all the military campaigns, forced labor, and masses of newly enslaved peoples had also arisen.

Indeed, extensive foreign campaigns meant that Egypt witnessed an increase in enslaved people coming into its lands. This meant that Ramses II's world was full of commodified foreign peoples owned by and working for Egyptians.[41] It's not that slavery hadn't existed in Egypt before; as soon as governments and cities sprang up there, slavery accompanied them. But the population was so enormous that the practice was largely unnecessary, even when huge numbers of laborers were required. Why use slaves to build the pyramids when a king had a peasantry that could be drafted into service during months of river inundation when they were underemployed?

But with the rise of foreign empires to the northeast, and with increasing Egyptian campaigns into the Levant, kings such as Ramses II could flaunt their procurement of enslaved people, creating another channel through which foreign peoples could enter Egypt's population. Whereas the 18th-dynasty patrician might have bragged about 12 captives in his tomb-chapel autobiography, a king's campaign stelae during the Ramesside period would talk of tens of thousands of people brought into Egypt as future labor.[42] The xenophobia itself had not really changed, but the level of foreign humanity in servitude had.

If Ramses II's populist kingship rested largely on the welfare of empowered institutions and those in their employ, then the spoils of war—booty, official positions, and enslaved people—needed to be distributed to them. This zeitgeist is an origination point for the Exodus story in the Hebrew Bible.[43] The narrative of captive Hebrews forcibly laboring for Pharaoh, making bricks without straw, was said to take place in the city the Hebrews called Pithom—almost certainly the capital that the Egyptians knew as Per-Ramses. It was within this urban context that a disgruntled foreign populace wove a story of their enslavement by an Egyptian king, of the return to their homeland in the Levant, and of reclaiming their identity as a chosen people of their god.[44]

Not only does the Exodus story impart how these Levantine peoples exited Egypt; it also explains how the Egyptian king was forever enfeebled in the process, revealing a great ruler's insurmountable power to be nothing more than manufactured fakery. By the time the Israelites wrote down their narrative, the notion of one-god worship had been reified within the Levantine highlands: a one true god who was Hebrew, not Egyptian. While that Hebrew divinity was not sunlight, he appeared to Moses as fire in the guise of the burning (and speaking) bush with a face so overwhelmingly bright that no one could look at it.[45]

I am not saying that Ramses II was the pharaoh of the Exodus or that such a series of events actually happened in reality, supernaturally aided or not. But I am saying that the biblical narrative holds kernels of truth. Although the imagery of Ramses II shows him as a god-king incarnate, he would lose much of what his father had built in terms of territories, as well as any upper hand over foreign polities. Ramses II was a master at taking something perceived as negative (a difficult battle) and turning it into something positive (he engaged personally). His stories are extraordinary, but they could be perceived as fraud nonetheless. Ramses II took a territorial contraction and turned it into what his people perceived—and many Egyptologists still do—as the greatest empire Egypt had ever known. His method? Gaslighting, plain and simple. He played the alternative scenario again and again.

Remember, propaganda is not meant to work on your enemies; they won't believe you in any case. Such machinations only work on those dependent upon you, those who want to believe you, those who love you. Gaslighting may not only work for a year, or a lifetime, but also for generations. Atrocities can be turned into necessary victories.

Examples abound around the world. Consider the dropping of atomic bombs on the Japanese cities of Hiroshima and Nagasaki during WWII, which killed some 120,000 civilians instantly and left hundreds of thousands more to die slow and horrific deaths. Americans who had absolutely nothing to do with the bombing still fiercely justify it. Or the story now told of California's original inhabitants. On a recent field trip with my son to the Mission San Juan Capistrano, our tour guide cheerfully told us that the 16th-century Spanish mission had created thousands of jobs for the Native Americans, taught them how to use clothing (they were apparently naked before), and introduced Christianity and marriage. All that apparently justified Spanish land theft from and enslavement of the Indigenous peoples.

Gaslighting works over centuries because none of us wants to own that collective guilt. As James Baldwin said, we want to remain innocent. Supporters of authoritarianism know full well the man they support is morally flawed, but most refuse to see that the cancer is within them as well. We need to believe in our good kings, our good presidents, our good men—because we get something out of it. We choose to hate. Because if we don't, we must confront the pain we ourselves have inflicted.

RAMSES THE GASLIGHTER

Ramses II's gaslighting would be exhibited large. Imagine his heroic escapades on a temple pylon, in a public space, where crowds of people gathered to celebrate being Egyptian, having a strong king and an empire of wealth to rally around. The colorful images were like a movie from *Captain America* comics—a brilliant tale from which you could not look away. In the Kadesh reliefs, the king's men were given credit where it was due; even the foreign mercenaries who saved the day are mentioned. There is some text to accompany the cartoonlike images, though it is small and difficult to read—except for the king's name, which was carved so boldly into the stone that even those blinded by the sun could see it. This was Ramses II communicating his alternate facts to a semiliterate people through image and text, in which he himself was both one with his people and a victorious god-king triumphant over a battle disaster that he alone could fix. Ramses' loyal Egyptians saw scenes of many chariots driven by different men and transporting bowmen: his paid, professional army, his base. Elsewhere, carved scenes showed scribes—his bureaucratic elite whom he needed to remain by his side—working to count the enemy dead. His priests were depicted too, in attendance when the spoils of the battle were given as pious gifts to various gods: Ptah at Memphis, Atum-Re at Heliopolis, and Amun-Re at Thebes.

Now, think of the president of Egypt today in his suit and tie. He is clearly showing that he is one of millions of Egyptian men, all of whom can now think themselves an essential part of his regime because they are employed as his policemen, officers, security details, government bureaucrats, all benefiting from this strongman's power. Sisi can tell the story of how he saved his people from religious extremism at the hands of the previous regime, and how he saved Egypt from aristocrats like Mubarak and his cronies; he presents himself as the victorious everyman.

Perhaps as a result, Sisi's base supported him even when he took Trump's side in the relocation of the U.S. Embassy from Tel Aviv to Jerusalem, throwing their Palestinian allies far under the bus. But the Egyptian president had to support Trump, one of his best champions, and was able to spin the story to communicate how the ends justified the means. His base of populist support—all those people in his generous employment—didn't dissent. Perhaps by that point most Egyptians understood the transaction they had made and willingly submitted not only to the shift in global loyalty, but also to the gaslighting itself.

The social base of Ramses II was less concerned with expanding the borders of Egypt than it was with enriching itself within an institutionalized system of manufactured ideology that assured everyone they were doing the right thing—with no atrocities, with the blessings of the gods—and that they would be rewarded for it. This is how a leader turns formerly oppressed people into his best foot soldiers. He calls them out onstage for recognition, rewards them, includes them. They're like the Black men at the 2020 Republican National Convention who told everyone how Trump was the only one who could save the inner cities from gang violence, and the Miami Cubans who promote an ongoing battle against the evils of socialism that their families have escaped.

The most important people for Ramses II to influence, however, were the members of his extensive family. Thus, he included them in his colorful spectacles as never before, naming his many children as extensions of his own power, his own lineage. With these acts, he communicated that his might was their dominion too, imbuing them with their own mini-celebrity status, their own *Vanity Fair* photo spread. Inside his many temples, Ramses II ordered the depiction of his 50 sons and 50 daughters, along with their names and titles.[46]

The Egyptians had never before allowed royal children, particularly sons, to be put in the limelight—and yet here they were, depicted in a VIP list of political influence. Although earlier Egyptian kings had, we must presume, filled their harem nurseries with children, they never acknowledged their many sons openly; in the short term, sons could use their positions to compete with the king himself, and in the long term they could battle one another for position.

For these reasons, the 18th-dynasty kings considered it an extraordinarily dangerous thing to empower dozens of royal sons. (Indeed, some of them, including Thutmose IV, depicted themselves in statues and reliefs with only a mother—no wife, no children—which seemed the safest political course.) The only 18th-dynasty sons featured in their fathers' monumental imagery were those who had been selected as heir during their fathers' lifetime. All the other sons were absent, invisible, never openly given the title "king's son" and expected to melt into regular elite society.

But in the 19th dynasty, Ramses II displayed his many children as extensions of his person. They could therefore be sent out into all of Egypt's different professional institutions to act on his behalf (and consequently, be enriched for their loyalty). Ramses II was publicly saying: My sons' will is my own. But behind the scenes, he needed them as a power bloc to be simultaneously enabled, threatened, and appeased.

Although Egypt's lower elites may have competed with one another as corporate professionals, Ramses II's top lieutenants were rewarded for their allegiance and canny political strategy, resulting in the king's carrot-and-stick approach of generous bribery and harsh demotion. The details are not clear, but some remnants of Ramses' firings and hirings are probably hidden in plain sight on the many statues and stelae of elites with erased names and on reused objects.[47]

In the end, Ramses was the only boss who mattered. He could fire all those entrenched aristocrats from their positions and replace them as he saw fit, often with his own blood. All those offspring would be more devoted to him than elite administrators who would put their own local communities first. And by placing his sons into those positions, Ramses II was inherently destabilizing provincial social systems throughout Egypt, infiltrating them with his own agenda from the farthest reaches of the Delta to the most southerly point of Upper Egypt. We can assume it worked brilliantly—in the beginning.

Families full of sons mean sturdy power blocs. Think of cultures in Ireland, Mexico, India, Pakistan, Saudi Arabia, and China that value large families. Part of the impact of Mao's infamous one-child policy was arguably to break the power of the extended family in the country-side. With many sons, you could create labor on a farm; you could protect that farm from outside threat; you could take over someone else's farm; you could steal livestock; you could stack the local councils with your guys. The advantages to royal nepotism seem obvious.

Under Ramses II, royal sons were both elevated and celebrated, holding titles such as Chief of Troops, Chief Scribe, Fanbearer on the King's Right, High Priest of Ptah, High Priest of Ra, Overseer of the King's Horses, First Charioteer of His Majesty, and Overseer of the Army. They filled the ranks left empty when the last generation of loyal officials died or, in the case of unknown or unrelated officials, were simply fired (though this is harder to prove in the given documentation). But this nepotism had its dangers. Although we commend Ramses II's prodigious production, Ramses' 50 sons may have created one of the largest extended families the world had ever seen. Such tribalism had to be fed, and there weren't enough tasty meals to go around.

In the same way that a 4th-dynasty king built pyramids to prove his divinity, this 19th-dynasty king needed loyal lieutenants clustered around him to carry out his will (the modern equivalent is Donald Trump's cultivation of his adult children Ivanka [and Jared], Don Jr., and Eric). That said, there is both power and danger in relying on family, and some authoritarian leaders understand the weakness inherent in such nepotism. Vladimir Putin doesn't name his family as supporters of his rule, and naming sons in North Korea is done discreetly. On the other hand, Saudi Arabia, the United Arab Emirates, Brunei, and Qatar enrich and empower family members willing to adhere to the rules. But those same sons can be the undoing of any dynasty if they turn on one another in the battle for ever diminishing resources. With each generation, more men with ties to the king fight over the same shrinking assets—and the king must play them all with promises and positions of real and phantom power.

No female empowerment was featured under Ramses II, however. Most of his queens, including the Great Royal Wife, Nefertari, were depicted in statuary on a much smaller scale than their colossal husband, appearing as tiny figurines between his knees or along his lower leg, not as near equals like Nefertiti with Akhenaten. Nefertari is more famous today for her breathtaking tomb and remarkable beauty than she is for any actual power. She was celebrated as Ramses II's dutiful consort, his beloved—a good woman, maybe head of his harem, but nothing more. She was the handmaiden to her lord, a wife, and a producer of children, not politically engaged. Like today's first ladies around the world, such women are meant to signal support of the larger competitive patriarchy without infiltrating it. Their mere presence broadcasts that their husbands are family men, capable of affection and love, and not rapacious warlords hungry for scorched earth.

In the 18th dynasty, kings had married their sisters with regularity. The offspring of those incestuous unions were often preferred as heir, which gave those royal women extraordinary power as mothers of kings. But as we move into the Ramesside period, that feminine power had all but vanished. Although, in an overt show of sustained masculinity, Ramses II would marry two of his daughters as his reign moved into its third decade—demonstrating, presumably, a sun god–like ability to sire his future self with his own daughter—there is no evidence for royal brother-sister marriage.[48] The king's sisters were afterthoughts, not power players. (Although there is documentation for a female king at the end of the 19th dynasty—a woman named Tawosret, who ruled for a couple of years—she seems more a pawn of male competitors trying to use nonthreatening and long-trusted female power to their benefit. Tawosret was quickly removed from power by the first king of the 20th dynasty, and she remains a blip on the Egyptian political time line, a remnant of the female power that once was.)

Despite (or because of) the obvious nepotism he employed, Ramses II manufactured a connection to the populace as a savior who could drain the swamp. As such, he was obsessed with his own celebrity, concerned with how many people saw his heroics and paid homage to his statue cults. He manufactured a new demagoguery that Egypt had not seen before, feeding into the desires and prejudices of his officials and soldiers and using divine backing to differentiate the kingship of the past from the kingship of the present. He reveled in defining who was loyal and who was not, placing his celebrity at the center of the whole show. Ramses II created a superstar kingship that only he could inhabit. That is why we call him Ramses the Great—not because he did great things, but because he created the pageant of greatness from which no one can look away. And we still love him for it.

We can suspect that Egypt's intellectuals were not at all happy with Ramses' modus operandi—both filled with anxiety about how norms were being discarded and concerned that the king was getting away with cheap and false narratives of winning. But the power of the aristocrats was dwindling. All the professionals that the Ramesside kings had empowered loved Ramses II for his celebrity; he was their guy, one of them, from a family like theirs, and he was making them richer than ever before. These same men might have remembered their grandparents speaking about how they'd had to bow down and touch their lips to the floor in front of a king who had no one else's interests at heart, or about the dark days when the king's men arrived at their temple to destroy the sacred images while all the town elites had just stood by, helpless to stop them. But no longer. This new dynasty was making Egypt great again.

Ramesside Egypt was undergoing a shift, all based on the empowerment of a people at the grassroots level—maybe not the peasant class, but a much broader swath of society who appreciated the fact that their beloved king was pulling them all up with him. Ramses II's authoritarianism was weak in comparison to kings such as Khufu, Senwosret III, or Amenhotep III. But he used his popularity within Egypt's lower social ranks, and within his own family, to remove or weaken those great landholders whose power rivaled his own, preferring lackeys willing to hustle and show their loyalty.

As an example of how Egyptian society now worked, let's return to Bakenkhonsu. He was the son of a simple priest of Amun at Thebes,[49] and his career provides indirect evidence that Ramses II was inexorably squeezing his upper elites. After working in the stables of King Seti for a decade, he soldiered for a bit until starting work as an entry-level *wab* priest for Amun. Rising through the temple ranks, Bakenkhonsu ended up in the illustrious position of High Priest of Amun. On an inscribed statue of him, we learn that he was responsible for overseeing the construction of Ramses II's popular east Karnak Temple. The text notes that "I performed the excellent duties in the house of Amun, being chief overseer of the works of my lord. I made for him a temple (called) Ramses Meriamun-Hearer-of-Petitions, at the upper portal of the house of Amun. I erected obelisks therein of granite, whose beauty approached heaven. A wall was before it of stone over against Thebes; it was flooded, and the gardens were planted with trees. I made very great double doors of electrum; their beauty met the heavens. I hewed very great flagstaffs, and I erected them in the august forecourt in front of his temple."[50] Bakenkhonsu had a simple background, but he ended up one of the most powerful operators in Egypt. Such radical social mobility smacks of a profound shift in royal court strategy, favoring the men who were willing to agree and flatter.

Decisions based on loyalty instead of ability have a way of coming back to haunt you, as when, in 2020, Donald Trump sidelined widely respected epidemiologist Anthony Fauci in favor of loyalist Alex Azar—a Stanford, Hoover Institution doctor-entrepreneur, a yes-man with absolutely no infectious disease qualifications—to head up his coronavirus task force. Empowered loyalists and former corporate leaders are often brought in to serve their leader precisely because their agendas merge, which furthers their own enrichment.

In Ramses II's case, the more loyalists he placed into power positions, the faster the cancer grew. For us, some 3,000 years distant, it only seems as if he was creating a broader professional class of previously excluded men. But no ruler has any real authority if a combination of loyalty and payoffs is the modus operandi. In the end, Ramses' base held the real power within Egypt's bloated institutions and all the people in their employ. People needed their plebeian king to serve, and indeed that was the only reason a family of mercenaries held the crown at all. The new populism had created an unregulated mess of self-interest.

Sometimes it looks as if Ramses II's celebrity was the only glue holding the whole house of cards together. We have moved away from an 18th-dynasty scenario in which the gods chose the king, to a 19th-dynasty reality in which the people chose their god. In image after image, Ramses II advertised his connection to his army and to his people.

Ramses ordered purpose-built temples so that his people could connect with his fame in person. At the Temple of Amun-Re Who Hears Prayers at Thebes, the king was styled as an Osirian divinity who could intercede on behalf of his people.[51] His statues there were bedazzled with jewelry, a testament to all the material improvements that loyalty to this king would bring. Ramses ordered multiple "contra-temples" like this: special places of worship open to more people that were situated behind Egypt's great temples. There he was, larger than life—not as an unapproachable divinity that you couldn't touch or look in the face, but someone you could see, work with, have a beer with, fight alongside, his chariot beside yours. This was bread and circuses, Egyptian style.

Many stelae show how Egyptian men memorialized their worship of Ramses II, depicting their pilgrimages and personal veneration of his statues, illustrating their offerings of flowers and incense to their god-king. One stela from Qantir shows Ramses II himself standing on the lap of one of his own seated colossal statues, his men arrayed below him in a massive rally to his kingship as he lobs all kinds of awesome stuff down to them.[52] The man who ordered the stela stands in front of the colossal statue, catching baubles. The scene was like displaying a picture of yourself and the president, advertising the fact that you were able to see and touch him.

This is demagoguery at its most effective. All this populist building—and especially the rallies and worship that occurred around it—removed aristocratic power from temple spaces. Before, a set of initiated priests had limited access to the sacred houses of the gods, carefully parsing the divine words, keeping out the unclean, uneducated masses. Now, people could crowd into temple spaces as never before. These contra-temples and colossal statues drove a wedge between the old patricians and the kingship. In the divide were a mass of grateful men who got new incomes and new temple festivals just for them.

Remember Akhenaten making everyone bow down? Ramses II would not be so stupid. He was one of the people—just the best, biggest, and most divine. He demonstrated this at the site of Abu Simbel, situated at the border between Egypt and Sudan. Cut into the rock above the Nile's second cataract in Nubia, we see a temple fronted by massive images of the monarch. Here, people could look up from their boats on the Nile and see four huge seated Ramses II images on either side of one tiny image of the god Re-Horakhty. Princes and princesses, queens and daughters were also depicted as inconsequential compared to the colossal body of the king. Inside, Ramses was shown in the back sanctuary sitting alongside Amun-Re, Re-Horakhty, and Ptah as a co-equal god. In 1960, when modern Egypt built the Aswan High Dam, this temple was moved, block by block, to a higher location on a custom-built fiberglass mountain. But even relocated, Abu Simbel remains a monument to Egyptian populist military might.

Abu Simbel was not built to terrorize an indigenous Nubian population. It was fashioned to rally an army of Egyptian occupation in Nubia, all loyal to their god-king and savior. It was red meat to his military professional class stationed down south to keep control of Nubia and its resources. Like U.S. troops in Iraq and Afghanistan treated to a USO spectacle, the guys sent down to live here permanently or semi-permanently needed to be reminded of just how Egyptian they were.

And what better way for the king to show them than with his physical celebrity? The Egyptian military men would see this grand temple and know it was for them, feel the connection to their patron, their guy, their god. He had been out in battle with them many times, after all, and his divinity had empowered them with riches and newly found professional bromance. For the patrician Egyptian, the tiny image of Re-Horakhty next to the king might have elicited shock. But for the professional military men, it was the right and proper thing to show—because it was their king who advanced them. No wonder Ramses II divinized himself most obviously on the frontier; it's where his most fervent supporters were located.

Abu Simbel was almost certainly a pilgrimage place for Egyptian and foreign soldiers stationed in Nubia. They would have proudly talked about their visit and brought mementos home as the selfies of their day. This was a miracle in stone that invited Egypt's people to partake in the king's glory in order to disempower those below them in a zero-sum game. Ramses II depicted himself victorious, but he was never alone. Look behind him and you see his princes in battle with him. His soldiers are there too. Charioteers. Foot soldiers. Bowmen. All of them included. Ramses knew to surround himself with his base.

The temple site evinced other wonders to prove the king's divinity. Twice a year the sun's beams shine directly through the temple's interior axis and light up the faces of Ramses, Amun, and Re, leaving the chthonic Ptah in the shadows as he preferred. What the significance of these days were, we do not know, but we can be sure the temple was purposefully sited for these moments of special ritual celebration. Some suggest one of the days was Ramses II's birthday; others believe the Egyptians might have been memorializing particular days of victory, perhaps connected to Ramses' beloved battle of Kadesh.[53]

This is the kind of celebration in which modern-day Egypt still participates. Cairo has a 26th of July Street, monumentalizing the day in 1952 when Egypt gained its independence from Britain. October 6 University, outside the city, marks the day in 1973 when Egypt crossed the Suez Canal to confront Israelis in the Sinai. Perhaps Ramses II was doing the same thing: inspiring his men to remember all the patriotic ideals connected to the state, forcing reflection on what it meant to be a good Egyptian as king, soldier, or priest.

Ramses II was no snob; he valued devotedness over intellectualism. No need to be initiated into the secrets of the priesthood; no need to learn all the intricacies of Egyptian writing systems. He would open these religious guilds up like no other. Ramses used religion to focus worship on himself as god-king, accompanied by the requisite ridicule of his vanquished losers.

This strategy is arguably similar to those of today's most successful authoritarian personalities—in Russia, Poland, the United States—which rely on Christianity as one of their most effective tools of persuasion. Christianity is no meritocracy. It is based on faith and contrition, following one's lord and savior. No critical thought is required, just taking Jesus into your heart. Indeed, the more slavishly the doctrine is followed, the better.

Authoritarian Christians in the United States believe the devil is active. According to modern Christian political websites, that anti-Christ will seduce people to empty the prisons, destroy the traditional family structure of one man and one woman, invite Sodom-and-Gomorrah sexual license, take away guns, give citizenship to those not worthy of it, and remove the privileged power from those marked by God. Religion and authoritarianism are inextricably intertwined.

Ramses II presented himself as the savior fighting against those who would oppress righteous Egyptians. Remember, just 60 or 70 years earlier, Akhenaten's henchmen had marched through Egypt's temple spaces, north and south, gouging out the names and images of Amun-Re, the word "gods," and countless images of other divinities. Ramses II would make it his life's work to repair that damage, to return the gods to their rightful homes while broadcasting his extraordinary piety. He used these rebuilding efforts to link himself personally with gods like Amun, Re, Ptah, and Atum, building a bridge between his eastern Delta 19th dynasty and esteemed southern kings of the 18th dynasty such as Thutmose III.[54]

Ramses II set out to win popular affection in Thebes, Memphis, Heliopolis, Elephantine—everywhere Akhenaten's damage had been done. As king, he positioned himself to implement Egyptian ma'at, or "justice." It was, in a sense, his means of marrying into the 18th-dynasty royal family, manufacturing their honorary adoption of him while putting them down at the same time. Akhenaten gave the family of Ramses II a mighty gift by breaking the norms of kingship so egregiously that a Delta king was now allowed to rebalance Egyptian society.

Ramses II also set himself up as a champion of the good old Amun-Re religion. Even though Amun-Re was a southern god and Ramses II was a Delta king, he was the one saving the Thebans from themselves, correcting the iconoclasm of their man Akhenaten. He was declaring his singular ability to right the wrongs of the past—to rescue his people from the previous overreach, patrician debauchery, and decadence. He was definitely sticking it to the Theban aristocrats, putting up numerous statues of himself embracing their beloved divinity, showing them that he could worship Amun more piously than they could. Amun-Re was only the king of the gods because Thebes was the birthplace of so many kings. Ramses II would take this idea of "king of the gods" and turn himself into a god of kings.

If you visit Luxor Temple today, you have to imagine the Kadesh scene on the front pylon—displayed as on a giant screen in Times Square in New York—with the courtyard full of supporters staring up at the king's imagery. With all the obelisks and colossal statues—there would have been as many as six before the front pylon—Ramses' unprecedented power was palpable. Today the Egyptian Ministry of Tourism and Antiquities has reconstructed many of Ramses' statues in front of Luxor Temple, perfecting what had been, aligning Egypt's current zeitgeist with Ramses the Great.

The king didn't have to impress any of the old aristocrats—just his own family and his people. But make no mistake: Half the colossal figures in the first court at Luxor Temple were reappropriated from the era of Amenhotep III and recut to Ramses II's liking.[55] Ramses didn't want to limit himself to using raw, quarried stone; he didn't need to work toward a space characterized by symmetry, proportions, elegance, and quality of carving. No, he needed size and numbers, and he needed them now. His statuary reflected that as he depicted himself again and again. This way, his newly empowered people could get their fill of their great savior, the warrior-king.

Ramses II even made liberal use of a hieroglyphic symbol known as the *rekhyt* bird, which stands for "ordinary people."[56] The sign is visible everywhere in Ramses' temples—on the columns of the Great Hypostyle Hall at Karnak, on the columns of Luxor Temple's first court, at his Temple of the Hearing Ear, potentially signaling that folks were now welcome in a place from which they had previously been barred. The incised birds may very well be clues that a spike had been driven into the heart of the old patronage systems. Ramses II may have been showing the old patricians the true source of his might when he invited his newly empowered professional class of priests and soldiers into his temples.

The social landscape of religiosity was quickly changing. Egypt's temples, tombs, and statues displayed profound transformation—one might even say destabilization—as a wider variety of people were able to participate in more divine activities than ever before. In Ramses II's Egypt, we see more direct worship of gods by the people, something that had been tightly controlled in the 18th dynasty. Egyptologists have argued for a religious awakening in Egypt, a new and heartfelt personal piety. But it's quite possible that the so-called religious changes were more about money and institutions than they were about some new kind of spiritual fervor.[57]

The scenario is reminiscent of the top caste in the United States signaling its power with over-the-top Christian zealotry. Americans have systematically manipulated Christianity throughout the country's history—as the means of expelling and assimilating Indigenous peoples, maintaining systems of enslaving people with moral impunity, and today, signaling loyalty to populist policies that purge unwanted social elements. American evangelical Christianity is not about following the Gospels, which might actually create a set of policies akin to socialism. Instead, American Evangelicalism signals that a person is willing to be faithful to a particular tribe. And such piety must be publicly and openly displayed—on social media and in person, with the right jewelry and hats, using the correct Bible verses and cipher turns of phrase—because Fundamentalist Christianity is completely intertwined with American patriotic power. Christianity is still used to demonize those who do not follow the established rules—intellectuals, educators, community activists, and any doubters. This is why some people went apoplectic when, in 2016, star quarterback Colin Kaepernick took a knee on a football field during the national anthem. That act was an open affront to established stakeholders.

Ramses II needed to signal his own piety to his base. He achieved this end with the most archaic of Egyptian festivals, including the 3,000-year-old Sed ritual, the renewal of kingship. He would use such ceremonies as a means of redistributing goods and resources to as many people as he could—likely to his sons, grandsons, and great-grandsons, but also to the professional priests, soldiers, and bureaucrats. Ramses II's Sed festivals were probably much less elegant and restricted than Amenhotep III's because they were about empowering his men and a new patrician elite in his own family.

Ramses II's reign would continue for almost seven jaw-dropping decades, allowing the aged king to celebrate an unprecedented 13 or 14 Sed festivals.[58] All the while he used the rituals as excuses for massive building programs that allowed the nationalization of such industries as faience and metal production, created countless new jobs, and provided an excuse for huge parties. Essentially, Ramses instituted gangbuster government spending for Egypt's people who were, for their part, essentially waiting for the king to just die already. One could compare it to Franklin Roosevelt's bloated budget during World War II—a massive reallocation of wealth not only from the government, but also from the Gettys and Rockefellers, to "the people." Like Roosevelt, Ramses II also did not want to relinquish power. He would find a way to hold on for a few more decades.

Ramses planned for a burial in Thebes, the expected and conservative course of action. But he would lay overt claim to the sacred space of the dead kings by siting his tomb (KV 7) in the most visible location, at the entrance to the graveyard itself. The ostentatious site suggests that the king may have even opened the sacred valley to the public, breaking with tradition that had offered entrance to no one but the initiated. Scandalous for some, to be sure—but because of its location directly in the middle of the wadi, the tomb ended up being brutally damaged by floodwaters, probably after the king's lifetime, making the structure so unstable that modern tourists have not been allowed inside. Although his engineers must have relayed the risks to him, Ramses II needed the biggest possible audience for his tomb. This was a king who valued a big impact now rather than safety for eternity.

What the 18th-dynasty kings had built as secret and hidden from view, the 19th-dynasty monarchs used as a public showpiece for the death rites of a populist leader. Ramses II wanted a tomb that was public and up front, and he got it. He even added a massive tomb for all his sons (KV 5). The mass sepulchre was an insane architectural feat and an unprecedented addition to the sacred valley that had previously been exclusive to kings and a few high-ranking courtiers, likely causing con-niption fits among Egypt's most conservative members who worried about the safety of their ancestor-kings' tombs.

Modern excavations began in KV 5 in the 1980s. With at least 130 chambers, the tomb is so big that not all of it has been investigated. The public ate up the spectacle of archaeology in the tomb as the media covered it;[59] we can be sure that the ancient Egyptians were similarly engrossed in the news of the wonders being built in the royal cemetery. Another notch in the belt for Ramses' celebrity.

Ramses II built his Temple of Millions of Years in western Thebes so his cult could be celebrated after his death—but he would do so differ-ently from 18th-dynasty kings. No strange astronomical statue gardens, like the ones Amenhotep III had built, that appealed only to a limited, intellectual audience of aristocrats. Ramses II would instead create an outward-facing temple with a simple, manly, heroic story. This was his space. And here at the Ramesseum, we see another colorful Kadesh relief advertising his greatness with multiple colossal statues out front.

Ramses II also made it a priority to systematically publish sacred texts previously kept under wraps. Seti I and Ramses II let out more religious secrets than any other New Kingdom monarchs, wresting control of sacred knowledge from the "experts" and giving it to the people. This was like England's King James commissioning a Bible in English, allowing the people to interact with the texts directly and cutting out the exclusive control of priests knowledgeable in Latin, Greek, Aramaic, and Hebrew.

END OF AN ERA

Ramses II's death had been long awaited, and the Egyptians seem to have had everything prepared. When his corpse was found among a cache of royal coffins at Deir el Bahri at the end of the 19th century, the king was so well preserved that his profile still evinced fierceness and pride. But the strange circumstances of the mummy's discovery were an indication of what his reign had wrought: The corpse had been re-interred in a coffin that did not originally belong to him. The man who had ruled as a god of his people for seven decades, whose body was perfectly embalmed, ended up wrecking his own lineage with his populist strategies to such an extent that generations later the inheritors of his failed administration would cannibalize his tomb's treasures to finance their own regime, reburying his mortal remains in an 18th-dynasty coffin. Today, visitors to the National Museum of Egyptian Civilization in Cairo can see the king's body, displayed like other larger-than-life figures such as Chairman Mao (in Beijing), Ho Chi Minh (in Hanoi), and Vladimir Lenin (in Moscow).

In the end, Ramses II had lived too long. The stretch of his reign trashed a system carefully constructed by his grandfather, Ramses I, in which son and grandson stood by as necessary heirs for dynastic succession. Though Ramses II named 50 sons in his temples, hundreds more men must have vied for power at his death; all had been waiting for the demise of the monarch so they could jump at their chance for power. Not only would most of the named heirs of such a long-lived ruler have predeceased him, but his sons would also now have had sons and grandsons of their own, increasing the rivalry of succession exponentially. The king's death meant competition not just among the remaining princes (who were mostly old men at this point), but also regionally and intergenerationally, as the young men below tried to muscle into the game to get positions and payoffs of their own.

The longer Ramses II had stayed on the throne, the more he destabilized the 19th dynasty. The structure that had seemed so impervious to any sort of vulnerability during all those years would crumble into civil war just two short reigns later. Ramses II's 13th son, Merneptah, took the throne after him. He may have been 70 years old himself at that point, having waited a dozen years after he was named the king's crown prince. We should perhaps congratulate Merneptah for ruling a full 10 years at all. His reign was punctuated by the continuing crisis of the Bronze Age collapse, including significant incursions of Sea Peoples and Libyans; the invaders were beaten back, we are told in inscriptions, by Merneptah's defensive campaigns to the southern Levant.

One stela, reused from the time of Amenhotep III, was etched with Merneptah's Levantine exploits, with all the details of whom he had defeated and how badly. It includes, at the very bottom, the first known contact with a people called Israel. Merneptah proudly recorded that he annihilated them: "Israel is wasted, bare of seed."[60] Ironically, the stela does not presage the end of Israel, but rather its beginnings, as its people would grow into one of the most influential religious wellsprings the world has ever known.

But the stela signals the death knell of Egypt as a globalized power. After a complicated and messy civil war, Egypt's 19th dynasty moved into the slow and steady decline of the 20th dynasty, punctuated by incursions of more Libyans and more Sea Peoples, more mercenary soldiers, more impoverishment, and more government destabilization. It was during the 20th dynasty that Egypt's elites, so used to displaying their family power with painted and inscribed funerary trappings, were relegated to reusing the coffins of their ancestors, taking them out of tombs, removing the mummies, and bringing the containers to a workshop to be updated with the latest styles. Even at the end, the Egyptians denied there was anything wrong.[61]

Meanwhile, the palace infighting among the king's descendants would become so fierce that Egyptian stakeholders took up arms against one another again at the end of the 20th dynasty. There is evidence that a southern Egyptian coalition felt so excluded and embittered that Ramses III, another king of eastern Delta lineage, was murdered in his harem at Thebes, his throat slit in what seems to have been an attempt to take the throne for the south.

How much did Ramses II's creation of a celebrity kingship sow the seeds for such rancorous discord? Even though none of the later Ramesside kings could build (or even reuse) on the scale that Ramses II had, his lineage did its best to maintain his celebrity reputation. They emulated him in simple things such as using the same name. Before the end of the 20th dynasty, every succeeding king but four was a Ramses; history now counts 11 of them. They imitated his persona, too. Every king tried to be just like Ramses, copying his portrait, his outfits, putting their own statues in his temples, trying to claim their rites and sacredness because they didn't have the means to build their own massive structures. They were all running futilely and desperately after Ramses the Great. But they would never catch up. He had made sure of that.

At the end of the New Kingdom, where did the power go? The kings' men, within their institutions, would be the recipients of Egypt's might. The priests and soldiers had played it well over the long term—saying, "Yes, my king, we will build this new temple," and "Yes, we can embark on this campaign to Nubia," and so on. Eventually, as the kingship weakened, the institutions would step into the void. By the end of the 20th dynasty, a bloc of priests would rule Egypt outright.

The Temple Complex of Amun-Re in Thebes is a case in point. Because the king had aggrandized his power with temple constructions that required so much funding and upkeep, he had inserted vast wealth into the corporations of Thebes, eventually allowing the priests to run a decentralized government in the absence of strong kingship. Late Ramesside Egypt would be ruled by temples more than kings, by institutions more than individuals. Amun-Re, king of the gods, would transform into a king of the people as well.

Ramses II had stamped all of Egypt—the desert and river, north and south—with his name and image. He built so much and so widely that his propaganda continues to work on our minds today. We still believe his press, his manufacturing of false realities—battles won, vast riches earned, an empire of extensive territories held within an iron grasp. Who are we to doubt what the great leader has inscribed in stone? We only know what the kings decide to tell us, after all.

CHAPTER 6

TAHARQA:

No Zealot Like the Convert

Documentaries about ancient Egypt would have us believe the high points of Egyptian history involved the reigns of Khufu, Tutankhamun, and Ramses. Not many people can name a king of the 25th dynasty, but surely those rulers also deserve our attention. Rooted in the land of Kush, in modern-day Sudan, their empire was vast, covering an expanse of territory that stretched from the Mediterranean Sea to Khartoum. Their dominion over Egypt would last a century—as long as Khufu's 4th dynasty.

King Taharqa (r. ca 690–664 B.C.), the fourth king of the 25th dynasty, was the Kushite ruler with the most extraordinary ups and downs. He controlled Egypt and defeated Assyria in noteworthy battles, but he also saw a royal son kidnapped as well as the beginning of the end of his kingdom's once mighty empire.

Taharqa depicted himself tall and strong, every taut muscle defined in his statuary. He inherited a mighty kingdom from his father, Piankhy, whose dynasty in Egypt boasted many achievements—among other things, doing away with a confusing mess of overlapping Libyan-Egyptian kingships and restoring centralized rule. It also took on the trappings of monumental temples and propagandistic inscriptions. Along the way, these Kushite kings proudly informed the Egyptian people why they should be grateful for the good fortune of kind authoritarianism that would once again embellish the land with beautiful images of god-kings.

Taharqa ruled for a healthy 26 years. He campaigned in the Levant and commissioned hundreds of temples, statues, and stelae. He also ordered the biggest-ever Sudanese pyramid for his burial (becoming, in essence, the Khufu of the Kushites). He was a canny imperialist, a king able to unify and tame Egypt from his base in Kush, who attempted to win hearts and minds with a stout religious zeal.

An heir to generations of Egyptian oppression, Taharqa hinted at his aspirations to wield a benevolent force over his homeland's erstwhile conquerors. Full of fatherly admonitions, tough love, and pious goodness, he wanted to be the kind of patriarchal leader who really does know what's good for everyone. But in the end, his efforts unraveled. Any knowledgeable Egyptologist will pause at the mention of the year 663 B.C., which continues to live in infamy as the date of Assyrian king Ashurbanipal's sack of Egypt, when divine effigies were stolen, temples burned, and the population brutalized. Taharqa's successor pushed back against the Assyrians, but he couldn't prevent the inevitable end of Kush's imperial control.

ORIGINS WITHIN A SACRED MOUNTAIN

Eight hundred miles south of Thebes, at the Nile's fourth cataract—one of six rocky areas that interrupt the flow of the river—King Taharqa cut a chapel into the mountainside of Jebel Barkal. There he communed with the god of Nile Valley kingship. Today, archaeologists simply call the place Temple B300. In ancient times, it allowed the king to enter the sanctified *dju wab,* the "pure mountain," and connect with the source of both worldly and supernatural power.

Jebel Barkal was located two weeks' travel upriver from Thebes, but the local Kushite people used the same name for its temples that had been used for Amun-Re's consecrated home at Karnak—*Ipet-Sut,* "most select of places." The two locations were ideological twins, home to two manifestations of the same god some 700 miles apart. There was apparently little second-guessing of Egypt's colonial imposition onto this sacred space.

King Taharqa was a southern emperor who ruled Egypt as well as Kush. Jebel Barkal was his home temple in his capital city of Napata,[1] and it was thought to be marked by the gods. The sacred mountain there displayed a natural outcropping with a strangely familiar shape—an unfurled cobra with a sun disk on its head when viewed from the western side, or a cobra wearing the white crown, the symbol of Upper Egypt, when seen from the northeast. Believed to be the wellspring of the annual Nile flood that brought forth new agriculture, Jebel Barkal embodied a kingly origin story in which the power to rule actually came from outside Egypt's traditional dominion.

This was a place of new beginnings and unexpected powers. Even the Nile offered evidence that Jebel Barkal was a sacred origination point, because the river made a giant loop here, flowing north to south for a stretch, opposite from what it did in Egypt. In Egypt proper, the sun rose on the river's right bank and then set on the left bank (in the land of the dead). But here in the south, on the upside-down stretch of the river at Napata, it seemed that death was life and life was death.

The land of Kush was believed to be the source of many things—the sun god's regeneration, for example, and pestilence and discord in the form of the Eye of Re. It was also the proven source of gold and vast mineral deposits. In short, it was the originator of everything that created power, ground zero for a king.

The Egyptians knew that their greatest blessings came from outside their homeland. Long before Taharqa, colonizing Egyptian kings had claimed the sacred mountain at Jebel Barkal as their own, constructing temples there, seeing it as a fountainhead of their own royal divinity. In the middle of the 15th century B.C., Thutmose III of the 18th dynasty was the first Egyptian king to build in stone at Jebel Barkal. Talatat stones have been found in the temple foundations here too—evidence of structures Akhenaten had built to his version of the sun god.[2] Ramses II came here to worship within the mountain of kingship as well, using the site as Alexander the Great did Siwa Oasis, when the latter made a pilgrimage to the oracle to prove his own divine right to rule.[3]

Ramses II was so proud of having been to this origin point of kingship that he depicted himself before Jebel Barkal's sacred cobra on the reliefs of his rock-cut temple at Abu Simbel. The king stands before the cobra emanating from the mountain, which hides the double-plumed Amun-Re behind it.[4] Ramses' arms are upraised; he holds a *sekhem* scepter of power in one hand and a pot of smoking incense in the other. It's a photo-like documentation that the king had well and truly tapped into the deep powers of the kingly mountain. In Ramses' accompanying captions, the god of Jebel Barkal is called a manifestation of Amun-Re, "Lord of the Thrones of the Two Lands." The god is shown as an enthroned humanlike divinity tucked away inside his mountain, safe behind a female cobra bodyguard of stone.

Centuries later, Taharqa would feel compelled to build and worship at Jebel Barkal too, despite—or because of—all the previous Egyptian stakeholders. He actually decided to renew many of the temples that the old invader pharaohs had built, commissioning new reliefs that also showed himself worshipping the god of the mountain. If Taharqa modeled his scene of worship on that of Ramses II, he does not tell us. All the same, the Kushite king is shown standing before the holy mountain, his arms upraised with an offering of wine, much like Ramses II. But in his relief, Amun-Re is depicted as a ram-headed human—a particularly Kushite form of the god. The caption in the accompanying hieroglyphic text names the divinity in Egyptian as "Amun-Re in the midst of the pure mountain."[5]

This sanctuary was a place for appeasement of forces of abject destruction. It was where the solar divinity Amun-Re dwelled, but it was also where the Eye of Re was believed to find her refuge. The Eye of Re was thought to be the daughter of the sun god; if traitors rose up, her father would send her forth, full of horrific fury, to vanquish any enemies on the horizon. She took the form of a maddened lioness, raging through the deserts and towns, gobbling up humanity as she went. So great was her frenzy that, at a certain point, she was not able to distinguish friend from foe and had to be calmed with beer.[6]

The Jebel Barkal mountain was considered the goddess's safe space and was thus an especially vital offering point when the world was most imperiled. That was particularly the case on the five days of the Egyptian new year when the fierce spirit of the lioness was believed to roam abroad, leaving upheaval and crisis in her wake.[7] Every Egyptian king needed to pay heed to the Jebel Barkal peak for the matter-of-fact reason that it was the shelter of the Eye of Re, who protected her father, Amun-Re, the king of the gods, and by extension his earthly king.

And so Egyptian and Kushite rulers alike filled the space in front of the mountain with temples to Mut, Hathor, and Sakhmet, all manifestations of fierce female forces. They decorated the halls with massive sistrum columns evocative of the rattles that calmed the angry goddess, and they set up giant figures of Bes, the dwarf leonine divinity whose fierce face and hybrid body frightened away misfortune and disease.[8]

Taharqa was one of the mountain's many embellishers, but he was not satisfied with only building at ground level. He also made sure to leave a grand display of his piety high on the peak, near the top of the cobra-shaped outcropping itself. There, he affixed to the mountainside thick gold sheeting with an inscription that proclaimed his victories over his enemies. Even from a great distance, everyone would have seen the king's godliness, his great wealth, and his audaciousness, as the gold glinted in the sun. Today, only the attachment holes are left.[9]

Taharqa tells us in other Jebel Barkal temple inscriptions that his new constructions replaced old temples built by "the ancestors." These apparently referred to Egyptian kings of the 18th and 19th dynasties who had put up the first structures there, but perhaps also to less permanent shrines built by his own Kushite brethren. Now Taharqa would claim this sacred mountain for his own kingship. In his new shrines, he ordered himself depicted as the god Shu, wearing the four tall plumes, ready to propitiate the goddess and bring her back to her father inside the mountain. This was the mission of a good king.

The southern location of Jebel Barkal, tucked away at the Nile's Great Bend, was where the positives and negatives of Egyptian kingly power originated, enshrining both the curses and blessings of any monarch's reign. As a Kushite ruler, Taharqa would claim its karmic force too. He depicted himself as a hybrid Egyptian Kushite king, picking and choosing which Egyptian elements he wanted to co-opt and which he would abandon;[10] images show him wearing a cap-like crown created specifically for the rulers from the deep south, complete with two cobras rising from the king's brow—one apparently to represent the kings' rule of their homeland of Kush, and another to represent dominion over Egypt, a crown of imperial power.[11]

CONQUERING A GOLDEN LAND

So powerful were the legends of Kush that the first-century B.C. Greek historian Diodorus Siculus wrote that the men from that region—whom he called Ethiopians—had been the originators of Egyptian civilization, preceding the Egyptian people. According to him, Osiris was the first Nubian king, and the Nubians colonized Egypt from the south, inserting their culture, religion, and rule into the Nile floodplain.[12] The historical narrative put forth by Egyptologists, on the other hand, is one of Egyptians regularly exerting their dominance over the region to the south and cruelly extracting what they needed with no thought to the well-being of the land's inhabitants.

Kush was part of a region known as Nubia, a name that was an Egyptian imposition, not a local construct. *Nub* meant "gold" in the Egyptian language, and it reduced an entire part of northeast Africa to a source of mineral wealth.[13] But Nubia was not just a source of gold. It was also the location of granites, copper, incense, exotic animals, and other luxury goods that Egypt's kings so favored.[14] When it was strong, Egypt was able to exploit Nubia even south of the second cataract. But they generally didn't push their command much farther. They were happy to put their soldiers and forts at that spot, only sending advance divisions south to crack down on rising Indigenous power as the need arose.[15]

The bedrock of Upper and Lower Nubia is sandstone and granite; as a result, the Nile cuts a much narrower channel through Sudan than it does to the north. In Egypt, the bedrock is limestone, allowing the Nile to carve broad expanses easily and—before the Aswan High Dam was built—flood its banks every year, depositing masses of rich silty earth. Those muddy waters came from the faraway highlands of Ethiopia in a kind of cosmic imbalance that stole soil from one land and enriched another.[16] In essence, Egypt was geologically set up for wealth, population growth, consolidation, and political dominance, allowing centralized kingships to repeatedly launch military expeditions to the south and take what they wanted.

Egypt's easy, naturally fertilized farming allowed its kings to draft multitudes of men into the army, supporting regular and systematic hegemonic control; Nubia supported a much lower population in comparison. Many of those long-standing geographical power dynamics are now being challenged by modern development as both Ethiopia and Sudan build great dams along their stretches of the Nile, capturing and rechanneling the river's waters before they can flow north and thus competing with Egypt's dam at Aswan.[17]

When strong ancient Egyptian kings exerted their authority, Lower Nubia was often devastated. The brutality of Egyptian hegemony was real. Conditions in the gold mines there were deemed so horrific that one of the oaths sworn by people of western Thebes in the 19th and 20th dynasties referenced the potential punishment of being sent to Nubia[18]—an oblique glimpse of the hellscape the Egyptians had created in the land of exploited minerals.

Countless Egyptian images dehumanized Nubians as abominations to humanity itself.[19] The Egyptians described and depicted Nubian enemies hanging upside down from fortification walls, a means of damning backward people both in this life and the next.[20] The Egyptians often called their enemies "the ones who are upside down," implying that the folk themselves had backward bodily functions, eating shit instead of food, drinking urine instead of beer.[21]

The handles of walking sticks found in the tomb of Tutankhamun represent stereotypical Nubian men curved in such a way that they were bound by the might of the king's grasp with every step. A painted box found in the teenage king's tomb is a masterpiece of artistic production that depicts the slaughter of Nubians on one side and the dispatch of West Asians on the other. It was the kind of palace furniture that reminded an Egyptian king of his military entitlements. The Saqqara tomb of Horemheb included scenes of Nubians being beaten, mocked, and poked in the eyes.[22] This was high Egyptian culture.

In their own tomb chapels, Egyptian elites gloried in depriving such southern people of their human qualities. The early 18th-dynasty tombs of Djehuty (Theban Tomb 11) and Montuherkhepeshef (Theban Tomb 20) show Nubians being strangled.[23] In other tomb chapels, Thebans proudly depicted the murder, mutilation, and display of dead Nubians and Kushites alongside the peoples of west Asia. They also showed the dismembered hands of their slain Nubian foes, virtuously collected. The images are akin to Americans from the Jim Crow South having themselves photographed next to the body of a lynched Black man hanging from a tree.

The examples of Egyptian cruelty in Nubia are many.[24] King Thutmose I hung a defeated Kushite chieftain from the prow of his boat; historians believe he killed the man before stringing up his body, but perhaps the deed signified a gruesome and slow death. Amenhotep II displayed a Kushite chief dangling from the fortification walls of the Kushite capital of Napata, the decomposing corpse a sign to those who might rebel against Egypt. In the early reign of Amenhotep III, the king killed scores of people from Kush, capturing hundreds of elite women and children in a battle near Semnah, taking them all back to Egypt as high-value captives to be raised in the palace, brainwashed, educated in Egyptian ways, and later returned to Kush as loyal vassals to Egypt.

The oppression continued with Akhenaten. A stela from the first 10 years of his reign mentions military action against Nubian rebels between the first and second cataracts, making sure to mention that multiple captives were impaled—that is, placed on a stake at the ribs and left to die a public and agonizing death: a warning to any who would try their luck against mighty Egypt. In the 19th dynasty, Merneptah left an inscription at Amada about a defeat of Nubian rebels in Wawat. He burned the bodies of enemy dead, thus denying them an afterlife.[25] Those unfortunate captives not killed had both hands, both ears, and both eyes ripped away, and "they were made into heaps in their towns" to suppress further rebellions.[26]

Ramses III of the 20th dynasty met Nubian bowmen in battle, telling us he vanquished them like women, a reference to emasculation, rape, or both.[27] And one of the last inscriptions of Egyptians in Nubia was left by the Theban High Priest of Amen Menkheperre of the early 21st dynasty, a remnant of brutal Egyptian civil wars fought on southern lands.

In about 800 B.C., some 200 years after that last Theban inscription, the Kushite kings would arise, following a reverse of the previous trend: When Egypt was weak, Nubia became strong. Every so-called "intermediate period" in Egypt, punctuated by drought, unrest, and/or political fragmentation, meant a time of flourishing cultural explosion in Nubia. The southern lands lent themselves to more decentralization and local control geographically, because the rocky cataracts interspersed along the Nile created rapids that made royal hegemony and political unification more difficult.

Geopolitically, Nubia was, and is, a less passive place than Egypt. In Egypt, authoritarian control was aided by straight, unobstructed river channels from which to impose a ruler's will. In Nubia, archaeologists find a variety of material cultures thriving in the absence of centralized hegemony: diverse, disunified, not following one script.[28]

We also have proof of extraordinary innovations in military technology and strategy in Nubia, which the locals so often used defensively against the Egyptians. To survive, generations of Nubians honed their skills in battle and sold that prized asset to the highest bidder, working for Egyptian overlords as police, mercenaries, or bodyguards when the kings there were strong, but taking that military ability back to their homeland when Egypt again fell into ruin.[29]

As the power of the Egyptian kings waned in the 20th dynasty, their colonial incursions into Nubia and Kush became more infrequent and the violence less brutal—not because Egypt was any kinder, but because its economic and political destabilization stopped the kings from pushing their forces south. As the Egyptians themselves suffered from repeated invasions of Sea Peoples from the Mediterranean and frequent Libyan raids from the Western Desert, their hegemony in Nubia contracted from the fourth cataract to the second, and then farther north still until Egypt's once mighty occupation was gone, its forces relegated to staying behind its historic southern boundary at Elephantine, at the first cataract.

The brutal incursions of Ramses III were only a few hundred years in the past by the time the Kushite hegemony began its rise.[30] We can imagine that the dehumanization, captivity, burnings, stranglings, dismemberments, and killings remained firmly fixed in the cultural memory of the Indigenous peoples, whether they were of the co-opted ruling class or members of the diverse groups of pastoral nomads, farmers, and miners who occupied the region. With the fall of Egypt's 20th dynasty, Nubia would regain control over its gold resources and conduct its own trade with regions farther to the south as well as with the land of Punt—probably located in Eritrea, Ethiopia, or even Yemen, and the source of frankincense and myrrh, ebony and ivory. With that wealth, Kush could finally grasp its destiny.

THE CULTURAL ADAPTATION OF A BRUTALIZED PEOPLE

Because the Kushites had been so ruthlessly colonized for so many thousands of years, we might imagine them repelled by all things Egyptian, holding a deep-seated hatred in their breasts for the cruel overlords and enslavers. We'd be surprised, then, to find King Alara—the eighth-century B.C. founder of the Napatan dynasty—calling himself a "son of Amun," after the Theban god of pre-creation. Or to see that one Kushite chief took on the throne names of the warlord king Thutmose III, who had inflicted so much pain on the Nubian people—a decision comparable perhaps to naming an Indigenous American Christopher Columbus. How are we to understand such Egyptian ciphers of control in the hands of the Kushites?

Xenophobia is obvious and easily recognized for the cruel indignity that it is, transforming someone with skin color, dress, physiognomy, or general appearance that's different from the dominant culture into something inhuman, even immoral—something that needs a firm hand to control it or even expunge it from the world. The Egyptians reminded foreigners of this on every temple they ever built, documenting their destruction of un-Egyptian peoples with the mace, the scimitar, the chariot, and the spear.

Colonial occupation, on the other hand, is messy and entangled, with both the dominant and oppressed segments of society borrowing from one another with mutual influence. Cultural adaptation allows people to deliberately take on elements of the dominant culture of power while maintaining some of their own ways and abandoning others. During the time that Egypt occupied Nubia, Nubians could enter into Egyptian society by engaging in complicated borrowings and synthesis of cultural identities, adopting proper dress and cultural traits, using accepted language and names, while maintaining elements of their Native identity. Maiherperi, for example, was a tall, Black man from Nubia who became one of the royal bodyguards during the reign of Hatshepsut. He was a man so valued that he was afforded the honor of burial in the Valley of the Kings itself.[31] His mummy shows the differences in his physiognomy—facial features, tighter curled hair, darker skin, height. Even his Book of the Dead papyrus depicts him as a darker man compared to the Egyptians—themselves people of color to be sure, but not that dark.

Maiherperi probably originated from the Medjay tribe of Nubia, a group of bowmen and pastoral nomads prized for their martial skills. But he was buried in an Egyptian coffin in a rock-cut tomb, not a pan grave typical of many of his people.[32] His grave included all the elements of traditional, elite burial, and proof of Egyptian religious beliefs, indicating that he, too, could enter the Field of Reeds, the Egyptian name for the afterlife. By co-opting the dominant culture, Maiherperi engaged in a complex game of identity blending. And he did all of this actively, to improve his station and status. He was connected. He was rich.

But cultural borrowings were ideologically fraught too, implicitly communicating to people who came from Nubia, Libya, the Levant, or farther afield that their ways were problematic, less than, discardable. Foreigners could only be a part of the show if they dressed like an Egyptian, spoke like an Egyptian, followed Egyptian elite mores, used the Egyptian legal system, and took on Egyptian styles of worship. Every Nubian moving in elite Egyptian circles of power knew he had to emulate Egypt in crucial ways, fraught or not. In that case, though, there could be agency in deliberate cultural borrowing.

At the same time, when one culture has been highly dominant for so long, retaining even the smallest elements of one's identity can be a form of resistance. Names in Egypt sometimes retained indications of a person's identity, for instance. Indeed, the ancient name Panehsy means "the Nubian" in Egyptian, just as the modern Egyptian name Nubi, common in Luxor, denotes a southern identity, a reminder of a culture retained in a new context. Migrant Sea Peoples and Libyans could also retain their foreign names with syllabic spellings in hieroglyphs. One 21st-dynasty coffin in the Vatican Museums, reused by a probable mother-daughter pair, betrays the Libyan names of Ikhy and Emdidit.[33] Neither has any meaning in the Egyptian language, but they were inscribed on an expensive coffin with complicated Book of the Dead scenes nonetheless, leaving no doubt that the owners had successfully blended Egyptian and non-Egyptian identities into an innovative synthesis. These women were Egyptian. But also something else.

Even the 18th-dynasty bodyguard Maiherperi bore a strange name broadcasting his Medjay identity. In the Egyptian language, his name meant "Lion upon the Battlefield"—a shout-out to his fighting prowess, to be sure, but also signaling his origins in the south, where lions still dwelled. His people proved themselves such sharp-witted fighters, in fact, that the name Medjay became the word for "police" in ancient Egypt—that is, paid strong men. Egyptian villages employed Medjay police whether or not they were actually Medjay tribesmen—and the ethnic designation became shorthand for "soldier for hire"—like the Sherden Sea Peoples working as mercenaries in the army of Ramses II, or the Bengali northern Hindus working in the Bengal Army for the East India Company in the 18th century.[34]

In the end, all peoples could be included in Egyptian society if they adopted some of its culture. But non-Egyptian elements were always maintained and integrated, many becoming seemingly Egyptian too—like the horse and chariot, an import from the Levant, eventually used as the main method of Egyptian kingly display in the Ramesside period.[35] As each wave of newcomers settled in, people's original identities slowly hybridized and transformed, blended into the melting pot that was this corner of northeast Africa, where fierce debate over ethnic identity, caste, and skin color continues to rage today.

Egypt's colonial occupation of northern Nubia traumatized the local population so much that the elites in power would have had to come from the less devastated southern reaches of Nubia—and even then, their leaders still relied on many Egyptian systems of religion, language, and governance. When Nubia was under Egyptian control, local social systems and cohesion were weakened, subjecting the people to savage exploitations. But with resistance, co-option, and adaptations, local elites could walk the long, hard road to recovery. Taharqa's native kingdom would rise—but when it did, it would retain many elements from its oppressors.[36]

In the same way, Martin Luther King, Jr., used the Christian Church as his chief tool of organization in his campaign for civil rights, even though that religion had been imposed upon his people after the African religions had been brutally suppressed.

In ancient Nubia, the origins of the Kushite Empire were at the fourth cataract. The peoples between the third and sixth cataracts were much more resilient compared to those between the first and second cataracts for the simple reason that it was harder for Egypt to reach so far south. The southern region was less devastated, more culturally whole. Horrible things had happened there too, but not the long, drawn-out systematic colonial destruction experienced by the north, which had felt the boot of Egypt's domination on its back for generations on end. In the south, Egypt's invasions had brought flashes of intense trauma, including the sacking of towns and Thutmose I's previously mentioned murder of their king. The Kushites might also have remembered the Egyptians carrying off their young princes to be reeducated at the Egyptian court and transformed into loyal, properly cowed vassals. Such misdeeds lived deep in the cultural memory of Kush, to be sure. But the land's social systems remained intact.

After the fall of Egypt's 20th dynasty, the Kushite region would go through a renaissance in military technology, economic connection, monumental building, and religious fervor, mixing local and Egyptian methodologies to their advantage. And from the city of Napata, the center of their military and religious power, the Kushites would lead Egypt's 25th dynasty as imperialists themselves.

THE LAW-AND-ORDER PARTY

The king who established the 25th dynasty was a certain Piankhy. This warrior from Kush would take on the competing Libyan Egyptian kings who ruled from different strongholds, defeating them all and establishing Kushite rule over Egypt. This was not the beginning or end of Kushite power. The 25th dynasty merely marked a 100-year period when the Kushites occupied their northern neighbor as an imperial force, starting with Piankhy's invasions.

On a massive granodiorite stela set up at Jebel Barkal to document his victory,[37] Piankhy lays out his detailed narrative. This object is almost all we have of his military narrative, and it is a delightfully innovative mash-up of blended cultural elements resulting in an extraordinary picture of transculturalism. The language and text are Egyptian. The stone is Kushite.

Piankhy's reign is such a mélange of cultural Egyptian Kushite construction that even his name is a confusing mishmash of two cultures, so much so that we don't know if we should pronounce it with the Egyptian *ankh* element, as Piankhy, or without it, as Piye. In any case, the Piye element was certainly Kushite, written phonetically; whether the *ankh* was an added epithet—"May he live!"—or a vocalized part of his name is still debated. No matter how it was pronounced, his Kushite Egyptian hybrid name was written in the Egyptian hieroglyphic script.[38]

The text of his stela is written in an archaic Middle Egyptian, showing the Kushites' interest in utilizing an older, ostensibly purer, Egyptian language of the past—with the intent of making the king's actions seem part of something greater, more profound. Piankhy's use of Middle Egyptian is as affected as Joseph Smith using his own made-up version of Elizabethan English in his Book of Mormon, grasping at the cachet of an older tongue to connect his beliefs with the gravity of a bygone age.

Piankhy's language is stilted and strange, since Middle Egyptian wasn't in use anymore and must have been very different from what people were actually speaking. The stela reads like a U.S. presidential speech written in Shakespearean or even Chaucerian English. No matter what form of the language Piankhy used, though, it is telling that he chose Egyptian for his declaration of victory over Egypt. Without any Indigenous writing system of his own, Piankhy naturally gravitated toward the script and language of power, the region's lingua franca, in the same way that Native peoples of Mexico might use Spanish, not Mixteco or Náhuatl, in formal legal documents.

Piankhy displayed other Nubian cultural traits on his stela. The artifact itself is unusual—round-topped like an Egyptian stela, yes, but much thicker. Also, strangely, inscriptions appear on the edges as well as the flat sides. In Egypt, such a stela would have been placed against a wall, but this document apparently was meant to be read by someone walking around it in the center of a temple courtyard.

The images at the top are also unabashedly Nubian, depicting extraordinary details never seen on a traditional Egyptian victory stela. We see a number of men bowing down on the ground, some of them wearing a cobra on the forehead, as if Piankhy were collecting defeated and humbled kings. Other kneeling figures are wearing feathers on their heads. In the text, Piankhy derisively calls these Libyan Egyptian rulers "feather wearers," a moniker probably comparable to many modern ethnic dehumanizations such as "towelhead" or "wetback." Obviously, just because his Nubian people had been the object of derision from Egyptian colonists didn't mean he couldn't serve up his own xenophobic epithets.

The victory stela shows a horse, too, in the process of being led to Piankhy as an offering of surrender by one of the defeated Libyan Egyptian kings, a certain Nimlot. It's an honest depiction of a moment in his conquest of which Piankhy was obviously proud. But no Egyptian victory stela has ever shown such a detail; Egyptians generally save such things for the textual description. This was a hybrid Kushite Egyptian monument for a hybrid Kushite Egyptian audience.

At the center of Piankhy's stela is the more recognizable and acceptably formal Egyptian figure of Amun-Re, king of the gods, the double-plumed divinity whose home base was originally Thebes but who was also fervently claimed by the Kushites. He is depicted in the Egyptian manner here, not in his pastoral, ram-god form. Behind him stands his consort, Mut, the fiercely strong mother goddess, also in human form, not her local leonine self.

The ruler, purposefully erased by a later 26th-dynasty conqueror, wore an innovative crown to mark himself as not just a Kushite king, but also as emperor of northeast Africa. He showed himself with the kilt and bare chest of an Egyptian king, but his headgear would have been clearly Nubian—the cap crown with two cobras on his brow.

Ideological symbols of "good kingship" also worked on the minds of Nubian people. The Kushite cap crown was never relinquished by the 25th-dynasty kings; they rarely wore the classically Egyptian cloth nemes headdress and never the blue crown, which was perhaps too evocative of the invading Egyptian warrior-kings who had caused them so much distress in years past. The cap crown was the Kushites' way of maintaining their Nubian identity while simultaneously claiming the power of Egyptian divine kingship.

The Egyptians had dominated Piankhy's ancestors for millennia, but now, as king, he nonetheless picked from an array of royal emblems, Kushite and Egyptian, choosing what worked for him in his current circumstances. His rule is a construct of diverse contradictions that make sense in the vortex of colonialism, resistance, and resilience.

Other details from the stela speak to Piankhy's cultural hybridity: The composite Egyptian-style bodies are retained for the formal figures of king, god, goddess, and standing supplicants. But the kneeling kings and princes are shown in perspective. The four men with cobras on their brows and cartouche names above their heads have confused many an Egyptologist who sees a simplistic lack of understanding of Egyptian kingship on the part of Piankhy, because he allowed those men to keep their royal symbols of kingship rather than claiming them for himself. But if we view Piankhy's stela as a creative manufacture of power, not a series of gauche mistakes, perhaps we can understand that this Kushite king was visually establishing himself as not just a king, but also as a king of kings, an emperor.

There are other little tells: Piankhy ordered the stonecutter to carve the rebellious Nimlot following his wife, rather than preceding her, presumably a Kushite insult to the supplicant's manhood, if there ever was one. Nimlot trails the woman, debased, leading the horse and holding a sistrum, the instrument of a woman. His wife is shown nearly a head taller than he, a visual put-down of a king whose defeat is told in excruciating detail on the stela.

A DECENTRALIZED WORLD

Entering the first millennium B.C., Egypt had just been through a time of drought and mass migration. Repeated influxes of people into the country had culminated in a mixing of many different cultural and ethnic identities, resulting in perhaps the country's most diverse population to date. Some people identified as Libyans, some as Canaanites, Nubians, or Kushites, but many now incorporated, blended, and borrowed cultural elements from the Egyptians. Many Egyptians must have had mixed parentage, part Egyptian and part immigrant—especially if they grew up near Egyptian garrisons along the Nile in Nubia or in the Levant.[39] Some probably even had clever methods of moving between identities, just as people today code-switch from a migrant ethnic identity in the home neighborhood to another "Whiter" identity of dominant American culture in the professional workplace. It all depends on which identity holds the most power.

The lead-up to the 25th dynasty was a time full of all the fragmentation, conflict, and competition associated with not having a strong king. Politically, Egypt was ruled by about seven different factions, the land carved up by chiefs and kinglets. Few monuments were built. Elites had no fine tombs. Statues were few and far between. Gold mining and crafting were luxuries few could afford.

Piankhy would change all of that. And he would tell the people to be grateful for his intercession. Piankhy may not have monopolized the symbols of kingship on his stela—including the cobra and the cartouche—as an Egyptian would have, but he did claim a superior knowledge of the patriotic ideals of ma'at. He equated a lack of strong kingship with immorality. His victory stela is a master class in demonstrating how people need a good king to be good themselves.

Egyptologists tend to denigrate the nuanced political wheeling and dealing of such decentralized periods as nothing more than a time of lawlessness, a lack of beauty, a dearth of temple building, an increase in dangers and aggressions from without and within. But such times were also characterized by political creativity, coalition building, and a lack of effective ideological control within the political arenas. We Egyptologists are members of the ancient Egyptian law-and-order party, disturbed when we cannot identify authoritarianism because we believe it the only sustainable driver of an ancient civilization worthy of our notice, and without a strong king, culture was impermanent and primitive and lacking ma'at. Maybe it's time to see the good king as the long-term source of intense human discord and deprivation in the first place.

We Egyptologists often become apologists for a return to good kingship as the only thing that can save people from themselves. We want the ancient peoples to reconnect with all those elements that provided a kind of national pride, believing that those great temples, tombs, monuments, and kings really did create trickle-down wealth to everyone else.

In effect, the ancient Egyptians have hoodwinked us into believing that those periods of monarchical centralization were exactly the times when most ancient Egyptians themselves would have preferred to live. The ideology of authoritarianism is so seductive that it continues to work on us from thousands of years in the past, making us believe that uniformity, monumentalism, and job creation were preferred—even if freedoms and fairer distributions of wealth were taken away, even if the jobs paid the ancient version of minimum wage.

This is exactly the kind of conversation we are having now about the role of government in the United States, and society's balance between controlling wealth for the few and equitable distribution to the many. It is perhaps no surprise that those on the side of the status quo use the ideological phrase "Give me liberty or give me death," when the "freedoms" currently demanded—defending men's rights, owning assault weapons, imposing Christian fundamentalism, enacting abortion restrictions, and purveying social discrimination—support a dominant White caste in maintaining wealth inequality to their benefit. "All lives matter," they say, when even the aversion to wearing masks during the COVID-19 pandemic is wrapped up in an ideological call for individual freedoms that are really caste power (especially as the novel coronavirus disproportionately killed more people of color in the United States than anyone else[40]).

It may seem, on the surface, that the liberty-or-death party would rather not have their government step in with a strong hand, but that's not the case at all. Instead, they want a crackdown on their enemies—that is, a government that maintains power only for its entitled culture of dominance. And so White supremacists in full assault gear stormed the

Capitol Building to demand freedoms while implicitly communicating that only their authoritarianism can save the nation. Ideologies are conflicting, complicated, confusing, veiled with morality and fear, and always obfuscating who is actually being served by the belief system.

The kings of Kush would also utilize a law-and-order ideology of good kingship and ma'at, not really recognizing that their own unimpeded growth in the south was the result of Egypt's decentralization and the cessation of its toxic incursions.

The Kushites now imposed much the same authoritarian system that had been thrust upon them—but from the opposite direction, using all of Egypt's ideological tricks to reimpose authoritarian government on the country itself (though interestingly, not with the same violent cruelty that had been forced upon them, if we are to believe texts like Piankhy's victory stela). The Kushite kings were on a mission to prove that true Egyptian beliefs existed in their hearts and originated in their lands. They were perhaps the first Afrocentrists: patriarchal adherents to proving not only that they were the first, but also that they were the best.

A TIME WITHOUT MONUMENTS

Egyptologists have invented a handy term for dynasties 21 to 25: the "Third Intermediate Period," with the focus being on the "intermediate" state between good Egyptian kingships. So weak were the rulers of dynasties 21, 22, 23, and 24 that they overlapped, competed, and carved Egypt into pieces. Instead of a centralized government, political fragmentation was the order of the day, characterized by repeated influxes of non-Egyptian migrants in waves and almost no construction of monuments such as pyramids and stone temples.

But the 25th dynasty doesn't quite belong in the category of the Third Intermediate Period. Indeed, those last 100 years saw the return of strong, centralized, Kushite kingship with its concomitant monumental building, political centralization, elite co-option, and military campaigns, all the things a good Egyptian authoritarian would want. By the time King Taharqa ascended the throne in 690 B.C., temples were being built all around Egypt, and from scratch, not from reused stones and statuary. Indeed, the main reason Egyptologists insist on calling Kushite rule "intermediate" is because it is not Egyptian. Lasting from about 750 to 650 B.C., the 25th dynasty was anything but decentralized, as the previous dynasties had been. It just wasn't Egyptian.[41]

The idea that the 25th dynasty belongs to the Third Intermediate Period, and not to the so-called Late Period with its classical texts and cultural revitalization, is a result of Egyptological racism, plain and simple.[42] Through that racism, the Kushite rulers were viewed as less centralized, weak, and foreign. But the Kushite kings, ruling from Napata, united Nubia and Egypt in a grasp that stretched for thousands of miles, from the Delta shores to the sixth Nile cataract and even farther south.

To make that governance work, the Kushite leadership had to be imperial in its organization, demanding a true delegation of power to vassal kings and local mayors so the king could administer over his vast expanse of territory from his capital city of Napata. Nevertheless, many an Egyptian history book says that because the Kushite kings left local men in charge of important regional centers, the 25th dynasty never had full direct control of Egypt at all, overlooking the fact that vassals were part and parcel of imperial rule.

Those history books do not make the same disparaging conclusions about West Asian imperialists such as the Assyrians, neo-Babylonians, or Persians—and certainly not about the Great White Hope, Alexander the Great, the king of political delegation. In fact, direct control of Egypt through loyal lieutenants only functioned within its traditional boundaries, in a country united by quick travel on an unobstructed Nile. The Kushite kings thus utilized an imperial structure because they ruled a massive, disconnected, and diverse region. In other words, the Kushites ruled from Napata not because they were too weak to rule Egypt personally, but because they did so as imperialists who delegated power. They would rule like any good imperial overlords, through a co-opted set of elites who could administer local places, report to their imperial leaders, pay their taxes, and draft men into the imperial army.[43] How else was one supposed to rule a territory that stretched 1,500 miles from tip to tip?

The Kushites were, arguably, ahead of their time, creating a flexible imperial structure on the African continent, using military strikes expeditiously, and largely relying on established elites as political connectors. It is the Egyptological unfamiliarity with imperial rule in its most basic forms that makes us unable to recognize the Kushite genius. Also overlooked is the ideological glue holding their imperial system together: the morality of a good kingship that could keep everyone safe.

A KINDER, GENTLER IMPERIALISM

Kings Alara and Kashta were the first known Kushite rulers to embrace the stereotypical vision of the Nubian warlord, able to strategize and overpower other polities at will. Nubians had been acting as paid strongmen for Egyptian kings for millennia; now, they would capitalize on the Egyptians' fear of their military abilities.

When King Piankhy ascended the throne, he decided to send his Kushite army north into Egypt, intending to sweep all those different Libyan Egyptian factions aside and consolidate the land for Kush. In 750 B.C. the Kushite Empire was born, and its first foreign territory was Upper Egypt. With hardly a battle, Piankhy claimed the religious center of Thebes and its adjacent territories along the Nile. He allowed the erstwhile ruler of Thebes, Rudamun, to retreat to Heracleopolis after the latter pledged his loyalty to his new overlord. The Libyan Egyptian God's Wife of Amun, Shepenwepet I, was allowed to stay on in her position at Thebes as Egypt's most important priestess, but she was made to adopt the Kushite royal woman Amenirdis I as the next God's Wife.[44] Perhaps the Kushites thought it impious to shove such a sacred woman aside. But they knew they had to infiltrate the high priesthood of Amun nonetheless.

King Piankhy then moved north, where Egypt had been carved into a number of different political regions, each ruled by a different Libyan warlord. Many of the warlords called themselves king. Others were Chiefs of Ma, according to their tribal heritage. There was also a powerful ruler of the western Delta city of Sais, a man named Tefnakht, who didn't even bother to call himself "king," just the "Great Chief of the West." Tefnakht had the Delta under his control and was the main competitor to Piankhy and the Kushites. When Tefnakht started to move south into Theban territory, Piankhy ordered his forces to meet him. But first, Piankhy said, they would pray; nothing could diminish King Piankhy's righteousness—or his need to tell us about it—and he promptly engaged in sacred ablutions in Thebes to gain the blessings of Amun.

As Tefnakht proceeded up the Nile, he formed a coalition against Piankhy that included many Libyan Egyptian chiefs, including Nimlot of Hermopolis who had previously sworn his allegiance to the Kushites. Vexed, Piankhy tells us in his victory stela that he immediately laid siege to Nimlot's city, bombarding it daily until the stronghold capitulated; the Kushites describe how the foul smell of death emanated from inside the city walls at its surrender.

Piankhy made his way inside and claimed everything in the storehouses and treasuries. The city's female residents brought him a special horse as a gift, begging for lenience with the best they had. When Piankhy entered the stables and saw that the horses were starving, he remarked that it was the foulest crime of all. The Kushites cunningly and deliberately set themselves up as kinder, gentler authoritarians.

With Hermopolis in hand, Piankhy moved farther north, forcing the surrender of King Peftjauwybast of Heracleopolis, as well as the capitulation of multiple strongholds near the entrance to Fayum, including the old Middle Kingdom town of Itjy-tawy. Piankhy tried to persuade the recalcitrant leaders of Memphis to surrender, and his victory stela mentions this famed lenience: "Look at the nomes of the south! No one was slain there, except the rebels who blasphemed god."[45] Piankhy pushed his Kushite compassionate conservatism, which put respect for divinity first and treated human life with the dignity he believed it deserved.

When Memphis finally fell, every other rival king and chief relented and finally gave their allegiance to Piankhy, we are told. The pious Kushite king made time to give offerings to the god Ptah in Memphis and then to Atum in Heliopolis. Piankhy had been trained from childhood, apparently, that war victories had to be dedicated to the gods in a temple. Finally, he headed to Sais, where he received the allegiance of Tefnakht in person.

By moving north, Piankhy was drawing the attention of rival empires. The first millennium B.C. was an age of imperialism. The Assyrians were on the rise in West Asia, looking to expand their vast empire with more territory in which to rape and pillage. As for the ancient Egyptians— well, they never really got the hang of the whole empire thing, having never really held one themselves. Even with the southern Levant and Lower Nubia in its grasp, Egypt had no stomach for the constant expansion, diminishing returns, and deputation of power. Egypt had no need for multitudes of enslaved people and, one could posit, little tolerance for the coexistence of different cultural and religious groups. The Egyptian system was more of a nationalistic hegemony that would sometimes expand into the Levant and Nubia, always stopping at its preferred boundaries: as far northeast as Megiddo or Kadesh in West Asia, and as far south as the fourth cataract on the upper Nile.

When its kings had been strong, Egypt instituted a colonial occupation of those foreign places, taking the resources that it wanted and putting up forts to protect and control the movement of goods.[46] But that was about it as far as imperial structures were concerned; the country had no need or will to expand farther like Assyria and Kush were now doing. Agricultural production was so high that it fed a large population from which to draft ample labor. Once it got gold from Nubia and wood and tin from Syria, Egypt had just about everything it needed.

The empires of West Asia, on the other hand, were ever hungry, willing to go to faraway regions to gain territory—and Egypt was the grand prize, with all of its ample wheat, gold, and stone. West Asian empires were honed on competition and constant warlording, coalition breaking and building, cycles of domination and cruelty against which Egypt had little defense. West Asia was a place of short dynasties, where kings were never really considered divine, no matter what they claimed, because they never stayed on the throne long enough.[47]

Like West Asia, Kush was a hardscrabble place, largely lacking agricultural resources; Kush would now look to Egypt as a territory to provide what it did not have.

Once empire had become an established political machine in East Africa and West Asia, Egypt would find itself hopelessly squeezed between the two, with no hope of withstanding such brutal military forces. It had been spoiled by two millennia of easily gotten grain, beer, and mineral wealth beyond the imagination of most ancient peoples; its kingship was so divinized that the monarch had forgotten how to fight at all, and was no match for the warrior-kings who would come its way from north and south. Regicide had been so rare in Egypt—the known instances could be counted on one hand—that courtiers were hopelessly unskilled in the arts of assassination or coups and thus easy targets for infiltrators with darker methodologies.

Egypt had a bright target painted on its back. Any invading imperial army that managed to get through the natural boundaries of sea, desert, and cataracts to control this place—and somehow ship goods back home—would be wealthy beyond belief, because Egypt was endowed with precious minerals and ample wheat. For millennia, rulers had bragged about their access to the mines in their eastern deserts and in Nubia. Now that imperial armies had fine-tuned the ability to move troops, forge iron weapons, develop fast chariots, domesticate the horse and, in some places, even the camel, Egyptian gold would draw empires like flies to a rotting corpse.

To this point, grain was not generally something that had been shipped around the ancient world. It was heavy, cumbersome, local. But once transportation technologies on land, sea, and river improved, distant empires had more and more reason to invade Egypt and develop mechanisms to exploit all the wheat and barley the country could produce.

In many ways, the fat, juicy kernels of grain gave Egypt its divine kingship in the first place. The land's first king was said to be Osiris, a grain god of death and rebirth, of black earth ready to miraculously sprout, of green shoots and new harvests, of beer and wanton drunkenness. Egypt's divine kingship advertised its wealth in grain.[48] Although that was a useful ideology at home as an internal control mechanism promising riches to the people, it was not necessarily the kind of thing one wanted to broadcast to hungry foreigners with fierce invading armies. Now, Egypt was on every imperialist's hit list.

Divine kingship only worked when there were no outside threats.[49] It was a system of gaslighting that communicated best to those on the inside—the king of his castle manipulating his nuclear family within four walls, so to speak. Divine kingship had little effect on outsiders who remained unmoved by its powers, especially when some invading forces could so easily beat the Egyptian armies. Worse still, divine kingship attracted those foreign authoritarian personalities seduced by a place that allowed its kings to be not just chosen by the gods, but also to become one of them.

The era repeatedly forced Egypt to feel the bite of empire—and once the outside realms had the ability to breach geographic barriers more easily with mobile troops, it was done for. The country could not maintain its god-given right to rule internally and would be forever forced to give it away to foreigners, including Darius, Alexander, Caesar, Antony, and Hadrian—all of whom were inducted into secret rituals of Egyptian kingship. The Kushite 25th dynasty was only the first of a series of imperial aggressors longing for Egypt's divine kingship. It would also be the most forgiving.

MORE EGYPTIAN THAN THE EGYPTIANS

From their capital of Napata, the Kushites now held Egypt in their grasp. In his victory stela,[50] Piankhy felt the need to justify and share a long and involved narrative of his takeover of Egypt, how some of the kings capitulated immediately, and how the king of Heracleopolis wouldn't give in. Piankhy is a moral compass. Excuses for violence were carved into stone. Heracleopolis's recalcitrance demanded a siege from Piankhy's forces, who let nothing in or out and bombarded the city every day until it fell.

In his monumental communication, Piankhy discusses his ability to defeat Egypt militarily and highlights how he brought back religious righteousness and the rule of law, showing the feather-wearing Libyan

Egyptians what it truly meant to worship god properly, how to rule a people with morality. Piankhy used religion as his chief means of claiming power, displaying his fundamentalist ways for all to see. There is even a section on the victory stela describing how he did not allow some of the Libyan chiefs to enter the Temple of Amun-Re because they had not been circumcised and—worse yet—had recently eaten fish.

The stela displays how Piankhy was a better follower of complex ritual demands than those living in Egypt. In an Egypt now buffeted by different ethnic groups, the Kushite king could transform himself into the pure Egyptian leader teaching a bunch of men who self-identified as Libyan how to Egyptianize—like saying "Speak English!" to recent immigrants in the United States—and pointing out that they were doing it wrong. This likely set the Libyans against the native Egyptian population, to whom Piankhy was signaling his greater piety.

In practice, this Kushite king was out-Egyptianizing the Libyans, using religious weight, decorum, formality, and even superior cultural familiarity to present himself as the ruler whose homeland was the true originator of Egyptian divinity, the source of its Nile flood, and of creation itself. Piankhy's message was, essentially, that the Kushites were the real Egyptians, and the Libyans should go back where they came from.

Piankhy's monumental legitimization had to be done in the Egyptian language with the support of Egyptian gods. On his victory stela, he tells us: "Hear of what I did, exceeding the ancestors, I the king, image of god, Living likeness of Atum! Who left the womb marked as ruler, Feared by those greater than he! His father knew, his mother perceived: He would be ruler from the egg, The Good God, beloved of the gods, the Son of Re, who acts with his arms, Piye [Piankhy] Beloved-of-Amun."[51]

The victory stela communicated how Piankhy's army had overwhelmed the city of Memphis like a flood, killing many and taking many more as living captives. But Piankhy was clear that he did not harm the Temple of Ptah, instead making sacred offerings to the gods there, complete with the sacrifice of bulls, calves, fowl, and all good things. He also made sure the temple priests were paid and maintained: a clever political tactic to win over people, or perhaps even to set the Egyptians working in the temples against their Libyan overlords.

Piankhy's stela was all about order—religious and political—and an attempt to get people to break up with their previous patrons and follow him instead. But his cultural insecurity was palpable in an Egyptian world that treated Nubians like second-class citizens. He was like America's first Black president, who had to respect every rule of White House decorum times 10 (even a tan suit was considered an abomination[52])— though presidents from the dominant White caste could (and did) get away with all kinds of norm breaking.

At Jebel Barkal, Piankhy also renewed a temple (B500) in which he documented his takeover of Egypt and the surrender of Hermopolis after the siege, again proudly showing that same scene of the horse being brought to him by the defeated women as a peace offering. He also ordered monumental scenes of himself on a chariot mowing down Egyptians—a reverse Ramesside smiting motif of extraordinary proportions in which the southerners dominate the northerners. In another scene, all the collected Libyan Egyptian kings are on their bellies, kissing the earth before their Kushite conqueror. Behind them are dozens more horses, brought as tribute to this equine-obsessed king.[53]

Piankhy also built a new temple pylon at Jebel Barkal, which he embellished with four massive cedar trunks from Lebanon, shipping them across the Mediterranean and a thousand miles upriver to the temple. Each trunk became a flagstaff, covered with gold and electrum and placed on a bronze disk upon which the name of a particular enemy was written—in the Meroitic language, but using a modified Egyptian script.[54]

The Kushite kings now went from being leaders of "wretched Kush," as Egyptian texts often described them, to presenting themselves as the chief guardians of the true Egyptian way of life in the face of foreign interlopers who were not keeping the temples ritually protected. In other words, the new line of Kushite rulers was openly signaling, in conservative Egyptian fashion, that the gods were on their side, that they were the true keepers of the Egyptian cultural flame. Piankhy tells us in his victory stela that he cleansed temples with natron and incense, clearly implying that they needed to be purified after the desecrations of the Libyans. His conquest was presented as one of piety, not personal ambition, and was never pursued with gratuitous violence.

Kush was what historians often call a secondary state—a fancy way of saying that it had acquired complexity and methods of rule from a primary state (in this case, Egypt).[55] Secondary state formation explains how the oppressed can use the tools of their oppressors to beat them at their own game, learning from the systems imposed upon them and developing their own work-arounds.

Egypt brought systems of exploitation, taxation and bureaucracy, government, and military control to Nubia. It was in the primary state of Egypt that divine kingship was first invented and perfected. When Egypt colonized Nubia, it brought those systems with it, and the Kushites would learn how to manipulate people, piously imperializing Egypt in its turn.

At the same time, the Kushite kings weren't slavish to Egyptian ways. They were no mere copyists; they used their own names, placing the monikers Kashta, Shabaka, Shebitku, Taharqa, and Tantamani—all of them obviously phonetically spelled and not Egyptian—into the ovals of Egyptian royal cartouches in a deliberate blend of cultural powers.

The Kushites did their homework, too, delving into the deepest reaches of Egyptian history to manufacture ideological power. Each of these kings took on Egyptian throne names obviously reminiscent of Egypt's 4th and 5th dynasties, evoking the pyramid-building, sun-worshipping kings of many thousands of years ago, giving these rulers a hybrid identity that allowed them to code-switch between Egyptian and Kushite monikers.

We can never know to what degree the Egyptians implanted their religion in Nubia, or if they were, in actuality, linking to preexisting religious beliefs from Nubia. But by imposing Egyptian versions of Amun onto Napata, and by claiming Upper Nubia as a wellspring for kingship and the Eye of Re, the imported Egyptian ideologies would end up empowering the Kushites in the end. The Kushite monarchs could claim to be not just imperial rulers of the Egyptians, but also the inventors of perfected Egyptian kingship itself. They had been the first, the Kushites could claim, and without their homeland, Egypt and all its agricultural riches and temples would not even exist. Without Nubian gold, Nubian floodwaters, Nubian sunlight, Nubian patriarchy, Nubian feminine protection, and Nubian culture, none of Egypt's majesty would have been even remotely possible.

This was the message of Piankhy as he established the 25th dynasty with his imperial invasion. He expressed his schemes through a religious lens, a temple lens, a divine lens. Taharqa would do the same.

TAHARQA'S POWER GRAB

Taharqa had grown up watching his father, uncle, and brother run a huge empire, and lending his strength and strategy to the cause as a young man. In 701 B.C., possibly during the reign of his brother Shabataka, he was dispatched north to the Levantine town of Eltekeh as general of the Kushite forces facing the Assyrian foe Sennacherib. It was a move that pushed Kushite imperial aspirations farther than ever before. Assyrian texts tell us that the armies met on a plain, and that Sennacherib claimed unmitigated victory.[56] That being said, the actual outcome of the battle remains unclear to historians. Jerusalem would be besieged by the Assyrians, but not taken—perhaps saved by Taharqa's army, or by an epidemic that ravaged the ranks of the Assyrians, or even by the palace coup that would end Sennacherib's life. The more conflicting the sources, the more complicated the historical narrative becomes. Whatever the details, the Kushites were now engaging in the Levant against an Assyrian war machine that slaughtered, impaled, and deported multitudes of people as it plowed through the region. West Asia was a shark zone of trouble, and the Kushites were wading in.

Piankhy had ruled for 31 years, the perfect amount of time to cement power and alliances. After Piankhy, his brother Shabaka, and then his son Shabataka, took the throne. The circumstances of Taharqa's subsequent ascension are unclear—How did he take power? Was there violent competition for the top spot?—but it was presented as divinely sanctioned. Taharqa only tells us that the king (whom he does not name) called him together with other candidates and chose him from among them, recording in his Kawa Stela V, "I had captivated the hearts of the patricians, and love of me was with everyone."[57] Vague enough, but telling. Kushite kingship was bestowed through merit and grace.

When that unspecified king died, it was Taharqa's chance to show his might. He said, "It was after the falcon had departed to heaven that I received the crown in Memphis, when my father Amun commanded me to place all lands and all foreign countries beneath my sandals . . ."[58] Apparently, Taharqa needed to be chosen by god, king, and courtiers—and perhaps it was his military leadership that set him apart.

Taharqa would combine elements from both Egyptian and Kushite cultures in every relief and statue of himself. He showed himself idealized and strong with the broad shoulders and trim waist of Khafre, the 4th-dynasty king, wearing the typical Egyptian royal kilt. But he was clearly a Kushite—in body, headgear, even facial features—claiming Egypt as part of his imperial domain, openly marking the foreign origin of his rule. The Taharqa name was Kushite, and he always wore his Kushite headdress, the cap with two cobras on the forehead. Even his succession was openly un-Egyptian, not following the typical father-to-son lineage. These Kushites followed a different way, a more practical way in a more competitive arena, choosing the most powerful warlord to rule instead of birthright.

When King Taharqa was reunited with his beloved mother in Kush after his coronation in Egypt, he tells us that "she found me crowned upon the throne of Horus, having received the diadems of Re, the two uraei [cobras] joined at my head."[59] A tearful reunion, we can be sure, but his mention of her was also politically expedient. A good mother standing front and center in support implies a good son. Taharqa used all the propagandistic methods at his disposal to show that his reign was blessed by the gods and their moral codes.

But events transpired in his sixth year that proved beyond a shadow of a doubt that he benefited from visible divine intervention. In another stela set up at the Nubian Temple of Kawa, Taharqa documented a massive Nile inundation, supposedly bigger than anyone had ever seen before:

> When the season occurred for the rising of the inundation, it was rising abundantly every day. It spent many days rising even at the rate of one cubit per day. And it entered (even) into the mountains of Upper Egypt, and it overtopped the mounds of Lower Egypt. The land was within the primordial ocean, the inert waters, and one could not distinguish islands from the river. When it rose by 21 cubits, 1 palm, and 2½ fingers at the harbor of Thebes, his Majesty caused that there be

brought to him the ancestral annals to see if such an inundation had occurred in their era, but without anything similar being found there.[60]

Though we know such high floods could be disastrous—the waters might wash away towns or not recede in time for a proper harvest—Taharqa focused only on the positive, particularly noting that "everything that issues from upon the lips of His Majesty, straightaway his father Amun causes that they happen."[61] Taharqa could speak to god, apparently, and god listened.

This great flood was presented like a surge in the stock market during an election year, appeasing all the elites in his imperial system. Taharqa went out of his way to document his great wealth in grain and gold throughout Egypt, broadcasting his spending at temples and palaces. His Kawa stela at the Gem-Pa-Aten Temple to Amun reads like an Instagram post of fashion designers, brands, and prices: "As his monument for his father Amun-Re, Lord of Gem-Aten, he made: 1 silver altar, amounting to 220 deben [a unit of currency], 1 gold censer, amounting to 10 deben, 1 gold ewer, amounting to 10 deben and 5 kite, 1 gold mirror, amounting to a deben and 2 kite, 7 large bronze vessels, 50 veils, 38 kilts, 12 garments, and 20 pieces of fine linen amounting to 120, 1 lapis lazuli figure of Maat, 1200 Cyprus seeds, an incense tree of sycamore . . ."[62] and on and on. The record of all of this wealth was painstakingly carved into hard granite.

Taharqa had the money to show off extraordinary real estate developments and significant temple constructions, making sure that everyone knew exactly how much everything cost. He also made sure to declare that every temple he now embellished "had fallen into ruin" and needed his intercession,[63] as when modern populist leaders criticize the inattention of local governors and mayors to take emergency powers.

Taharqa staffed his temples with "the children of the rulers of the

Libyans."[64] He thus relied on a clever method of deportation used by other imperial dynasts intent on destabilizing rival power centers as he moved elites of the north down to the south and gave them jobs in his own homeland to administer his temples and lands. He was apparently using some of the same tactics the Egyptians had inflicted upon his own people for millennia: capturing the children of important combatants and raising them at a faraway court to be loyal supporters of the dominant regime.

At the Nubian temple of Kawa, Taharqa included reliefs of himself as a sphinx trampling Libyan enemies that were copied precisely from the pyramid temples of the 5th-dynasty kings buried near Memphis. He imported artisans specifically for the task, and they must have brought their pattern books with them so they could copy the millennia-old captions word for word.[65] Taharqa needed to emulate the archaic images to connect himself to the Egyptian founding fathers, though he was careful about how old-fashioned he styled his portraiture. (Just to compare, today's politicians would have a hard time dressing up in the short trousers, tights, and gray wigs of the writers of the U.S. Constitution without looking ridiculous—but they can pick up other symbols and codes to show loyalty to that brand.)

Taharqa didn't want to look out of place. He was well aware that archaism can be pushed too far, and he updated old Egyptian imagery while maintaining his Kushite identity, giving people some of the old ways yet not becoming a mere copyist.

NOSTALGIC PIETY

Taharqa was a master at connecting with the halcyon days of Theban dynasties of yore—the 11th, 12th, 17th, and 18th dynasties, the royal lines of Mentuhotep, Senwosret, Ahmose, Thutmose, and Amenhotep. He ordered image after image of himself associated with Amun-Re, the favorite god of both the Kushites and the Thebans. He commissioned statues of himself standing between the legs of a giant ram version of the deity Amun.

To Taharqa, piety was a sacred political exchange, but also a proof of violent, sacralized might. He explained the divine providence of his kingship in another one of the many stelae he set up at Kawa Temple. This divine act was the result of a decision made by his grandfather Alara, who had dedicated his own twin sister—Taharqa's grandmother—to the cult of Amun-Re by saying, "May you look after my sister-wife for me, she who was born together with me in a single womb. You have acted for her just as you have acted for the one who acted for you, as a wonder unimagined, unbelieved by plotters, when you repelled for me evil plots against me, and you elevated me as king."[66] In other words, it was a pious dedication of the girl to Amun-Re before Taharqa was even born that determined his future kingship. The piety of the donation, we are told, caused the god Amun to later mark Taharqa for power.

Taharqa perceived his rule as a rebirth of Egyptian divine kingship, and himself as

> a master of rejuvenations, a champion, one uniquely valiant, a powerful king who has no equal, a ruler like Atum, love of whom pervades the lands like Re when he appears in the sky, a Son of Re like Onuris, whose kingship is infinite like Tatenen, with open stride, wide sandals, who sends forth his arrow that he might overpower chiefs, who tramples the mountains in pursuit of his enemies, who fights with his strong arm, slaying hundreds of thousands, at the sight of whom every face is dazzled, for whom everyone rejoices when he appears with fighting in his heart daily.[67]

Quite a king.

In many ways, the 25th-dynasty rulers had to work an ideological battle on two fronts. First, they had to become more Egyptian than the Egyptian kings by exposing the Libyan rulers as Egyptianized frauds. But they also had to pull Egyptian images into their homeland of Kush to aggrandize their power among their own people.

We can only wonder at the Kushite perception of so many Egyptian ways entering Nubia, which must have maintained a cultural memory of past wrongs. But oppressed peoples often use hyper-instantiations of colonial culture to gain power over their own. Colonial culture can even take shape in quotidian fashion, with food and drink. It's reminiscent of the way Japanese Americans in Hawaii continue to embrace Spam and canned Vienna sausages long after they and their relatives were sent to internment camps on the U.S. mainland during WWII (while their men defied that cultural bias and heroically fought battles in Europe and Asia). Most Japanese Americans probably don't think eating foods from U.S. corporations is problematic, given that history. But it is part of complicated, daily-life colonialism.

As for Taharqa, he followed a conscious return to Egyptian styles of past glory. Using old language, old official titles, old methods of cutting relief and statuary, old architecture, he reminded everyone—Kushite or Egyptian—of the historic greatness of kingship. These 25th-dynasty kings set themselves up as the rediscoverers of ancient Egypt, even if they had to manufacture that antiquity.[68]

Taharqa would even build a pyramid as 4th-dynasty King Snefru had intended, with an angle approaching 60-some degrees. (Snefru, remember, was foiled by cracked foundations, which forced the angle to be lowered.) Taharqa's pyramid project would fashion the king's sacred resting place as it was originally supposed to be, perhaps, succeeding where the Egyptians themselves had failed. Choosing a burial in his Kushite homeland, he seems to have taken inspiration from the Meidum and Bent Pyramids, perhaps even the sacred Benben stone of Heliopolis, which symbolized the primordial mound. But at the same time, Taharqa created a Kushite innovation: a high-angled, massive pyramid of stone for the royal burial.[69]

The Kushites made it fashionable to use religious piety to maintain power. Montuemhat, mayor of Thebes, followed suit and displayed his knowledge of arcane religious texts and piety in his massive tomb in the Asasif Valley of Thebes. In his inscriptions in Karnak's Mut Temple, he stated, "I placed Upper Egypt on the path of its god, when the whole land was in upheaval" because he "purified all the temples throughout the nomes of Upper Egypt to its full extent in accordance with the ritual scroll." Montuemhat created ritual implements, opened the holy shrines, served the god, and followed every holy regulation.[70] Religion was in vogue.

Taharqa himself looked to Amun, Ptah, and other gods to legitimize his power. He tells us that working for god is essential: "How good it is, then to act for the one who has acted!"[71] Kushite religious zeal had touched everybody, with citizens motivated to display how much they understood the secrets of certain underworld books or archaic rites. Suddenly everyone wanted to become an expert on orthodoxy.

In the Kushite empire it was now trendy to be overtly religious in tomb decoration and statuary, much in the same way that it's currently in vogue to impose and practice proper Hinduism in the modern state of India. Following religious orthodoxy—whether in Christianity, Judaism, Islam, Mormonism, Buddhism, or Hinduism—works to support a kind of nationalistic zealotry in which religious zeal becomes linked to state identity. Displays of overt piety, absolutism, or even fundamentalism are shorthand signals, telling everyone where you belong within authoritarian systems.

Consider, for example, modern Christian leaders who say that gay people are an abomination to good family values, using religious zealotry to gain political power through scapegoats. Or observe how Israel uses a fundamentalist reading of Judges in the Hebrew Old Testament to take land from Palestinians with impunity. Think of fundamentalist use of the Koran to support takeovers of elections and parliaments. Look to the use of Catholicism in Hungary and Poland in support of law-and-order parties cracking down on a free press and dissent, or how Putin's connection to the Orthodox Christian Church creates a moral right to continued authoritarian power in Russia.

Is this the kind of agenda the Kushite kings were pushing during the 25th dynasty? Such a dark side of their piety is not readily apparent, but their fierce reproaches of past immoralities do come through in their texts. And with everyone in Egypt seemingly engaged in overt religious displays, zealotry may have been the key to showing who truly belonged in Egypt and who did not—which, of course, would have ramped up even more elaborate religious displays in every level of society. Whatever the nature of the beast, Kushite kings led the charge.

For 26 years, Taharqa built all around Egypt and Nubia, north and south. He would update and beautify his realm, with the following effect: Taharqa, "the one who loves the god, he spends the day and lies by night seeking what is useful to the gods, building their temples fallen into decay, giving birth to their statues as the primeval times, building their storehouses, endowing altars, presenting them with offerings of any product, making their offering tables of fine gold, silver, and copper."[72]

The king made sure to show his piety in the most public ways possible, not hiding it in the back sanctuary of a temple space only visible to the highest of elites. His best preserved projects stand at three sites: Thebes, Jebel Barkal, and Kawa.

At Karnak, in Thebes, he put his constructions right up front where everyone would see them, presenting everything new, everything jaw-dropping, everything pious as he ostentatiously enhanced the ancestral temples.[73] He fronted every public temple entrance with a kiosk or colonnade covered with images of his ritual actions for the gods. He often built small chapels to Osiris here and there, but on the most public processional ways, always keen to connect himself to the next parade.

The Temple of Osiris Nebankh at Karnak, for instance, is located on the north-south festival route from the Khonsu Temple to the Mut precinct. Taharqa's monumental two-rowed colonnade stood in front of Karnak's front gateway, where everyone gathered for processions and festivals and would be sure to see its glory. He also built a kiosk in front of Ramses II's temple to the God Who Hears Prayers, located on the opposite side of Karnak, which connected with the larger populace there. And finally, he built kiosks in front of the Ptah Temple, the Monthu precinct, Khonsu's religious structure, and the Mut Temple to the south. Taharqa was knocking at every god's front door.

The king needed to impress more people by constructing publicly and strategically. He also built to reach particular audiences, as with his structure near the more intimate and exclusive Sacred Lake. There, he garnered the attention of the priesthood, whose homes and service locations were nearby. His Sacred Lake edifice was also located right next to the nilometer, a ritual stairway to the groundwater where Nile flood levels were measured.[74] If Ramses II would never let anyone forget about the Battle of Kadesh (he won, right?), then Taharqa wouldn't allow the miraculous flood of his sixth year to leave anyone's memory either (and it wasn't that destructive).

The embellishment of ritual spaces must have won over the high priesthood of Karnak. Every priest wanted to be seen as an indispensable expert performing the necessary rites to keep the gods happily ensconced in their temple homes, and Taharqa would build the stages on which to showcase their hard-won talents. Ritualist positions throughout Egypt now became even more important as avenues to political power. The high priests of different gods became dealmakers, working to link local elites to the royal Kushite court.

The 25th dynasty had made sure to place its own female relatives into the position of God's Wife of Amun at Thebes, using that important dedicatory role as an avenue to riches and political decision-making. Two Kushite God's Wives had already served: Amenirdis I, a daughter of King Kashta, and Shepenwepet II, daughter of Piankhy. Now Taharqa would appoint his own daughter, the second Amenirdis (whose name meant "Amun Made Her") to act as an extension of his own royal power. The high priesthood of Amun had effectively been infiltrated by members of the Kushite royal court. Those women would even be buried inside the walls of the old mortuary complex of Ramses III at Medinet Habu, on a site believed to be no less than the burial place of the gods of creation.[75]

THE CULTURE OF OPPRESSION

Taharqa was engaging in a propaganda of materiality, showing people through temples and buildings that they could have access to power too, that wealth would trickle down. Such authoritarian personalities like to show that they are fabulously wealthy, dangling goodies in front of everybody—gold, stones, metals, timber, medicines, money, statues, buildings, technology—so that people understand their ruler has monopolized access to all those riches. If people want to share in any of it, they must go through him.

Taharqa's elites would participate in those monopolies too, showing off their own access with commissioned statues and stelae, and gaining their own power. Fabulous wealth during the Kushite period was virtue signaling of political loyalty, and it remains a key factor of all authoritarian regimes.

Today, we try to pretend that such self-dealing doesn't exist, that we depend on fair bureaucracies. But our denial about elite corruption is as ideological as anything else. Whether or not we lie to ourselves about it, all elites support their ruler if that allows them better access to goods and power. In the 25th dynasty, elites were just more open about broadcasting the kinds of things that one could get by being a good lieutenant to a great leader.

Displays of wealth and religion can warp our thoughts, though, making us identify with bullies and oppressors. Take an incident from my own family, for example. After my son learned in third grade about how the local Native peoples in California labored for the Spanish, he asked me where all the Native Americans had gone. He posed this question in front of a Mexican American friend of ours who has features that evoke the long-ago Aztec of his homeland. I said, "They're right here." But when my son asked, "Are you a Native American?" our friend answered, "No, I'm Spanish."

And with that, we see how ideology, cultural impositions, and colonization can make Indigenous people disappear. My friend felt he had no Indigenous culture left with which to identify—no language, no religion, no name—and this only some 300 years after the first European contact with the peoples of the Americas. He had so completely associated with the Spanish colonizers that his own identity had become that of the erstwhile oppressor. His people had been persecuted cruelly by Spanish soldiers, priests, bureaucrats, and elites, but he had no memory of that oppression, no victimhood, no real feeling that his own people had ever been enslaved, died en masse, lost their Indigenous lifestyles, had their lands and homes stolen, were denied their religion and languages, or were forced into European institutions on fenced land.

Unable to keep their own cultural traditions, Indigenous people have had to systematically learn from and identify with the dominant culture of power—and with each passing generation, the details of the tyranny have moved farther and farther into the past. It should come as no surprise that so many colonized people connect with the cultures of their oppressors, identifying with them, becoming them, speaking French in Mali, English in Egypt, Dutch in South Africa.

But the colonial overlays go beyond language. In the United States today, people of color might feel compelled to cooperate with White power systems. And we encourage women to "lean in" to the masculine culture of interruptions and after-work drinking. All of us are apologists for the powerful if we can be one of them.

Is this what happened to the Nubians? Did they identify so strongly with power that they gravitated toward Egyptian systems of politics, religion, language, and culture, eventually seeing it as their own? To some extent, yes. It was unavoidable. But what is chilling is the propensity of those co-opted Nubians to inflict the same dominance on others, using the same tools of ideology that had been used on them. In a similar scenario, Italian Americans, once reviled as backward papists, are now some of the strictest socially conservative, law-and-order candidates in the hard-right wing of U.S. politics.

The ideology of co-option is insidious because we often cannot even recognize that it has happened to us. But this is how the ideology of authoritarianism gets us to turn away from our own better interests to grasp at power individually. Perhaps the Kushite kings believed that if they truly had god on their side, if they performed every rite in the orthodox manner, if they showed themselves to be the true originators of the Egyptian religion, if they were really pious, then they could win in the end. If that was the case, then the 25th dynasty is a study in the political-cultural Stockholm syndrome of colonialism felt by so many.

This is dark stuff. We know of the psychology of the master-slave relationship in which African Americans are told to be grateful to their fatherly caretaker for providing food and shelter, or the brutalized women told to appease their men. This relationship of patronage has been mythologized, masked behind the morality of work and the label of "family."

In modern Egypt, the ancient Egyptian language was forgotten long ago, discarded as the country was colonized by Arabs, then Ottoman Turks, then the French and British. But here's the paradox: Most Egyptian elites teach their children to read and write a European language before Arabic. The abused become abusers because it is too damaging to choose the path of scorched earth and reject the system outright. Though violent resistance does happen, rebels are systematically and irrevocably shut out of power. This is a fact that Black Americans have experienced firsthand, as the police, prison, housing, education, and employment systems can all be made to work against them. Fighting back comes with a steep price—and even remembering past indignities comes with a problematic psychological cost.

Colonization is powerful because of how pervasively it works on the mind over the long term—not just over hundreds of years, but thousands. The Britons, for example, colonized by Rome beginning in the year A.D. 43, when the Roman troops first invaded. The Britons did fight back; we have stories of Queen Boudicca, for example, who led her people against the Romans, but to no avail. And yet despite the obvious retained knowledge of this horrific past, Roman leaders such as Octavian and Julius Caesar, Claudius and Hadrian, are presented as the good guys, the heroes, in British school textbooks.[76]

Even a couple thousand years after the fact, the British still identify with their oppressor's morality, cultural superiority, education, and fine manners. The Latin language, taught at private schools, becomes a means of gaining power, of participating in a communal gaslighting of systematic subjugation. The words of this book are written with an imposed Latin alphabet to write a barbarian language that had no writing system of its own.

The Britons, themselves so cruelly victimized, had arguably learned ideological strategies to inflict the same oppression on their own neighbors in Scotland, Wales, and Ireland—and that was just to start. They would use ancient Roman ideals to colonize half the globe. What's extraordinary is how we can't even recognize the pattern with the passing of so many generations.

Taharqa's ancestors seem to have associated so much with their Egyptian overlords that they used many of the same strategies for their own empire. And Taharqa himself ruled over vast territories using Egyptian institutions, language, military strategies, economic systems, religion, and divine kingship to control it all. In many ways, this king took the colonial bribe; his Nubia was not Egyptian, but he had adopted Egyptian ways, nevertheless.

THE REVENGE OF ASSYRIA

Development projects and government spending work beautifully to create a happy and pliant co-opted elite—but the flip side is that they tend to attract unwanted attention. All the Kushite wealth soon drew the gaze of Assyria, putting Taharqa on the defensive like no previous king of Egypt. The Assyrian king and his massive army were on the march.[77]

Empire building was (and is) a dangerous game, because everything that goes up must come down. The Assyrian king Sennacherib had been killed by his elder sons, who were upset that they had been passed over as heir apparent in favor of a younger son, Esarhaddon. The first part of Esarhaddon's reign was spent shoring up support for the new king—a welcome relief for everyone in the region. But in 677 B.C., Assyria was again in battle mode, taking the Phoenician cities of Sidon and Tyre and setting its sights on Egypt. In 673 B.C., in Esarhaddon's sixth year of rule, Taharqa's troops met the imperial invaders at Ashkelon in the Levant. Taharqa was victorious, sending the young Assyrian king back to Nineveh and buying the Egyptians a few more years of peace.

In 671 B.C. Esarhaddon returned. He won the first battle, only to let paranoia get the better of him as he went into hiding for the next hundred days. But he rebounded to finish the job, driving into Egypt itself, sacking Memphis, and sending Taharqa scurrying back to Napata. Esarhaddon even captured Taharqa's crown prince, wife, and courtiers, and sent them back to Nineveh as captives. The stela that Esarhaddon commissioned to celebrate his victory shows Taharqa's son with a rope around his neck, kneeling in supplication at the Assyrian king's feet.

There could be no more tragic defeat for Taharqa. We read the gory details in Esarhaddon's own words: "Memphis, his royal city, in half a day, with mines, tunnels, assaults, I besieged, I captured, I destroyed, I devastated, I burned with fire. His queen, his harem, Ushanahuru, his heir, and the rest of his sons and daughters, his property and his goods, his horses, his cattle, his sheep, in countless numbers, I carried off to Assyria."[78]

Everybody wanted this corner of northeast Africa for its grain, minerals, and gold. Taharqa had taken it from the south. The Assyrians came from the north. And now the Kushites had lost, the Assyrians had won, and Memphis saw its treasures listed in a victory stela as if they were assets in a spreadsheet during a hostile corporate takeover.

If it were not for the invasion of the growing imperial force in West Asia, the 25th dynasty would likely have thrived for many more years—

but instead, it was snuffed out in the midst of its greatest glories. Taharqa faced the Assyrian war machine and lost badly. His sister Amenirdis and his daughter Shepenwepet were left to rule Thebes in his absence. A Kushite relative named Harkhebi still served as High Priest of Amun at Karnak, but with the loss to the Assyrians, it was only a matter of time before that job, too, came to an end.

Taharqa fled south with his army, heartbroken at his family being taken away, at the loss of life. He would continue his worship of Amun-Re at Jebel Barkal, building temple spaces and constructing a pyramid for himself at Nuri—an Egyptian symbol of sunlight 20 stories high—even though he ruled Egypt no more. This would be the first and largest pyramid ever built in Kush, reinvigorating a long history of pyramid building, but in the south.

Taharqa died in 664 B.C. and was interred under his pyramid. The tomb was oriented to have a solar alignment with Jebel Barkal's cobra-shaped outcropping twice a year—including July 31, the start of the Egyptian new year. On that day, the sun shone directly upon the outcropping when viewed from the pyramid, thus highlighting the king's claim, in life, that he was the true Osiris.[79]

Taharqa's underground pyramid chambers situated the sarcophagus in the midst of the Nile floodwaters, surrounding the king with life-giving waters. In light of the tragic outcome of Taharqa's reign, the parallels to Osiris—Egypt's first king brutally cut down by his own brother—were perhaps on everyone's mind as they buried this imperial warlord of greatest territory, greatest construction, and greatest defeat.

Temple B700 at the Jebel Barkal mountain displays a hymn commissioned by Atlanersa, Taharqa's son, in which he refers to his father as Osiris, the creator of the flood, food, and prosperity, a king whose corpse was placed back into the waters of cosmic generation:

Greetings to you, Osiris, Lord of Eternity, King of the Two
Lands, Chief of both banks, . . . Youth, King, who took the
White Crown for himself . . . Who makes himself young again
a million times . . . What he loves is that every face looks up
to him . . . Shining youth, who is in the primordial water, born
on the first of the year . . . From the outflow of his limbs both
lands drink. Of him it is arranged that the grain springs forth
from the water in which he is placed . . . [80]

As for the Assyrians, they would appoint men in the city of Sais
as their Egyptian puppet dynasts. A man named Necho, a loyal vassal
to Assyria, was named king, and the 26th dynasty of Egypt was born.
The succeeding ruler, Psamtik I, would reclaim Thebes and install
his own daughter Nitikret (Nitocris in its Greek form) as God's
Wife of Amun at Karnak, transferring all the wealth and power to
his own family lineage.

After the Kushites tried to move into Egypt again under King Tantamani, the Assyrian king Ashurbanipal stormed into Egypt, sacked
Thebes in 663 B.C., laid waste to the land, and destroyed most of its
elite base. Ashurbanipal even ordered the temples burned. The scars
of the devastation are still visible in Luxor today: The burning flag-
poles melted the stone of Karnak's second pylon, and at least one
colossal quartzite statue exploded in the fire, sending chunks of stone
in multiple directions.

The Assyrians had no interest in becoming Egyptian or in winning
local hearts and minds; their ideology was one of military domination. The statue pieces remained where they lay. They are currently
spread from the 10th pylon to the courtyard of Khonsu Temple: a
giant foot here, a monumental hand there, signs of a kingship torn
asunder.

THE GOOD KINGS

The Kushites were now relegated to a Nubian kingship. King Aspelta did attempt to take his empire back from the 26th dynasty, massing his forces to sail north. When he heard of the impending invasion, the Egyptian king Psamtik II sent his mercenary forces down to Napata, where they killed so many the king claimed to have waded in Kushite blood like it was water.[81]

The temples at Jebel Barkal still bear the remnants of Psamtik II's campaign, with statues systematically destroyed, heads severed from bodies, crowns removed from heads, hands separated from arms—all the pieces unceremoniously dumped into a pit at the temple site. The Saites left the city of Napata as a heap of ash and rubble, having burned the royal palace, ritually murdered the stone statues of kings, and smashed the Kushite sacred monuments. What Egyptian kings had first erected at Jebel Barkal, a king from Sais would destroy.

The Kushite kings would never invade Egypt again. They would retreat south, building a new capital at Meroë, beyond the fifth cataract and far from the threat of repeated invasions from whomever held the throne in Egypt. But the Kushites brought their pyramid tomb–building ways with them, enthusiastically continuing what the Egyptians had long ago abandoned.

As for the Assyrians, they were largely done with Egypt, as they were themselves defeated by yet another empire—the neo-Babylonians of the sixth century B.C., who would in turn invade and sack Egypt. Poor Egypt would fall to every single imperial advance to come their way.

The onslaught was ferocious as the age of empires got under way. After the neo-Babylonians, the Persians would come in, occupying Egypt, setting up a satrapy, and building gardens in the western oases— only to be defeated by the Macedonians under the command of Alexander the Great. The imperial domination of Egypt by Greek-speaking elites, known as the Ptolemies, would be the longest yet at more than 300 years.

But outside powers were not done with the land of the pharaohs—not by a long shot. After the death of Cleopatra, Rome would claim Egypt as its breadbasket. The Nile kingdom was handed from empire to empire, buffeted about, claimed and reclaimed. It did not matter which empire it was; Egypt would be no match for it. The people of the Nile were ever on the defensive, constantly fighting for their survival, ready to identify with any new occupiers and oppressors, adapting just as the Nubians had done some 1,000 years before. (Karma is, indeed, a bitch.)

But Egypt still held a special place in imperial hearts as the originator of a perfected divine kingship. Most invaders wanted to associate with just such an ideology of good kings and perfected men. Ashurbanipal of the Assyrians may have been an exception; Darius of the Persians and Alexander of the Macedonians were the norm, looking to Egyptian ideological systems to strengthen their own kingships.

Julius Caesar would use the might of Egypt to grow his own authoritarian powers against rival Roman elites in a messy civil war; it would be his downfall. Mark Antony, too, would build a foundation of kingly rule on Egyptian soil, also at his peril. Octavian would use Egypt's wealth to perfect Rome's first imperial rule consolidated under one man. The Roman emperor Hadrian also found ideological power—and lost a lover, Antinous—along Egypt's sacred river.

Byzantine kings, Arab warlords, Ottoman sultans and governors came and went after the Romans. Napoleon, too, was seduced by Egypt's siren song. Each one of those men looked to the perfected authoritarian rule that Egypt had created: craving it, grasping at it, wanting a part of its divinity and the incontestable connection between religion and politics.

Egypt had created something that had become intensely useful for authoritarian rulers all over the world looking to justify themselves as good and moral. This is why we are still obsessed with Egypt today, our wealthy oppressor, powerful to a fault, morally justified, perfect. No one could do anything against Pharaoh; his was a seductive power. Indeed, if someone asks us to name the most powerful human being ever to rule the earth, it just might be the Egyptian god-king who could never be told no.

CHAPTER 7

SMASHING THE PATRIARCHY

Ideological manipulation was ancient Egypt's most effective tool of patriarchal power. It's the very reason, in fact, that we are so attracted to the culture's mummies, pyramids, coffins, and statues. Those pharaohs of northeast Africa created rituals, sacred texts, and temples to manufacture a noble and ethical leadership. People bowed down to them not just because they thought they knew what was good for them, but also because they believed in the sanctity and goodness of the men in charge.

Ancient Assyria, Iran, Israel, Greece, Rome, China, the Moche, Maya, Inca, Aztec—all of them engaged in the same ideological power plays, using father-son lineage, manipulation of women's labor, the monopolizing of resources among a few men, and the manufacturing of ideologies to support their rule. But none of them, arguably, were able to perfect the packaging of their power like the ancient Egyptians. This is why so many ancient peoples seem much more violent and vicious than the pharaohs. The Egyptians had cracked a code of presenting power as something beautiful, something good, something wonderful.

Make no mistake: The systems of power in Egypt were just as brutal, just as unfair and cruel, as in other ancient societies. But the pharaohs ably marketed themselves as nothing less than the saviors of the world, the thoughtful managers of scarce resources, the genius controllers of technologies that built pyramids and obelisks, the initiated priests who understood the secrets of the universe, the moral dictators.

Their propaganda was so clever, so successful, that everyone believed them in the end, even though those gold-encrusted kings lied just like every other ancient monarch. They lied to their people. They lied to themselves. And we still believe them. We love them for the success of their righteousness. This is the key to ancient Egypt's cultural power in the past and today—their ability to make patriarchy's hallmarks of aggression and hoarding seem not just necessary evils, but also tactics deployed for the ultimate betterment of all.

Egyptian patriarchal power is perfectly encapsulated in the second division of the Book of Gates. The sun god Atum-Re, having set in the west and entered the land of the dead inside his mother-lover Nut, needs to find the strength to rise again. He addresses his enemies in the underworld:

> My father Re is triumphant against you, I am triumphant against you! I am the son who emanated from his father. I am the father who emanated from his son. You are fettered, you are bound with firm ropes. I have ordered that you be fettered; your arms will not be opened! Re's magic is against you, effective is his Ba spirit against you, powerful is my father against you, strong is his Ba spirit against you! Your evil belongs to you; your slaughtering is against you, your punishment is upon you, you are summoned to evil![1]

The father-to-son lineage is called out in this spell as a justification for taking power. My father did this, thus I can and will do it too. Lurking underneath is the patriarchal insistence that the sun god's abilities alone have gotten him through these trials, that there is no entitlement or systemic advantage, that he wins only because of hard work and inborn righteousness we cannot comprehend. This is the same kind of legacy under which the world continues to live today: the identity of name, wealth, and power conferred upon people by pedigree, All Lives Matter privilege, and color.

The Book of Gates incantation connects the patriarch's use of violence to maintain a cosmic purpose—namely, the ability of our father, the sun, to keep us warm, safe, and prosperous. Even the most tortuous of deaths are openly displayed as a moral and necessary brutality, with the patriarch keeping a calm demeanor until the despicable actions of his bloodthirsty enemies become so overt that they must be neutralized with all the blinding force of his legitimate rage.

The sun god's enemies are called evil, and well they should be. They have been trying to stop Atum-Re from rising again in the east, attempting to grasp power for power's sake, we are told—not doing what is right and true, not following along obediently. This is where the patriarchy's fearmongering takes its cleverest turn, because we understand that if the enemies somehow win, the sun will cease to shine, and we will die, shivering, alone in the dark.

The stakes of this magical incantation are the highest imaginable. Nothing less than the creation of a sunlit world depended on this transfer of power from father to son, on the son's rebirth from death. In Egypt, the narrative pitted ma'at (truth or right) against *isfet* (disorder). The parallel narrative today is composed of light versus dark, good versus evil, clean versus dirty, straight versus crooked, White versus Black, Shining City on a Hill versus Axis of Evil. It's the Catholic priest telling you of an afterlife in hell if you abort or divorce, and the evangelical leader intoning that pandemics and natural disasters can all be laid at the feet of gay, lesbian, and transgender aberrance. It is QAnon telling us we must fight against a pedophile sex ring running rampant among Democrats in Washington, D.C. This binary framework manufactures deep emotional investment. There is no gray area.

The Book of Gates text was placed on the sarcophagi and tomb walls of pharaohs, forever linking good kings' leadership with the continuance of the created world. All the pharaohs' people were given seats in this theater of power—some close to the stage, some in the nosebleed seats at the back, barely able to glimpse anything. But everyone was meant to be petrified at the potential of their father's loss, too afraid to doubt or judge or second-guess their great leader lest they lose the warmth of their father's light. When the equation is set that the father is the ultimate good, any and every violent act that any father anywhere does is essential and justified; it doesn't matter how horrific and bloody the action seems if it will make the sun rise again. An ideology of fear and beauty is the most essential tool of the patriarchy.

This particular afterlife text fails to mention how the sun god must impregnate his own mother with his future self, a divine self-creation that arguably spawned the notion of Jesus' virgin birth in the New Testament, another patriarchal trope that robs women of agency. In such schemes, the divine feminine does not create; she only contains and protects. Her fierce desire to shield her son, her father, her brother, or her lover can become so overpowering to the supposedly weaker feminine mind that she can lose all sense and reason, becoming hysterical, needing to be calmly led back home like a child.

The Egyptian divine feminine surrounds her patriarch with her body, conflating lover, mother, and daughter, willingly sacrificing her own power for the sun god's healthy rebirth. This corresponds to the message so many women in our society today take on board, that we are put on this earth to fight for our menfolk, that they know better than we do, that we must be caretakers. According to this philosophy, all our energy, service, knowledge, skills are a cosmic gift to our fathers, our sons, our husbands, and our brothers.

The whole patriarchal scheme is our scheme too. It is visible in the surnames women take to make themselves legible to the state, in citizenships that pass primarily through the line of the father (How many of us cannot get a passport to another country because our lineage travels through our mother's side?), and in patronizing divorce laws written to protect the stay-at-home mother from the potential exploitation of the male provider. The patriarchy demands women's exclusion from power because our great leader has monopolized both it and the resources attached, making ideas such as "socialism," "community organizing," and "feminism" akin to treasonous rebellion. We are to believe that only the leader and his representatives have psychic and ritualized capacity for the messiness of politics, that they must shield women's childlike eyes from the ongoing series of cosmic battles fought for our own good, that they will keep women safe from the dealmaking in which they must engage on our behalf, dirtying their hands for us, that women who do engage in politics are duplicitous and immorally ambitious. And only our fathers can wield the necessary violence, that "good" smiting meant to get the sun god through the dark hours of night unscathed.

With my last book on female pharaohs, *When Women Ruled the World,* I started down the path of a skeptic, a nonbeliever, a betrayed lover, a recovering Egyptologist. I had been enraptured by the gold, the divinities, the miracles in stone. But as I examined how the clever ideology of Egyptian pharaohs worked upon my own mind and soul, I began to recognize how so many of us acquiesce to these ancient spin doctors.

Critical thought will be our salvation, and I believe in the profound power of education. I have stood in the classroom many a time watching the light dawn on the face of a student who grasped a concept for the first time. Teaching—and thus being taught in turn—challenges our assumptions, demanding that we question why we find these gold-encrusted kings so fascinating in the first place.

I tell my graduate students at University of California, Los Angeles all the time that Egyptology is dead. Why? This discipline was largely created to discover, document, and celebrate ancient Egyptian power and its creations. But now the field of Egyptology—mirroring a larger global shift—is quickly entering something new, in which its practitioners think holistically, comparatively, stepping into the realms of the excluded on the fringes of "good" Egyptian society, working with Egypt's time periods of crisis as much as its heights of centralization.

That said, I don't want to just push a simple thought exercise of whether Akhenaten was "bad" or "good," or whether Khufu was "despotic" or a "jobs creator." Binary takedowns just enable more of the same system of browbeating and ideological control. Instead, I want to turn over all the stones, examine all the papyri, expose all the veiled data to recognize how power worked in this ancient system. This way, I can subject our extensive knowledge of Egyptian power to new scrutiny so that we can bend our own arcs of intolerance, identify and smash our own patriarchies, expose our own carefully constructed propagandas.

Today, I have become the student who finally realizes something she didn't understand before, and it has shifted everything. Of course, I can't unsee that we are willing subjects to pharaohs too—that I myself have power in an academic system I might not want to upend because its carefully constructed (ivory) tower protects my personal interests now that I am inside it. Such franchises—all too big to fail—are embedded throughout our social fabric. So now, I would like to examine how we uphold our own obsolete pharaonic system—our own franchise.

The patriarchs' lieutenants are our mayors and governors, our congressional representatives, our police chiefs and beat cops, our Green Berets and black ops agents, our CEOs and financiers. They show us parts of their access but they don't declassify the files, revealing just a flash of imagery as their hand sweeps aside the curtain for a moment. The dash cam on the cop car wasn't working, and the Black man had pulled a gun, we are told, necessitating brutal action. Or the socialist Dems were demanding trillion-dollar relief packages to give money to illegal immigrants, they tell us, as they kill another bill to support working people during a pandemic.

The patriarchy demands that the privileged monopolize the violence, because it would be too much for the rest of us. To allow the patriarchy unfettered access to its semiautomatic weapons, we live in a wildly unregulated place where anyone can procure a gun at any time. The difference is in the punishment doled out by the state. If you are arrested with such a weapon and are Black, Indigenous, or Muslim, or an undocumented immigrant, you are in grave danger. If you are confronted while White and armed, you can stand your ground. The patriarchy gives our police forces military gear—tanks and assault machinery—to use on the unwanted of our own society.

The patriarchy keeps control of resources, land, and the stock market; only the ones in charge know how to manage it all wisely. Home buying is just for the patriarch's favored lieutenants, not for the excluded; banks help create brilliant strategies such as redlining (denying loans based on identifying "risky" neighborhoods). The patriarchs funnel decision-making to their loyal followers, using gerrymandering and voter suppression to make sure only the righteous cast votes. To maintain their hoarding of resources, knowledge, and power, they construct an education system that is semiprivatized for the few, based on property-tax revenue and neighborhood inequalities that maintain established social boundaries, and hamstringing many with student loan debt so deep and so wide it takes a lifetime to wade through. In the United States, the ideology of equality is essential to the whole game. It's what gives members of the lower classes the audacity to try to get college degrees at all, but their debt only enriches the good fathers.

Our American pharaohs are skilled at manufacturing their own moral displays to create solidarity, righteous indignation, and fear. For instance, we are told that people are taking away our heritage when they attack our Confederate statues, that they're disrespecting our dead, our veteran soldiers, fathers, uncles, and brothers as they try to change the facts of history itself. When the U.S. Civil War is discussed, battles and outcomes are seen as objective, scriptural truths, not a mythology crafted by the winners.

Thus, Colin Kaepernick must be punished for disrespecting our sacred flag, effectively drawing our eyes away from any societal consternation about police killings of unarmed Black men. Evangelical and Catholic Christianity has been mobilized to fight for the lives of the unborn by focusing on the baby, claiming that only perverse people would happily rip the child, limb from limb, from the body of a mother who doesn't understand her place of service to her impregnator. Her body must be sacrificed to serve society's innocence. If we believe our leaders are fighting a cosmic battle on our behalf that we cannot see or understand, then we will do whatever we can to aid them.

Our obsession with ancient patriarchs, like Egyptian pharaohs, tells us more about us than it does about them (and if you don't believe the past is relevant, then the propaganda machine is working on you as well). Countless history books carefully parse the evidence from the reigns of Egyptian kings, when it's all just a collection of mythologies, a study of optics, histories unwittingly respinning old stories of patriarchal power that draw us in the way they did the ancient Egyptians. We believe because we still take the ancient kings at their word, because that is what the documents say and who am I to speculate, and because—even now— we think the ends justify the means.

This book is about recurring human systems of power—an attempt to use the messaging of ancient Egypt to crack open our own patriarchy, and to recognize that divine kingship is not so very different from some of today's systems of rule. In it, we have seen how nationalistic ideologies, democratic populism, and patriotism cloak the machines of power—much like how the perfect skin of the Red Delicious apple masks a mealy, corporatized interior.

The kings of ancient Egypt can help us decode the tactics of the patriarchal system under which we all live. There was Khufu, the tax-and-spend creator of pyramid propaganda; Senwosret and his absolutist crackdowns; Akhenaten, the evangelical king; Ramses, the needy populist; and Taharqa, the colonized imperialist. Those rulers were all products of their time. Today, we create our own kings (perhaps at a faster clip, because technology speeds up our political development). If we were to categorize the Egyptian rulers in modern terms—as in a Breakfast Club with a brain, an athlete, a basket case, a princess, and a criminal—then our story consists of a builder, a bully, a zealot, a narcissist, and a missionary. We should recognize these men in ourselves; their stories are ours too.

History lives and breathes today. As I reflected on the schematized methodologies of those long-ago pharaohs, it sometimes seemed as though I were analyzing modern politics. The intent of Khufu's pyramid of phallic proportions is akin to Joseph Stalin and his military-industrial complex of collective toxic masculinity, mass repression, ethnic cleansing, famine, and work camps, all of which set up the very reasons for the

Soviet Union's eventual downfall. Senwosret III is that abusive father figure whom you love but who makes people debase themselves to share in his riches. He is Hollywood mogul Harvey Weinstein, who preyed on wannabe stars, and Harvard professor Gary Urton, who reportedly abused young female students—men who presented their victims with a seductive quid pro quo through monopolized access to agents and development money, archaeological data sets, and research grants. They could behave that way because, "When you're a star, they let you do it."

Akhenaten is reminiscent of our own monotheistic evangelicalism as revealed by Pat Robertson, Jerry Falwell, Jr., and Joel Osteen, all of whom bifurcate the world into the powers of light and darkness. These good fathers ostentatiously pray for their enemies while righteously supporting cruel policies to take down those same people, demonstrating to their followers that they have been truly touched by God—and that their acolytes could be too, if they only gave a little donation. Ramses II, our jobs creator par excellence, is a builder of his own narcissism—the most obvious Donald Trump–like character, had he held the reins of power for decades. And then there is Taharqa, a product of colonialism who overthrew tyrants only to lead with more of the same. He is like Zimbabwe's Robert Mugabe casting off the yoke of the British patriarchal empire only to use the former oppressors' tools with righteous zeal.

It is almost impossible to see through the mythologies of kingly goodness. But even the most skilled of poker players has the rare tell—a movement of the hand, a flick of the eye, a crossed leg—something that reveals all is not right, that a storm is raging beneath the calm surface. Even in their perfected landscapes, Egyptian kings have tells too, thousands of years removed. Here, I wanted to condense and simplify 1,500 years of human power plays like a time-lapse camera—not to denigrate, but to reveal actions no one can appreciate while embedded in the game.

The pharaohs cloaked themselves with an ideology of divine kingship that included crowns and staves, Horus and Seth mythologies, thrones and Sed festivals; we have an ideology of Founding Fathers, flags that cannot touch the ground, hands on hearts, and constitutionality, all cemented with pledges of allegiance, churchgoing piety, and disavowals of personal racial hatred. We write and consume our own propaganda. We manufacture our own mythology of exceptionalism and righteousness. We present ourselves as innocent. We clothe our leaders with tokens and myths to make them unassailable, unstoppable, and it is seen as immoral to draw aside the curtain and reveal the frail old men behind it.

We can pull many useful patterns from ancient Egypt to shed light on American culture today. For one, the reigns of the most authoritarian Egyptian kings—like Khufu, Akhenaten, and Ramses—do not mark the steepest jump toward that authoritarianism, but rather, the beginning of the end of it. That is, the apex in centralized power usually occurs right at that moment before it all falls into a decentralized heap of failed lineage, deep state takeovers, and warlords battling for the crown.

If we use history to prognosticate our own endgame, then the current flirtation—or the outright love affair—that some Americans are having with authoritarian populism is, in fact, the calm before the storm. We could end up with a second civil war if we don't recognize the ominous patterns and change course. Or we could lock ourselves into an inescapable, repressive regime.

Ancient Egypt proves that fearmongering works best long after the time when there is actually something to be afraid of. The Egyptian kings could teach a master class in whipping up a population's terror—of disorder, of the foreigner, of roving bands of armed thugs, of uprising, of social upheaval. The fear of a leaderless Egypt was ably weaponized by kings who ruled much later than the actual moments of lawlessness took place. They constantly reminded their citizens of past depravities, like a parent harping on old mistakes: that time you wrecked the car or failed the exam. Those kings were the strict fathers who made sure bad things would not happen again, even though their very authoritarianism would create the next fall into disorder. Even the natural cycles of the Nile floods could become potential apocalypses of bad times if people did not do as they were told. The gods were watching, after all. This was statewide recriminatory parenting at its most skillful.

In the United States of 2020, we saw angry demonstrations in the wake of the killing of yet another unarmed Black man that sometimes devolved into sprees of looting and rioting by an angry, disenfranchised young populace. Those events were politically transformed by White patriarchal leaders—as if by magic—into rampages of evil, drug-addicted, parentless, rudderless youths ready to invade people's homes with their illegal firearms, raping and murdering as they went. With such fearmongering, the brilliance of the propaganda rests in recalling a mythical deep past to remind people that the same pain will return if they do not bow down to the fatherly abilities of the great leaders.

We can use another pattern from ancient Egypt to understand our own times. Close analysis of pharaonic rule proves the strategies of authoritarians to be more blunt instruments and less the surgical, expert incisions that the patriarchs aspire to make. Authoritarians are short-term thinkers. There is always collateral damage as they intend to do one thing yet create another problem. The authoritarian is usually not some kind of evil genius but rather the bumbling fool, who in an attempt to become the biggest, most wealthy, most successful king of kings, ends up bringing down the entire system.

We have inherited the same kind of stark inequality in our modern world. A few people can inherit or invent billions while the unnamed, unsung, uneducated masses endlessly perform multiple jobs for those few overlords, never catching up, never meant to catch up, destined to trip and fall in service to the rich. Egypt proves to us that the patriarchal game has never stopped, that our booms and busts can be laid at the feet of our pharaohs. Whatever we call it—a monarchy, an oligarchy, a democracy, or a corporatocracy—our social system is headed up by just a few men running the same schemes that drive us all to rise and ruin again and again.

This dive into Egypt's history has revealed the ups and downs of the country's kingship over the millennia, with the patriarchy always coming back to life like a TV movie zombie, its authoritarianism an ever present, unavoidable feature of human life. No matter how we repackage it, though—no matter how strong our denial is that we do not worship kings—most of us do (or are made to bow down to them in spite of ourselves).

Details of individual ruling strategy aside, each Egyptian king set up the same basic story: smashing and grabbing power unsustainably, then setting up the fall for everyone (which usually occurred after the king himself had passed on). Ideologically, the Egyptian kings excelled at pushing a kind of collective cynicism, demanding from their people a fatalist surrender to their greater powers.

We in the United States might think ourselves immune to such defeat-ist narratives because we have embraced our individual selves, our ability to pull ourselves up by our bootstraps, and the erudition of our techno-logical innovators. But a closer look reveals that our own narcissism has simply been commodified by those same overlords. Every Instagram post, every mascara purchase, every exercise subscription, every Netflix view, enriches them.

Maybe the reason we are so obsessed with the ancient Egyptians is because our own capacity for self-deception is as finely honed as theirs. Instead of believing in a ruler who can make the sun rise again, we prefer leaders who can make us cellulite-free, testosterone-pumped, ever employed, numbed-out, oversexed, overstimulated, ostentatiously virtuous, armed to the teeth, full to bursting, and completely purged.

The Egyptians gave their labors to their god-kings. We do the same. That is excruciatingly obvious to everyone as we all slog and hustle while worrying about our livelihoods and futures and health care packages and retirement plans, if we have them at all. And the more work, caretaking, exhaustion, anxiety, and fear we take on, the more susceptible we are to the authoritarians' siren songs of painkillers, entertainment, social media, materialism, righteousness, AR-15s, and American beer. We become lost, subsumed by the power of our own pharaohs that turns us into apologists for bright and shiny new strongmen, for the beauty and safety they could create for us by taking us under their wing—if only we have a childlike faith in them. We are told that our amassed goods for which we have worked so hard—fast fashion, overstuffed couches, and endless gadgets so overflowing in our lives that we need to rent storage units to hold everything—will be stolen by people who don't deserve them, who didn't work for them, who are not chosen by God.

The current political landscape is a clear indication that the more unequal society becomes, the more we are seduced by the patriarchs who created it. This next leader will be different, we tell ourselves, because he says things openly that we have been thinking for some time. His fear is our fear; his hate is our hate; he will provide just the edge we need to finally get ahead, to keep what we have, to stop others who never had anything from getting something, to keep everyone in their place so we can maintain our power, uphold the franchise.

Just as in the stories of the ancient pharaohs, we give our good fathers emergency powers to quell sectarian divisions and halt the extremes of militias and fanatics, even while those leaders engage in exactly the same misdeeds. Our leaders aggrandize the evils of perceived enemies and foreigners, excluding peoples whom we don't understand—particularly those who don't play by patriarchal rules: the nonbinary people, uppity women, and lower-caste individuals who don't know their place anymore. Patriarchy wants to force people into strict male or female roles, family hierarchies, support for law and order, and traditional religions as a condition of participating in a culture's wealth and power. And those who speak against it—those calling to change police funding, for example, or grant LGBTQ rights, or allow access to birth control and abortions—become the enemies the patriarchy righteously opposes every day.

Breaking Up With Pharaoh

We now find ourselves in a moment of great change and extraordinary choice, when we can all feel our feet poised on the edge of the diving board. Today, people are opting out of patriarchal rules for the simple reason that they can. The pharaonic franchise lasted for three thousand years; its modus operandi is still with us today. Why are humans suddenly finding new power beyond the realm of their good fathers when they couldn't before? To answer that, we need a primer on the patriarchy's identity and nature.

A patriarchy represents the control of a community's scarce resources by "the fathers"—that is, by a minority of the male of the species. The resources in question are money or wheat, political might or religious power, military or police force.

Patriarchy is economically established by three main biological elements: First, there's human reproduction, which demands the female use her body to gestate and care for babies who have a long maturation time. That includes all the menstruation, pregnancies, breast-feeding, and load-bearing that a female has to endure to have a family. Second, the human species is characterized by sexual dimorphism, in which the female has less muscle mass than the male. Unlike the gibbons, higher apes whose females and males have more or less the same size and mass, female *Homo sapiens* can easily be overpowered and physically controlled by males. And third, economic circumstances. In the not-so-distant past, earning a living through agriculture demanded a large family to protect and work the land profitably; this put women into the repeated cycle of pregnancy, childcare, and overwork.

So we're biologically hardwired for patriarchy? Not necessarily. Those biological realities don't need to spell eternal doom for human females. Strong patriarchal structures are only 10,000 years old on this planet, and far younger in places such as California, where the agricultural revolution came much later. Power distributions depend on what scarce resources women and men can bring into their communities. Before farming, the norm for the human species was hunting and gathering—small bands moving from place to place, following seasonal resources such as game and wild plants. In most hunter-gatherer societies based on game hunting, women bring in 80 percent of the calories for their tribe, men 20 percent. Though it seems like that should translate into women amassing 80 percent of the power, the calories they provide are plentiful, not scarce—and that makes a difference in the power structure.

In such a society in Papua New Guinea, for example, the women collect masses of wild plants, while the men bring in wild pork in far smaller quantities. But the pork is much scarcer, so the men end up having much more political power. We might also consider the hunter-gatherers of Canada's Pacific coast, who were dependent on hunting seals and whales on journeys that lasted for weeks. Women were excluded from the hunt and were relegated instead to handling the blubber and skins of captured animals, as well as doing housework, caring for children, and preparing food. Not surprisingly, they had little power.

On the other hand, the Tongva people of Southern California fished at the riverside. There, a menstruating, pregnant, or breast-feeding woman could bring in as many fish as the man next to her, translating into nearly equal power within her community.[2] More on the Tongva in a moment—but for now, we can see that power often comes down to how women contribute hard-won resources to their larger groups. In modern times, that often means women's ability to make money.

Anyone who has ever found themselves trapped in an unequal relationship will understand this in their bones. The patriarchy can trap a woman caring for young children into an abusive, dependent situation. Unequal economies can trap children in cycles of corporal punishment, overwork, and neglect. But recent economic changes in today's societies are demanding that both men and women work for wages. We are all becoming more like the Tongva, because people of any sexual identity can be equally successful in the current economic system as they sit at a computer terminal, engage in cognitive work, operate machinery, and create the same scarce products.

I know a woman born in the early 1970s in a rural town on the border of Pakistan and Afghanistan. As a girl, she was denied food and education so that the males in her family could get resources and attention, so necessary were the boys for a family's survival. But this girl's mother secretly saved her money and made sure her daughter was educated. The little girl tested so well in elementary school that she was sent away to a prestigious school in Islamabad, and then went to the United States for her education in math, science, and engineering. After she got her Ph.D., she landed a postdoc and then a tenure-track position at a well-known university. She has excelled because of her keen scientific mind, and because the current economic system rewards that mind, regardless of sex or size or national origin or color. Indeed, this particular woman is absolutely tiny, under five feet tall: the very example of sexual dimorphism in the human species, and someone who would probably have been manhandled and controlled in earlier times. But she now gets opportunities—not as a wife and mother, but as an engineer.

Although this woman felt a great sense of professional accomplishment, she nevertheless bowed to her family's wishes to honor cultural traditions and agree to an arranged marriage. Although her husband was a nice guy, the demands that he and his family made upon her were untenable in her position as a professor and campus leader. She avoided having children and soon opted for divorce, a move that allowed her to continue a successful career and grow in social power. A hundred years ago, the intellect of such a woman would have been suppressed or not even noticed. Now our society allows women to compete with men directly and leave patriarchy in the dust.

Long-established power dynamics are thus being upended in a revolution that really is all about showing skill and bringing in the cash. Sexual dimorphism is no handicap for weaker females—or disabled men—because we now rely on automobiles and machines, computers and wheelchairs.

As more people are earning their own keep, so to speak, fewer need to find refuge in the old patriarchal standbys—marriage, being a stay-at-home wife, even keeping a nonbinary identity hidden. In fact, people are deciding they don't need to identify as male or female at all; technological innovation and capitalist economic shifts have been key movers in breaking down traditional gender roles and identities. Children are no longer necessary to economic success; indeed, they have become an expensive luxury. Unlike couples with a family, partners who choose not to have children are able to invest and save, funneling their resources directly into their own emancipation.

In a traditional pairing, the new economic equality can lead to a male partner resenting a female breadwinner because he feels his shortcomings according to the expectations of the old gender-based distribution of power. Also, recent demands for equality in marriage have led to nonbinary legal unions, a bitter reality for traditionalists who believe marriage can only be between a man and a woman. Anger about such developments is on ferocious display in modern societies as the rules of the game continue to change.

At the same time, overly active males of the human species find themselves increasingly diagnosed with attention deficit/hyperactivity disorder, unable to sit still and produce as they are expected to in this new service-oriented economy. Or they are labeled with anger-management problems as our corporatized economies increasingly demand compliance and teamwork. We might contemplate the irony that the patriarchal hoarders themselves have created the very industrialized, capitalist circumstances demanding such constant work from everyone that they have completely destabilized the traditional male-centered monopolization of scarce resources and the aggression typically used to get them. Most of us earn very little in comparison to our billionaire overlords—but we are all busting to earn that little bit extra, and that in and of itself is liberating us from our fathers' rules.

Traditional society is falling all around us, to be replaced with we know not what. We are finally breaking up with pharaoh; divorcing our controlling husband; coming out as gay, lesbian, transgender, bisexual, or asexual; exposing sexual harassers; naming child abusers; turning on morally compromised priests and politicians; leaving the church; defunding the police. Meanwhile, the jilted patriarch is reacting strongly as society goes through elemental—dare we say, scandalous—change, erupting in ways that for some people approach Bill Murray's celebrated line in *Ghostbusters*: "Human sacrifice, dogs and cats living together, mass hysteria!"

Human society has reached the point where the patriarchs are rising up to take back their power, simply because they always had it. We know the headlines well: "Florida Man Kills Self, Wife and 2 Children in Apparent Murder-Suicide,"[3] "Mass Shooting at Orlando Gay Club,"[4] "Gunman Opens Fire on Las Vegas Concert Crowd, Wounding Hundreds and Killing 58,"[5] "Man Raped Woman at Gunpoint After She Rebuffed His Advances,"[6] ". . . Anger Mounts Over Killing of Black Jogger Caught on Video,"[7] "No Retaliation in Walmart's Firing of Worker Who Reported Sex Harassment,"[8] "LGBTQ Military Service Members at Higher Risk of Sexual Harassment, Assault, Stalking,"[9] "A Rising Number of Homeless Gay Teens Are Being Cast Out by Religious Families,"[10] ". . . California Man Beats Teen Syrian Refugee for Speaking Arabic,"[11] "Woman Killed by Husband in Warren Had Recently Left Him, Filed for Divorce, Family Says."[12]

Such incidents are well known, as are the perpetrators who feel justified in their anger because of a loss of traditional power or confusion over upended social roles, just like the Egyptian king righteously displaying his dispatch of the rebel on thousands of temple pylons. To put it quite simply: Men have gotten used to inhabiting a macho identity and getting emotional care, a clean home, obedient children, sex, and even love without having to worry about being kind or desirable or attractive, simply because they have had all the resources. That is quickly changing, and the resulting disbelief is part of our societal stew.

We should note here that the patriarchy hurts men too, demanding strict adherence to a cis sexual identity, prioritizing anger and violence over softer emotions, frowning upon certain kinds of work such as nursing or teaching that are considered too womanly. Opposing the patriarchy isn't man-hating. It is an attempt to heal a society that has been sick for more than 10,000 years.

We all feel the paradigm shift happening around us—in our own fields, our own franchises, our own fiefdoms—but we don't quite know what to do about it. Indeed, the fall of the patriarchy could be the very reason why everyone in the world seems to be arguing, blaming, demonizing—not just in the United States, but globally. The issues are fiercely fought, with the two polarized sides each arguing for their position: Abortion. Gun rights. Men's rights. Women's rights. Intersectionality. LGBTQ rights. Gays in the military. Gay marriage. The wage gap. The glass ceiling. Women in politics. Religion in politics. Money in politics. Climate change. Birth control. Sex education. America first. Britain first. Caste systems. And whose lives really do matter.

There can be no better image of the shifting sands beneath our feet than a Black Lives Matter demonstration in St. Louis, Missouri. It passed the marble-clad home of Mark and Patricia McCloskey, two wealthy White lawyers each aiming their precious firearms directly at the crowd: an AR-15 rifle in the arms of Mark, in a pink polo shirt, and a tiny silver handgun held by Patricia, in a striped Hamburglar top. The couple had the weapons cocked and ready to shoot because they believed that the BLM marchers would break into their home, take their things, and do them grave harm. This visualized death threat directed at the protestors was their right, they believed, their privilege to show to society.

Or consider 17-year-old Kyle Rittenhouse, who used his semi-automatic weapon to kill two Black men in Kenosha, Wisconsin, while waging a glorious race war on behalf of his inherited White power. That's not to mention the White people who rallied behind him to post his bail. Fear has gripped the patriarchy, and the threat of righteous violence—or the lethal use of it—is the patriarchy's response.

The rage is real and inflicted with all the power that the system can muster—through the office of the presidency, the police, the church, the courts, the drawing of county lines, voting laws, and privately owned firearms. Patriarchal anger exists in a purely binary space in which the male of the species has been the good king for so long that he sees no other way. The morality of the authoritarian regime is the most powerful part of the game, veiling the overt controls. We continue to be seduced by the principles of it all—the ethics of our rulers, the virtuousness of our wars, the righteousness of our exploitation of others, the necessity of harsh punishments for those with addictions, who are poor, have mental illness, are Black, gay.

Authoritarians will make us stifle not only our back talk and rebellion, but also our idle thoughts, our joyful dances, our music making, our queerness, our bad words, our strange clothing, and our purple hair. We are meant to engage in the necessary beating and academic drilling of our children for their own good. If we belong to the power brokers, we consider ourselves members of the same "family," a code word for the license to constrain and exploit others with impunity. "Family" is the authoritarian's food and drink, his sex and labor, his wealth and afterlife. "Family" demands that we blame the victims for the powerlessness we have imposed upon them. We have all learned the hard way that when a leader says you are part of a "family," or that we need to re-instill good "family" values, a crackdown is ahead.

Patriarchy's most skillful retort is its reminder of the coming discord, civil war, the next *Mad Max*-like reality. Every fetishized trope in the latest apocalyptic film—the cannibalism, the incest, the gore—is injected into our imagination. Every discussion of societal collapse drives home the possibility of our ultimate destruction without the presence of our protective fathers, our lords and masters, for whom we should be most grateful.

Indeed, the specter of collapse is the fertilizer of the whole authoritarian system. Armageddon is meant to scare us straight, the scorched earth of keeping us in line, the terror that the sun might not rise again if Apophis is not dispatched, causing everyone to go scurrying for new strongmen to keep us safe. Collapse empowers the emerging overlord. But authoritarians do not like to recognize the collapse of their own making. Human-induced climate change is denied. Its gangbuster hurricane seasons are downplayed. The viral nature of a pandemic is discounted. Acts of God undercut the patriarchy's divinely endowed power. None of the ancient Egyptian tales of woe reminded people of droughts or epidemics, for instance—only the vile foreigners and the tomb robbers.

Clever authoritarians look for scapegoats, stirring up fear about Mexicans massing on our borders or "decadent" social liberties. We have only ourselves to blame, we are told, taking on the responsibility for the next apocalypse before it has even started. The coming Sodom and Gomorrahs are gay marriage and nasty women, libtards and snowflakes, Black Lives Matter and antifa. Blame it on them.

There's a reason that conservative factions in society obsess on social collapse as they cling to traditional gender roles and prep for the apocalypse with glee, creating custom-built fallout shelters, exhorting their women to can food and engage in do-it-yourself medical care while they stockpile assault weapons. It's a way of returning everyone to the hard line emotionally, ideologically, without any impetus except the memory of the last spate of bloodshed—caused by those same hard-liners.

Ancient Egypt has been to those apocalyptic places before. Its so-called intermediate periods are characterized by a lack of strong kings, unclear histories, civil wars, and atrocities as warlords fought for the top spot. Egypt went through at least three such interludes—the nadirs of the country's long existence, the histories tell us.

But the dark days never allowed a society to break up with their pharaoh. Each time a new king reconsolidated, he included more people in his administration, making the pie bigger, giving the appearance of social inclusion, communicating to everyone that wealth really and truly would trickle down this time. Thus the ancient Egyptian booms and busts continued apace, allowing the kingship to present itself with updated ruling personalities, a repackaged look, a new name.

But whether Khufu's monarchical divination, Senwosret's absolutism, Akhenaten's fanaticism, Ramses' populism, or Taharqa's pious orthodoxy, Egyptian pharaonic history was largely a patriarchal rinse and repeat with approximately the same result. The modern world has been tossed around in the same cycle, albeit with more stark philosophical differences—communism or capitalism, socialism or democracy, fascism or theocracy, totalitarianism or oligarchy, with all the bloodshed in between—and yet it's all still essentially the same patriarchal system. And with every new cycle, each leader uses the pain of the last fall to cement his nascent rule. Rinse and repeat.

The patriarchy is the water in which we all swim, unknowable to most, normalized for all. Humans have been thinking in these unequal, controlling, spreadsheeting, market-driven, power-obsessed, smash-and-grab, consumptive, accumulating, domesticating, competitive ways for so long that we feel we don't know any other way. We find ourselves looking up from our hard labors only to see that the landscape has been clear-cut while we weren't looking, that the toxic smog of industry suddenly hides the blue sky, and that a few billionaires have carved out pleasure gardens with beautiful furnishings, air purifiers, and high walls. In response, we have cleaved into two factions: one group that wants to walk forward to find a different way and another group that just wants a king, like the one Israel asked for in the Book of Samuel 1:8.

You might insist that we modern humans are elementally different from anybody in the ancient world, that any comparison between then and now is cheap and facile. We have vaccines, spaceships, iPhones, factory-made clothing, single-use plastics, flush toilets, and one-day delivery. We don't suffer from the overmasculinized vagaries of power with harems and phallic imagery.

Or do we? Our superstar culture of youth and vigor and sexual strength appears in every celebrity social media post. Our pedigreed

power (M.A. from Yale! Ph.D. from Harvard!) is written into our academic dossiers. Egyptologists buy into their legend that we are the best
purveyors of true, unbiased history because we claim to have no political
agenda over that history—and yet we shut out most non-White practitioners who dare to conflate modern and ancient power.

We Egyptologists benefit from the positive optics of great kings so far
removed from us that we can buy into their history as its quiet advocates.
We dress up in our colonial button-down shirts and khaki trousers, with
fedoras or pith helmets on our heads,[13] and lead the charge to learn about
the ancient past for "its own sake." There is no real understanding that
almost all our scholarship is uncritically supportive of authoritarian
policies. There is little appreciation for the fact that the economics of
preparation for Ph.D.'s serve as gatekeepers to the field. No surprise,
then, that women have been let into the academy right when the entire
structure of higher education is being carpet-bombed with privatization
and gig capitalism.

If you say you want a revolution, well, you know, that's just patriarchy
too. Revolutions have done nothing more than replace one unequal and
exploitative male-dominated system with another, installing another
impenetrable layer of ideology that we can squabble over. We have tried
out all the governments—each seemingly the last, best solution to our
human situation. We hit upon democracy in our epic battle against
monarchy. Then communism arose in its cosmic fight against capitalism.
Liberal capitalist democracies, with their conveniences and abundance,
made us feel like we had finally solved it all until we started to suspect
that our billionaires had become kings, that the stock markets were not
the equalizers we thought they were, and that our unbridled consumption was destroying our one and only home. We may think we are more
clever than Egyptians worshipping god-kings. But it is only that our
latitude for damage is that much greater.

Only when we figure out how the patriarchy wields its mesmerizing power can we smash it. But just as it's being revealed for the alcoholic, abusive father that it is, the old man is fighting back with the most fierce of ideological weaponry. Socialism is categorized as the ultimate societal evil. Female leaders must masculinize to succeed, but are paradoxically put down for being ugly and deceitful. Patriarchal systems malign gay people as weak, mercilessly mistreating them as aberrant.

Perhaps most disturbingly, the prepubescent virgin female body is put on a pedestal as the ideal. It is commodified by plastic surgery and the weight-loss industry, deemed something to be owned, shielded, and veiled yet simultaneously displayed and penetrated: perfect for a patri-arch to sow his seed in. Patriarchy categorizes the unmarried woman as a dried-up, unwanted, unprotected, and crusty old maid, while the woman past her sexual use-by date is considered an invisible and useless crone. Conversely, the male-dominated system sees the woman who has had sex as used goods at best, a slut or whore at worst; she is someone to be eventually cast aside in favor of a newer model, as 67-year-old actor Dennis Quaid has demonstrated with four marriages, most recently to a 27-year-old woman.

THE FUTURE WE HAVE FORGOTTEN

We are like children who can hear our parents fighting, knowing something is terribly wrong, but no one will tell us what is going on. Some people are shouting with angry voices for us to go back to when things were great and moral, if we know what's good for us. Others—an increas-ing majority of us in many places—keep stepping forward, another step and then another. We can see the rules of a new game emerging as we move back to norms and values that are so ancient they seem new.

It is time to forget what we think we know and remember what we have forgotten. The patriarchy is an unsustainable human experiment whose endgame is quickly coming. Earth's abundance will run out if we keep amassing resources, cutting down trees to make us rich only to be surprised that what we've done has choked off the very air we breathe. We need to look to the time before humans invented pyramids and obelisks, colossi and skyscrapers, combustion engines and plastics, constitutions and good kings, and settle into a future version of what we used to be a long, long time ago.

Humanity has been sick for a long time: oppressed, beaten, and racked by demands for constant growth. Over the last 10,000 years, we have craved a forgotten home, glimpses of which we somehow remember from long ago and into whose comforting arms we quickly return when given half the chance. We are not talking about a matriarchy, something so mythical it can only exist in Wonder Woman comics. Instead, we crave societies in which males do not repressively dominate females, in which different sexualities are celebrated, in which strong goddesses are worshipped not as mere appendages of masculine creator gods but as agents in their own right.

Female divinities that seem to have been mainstays of most patriarchal religions were relegated to working on behalf of their good fathers as sexualized beings or violent protectors or nurturing mothers. In Egypt, we know of Sakhmet, Hathor, Isis, Nephthys, and Neith; in India, there are Kali and Durga; in Greece, Athena and Demeter. But the goddess is much more than that, and much older.

Historians study the tension between Egypt's Hathoric, sexualized, drunken feast days with the more sober pharaonic rule of the masculine sun god. They recognize how orgiastic Dionysius festivals clashed with the rigid patriarchal control of sexuality in ancient Greece and Rome. And they examine pagan European rituals, such as the winter solstice and spring festivals, that simultaneously threatened and combined with Christian celebrations of Christ's birth and death.

Our festivals have shown us how we long for unrestricted and equalized social identities. What we used to be is still there, though, biding its time. If the goddess is allowed to earn her own way, not serve her lord and master, maybe we can follow our own agenda too.

Marija Gimbutas was a 20th-century archaeologist who studied the inclusive and equalizing elements of Neolithic European human societies, a time before the Indo-European patriarchy rolled in and mowed down the old systems. Her work has been much maligned by some of today's best and brightest archaeologists. Scholars such as Ian Hodder and Lynn Meskell, with their post-processual theories and cognitive archaeological ideas, have cynically assigned Gimbutas to the category of a hysterical matriarchal revisionist dancing in her coven.[14] But Gimbutas was just remembering what we had all forgotten, hearing the faint whispers of a pre-patriarchal culture that worked in community with the landscape: not raping, hoarding, fencing, or commodifying, but living as one of its many animals, participating in its many cycles.

As early as 12,000 years ago, humanity began its trek through the Neolithic revolution. It happened first in the Fertile Crescent of West Asia, ushering in plant and animal domestication along with our beloved patriarchy and the first towns in Anatolia. Then came the urban revolution of 5,000 years ago, introducing the first regional state in Egypt and the first city-states in Mesopotamia. The industrial revolution of some 500 years ago helped us build stronger, better, faster. The sexual revolution is ongoing. (I think we are on the third Year of the Woman, at least.) What human revolution is next? We are finally discussing misogyny and antiracism, and *intersectionality* and *caste* are new buzzwords. Perhaps we now find ourselves poised at the brink of an antipatriarchal revolution of some kind, leading to . . . what?

Patriarchy has only ruled a few hundred years in Los Angeles, where the aforementioned pre-Hispanic Tongva peoples created a society in which men and women were practical equals in their council of elders. The Tongva fished the waterways that fed into the Pacific Ocean; a woman could spear just as many fish as the guy next to her, holding her own like my Pakistani engineering colleague. The ability of the Tongva female to bring in scarce resources translated to a seat on the elder's council within her society.

This isn't a parable of the good hunter-gatherer versus the bad agriculturalist, though. The takeaway is that the Tongva valued their women as leaders alongside their men, specifically because of the foundation of their economy. The region's geography allowed women to be active economic participants.

We have now covered over the Tongva tributaries with concrete and channeled the waters into farming and industry. But the ancient models of such people could be our salvation as we look to a future in which scarce resources are no longer monopolized by our fathers, sexuality is not an imposed sacrifice, marriage is not required, established religions with orthodoxies and hierarchies don't exist, population growth is not the backbone of economic soundness, and people live in sustainable companionship with other animals and plants. Many would see this as an over-romanticization of Indigenous peoples we have fenced in and assimilated. But others may see it as the way humans have lived for most of our species' existence, over hundreds of thousands of years—and a place we must find our way back to before patriarchal competition makes Earth itself unlivable.

If we are to change the patriarchy from within, we'll have to use different tactics from the ones we've tried before. Consider the example of the Black Lives Matter movement, whose radical inclusion of all manner of people is the jujitsu move against a more powerful opposition. We all remember that the fight against separate-but-equal segregation—at lunch counters, elementary schools, universities, and public spaces—

made Rosa Parks a hero when she took a seat in the White section of a public bus and started the Montgomery bus boycott. But the people who led the charge in the 1960s were male civil rights activists—Medgar Evers, Martin Luther King, Jr., Malcolm X, and John Lewis. In the 1960s, patriarchy combated patriarchy.

But when the optics of Black-White equality were created, the Black man bore the brunt of the backlash. For the White man, his Black counterpart became an ever more feared cipher of animalistic aggression and lawlessness, triggering racist abuse and exploitation in different forms: harsher sentencing, for-profit imprisonment, reduced employment and educational opportunities, poor medical care, and corporatized discrimination.

The current Black Lives Matter (BLM) movement is much broader, allowing gay and lesbian voices, Indigenous voices, women's voices. Indeed, this decentralized political movement calling for civil disobedience against police brutality is largely run by women. Alicia Garza, Patrisse Cullors, and Opal Tometi created the first 30 national chapters between 2014 and 2016. BLM's civil disobedience focuses attention on unfair practices, rather than broadcasting just another patriarchal claim that ramps up aggression on the opposing side. This has provoked the petulant reactions of White Lives Matter and Blue Lives Matter, making the patriarchy all the more recognizable and repugnant to many White Americans who now count themselves BLM supporters. When we include more voices rather than bowing to the basso notes of patriarchal traditions, things can shift.

Sometimes antipatriarchy tactics include using the moves of our opponent against him, as taught by martial arts. Take the case of Stacey Abrams. In 2018, she ran for governor of Georgia. Her opponent, then Georgia's Secretary of State Brian Kemp, was in charge of protecting and implementing all the voting laws. He accused Abrams's office of cybercrimes, canceled a scheduled debate at the last minute, and threw out hundreds of thousands of voter registrations—most of them from counties with Black populations. Abrams lost the election by only 50,000 votes, but chose not to call for a recount, even while stating that the election had not been free and fair (a fact later corroborated in court).

Abrams understood that demanding a recount would be perceived as unduly aggressive, something that stakeholders could easily oppose with fury and righteousness. Instead, she co-opted the voting system of the patriarchy by creating Fair Fight 2020, a methodical campaign to mobilize voters against state-funded voter suppression. This resulted in a razor-thin margin in Georgia for 2020 presidential candidate Joe Biden, and two Senate races so close they required a runoff election in 2021—which, through Abrams's calm and calculated efforts, ultimately fell into the Democratic column.

Abrams worked strategically against a patriarchal opponent much more powerful and better armed than she was. She moved in so patiently, so close, that she made him lose his balance, as the best karate practitioners do. In the end, Kemp's unfair tactics were outed, and Abrams's inclusivity and grassroots mobilization resulted in the fairest elections Georgia had seen in centuries.

Women are now gaining real political power, and the 2020 coronavirus pandemic has provided a useful rubric through which to judge whether society is ruled better when women are valued as change makers. The female prime ministers of New Zealand and Finland, for instance, differentiated themselves brilliantly from the old-school, competitive patriarchs of Britain and the United States by orchestrating a national management of community-based safety during the pandemic. They redefined politics as usual, rather than basing survival on fallacious denialism and individualist, sink-or-swim, herd immunity.

Kamala Harris is a precursor of what is to come—a woman with no dynasty, a mixed immigrant past, the wife of a divorced husband, a childless woman. She is a conglomeration of strong feminism incongruously originating within a traditional patriarchal society. One of the most extraordinary things about Harris's candidacy was how much she was criticized for her past harsh sentencing of people of color. But she has used the tools of the patriarchy—such as its strong prosecutorial practices—against it. She has now emerged as an effective figure on the national stage to lead us forward into antipatriarchal practices.

Meanwhile, change is happening everywhere—in our homes and schools, streets and businesses—as we leave the systems of our good fathers behind. More women are now earning college degrees and acting as the breadwinners for their families. Children who, until recently, were seen but not heard, are now included in the running of households, allowed to offer an opinion rather than being worked or schooled into silence.

Even more extraordinary, the nature of education itself is changing, and although we still have drilling and testing, teachers are also interested in experiment and play. Androgyny is celebrated. Feminism is not angry. Middle-aged plumpness can be beautiful. Childbirth is not commodified, controlled, or even necessary. Masculinity is not feared, moralizing, or violent. Cooperation is not weak. Everyone is a little bit queer. And manifest destiny, Christopher Columbus, and the totem of the American flag? We are questioning all of that.

"Haven't we been down this path before?" you might ask. The late 1960s created a similar thought revolution, but with little lasting impact on the patriarchy. Are we truly on the cusp of another human revolution? Or are we headed for more of the same, but with a thud after the next collapse that's even bigger than what ancient Egypt experienced after one of its intermediate periods?

We might remind ourselves here that the 1960s peace-and-love revolution was not inclusive; it was primarily for the benefit of White, Western males, as represented by the Grateful Dead lyrics, "We can share the women; we can share the wine." The casting aside of society's rules was really only for the sons of stakeholders. And when it was all over, many of those freethinkers just came home and got their M.B.A.'s, happily finding financial success as postwar baby boomers. Ironically, the marches and sit-ins of the 1960s brought additional White financiers telling us that unregulated growth was best, White politicians telling us that we can't rush the equalization of Black people or women, neoliberalists such as Bill Clinton enjoying his Oval Office mini-harem, and democratic populists such as Donald Trump surrounding himself with traditional women who find ongoing success in archaic patriarchal structures, and working a new ideological angle that what liberated women like Ivanka Trump really want are old family values.

But capitalism's rapaciousness is exactly what has released the kraken and altered our society fundamentally. It has created a population so stretched and so overburdened that most people have to work like crazy and use every brain cell to find an edge. We can now clearly see the patriarchy's oppression, inequality, and cruelty. Our good fathers try to throw an ideological veil over their game, using Abrahamic religion and patriotism—but it's not working the way it did before.

For example, we now realize that a few White male junk-food purveyors are making billions while others of the same ilk make similar fortunes from the medicines that treat the resulting diabetes. We see that wars are the solution to nothing, and we recognize the moneymaking capabilities of the military-industrial complex in a country forever at war. We even acknowledge how a pandemic can be super profitable, not to mention that some countries can buy up the new vaccines and decide who will get inoculated first, leaving poor countries in the dust of their gracious patronage to their economic liege lords. And we are finally seeing that our diverse population should be represented in the leadership of a presidential administration, demanding at least an attempt at a cross section of male and female, White and Black and Brown, gay and straight, old and young.

I was recently teaching a course on ancient Egyptian kingship, comparing the ancient kings to today, and one kid said with exasperation, "But every government in the world is authoritarian! What can we even do?" His despair was real; modern politics seem like the same story of Khufu and Senwosret and Akhenaten and Ramses and Taharqa all over again. But I found myself saying no—there are places and people trying to do it differently. This is not an exercise in futility. Not this time.

But you won't always see change at the top of society. Instead, look at what's bubbling up from the bottom. More of us want governments interested in equitable futures for everyone.[15] All over the world, the patriarchy is being deleted from the inside out. Fathers are not our only leaders; mothers have a part to play as well. And so do those who decide not to be parents at all. The American modern family is looking very different from the way it did just 20 years ago. Separated from grandparents, aunts, uncles, and cousins, we have started to build neighborhood pods of support, following what people are the bottom of society have always done by pooling resources—for the entire floor of an apartment building, or an entire block, or an entire tribe. Families, once built from the marriage of one man and one woman, have become mixed, communal villages coming together to care for one another.

If the good kings depend on the ideology of fearmongering and our faith in their singular ability to put everything back to rights, then this is one of the very things that is changing. Many of us are no longer afraid—of the Black family moving into the neighborhood, of the undocumented immigrant caring for our elderly mother, of the gay son who is moving in with his boyfriend, of our unmarried daughter who has just gotten pregnant. What we are afraid of—and incredibly angry about—is the obvious lack of social equality, systemic racism, capitalized health care, discrimination, warehousing of our elderly, neglect of those with mental illness, lack of housing for people experiencing poverty, punishments for those suffering addictions, and a cruel prison-industrial complex. The inequalities are now visible for all to see. And right now, it's hard to see much else.

More than anything, it's time for humanity to recognize that Earth—with all its viruses and bacteria, melting polar ice, burning forests, heat-driven hurricanes, and dying species—has an agency of its own. The planet has something to say about this whole patriarchy thing, and it's not good.

We humans have thought ourselves the masters of our universe for too long. The ideology of the pharaohs once reified the superiority of humans in our minds, as have countless religions and governments that have fashioned us as the sovereigns of world, lords of all plants and animals, able to infiltrate each and every ecosystem and pave it over to build McMansions and golf courses, factories and strip mines. We have plunged our fingers deep into our ears when experts said we were to blame for unlivable temperatures and rising ocean levels, or when research concluded that emerging viruses will decimate our population in the future.

But we are now beginning to realize that we're more dependent on the totality of Earth's life than Earth is on our human stewardship. All our patriarchal leadership has gotten us is eight billion people, a toxic stew of sludge, a pandemic to clean up, and a whole mess of plastic for future archaeologists to bulldoze through (because no one is sifting that shit in the next two thousand years). We are starting to re-appreciate how humanity is connected to the other animals and plant life around us, how we're not separate from or dominant over them. And we're seeing research into economic models built on sustainability, not growth for lucky insiders. Earth can't take much more of what we've been doing. It's time for all of humanity to break up with its pharaohs, find different leadership models, and craft something new.

Equal society, nonbinary sexuality, strong, powerful women, creating our own villages, having time for leisure pursuits, following the cycles of the sun and moon—these are powerful ideas. We are prone to ridicule such things because they seem a bit peace-and-love hippie-dippy, and more than a bit naive in the face of the next apocalypse. But if all these antipatriarchal shifts were merely the products of misguided sentiments, they wouldn't foment such hate among those in power. If they were all ineffectual and harmless, they wouldn't be considered such radical challenges.

In the end, the patriarchy had its 10,000 years. Our once beloved patriarch is getting old, and we can see now that he's not only controlling but more than a little abusive. We want out. His moralizing sermons and gaslighting don't work the way they used to, because we're not afraid anymore. We can earn our living without him, and we're ready to walk away.

Yes, our good king is angry, and he's ready to fight to the bitter end. He has always stalked us, terrorized us, bullied and moralized, tempted and bribed us to stay until he had us just where he thought we belonged. But now he's threatening to kill us. And the kids too. He's telling us he will burn everything down and turn the gun on himself.

What to do against such reckless insecurity? It's time for the whole family to get out of the abusive home, no matter how physically comfortable or secure it might seem. The patriarchy has become a toxic place for everyone living there.

The ancient Egyptian people never could figure out how to move on from the patriarchy, to their everlasting detriment. They kept doing the same thing, making the same choices—returning to the model of the good king after every chaotic apocalypse as if they might get a different result. We know that is the definition of madness; history allows us to see that pattern of human idiocy. But if we carefully consider the fact that the traditional path carved by ancient Egyptians over the millennia is the same one most people are currently walking, maybe we will at last decide to draw on the wisdom of our long-distant ancestors and forge new paths to places we thought we had forgotten.

Our survival and the future of our children depend on it.

ACKNOWLEDGMENTS

I owe an enormous debt of gratitude to a whole lot of UCLA undergraduate students who were subjected to the contents of a book on Egyptian kingship that I inelegantly forced into a class on Egyptian religion. My lectures were meant to be in person but ended up on Zoom during the COVID pandemic of 2020. Presenting my thoughts remotely on kingship, authoritarianism, and patriarchy to a class of 200 students and some six graduate teaching assistants forced me to quickly formulate my thoughts on power, and on how humans manufacture it, without the helpful give-and-take of a live class. Strangely, the safety of never leaving my Mar Vista office helped me to be braver with those ideas, and the weekly discussions with students allowed me to streamline the messaging.

I am thankful for my many social media followers who watched my live or taped lectures on these topics via Facebook, Twitter, and YouTube, always benefiting from lively (too lively, sometimes) back-and-forth discussion that helped me to better formulate my thoughts (and defensive strategies).

When I settled down to pull all this madness into a coherent whole, I relied on the indefatigable Amber Myers Wells, my trusty companion of footnotes and events scheduling and various high jinks, to transcribe my 20 hours of lecturing into some kind of prose that I could mess with. She had just been through some serious stuff herself, and I will forever be grateful for the single-minded way she threw herself into this task and the many others to follow. Don't you quit me, Amber.

So many of my thoughts on these topics have been informed and nudged along and batted down by constant and passionate discussion among our die-hard cohort of UCLA lecturers, graduate students, and colleagues who formed seminars of radical questioning. Those people include Dani Candelora, Nadia Ben-Marzouk, Jonathan Winnerman, Marissa Stevens, Michael Chen, Jordan Galczynski, Vera Rondano, Rose Campbell, Carrie Arbuckle, Andrew Danielson, Amr Shahat, Robyn Price, Jeffrey Newman, Nick Brown, Maryan Ragheb, Kylie Thomsen, Matei Tichindelean, and Hong Yu Chen. You all challenge me every day, and I wouldn't have it any other way.

To my UCLA crew—Diane Ohkawahira, Yadira Marquez, Barbara Van Nostrand, and Tiffany Chen—you are the best partners of department chairmanship ever. You all know I couldn't do it without you.

To my colleagues who understand that I need (we need) to make history relevant—Violaine Chauvet, JJ Shirley, Luigi Prada, and Paul Wordsworth—thank you for the feedback, support, and weekly chats.

For Rahim Shayegan, who also studies kings and power, but of ancient Iran, I am grateful for your advice along this crazy journey.

Profound thanks to my agent, Marc Gerald, whose counsel on all things literary is so valuable. I am indebted.

To my National Geographic editors Hilary Black, Ann Williams, and Moriah Petty, thank you for giving me free rein to be provocative, for catching me when I fell, and for supporting me when I pulled multiple all-nighters to finish that last draft, after which I promptly needed an emergency appendectomy. (Coincidence?! I think not.)

Thank you, Robin / Rebecca, whatever your name is, who is always there to listen to another worry or rant or idea or madcap scheme. We had quite a 2020, didn't we? And Cali and Rafi were there to help us be strong too.

Thank you, Julian, my antiauthoritarian boy, who has never stopped asking me why things are the way they are, isn't afraid of all the big topics so many of us avoid, and actually needs me to talk openly about them—racism, gender and sexuality, identity, power, shame, social class, economic demands, addiction, work ethics, religion. I am grateful for the long pandemic walks to get boba, and I hope we don't give them up.

Loving thanks to my stepchildren, Kimberly and Branden, who were there every step of the way, asking my opinion about whatever crazy thing had happened that day of 2020, entertained by the madness of my evening writing, ever joyful because it usually meant they got to watch one more *Naruto* or play one more Roblox.

Profound gratitude to Jim and Kelli, whose home is always open in New York when I pass through (and to Livy and Jamie, whose beds I often steal); to Elena and David (and Emilie and Luc), who feed and libate us all in Houston; and to Erin and Dominic for late nights by the fire in Los Angeles.

I send profound love and thanks to my mom and dad, who actually read drafts of this work. I will forever remember my mother joyfully saying, "This is the first one of your books I will actually really want to read!" Even though I suspect my dear mother will only make her way through the first and last chapters, my dad will read the whole damn thing. I'm curious to hear what they both think. That will be a fun night of talk and whiskey and red wine.

And finally, sincere thanks to Remy who well and truly *cared* for me while I wrote this book—forming a company to manage my speaking engagements and media projects, making me take breaks to eat Japanese curry or some other fabulous concoction, cooking the kids' food so I could crank out some more work, always making me laugh somehow, someway, during a difficult year in which I hardly left the house. Remy nonetheless managed to craft at least two dozen brilliant paintings and even a few dozen pots on his new wheel, all of which we will display soon in a bohemian pop-up gallery, I promise. I am even grateful for his forced marches on which we discussed everything from home decor to apocalypse. Remy never shoots an idea down; he gets thoughtful and says, "Have you thought about how . . . ?" and we're off. Remy commented on every page of the first draft and a whole lot of the second, and his insightful ideas helped to form the core of the book. I can be brave because he provides so much light.

NOTES

CHAPTER 1

1 Genesis 41:29-36.

2 This depiction of Akhenaten and Nefertiti in their window of appearances is seen, for example, in the tombs of Ay (TA25), Parennefer (TT188), and Ramose (TT55). For more information, see Cyril Aldred, *Akhenaten and Nefertiti* (Brooklyn Museum/Viking Press, 1973); Nicholas Reeves, *Akhenaten: Egypt's False Prophet* (Thames & Hudson, 2001); Dimitri Laboury, *Akhenaton and Ancient Egypt in the Amarna Era* (Cambridge University Press, 2017).

3 James C. Scott, *Seeing Like a State: How Certain Schemes to Improve the Human Condition Have Failed* (Yale University Press, 1998), 78. See Scott's discussion of the legibility of the Dutch state and how the information made it easy for the Nazis to find and put undesirables in camps. The state's ability to know and intervene, we should remember, is "a capacity that in principle could as easily have been deployed to feed the Jews as to deport them."

4 See Anne Applebaum, "History Will Judge the Complicit," *The Atlantic*, July/August 2020.

5 David Graeber and Marshall Sahlins, *On Kings* (HAU Books/University of Chicago Press, 2017).

6 William E. Scheuerman, "American Kingship? Monarchical Origins of Modern Presidentialism," *Polity* 37 (January 2005): 24–53.

7 Walter Scheidel, *Escape From Rome: The Failure of Empire and the Road to Prosperity* (Princeton University Press, 2019).

8 See Anne Applebaum, "History Will Judge"; John Bolton, *The Room Where It Happened: A White House Memoir* (Simon & Schuster, 2020).

9 Jan Assmann, *Ma'at: Gerechtigkeit und Unsterblichkeit im Alten Ägypten* [Ma'at: Justice and Mortality in Ancient Egypt] (C. H. Beck, 2006).

10 Thomas P. Bonczar and Allen J. Beck, *Lifetime Likelihood of Going to State or Federal Prison* (U.S. Department of Justice, Office of Justice Programs, Bureau of Justice Statistics, 1997).

11 For translation, see Miriam Lichtheim, *Ancient Egyptian Literature,* vol. I, *The Old and Middle Kingdoms* (University of California Press, paperback edition, 1975), 169–84.

12 James C. Scott, *Weapons of the Weak: Everyday Forms of Peasant Resistance* (Yale University Press, 1985).

13 The Narmer Palette, JE32169 and CG14716, is on display at the Egyptian Museum in Cairo. Whitney Davis, *Masking the Blow: The Scene of Representation in Late Prehistoric Egyptian Art* (University of California Press 1992), 162–63, fig. 38.

14 Michael Mann, *The Sources of Social Power,* vol. 1 of *A History of Power from the Beginning to A.D. 1760* (Cambridge University Press, 1986).
15 Carolyn Marvin and David W. Ingle, *Blood Sacrifice and the Nation: Totem Rituals and the American Flag* (Cambridge University Press, 1999), 63.
16 Bjørnar Olsen, *In Defense of Things: Archaeology and the Ontology of Objects* (AltaMira Press, 2010), 63; Ian Hacking, *The Social Construction of What?* (Harvard University Press, 1999), 24.

CHAPTER 2

1 Although B.C. and A.D. are used in this book, it is important to realize that most historians of antiquity prefer to use BCE, "Before Current Era," and CE, "Current Era." See Joshua Mark, "The Origin and History of the BCE/CE Dating System," in *Ancient History Encyclopedia* (2017), www.ancient.eu/article/1041.
2 Pyramid Text Spell 217. For discussion and translation, see James P. Allen, *The Ancient Egyptian Pyramid Texts,* vol. 23 (Society of Biblical Literature, 2005).
3 Pyramid Text Spell 373.
4 Ibid.
5 Pyramid Text Spell 253.
6 Pyramid Text Spell 263.
7 Pyramid Text Spell 337.
8 This story is from Papyrus Westcar. For a translation, see Lichtheim, *Ancient Egyptian Literature,* vol. I, 215–22.
9 *Herodotus,* bk. II, 124–27. A. D. Godley, *Herodotus, With an English Translation* (William Heinemann Ltd., 1931), 425–31.
10 Manetho is the Egyptian priest-historian who organized Egyptian history into 30 dynasties. W. G. Waddell, *Manetho* (Harvard University/William Heinemann Ltd., 1940), 49.
11 Rolf Gundlach and John H. Taylor, *Egyptian Royal Residences* (Harrassowitz, 2009).
12 Alexandra A. O'Brien, "The Serekh as an Aspect of the Iconography of Early Kingship," *JARCE* 33 (1996): 123–38; David Ian Lightbody, *On the Origins of the Cartouche and Encircling Symbolism in Old Kingdom Pyramids* (Archaeopress, 2020).
13 Alan H. Gardiner, *Egyptian Grammar* (Griffith Institute, 1957), 132.
14 For more on the ritualization of power, see David I. Kertzer, *Ritual, Politics, and Power* (Yale University Press, 1988).
15 Colin Jones, *Versailles: Landscape of Power and Pleasure* (Head of Zeus Ltd., 2018).
16 Klaus Baer, *Rank and Title in the Old Kingdom* (University of Chicago Press, 1960); Nigel Strudwick, *The Administration of Egypt in the Old Kingdom: The Highest Titles and Their Holders* (KPI Limited, 1985); Miroslav Bárta, "Kings, Viziers, and Courtiers: Executive Power in the Third Millennium B.C.," in *Ancient Egyptian Administration* (Brill, 2013), 153–75.
17 Although some scholars doubt the existence of such an institution in the early dynasties— see Vivienne Gae Callender, *In Hathor's Image: The Wives and Mothers of Egyptian Kings from Dynasties I-VI* (Czech Institute of Egyptology, 2012)—the king certainly had many wives who were documented in burial and temple reliefs. The "harem" as an institution is very controversial, as it conveys the judgment of those who think women should not be compelled to serve one man. Although I do not disavow the inequality such a structure

promotes, I do see the advantages it might provide to a hereditary kingship. We historians discount such advantages at our peril. I do not suggest that the ancient Egyptians had a harem like the Turks or the Chinese, but a harem provided its king with a collection of many young and fruitful women for his reproduction into the next generation. See also Kathlyn M. Cooney, "The Body of Egypt: How the Harem Women Physically Connected a King with His Elites," in *Ancient Egyptian Society: Challenging Assumptions, Exploring Approaches* (Routledge, 2021); Silke Roth, "Harem," in *UCLA Encyclopedia of Egyptology* (2012), escholarship.org/uc/item/1k366313; Elfriede Haslauer, "Harem," in *The Oxford Encyclopedia of Ancient Egypt*, vol. 2 (Oxford University Press, 2001), 76–80.

18 Hratch Papazian, *Domain of Pharaoh: The Structure and Components of the Economy of Old Kingdom Egypt*, vol. 52 (Gebrüder Gerstenberg GmbH & Co, 2012).

19 No Old Kingdom treasury remains, but we have titles and other information. See Nigel Strudwick, "Three Monuments of Old Kingdom Treasury Officials," *JEA* 71 (1985): 43–51.

20 See Katja Goebs, "Crowns," in *The Oxford Encyclopedia of Ancient Egypt*, vol. 1, 321–26.

21 For further reading see Mark Lehner, *The Complete Pyramids* (Thames & Hudson, 1997).

22 The debate continues about how the pyramids were built. See, for example, Jean-Pierre Houdin and Zahi Hawass, *Kheops: Les secrets de la construction de la Grande Pyramide* [Kheops: The Secrets of the Construction of the Great Pyramid] (Éditions du Linteau, 2007); Lehner, *The Complete Pyramids*; Dieter Arnold, *Building in Egypt: Pharaonic Stone Masonry* (Oxford University Press, 1991); Zahi Hawass, "Pyramid Construction: New Evidence Discovered at Giza," *Stationen: Beiträge zur Kulturgeschichte Ägyptens, Rainer Stadelmann gewidmet* [Stations: Contributions to the Cultural History of Egypt, Dedicated to Rainer Stadelmann] (Verlag Philipp von Zabern, 1998), 53–62; Martin Isler, "On Pyramid Building II," *JARCE* 24 (1987): 95–112; Nairy Hampikian, "How Was the Pyramidion Placed at the Top of Khufu Pyramid?" in *Stationen: Beiträge zur Kulturgeschichte Ägyptens, Rainer Stadelmann Gewidmet* (Philipp von Zabern, 1998), 47–51.

23 Donald B. O'Connor, *Abydos: Egypt's First Pharaohs and the Cult of Osiris* (Thames & Hudson, 2009).

24 Laurel Bestock, *The Development of Royal Funerary Cult at Abydos: Two Funerary Enclosures From the Reign of Aha* (Harrassowitz, 2009); Ellen F. Morris, "Sacrifice for the State: First Dynasty Royal Funerals and the Rites at Macramallah's Rectangle," in *Performing Death: Social Analyses of Funerary Traditions in the Ancient Near East and Mediterranean* (University of Chicago, 2007), 15–38; Ellen F. Morris, "(Un)Dying Loyalty: Meditations on Retainer Sacrifice in Ancient Egypt and Elsewhere," in *Violence and Civilization: Studies of Social Violence in History and Prehistory* (Joukowsky Institute Publications, 2013), 61–93.

25 Roselyn Anne Campbell, *Kill Thy Neighbor: Violence, Power, and Human Sacrifice in Ancient Egypt* (University of California, Los Angeles, 2019).

26 Ellen F. Morris, "(Un)Dying Loyalty," fig. 2.2.

27 Alice Stevenson, "The Egyptian Predynastic and State Formation," *JAR* 24, no. 4 (2016): 421–68.

28 Toby A. H. Wilkinson, *Royal Annals of Ancient Egypt: The Palermo Stone and Its Associated Fragments* (Kegan Paul International, 2000).

29 Kurt Sethe, *Denkmäler aus Aegypten und Aethiopien: Text* [Monuments from Egypt and Ethiopia: Text] (J. C. Hinrichs'sche Buchhandlung, 1897).

30 Boston Museum of Fine Arts, MFA 13.3448. Zahi Hawass, "The Khufu Statuette: Is It an Old Kingdom Sculpture?" in *Mélanges Gamal Eddin Mokhtar* [Gamal Eddin Mokhtar Collections], vol. 1 (Institut français d'archéologie orientale du Caire, 1985), 379–94.

31 Brooklyn Museum of Art, 46.167; Staatliches Museum Ägyptischer Kunst in München, ÄS 7086. See Dorothea Arnold, Christiane Ziegler, and Catherine Roehrig, *Egyptian Art in the Age of the Pyramids* (Metropolitan Museum of Art/Harry N. Abrams, 1999), 194, 219.

32 Rainer Stadelmann, "Le grand Sphinx de Giza, chef-d'œuvre du règne de Chéops [The Great Sphinx of Giza, Masterpiece of the Reign of Cheops]" in *Comptes rendus des séances de l'Académie des Inscriptions et Belles-Lettres* [Reports of the Meetings of the Academy of Inscriptions and Belles-Lettres], 143ᵉ année, 3 (1999): 863–79.

33 Egyptian Museum in Cairo, JE 36143; Alan B. Lloyd, ed., *A Companion to Ancient Egypt* (Wiley-Blackwell, 2010), 858, fig. 38.2.

34 Hawass, "The Khufu Statuette," 379–94. Perhaps we could carbon-date the ivory to be sure.

35 For all of these studies, see the Giza Archives at http://gizapyramids.org/static/html/library.jsp; Lehner, *The Complete Pyramids*.

36 Christopher Bartlett, "The Design of the Great Pyramid of Khufu," *Nexus Network Journal* 16 (2014): 299.

37 Strudwick, *The Administration of Egypt in the Old Kingdom*.

38 For a repository of pseudo-archaeological theories about the Giza Pyramids, see this website set up by Logan Miller, https://about-dev.illinoisstate.edu/glmill1/psuedoarchaeology-recources/.

39 For instance, see David O'Connor, "Political Systems and Archaeological Data in Egypt: 2600–1780 B.C.," *World Archaeology* 6, no. 1 (1974): 15–38; R. Müller-Wollermann, "Das ägyptische Alte Reich als Beispiel einer Weberschen Patrimonialbürokratie [The Egyptian Old Empire as an Example of (Max) Weber's Patrimonial Bureaucracy]," *Bulletin of the Egyptological Seminar* 9 (1987): 25–40; Chris Scarre, "The Meaning of Death: Funerary Beliefs and the Prehistorian," in *The Ancient Mind: Elements of Cognitive Archaeology* (Cambridge University Press, 1994), 75–82.

40 There were stone steps, doors, and emplacements, but the tombs themselves were mud brick. Toby A. H. Wilkinson, *Early Dynastic Egypt* (Routledge, 1999).

41 Cecil Mallaby Firth, James E. Quibell, and Jean Philippe Lauer, *Excavations at Saqqara: The Step Pyramid* (l'Institut français d'archéologie orientale, 1935).

42 Kate Spence, "Ancient Egyptian Chronology and the Astronomical Orientation of Pyramids," *Nature* 408 (2000): 320–24.

43 Jean-Philippe Lauer, "The Step Pyramid Precinct of King Djoser," in *Egyptian Art in the Age of the Pyramids* (Metropolitan Museum of Art/Harry N. Abrams, 1999), 12–19.

44 Peter Jánosi, "The Tombs of Officials: Houses of Eternity," in *Egyptian Art in the Age of the Pyramids* (1999), 26–39.

45 Peter Jánosi, *Die Pyramidenanlagen der Königinnen: Untersuchungen zu einem Grabtyp des Alten und Mittleren Reiches* [The Pyramids of the Queens: Investigations into a Grave Type of the Old and Middle Kingdoms], vol. 13 (Österreichischen Akademie der Wissenschaften, 1996).

46 Rainer Stadelmann, "Snofru und die Pyramiden von Meidum und Dahschur [Snefru

and the Pyramids of Meidum and Dahshur]," in *Mitteilungen des Deutschen Archäologischen Instituts, Abteilung Kairo* 36 (1980): 437–49; Ludwig Borchardt, *Die Entstehung der Pyramide an der Baugeschichte der Pyramide bei Mejdum nachgewiesen* [The Origin of the Pyramid Demonstrated by the Building History of the Pyramid at Meidum], vol. 1 (J. Springer, 1928).

47 Ahmed Fakhry, *The Monuments of Sneferu at Dahshur* (General Organization for Government Printing Offices, 1959), 611.

48 For example, we see this sentiment in a piece of didactic literature called the "Instructions of Ptahhotep." The only known complete version of this text comes from the Middle Kingdom, though Miriam Lichtheim proposes that this work would have been originally composed during the latter part of the 6th dynasty. Here, vizier Ptahhotep speaks to his son, saying, "Don't be proud of your knowledge, Consult the ignorant and the wise." See Lichtheim, *Ancient Egyptian Literature,* vol. I, 63.

49 Dennis Rawlins and Keith Pickering, "Astronomical Orientation of the Pyramids," *Nature* 412 (2001): 699.

50 Barbara G. Aston, James A. Harrell, and Ian Shaw, "Stone," in *Ancient Egyptian Materials and Technology* (Cambridge University Press, 2000), 5–77.

51 Linda C. Eneix, *Archaeoacoustics: The Archaeology of Sound: Publication of Proceedings from the 2014 Conference in Malta* (The OTS Foundation, 2014).

52 Hartwig Altenmüller, "Funerary Boats and Boat Pits of the Old Kingdom," *Archiv Orientální* 70 (2002): 269–90.

53 See John Baines, "Kingship, Definition of Culture, and Legitimation," in *Ancient Egyptian Kingship* (E. J. Brill, 1995), 7.

54 Lehner, *The Complete Pyramids,* 224–27.

55 Yannis Gourdon, "Les Inscriptions rupestres de Hatnoub [The Rock Inscriptions of Hatnoub]," in *Rapport d'activité 2015–2016,* vol. 116 (Institut français d'archéologie orientale, 2017), 238–50.

56 Pierre Tallet, *Les papyrus de la mer Rouge I: Le "journal de Merer" (Papyrus Jarf A et B)* [The Red Sea Papyri I: The "Journal of Merer" (Papyrus Jarf A and B)], vol. 136 (Institut français d'archéologie orientale, 2017).

57 Walter Williams, *Reaganism and the Death of Representative Democracy* (Georgetown University Press, 2003).

58 Philip J. Watson, *Egyptian Pyramids and Mastaba Tombs* (Shire Publications, 1987). For the decoration of these tombs, see Yvonne Harpur, *Decoration in Egyptian Tombs of the Old Kingdom: Studies in Orientation and Scene Content* (KPI, 1987); Hartwig Altenmüller, "Daily Life in Eternity: The Mastabas and Rock-Cut Tombs of Officials," in *Egypt: The World of the Pharaohs* (H. F. Ullmann, 2007), 78–103.

59 See Mark Lehner, "Labor and the Pyramids: The Heit el-Ghurab 'Workers Town' at Giza," in *Labor in the Ancient World* (ISLET, 2015), 397–522.

60 Egyptian Museum in Cairo, CG 3, 4. Abeer el-Shahawy, *Egyptian Museum in Cairo: A Walk Through the Alleys of Ancient Egypt* (Farid Atiya Press, 2005), 71–72, entry 42.

61 MFA 27.442. Lawrence Berman, Denise Doxey, and Rita Freed, *Arts of Ancient Egypt* (MFA Boston, 2003), 78.

62 See inventory no. 1962; Arnold, Ziegler, and Roehrig, *Egyptian Art in the Age of the Pyramids,* 229–31.

63 Betsy M. Bryan, "Portraiture," in *A Companion to Ancient Egyptian Art* (Wiley Blackwell, 2015), 375–96.

64 The Turin King List gives him eight years. K. S. B. Ryholt, *The Political Situation in Egypt During the Second Intermediate Period, c. 1800–1550 B.C.* (Museum Tusculanum Press, 1997), 13; Miroslav Verner, "Archaeological Remarks on the 4th and 5th Dynasty Chronology," *Archiv Orientální* 69, no. 3 (2001): 363–418.

65 The tale of Horus and Seth, in Miriam Lichtheim, *Ancient Egyptian Literature,* vol. II: *The New Kingdom* (University of California Press, 1976), 214–23.

66 Uvo Hölscher, *Das Grabdenkmal des Königs Chephren* [The Funerary Monument of King Chephren], vol. I (Hinrichs'sche Buchhandlung, 1912).

67 Rainer Stadelmann, "Royal Tombs From the Age of the Pyramids," in *Egypt: The World of the Pharaohs,* 47–77.

68 It is practically impossible to find a non-pseudoscience citation for this theory, an unfortunate reality of Egyptology being unable to grapple with stellar theories that are considered problematic.

69 Krzysztof Grzymski, "Royal Statuary," in *Egyptian Art in the Age of the Pyramids* (Metropolitan Museum of Art, 1999), 50–55; Dieter Arnold, "Old Kingdom Statues in Their Architectural Setting," in *Egyptian Art in the Age of the Pyramids,* 40–49.

70 The Mastabat el-Fara'un. Lehner, *The Complete Pyramids,* 139.

71 Massimiliano Nuzzolo, "The Sun Temples of the Vth Dynasty: A Reassessment," *Studien zur Altägyptischen Kultur* 36 (2007): 217–47.

72 Miroslav Bárta, *Analyzing Collapse: The Rise and Fall of the Old Kingdom* (American University in Cairo Press, 2020).

73 John Baines calls this new dynasty a "drawing apart of religion and kingship." See his "Kingship, Definition of Culture, and Legitimation," in *Ancient Egyptian Kingship* (1995), 4.

74 For more on the de-skilling process, see Scott, *Seeing Like a State,* 334–37.

CHAPTER 3

1 Georges Posener, *De la divinité du pharaon, Cahiers de la Société asiatique* [On the Divinity of the Pharaoh, Notebooks of the Asian Society], vol. 15 (Imprimerie nationale, 1960).

2 Two literary texts, the "Instruction of King Amenemhat" and the "Story of Sinuhe," describe Amenemhat's murder in his bed while Senwosret is away on campaign in Libya. See Lichtheim, *Ancient Egyptian Literature,* vol. I, 135–39, 222–35; Adela Oppenheim et al., eds., *Ancient Egypt Transformed: The Middle Kingdom* (Metropolitan Museum of Art, 2015); Waddell, *Manetho,* 57–94.

3 Wolfram Grajetzki, "Late Middle Kingdom," in *UCLA Encyclopedia of Egyptology* (2013), https://escholarship.org/uc/item/3gk7274p.

4 John P. Cooper, *The Medieval Nile: Route, Navigation, and Landscape in Islamic Egypt* (American University in Cairo Press, 2014); Kathlyn M. Cooney, "People of Nile and Sun, Wheat and Barley, Copper and Gold: Ancient Egyptian Society and the Agency of Place," in *Ancient Egyptian Society: Challenging Assumptions, Exploring Approaches* (Routledge, 2021).

5 In a rock stela of King Mentuhotep IV at the Wadi Hammamat, we read of this man's social and military power: "My majesty has sent the noble, mayor of the city, vizier, chief of royal works, royal favorite, Amenemhat, with a group of ten thousand men from the southern nomes of Upper Egypt and from the garrisons of Thebes in order to

bring me a precious block of the pure stone of this mountain." The fact that he is mentioned so prominently implies that the vizier Amenemhat may have been marked as heir, but given that the inscription was made under the direction of the same man, Amenemhat, ostensibly in the absence of the king, it could also indicate a competitive seizure of power. Translation after Lichtheim, *Ancient Egyptian Literature*, vol. I, 114.

6 Claire J. Malleson, *The Fayum Landscape: Ten Thousand Years of Archaeology, Texts, and Traditions in Egypt* (American University in Cairo Press, 2019). The name comes from Pa-yom, meaning "The Lake," and it is particularly associated with Egypt's 12th-dynasty kings.

7 Farouk Gomáa, *Die Besiedlung Ägyptens während des Mittleren Reiches 1. Oberägypten und das Fayyūm* [The Settlement of Egypt During the Middle Kingdom 1. Upper Egypt and the Fayum] (Reichert, 1986).

8 See Abigail Tucker, "Space Archaeologist Sarah Parcak Uses Satellites to Uncover Ancient Egyptian Ruins," *Smithsonian*, December 2016. Parcak has surveyed the area believed to be Itjy-tawy using aerial imagery. For more information on the city's associated necropolis, see Dieter Arnold, *Middle Kingdom Tomb Architecture at Lisht* (Metropolitan Museum of Art, 2008).

9 Dieter Kessler, "The Political History from the Ninth to the Seventeenth Dynasties," in *Egypt: The World of the Pharaohs*, 104–07.

10 Scott, *Seeing Like a State*.

11 Edouard Henri Naville, *The XIth Dynasty temple at Deir el-Bahari*. pt. I–III, *Egypt Exploration Fund Memoirs*, vol. 28 (Kegan Paul, 1907); Rainer Stadelmann, "The Tombs of the Pharaohs: Between Tradition and Innovation," in *Egypt: The World of the Pharaohs*, 108–17.

12 Dorothea Arnold, "Amenemhat I and the Early Twelfth Dynasty at Thebes," *Metropolitan Museum Journal* 26 (1991): 5–48.

13 Juan Carlos Moreno García, *The State in Ancient Egypt: Power, Challenges and Dynamics* (Bloomsbury, 2020), 67–72.

14 Lehner, *The Complete Pyramids*, 168–83.

15 Hans Goedicke, *Re-Used Blocks from the Pyramid of Amenemhet I at Lisht*, vol. 20 (Metropolitan Museum of Art, 1971).

16 A stela from Abydos now in the Cairo Museum (CG 20516), for instance, bears those two dates. William J. Murnane, *Ancient Egyptian Coregencies* (Oriental Institute, University of Chicago, 1977).

17 García, *The State in Ancient Egypt*, 33.

18 Josef W. Wegner, "The Nature and Chronology of the Senwosret III-Amenemhat III Regnal Succession: Some Considerations Based on New Evidence from the Mortuary Temple of Senwosret III at Abydos," *J NES* 55, no. 4 (1996): 249–79; Lisa Saladino Haney, *Visualizing Coregency: An Exploration of the Link Between Royal Image and Co-Rule During the Reign of Senwosret III and Amenemhet III* (Brill, 2020).

19 Claude Obsomer, *Sésostris Ier: Étude chronologique et historique du règne* [Sesostris I: Chronological and Historical Study of the Reign] (Conaissance de l'Egypte Ancienne, 1995).

20 William J. Murnane, "Coregency," in *The Oxford Encyclopedia of Ancient Egypt*, 307–31.

21 Anne Applebaum, *Twilight of Democracy: The Seductive Lure of Authoritarianism* (Doubleday, 2020).

22 Abdel Ghaffar Shedid, "A House for Eternity: The Tombs of Governors and Officials," in *Egypt: The World of the Pharaohs,* 119–31.

23 Dieter Eigner, "Tell Ibrahim Awad: Divine Residence from Dynasty 0 until Dynasty 11," *Ägypten und Levante* 10 (2000): 17–36; Eva Lange-Athinodorou, "The Issue of Residence and Periphery in the Middle Kingdom: Surveying the Delta," in *Middle Kingdom Palace Culture and Its Echoes in the Provinces,* ed. Alejandro Jiménez-Serrano and Antonio J. Morales (Brill, 2021), 256–83. Many of those aristocrats had the title *hery-tep,* meaning something like "head chief" or "top man." Egyptologists call these men provincial governors, or nomarchs if they use a later Greek word. But that title was not used consistently. Harco Willems, "Nomarchs and Local Potentates: The Provincial Administration in the Middle Kingdom," in *Ancient Egyptian Administration,* 341–92; Jessica Tomkins, "The Misnomer of Nomarchs: Οἱ Νομάρχαι and Provincial Administrators of the Old–Middle Kingdoms," *Zeitschrift für Ägyptische Sprache und Altertumskunde* 145, no. 1 (2018), 95–104; Juan Carlos Moreno García, "The Territorial Administration of the Kingdom in the 3rd Millennium," in *Ancient Egyptian Administration,* 85–151.

24 Harco Willems, "Nomarchs and Local Potentates," 341–92.

25 Instruction for Merikare. Lichtheim, *Ancient Egyptian Literature,* vol. I, 103.

26 Rita Freed, *The Secrets of Tomb 10A: Egypt 2000 BC* (MFA Publications, 2009).

27 Aurore Motte, "A (Re)investigation of Middle Kingdom Speech Captions in Wrestling Scenes," *JEA* 103, no. 1 (2017): 53–70.

28 The back walls of the tombs of Khety (BH 17) and Amenemhat (BH 2) have scenes of private armies. Percy E. Newberry and Francis L. Griffith, *Beni Hasan* (Egypt Exploration Fund/K. Paul, Trench, Trübner & Co., 1893).

29 Such as in the back niche of the tomb of Sarenput II at Qubbet el Hawa at Aswan. Elmar Edel, *Die Felsengräber der Qubbet el Hawa bei Assuan* [The Rock Tombs of the Qubbet el Hawa Near Aswan] (Harrassowitz, 1967).

30 Harco Willems, *Chests of Life: A Study of the Typology and Conceptual Development of Middle Kingdom Standard Class Coffins* (Ex Oriente Lux, 1988); R. O. Faulkner, *The Ancient Egyptian Coffin Texts* (Aris & Phillips, 1973–78); Carlos Gracia Zamacona, "Some Remarks on a Multidimensional Approach to the Unique Spells in the Coffin Texts," in *Middle Kingdom Palace Culture and Its Echoes in the Provinces* (Brill, 2021), 171–222.

31 Harco Willems, *Les textes des sarcophages et la démocratie: Éléments d'une histoire culturelle du Moyen Empire Égyptien* [Sarcophagus Texts and Democracy: Elements of a Cultural History of the Egyptian Middle Kingdom] (Librairie Cybele, 2008). However, see Mark Smith, "Democratization of the Afterlife," in *UCLA Encyclopedia of Egyptology* (2009), https://escholarship.org/uc/item/70g428wj, in which the author argues that nonroyal individuals had long had access to such secret religious texts.

32 Harco Willems, "A Fragment of an Early Book of Two Ways on the Coffin of Ankh from Dayr al-Barshā (B4B)," *JEA* 104, no. 2 (2018): 145–60.

33 Lichtheim, *Ancient Egyptian Literature,* vol. I, 223–24; Miroslav Bárta and Jiří Janák, "Sinuhe: Popular Hero, Court Politics, and the Royal Paradigm," in *Middle Kingdom Palace Culture and Its Echoes in the Provinces,* 101–18.

34 Lichtheim, *Ancient Egyptian Literature,* vol. I, 224.

35 Instruction of Amenemhat I for his son Senwosret I. Lichtheim, *Ancient Egyptian Literature*, vol. I, 137.

36 The vast majority of Egyptologists take the Egyptian kings at their word and buy into the double-dated inscriptional evidence despite its ideological context. Only Claude Obsomer seems to disagree with the co-regency theory—see *Sésostris Ier: étude chronologique et historique du règne* [Sesostris I: Chronological and Historical Study of the Reign] (Conaissance de l'Egypte Ancienne, 1995). For a full discussion of this topic, see Thomas Schneider, "The Relative Chronology of the Middle Kingdom and the Hyksos Period (Dyns. 12–17)," in *Ancient Egyptian Chronology* (Brill, 2006), 168–96.

37 Leather roll Berlin 3029 with a building inscription of Senwosret I; Lichtheim, *Ancient Egyptian Literature*, vol. I, 116.

38 Regine Schulz, "Between Heaven and Earth: Temples to the Gods in the Middle Kingdom," in *Egypt: The World of the Pharaohs*, 132–41.

39 Lintel of Senwosret I running toward the god Min, UC 14786; Oppenheim et al., *Ancient Egypt Transformed*, 282–83.

40 Wolfram Grajetzki, *The Middle Kingdom of Ancient Egypt: History, Archaeology and Society* (Duckworth, 2006).

41 Gae Callender, "The Middle Kingdom Renaissance (c. 2055–1650 BC)," in *The Oxford History of Ancient Egypt* (Oxford University Press, 2001), 148–84.

42 Labib Habachi, *The Obelisks of Egypt: Skyscrapers of the Past* (J. M. Dent & Sons, 1978), 46–50, plate 8.

43 Blyth, *Karnak: Evolution of a Temple*.

44 Pierre Lacau and Henri Chevrier, *Une chapelle de Sésostris Ier à Karnak* [A Chapel of Sesostris I in Karnak] (Institut français d'archéologie orientale, 1956).

45 Aidan Dodson and Dyan Hilton, *The Complete Royal Families of Ancient Egypt* (Thames & Hudson, 2004), 92–93.

46 The stela of Wepwawet shows Senwosret I at year 44 and his son Amenemhat II at year 2. Lisa Saladino Haney, *Visualizing Coregency: An Exploration of the Link Between Royal Image and Co-Rule During the Reign of Senwosret III and Amenemhet III* (Brill, 2020), 72–73. The Turin Canon gives Senwosret I 45 years of rule—Ryholt, *The Political Situation in Egypt*—so we can assume he died in in the 45th or 46th year of his reign. Again, Senwosret backdating his kingship would not discount such reign years being preserved in a later document.

47 Oppenheim et al., *Ancient Egypt Transformed*.

48 For some of the teachings and discourses of his reign, see R. B. Parkinson, *The Tale of Sinuhe and Other Ancient Egyptian Poems, 1940–1640 BC* (Clarendon Press, 1997).

49 For more on this portraiture, see Janine Bourriau and Stephen Quirke, *Pharaohs and Mortals: Egyptian Art in the Middle Kingdom* (Cambridge University Press, 1988); Dimitri Laboury, "Portrait Versus Ideal Image" (2010), in *UCLA Encyclopedia of Egyptology*, https://escholarship.org/uc/item/9370v0rz; Dimitri Laboury, "Senwosret III and the Issue of Portraiture in Ancient Egyptian Art," *Cahiers de Recherches de l'Institut de Papyrologie et d'Égyptologie de Lille* 31 (2016): 71–84.

50 As Dimitri Laboury ably argues in "Senwosret III and the Issue of Portraiture in Ancient Egyptian Art." See also Dorothea Arnold, "Pharaoh: Power and Performance," in *Ancient Egypt Transformed*, 68–72; Bryan, "Portraiture," 375–96.

51 Edouard Naville et al., *The XIth Dynasty Temple at Deir el-Bahari*, pt. I–III, vol. 28 (The Egypt Exploration Fund, 1907).

52 Erik Hornung and Elisabeth Staehelin, *Neue Studien zum Sedfest* [New Studies on the Sed Festival] (Schwabe, 2006); Eric Uphill, "The Egyptian Sed-Festival Rites," *JNES* 24, no. 4 (1965): 365–83; William J. Murnane, "The Sed Festival: A Problem in Historical Method," in *Mitteilungen des Deutschen Archäologischen Instituts, Abteilung Kairo 37* (1981): 369–76.

53 Grajetzki, *The Middle Kingdom of Ancient Egypt*; Pierre Tallet, *Sésostris III et la fin de la XIIe dynastie* [Sesostris III and the End of the 12th Dynasty] (Pygmalion, 2015).

54 Most of the mud-brick fortresses have been lost to the waters of Lake Nasser and the Aswan High Dam. Paul C. Smither, "The Semnah Despatches," *JEA* 31 (1945): 3–10; Bryan Kraemer and Kate Liszka, "Evidence for Administration of the Nubian Fortresses in the Late Middle Kingdom: The Semna Dispatches," *JEH* 9, no. 1 (2016): 1–65.

55 Boundary stela, Ägyptisches Museum 1157. *Ancient Egypt Transformed,* 167.

56 Translation after Lichtheim, *Ancient Egyptian Literature*, vol. I, 119.

57 Stuart Tyson Smith, "Nubia and Egypt: Interaction, Acculturation, and Secondary State Formation from the Third to First Millennium B.C.," in *Studies in Culture Contact: Interaction, Culture Change, and Archaeology* (Center for Archaeological Investigations, Southern Illinois University, 1998), 256–87; Carola Vogel, *The Fortifications of Ancient Egypt, 3000–1780 BC* (Osprey, 2010); Stuart Tyson Smith, *Wretched Kush: Ethnic Identities and Boundaries in Egypt's Nubian Empire* (Routledge, 2003).

58 Instruction for Merikare. Translation after Lichtheim, *Ancient Egyptian Literature,* vol. I, 101.

59 Josef W. Wegner, "Regional Control in Middle Kingdom Lower Nubia: The Function and History of the Site of Areika," *JARCE* 32 (1995): 144–49.

60 Translation after Lichtheim, *Ancient Egyptian Literature*, vol. I, 119.

61 Christoffer Theis, "Neue Identifizierungsvorschläge zu den Ächtungstexten des Mittleren Reiches [New Identification Proposals on the Prohibition Texts of the Middle Kingdom]," *Zeitschrift des Deutschen Palästina-Vereins* 128, no. 2 (2012): 121–32.; R. K. Ritner, *The Mechanics of Ancient Egyptian Magical Practice* (Oriental Institute, The University of Chicago, 1993).

62 Hymns to Senwosret III. William Kelly Simpson, ed., et al., *The Literature of Ancient Egypt: An Anthology of Stories, Instructions, Stelae, Autobiographies, and Poetry* (Yale University Press, 1973), 302.

63 André Vila, "Un depot de textes d'envoûtement au Moyen Empire [A Deposit of Spellbinding Texts in the Middle Kingdom]," *Journal des Savants* (1963): 146–47, fig. 6.

64 Grajetzki, "Late Middle Kingdom," https://escholarship.org/uc/item/3gk7274p.

65 Wolfgang Helck, *Die altägyptischen Gaue* [The Ancient Egyptian Districts] (L. Reichert, 1974).

66 Because not all men used the title *hery-tep,* many Egyptologists claim the crackdown on these elites was not as extensive as we think. Detlef Franke, "The Career of Khnumhotep III of Beni Hasan and the So-Called 'Decline of the Nomarchs,'" in *Middle Kingdom Studies* (SIA, 1991), 51–67; Stephen Quirke, *Titles and Bureaux of Egypt, 1850–1700 BC* (Golden House Publications, 2004).

67 See, for instance, Sidney Blumenthal, "Lindsey Graham, Reverse Ferret: How John McCain's Spaniel Became Trump's Poodle," *The Guardian,* October 11, 2020.

68 Ellen Morris, "The Civilizing Process and the Machiavellian Aims of the State in Pharaonic Egypt," *JEH* 13 (special issue: "Egyptology and Global History," forthcoming); Martina Bardoňová, "The 'Prince's Court Is Like a Common Fountain': Middle Kingdom Royal Patronage in the Light of a Modern Sociological Concept," in *Middle Kingdom Palace Culture and Its Echoes in the Provinces,* 77–100.

69 S. Allam, "Egyptian Law Courts in Pharaonic and Hellenistic Times," *JEA* 77 (1991): 109–27; Mahmoud Ezzamel, "Work Organization in the Middle Kingdom, Ancient Egypt," *Organization* 11, no. 4 (2004), 497–537.

70 William Beik, *Louis XIV and Absolutism: A Brief Study with Documents* (Bedford/St. Martin's, 2000).

71 Adela Oppenheim, "Elite Tombs at the Residence: The Decoration and Design of Twelfth Dynasty Tomb Chapels and Mastabas at Lisht and Dahshur," in *Middle Kingdom Palace Culture and Its Echoes in the Provinces.*

72 Silke Roth, "Harem," in *UCLA Encyclopedia of Egyptology* (2012), https://escholarship.org/uc/item/1k3663r3.

73 Some suggest that the rise of the title "King's Son" in the late 12th and 13th dynasties and into the Second Intermediate Period means that the king was taking the nomarch's sons as (semi-)captive hostages and raising them at court, as they would have done with a foreign king's son. J J Shirley, "Crisis and Restructuring of the State: From the Second Intermediate Period to the Advent of the Ramesses," in *Ancient Egyptian Administration,* 521–606.

74 The Loyalist Instruction. Translation after William Kelly Simpson et al., *The Literature of Ancient Egypt: An Anthology of Stories, Instructions, Stelae, Autobiographies, and Poetry* (Yale University Press, 1973), 173.

75 Stuart Tyson Smith, "Ethnicity: Constructions of Self and Other in Ancient Egypt," *JEH* 11, no. 1–2 (2018): 113–46.

76 See Dieter Arnold, *The Pyramid Complex of Senwosret III at Dahshur: Architectural Studies* (Metropolitan Museum of Art, 2002).

77 Jacques Jean Marie de Morgan, *Fouilles à Dahchour* [Excavations at Dahshur] (A. Holzhausen, 1895).

78 Amenemhat II was the first Middle Kingdom monarch to build at Dahshur; Senwosret III was following in his grandfather's footsteps.

79 Josef Wegner, "The Tomb of Senwosret III at Abydos: Considerations on the Origins and Development of the Royal Amduat-Tomb," in *Archaism and Innovation: Studies in the Culture of Middle Kingdom Egypt* (Yale Egyptological Seminar, 2009), 103–68.

80 Snefru had multiple pyramids, but it doesn't seem he claimed the others as simultaneous burials; they reflect his quest for the still unperfected straight-sided pyramid.

81 Josef Wegner proposes that there was a 19-year co-kingship between Amenemhat and Senwosret III. See his "The Nature and Chronology of the Senwosret III-Amenemhat III Regnal Succession: Some Considerations Based on New Evidence from the Mortuary Temple of Senwosret III at Abydos," *JNES* 55, no. 4 (1996): 249–79.

82 Lichtheim, *Ancient Egyptian Literature,* vol. I, 119-20.
83 Grajetzki, *The Middle Kingdom of Ancient Egypt,* 61–63.
84 Ryholt, *The Political Situation in Egypt.*
85 Lee Drutman, "How Corporate Lobbyists Conquered American Democracy," *The Atlantic,* April 20, 2015; Robert G. Kaiser, "How Lobbying Became Washington's Biggest Business: Big Money Creates a New Capital City, As Lobbying Booms, Washington and Politics Are Transformed," Citizen K Street (blog), *Washington Post,* May 24, 2012.

CHAPTER 4

1 Marc Van De Mieroop, *A History of Ancient Egypt* (Wiley-Blackwell, 2011), 199–200; Jürgen von Beckerath, *Handbuch der ägyptischen Königsnamen* [Handbook of the Ancient Egyptian Names of Kings] (Philipp von Zabern, 1999), 142–44.
2 The first known mention is actually in the 12th dynasty "Tale of Sinuhe," in which the death of the murdered King Amenhotep I is described as uniting with the sun. See Lichtheim, *Ancient Egyptian Literature,* vol. I, 223.
3 Barry Kemp, *The City of Akhenaten and Nefertiti: Amarna and Its People* (Thames & Hudson, 2012), 79–83; Richard H. Wilkinson, *The Complete Gods and Goddesses of Ancient Egypt* (Thames & Hudson, 2003).
4 Donald B. Redford, *Akhenaten: The Heretic King* (Princeton University Press, 1984).
5 *The Oxford History of Ancient Egypt,* 207–64; Van De Mieroop, *A History of Ancient Egypt,* 151–83.
6 García, *The State in Ancient Egypt,* 15–36.
7 José M. Galán, Betsy M. Bryan, and Peter F. Dorman, eds., *Creativity and Innovation in the Reign of Hatshepsut* (Oriental Institute, University of Chicago, 2014).
8 Lichtheim, *Ancient Egyptian Literature,* vol. II, 12-14; Mark D. Janzen, *The Iconography of Humiliation: The Depiction and Treatment of Bound Foreigners in New Kingdom Egypt* (University of Memphis: Dissertation, 2013), 144.
9 Danielle Candelora, "Entangled in Orientalism: How the Hyksos Became a Race," *JEH* 11, no. 1–2 (2018): 45–72.
10 David O'Connor and Eric H. Cline, eds., *Amenhotep III: Perspectives on His Reign* (University of Michigan Press, 1998), 223–70.
11 Arielle P. Kozloff et al., *Egypt's Dazzling Sun: Amenhotep III and His World* (Cleveland Museum of Art, 1992).
12 W. Raymond Johnson, "Monuments and Monumental Art," in *Amenhotep III: Perspectives,* 63–94.
13 Kozloff, *Egypt's Dazzling Sun.*
14 Egyptian Museum in Cairo CG 34025/JE 31408. Pierre Lacau, *Stèles du nouvel empire* [Stelae of the New Kingdom]: *Nos. 34001-34189* (Institut français d'archéologie orientale, 1909).
15 Lichtheim, *Ancient Egyptian Literature,* vol. II, 45.
16 H. Sourouzian et al., "The Temple of Amenhotep III at Thebes: Excavation and Conservation at Kom el-Hettân. Third Report on the Fifth Season in 2002/2003," *Mitteilungen des Deutschen Archäologischen Instituts, Abteilung Kairo* 60 (2004): 171–236; H. Sourouzian et al., "The Temple of Amenhotep III at Thebes: Excavations and

Conservation at Kom el-Hettân. Fourth Report on the Sixth, Seventh and Eighth Season in 2004, 2004–2005 and 2006," 63 (2007): 247–335.

17 Betsy M. Bryan, "The Statue Program for the Mortuary Temple of Amenhotep III," in *The Temple in Ancient Egypt: New Discoveries and Recent Research* (British Museum Press, 1997), 57–81.

18 For links to the latest Sakhmet conference, see Tara Draper-Stumm, "Sekhmet Omnipresent in Luxor and New Discoveries at Kom el-Hettan," in *Ancient Egypt Heritage*, April 2, 2017, www.ancientegyptheritage.wordpress.com.

19 Lawrence M. Berman, "Overview of Amenhotep III and His Reign," in *Amenhotep III: Perspectives*, 15–18.

20 Berman, "Overview of Amenhotep III and His Reign," 11–15; Johnson, "Monuments and Monumental Art," 75–76.

21 Berman, "Overview of Amenhotep III and His Reign," 15–18; Reeves, *Akhenaten: Egypt's False Prophet*.

22 John G. Oates and Eric Grynaviski, "Reciprocity, Hierarchy, and Obligation in World Politics: From Kula to Potlatch," *Journal of International Political Theory* 14, no. 2 (2018): 145–64.

23 Kozloff, *Egypt's Dazzling Sun*, 106–10, ep. 08, fig. IV.28; John Baines, "The Dawn of the Amarna Age," in *Amenhotep III: Perspectives*, 294.

24 Amarna Letter EA 26; BM EA 29794; Rita E. Freed and Yvonne J. Markowitz, *Pharaohs of the Sun: Akhenaten, Nefertiti, Tutankhamen* (Museum of Fine Arts, 1999); Kenneth A. Kitchen, "Amenhotep III and Mesopotamia," in *Amenhotep III: Perspectives*, 257–58. There is also the letter by the Assyrian king, Ashur-uballit, EA 16: "Gold is like dust in your land—one simply gathers it up . . . I intend to build a new palace. Send me gold enough for its decoration and its furnishing." Mark W. Chavalas, *The Ancient Near East: Historical Sources in Translation* (Wiley-Blackwell, 2006), 197.

25 Dodson and Hilton, *The Complete Royal Families of Ancient Egypt*.

26 Aidan Dodson, "Crown Prince Djhutmose and the Royal Sons of the Eighteenth Dynasty," *JEA* 76 (1990): 87–96.

27 Gretchen Dabbs et al., "The Bioarchaeology of Akhenaten: Unexpected Results from a Capital City," in *Egyptian Bioarchaeology: Humans, Animals, and the Environment* (Sidestone Press, 2015), 43–52.

28 Ben Haring, "The Rising Power of the House of Amun in the New Kingdom," in *Ancient Egyptian Administration*, 607–37.

29 Ben J. J. Haring, *Divine Households: Administrative and Economic Aspects of the New Kingdom Royal Memorial Temples in Western Thebes* (Nederlands Instituut voor het Nabije Oosten, 1997).

30 Elizabeth Blyth, *Karnak: Evolution of a Temple* (Routledge, 2006).

31 Such as ÄM 2072; see Friederike Seyfried, *In the Light of Amarna: 100 Years of the Nefertiti Discovery* (Michael Imhof, 2012), 206, cat. no. 7.

32 Redford, *Akhenaten: The Heretic King*, 102–36.

33 Reeves, *Akhenaten: Egypt's False Prophet*, 96–97; Jocelyn Gohary, *Akhenaten's Sed-Festival at Karnak* (Kegan Paul International, 1992).

34 Kemp, *The City of Akhenaten and Nefertiti*, 59–63.

35 Egyptian Museum in Cairo JE 49529. Dorothea Arnold, "Von Karnak nach Amarna: Ein künstlerischer Durchbruch und seine Folgen [From Karnak to Amarna: An

Artistic Breakthrough and its Consequences]," in *Im Licht von Amarna: 100 Jahre Fund der Nofretete* [In the Light of Amarna: 100 Years from the Discovery of Nefertiti] (Ägyptisches Museum und Papyrussammlung, Staatliche Museen zu Berlin, 2012), 143–52, fig. 2. See also W. Raymond Johnson, "Sexual Duality and Goddess Iconography on the Amenhotep IV Sandstone Colossi at Karnak," *Bulletin of the Egyptological Seminar* 19 (2015): 415–22.

36 Cyril Aldred suggests that Akhenaten suffered from Fröhlich's syndrome in *Akhenaten: King of Egypt* (Thames & Hudson, 1988). Alwyn L. Burridge offers another diagnosis in "Did Akhenaten Suffer from Marfan's Syndrome?" *Akhenaten Temple Project Newsletter* 3 (1995): 3–4. Dominic Montserrat believes none of the depicted deformities are to be read literally but rather metaphorically, indicating someone who is both male and female, in *Akhenaten: History, Fantasy and Ancient Egypt* (Routledge, 2000). For a distillation of these medical-Egyptological theories, see Megaera Lorenz, "The Mystery of Akhenaten: Genetics or Aesthetics?" (1996), www.heptune.com/Marfans.html.

37 Dorothea Arnold, *The Royal Women of Amarna: Images of Beauty From Ancient Egypt* (Metropolitan Museum of Art, 1996); Seyfried, *In the Light of Amarna*, 145–48.

38 For similar ideas that Akhenaten's artistic imagery is suffused with light and movement, see Montserrat, *Akhenaten: History, Fantasy and Ancient Egypt*; Erik Hornung, *Akhenaten and the Religion of Light* (Cornell University Press, 1999), 44.

39 H. Chevrier, "Rapport sur les travaux de Karnak (1927–1928) [Report on the Work at Karnak]," *Annales du Service des Antiquités de l'Égypte* 28 (1928): 114–28. See also Lise Manniche, *The Akhenaten Colossi of Karnak* (The American University in Cairo Press, 2010), 1–12.

40 Freed and Markowitz, *Pharaohs of the Sun*, 208–09; Reeves, *Akhenaten: Egypt's False Prophet*, 96.

41 From the prayers in the tomb of Ay; Lichtheim, *Ancient Egyptian Literature*, vol. II, 95.

42 Memphis: Stéphane Pasquali, "A Sun-Shade Temple of Princess Ankhesenpaaten in Memphis?" *JEA* 97 (2011): 216–22; Heliopolis: L. Habachi, "Akhenaten in Heliopolis," in *Aufsätze zum 70. Geburtstag von Herbert Ricke* [Essays on the 70th Birthday of Herbert Ricke], ed. Gerhard Haeny (Franz Steiner, 1971), 35–45; Hermopolis: Gunther Roeder, *Amarna-Reliefs aus Hermopolis: Ausgrabungen der Deutschen Hermopolis-Expedition in Hermopolis* [Amarna Reliefs from Hermopolis: Excavations of the German Hermopolis Expedition in Hermopolis] *1929–1939, Band II* (Gebrüder Gerstenberg, 1969); Jebel Barkal: Timothy Kendall, "Talatat Architecture at Jebel Barkal: Report of the NCAM Mission 2008–2009," *Sudan & Nubia* 13 (2009): 2–16.

43 EM JT 30/10/26/12. Freed and Markowitz, *Pharaohs of the Sun*, cat. no. 72, 226.

44 *Amenhotep III: Perspectives*. For the bowl of Khafre, JE 59456, see Geoffrey Thorndike Martin, *The Rock Tombs of el-'Amarna*, pt. VII, *The Royal Tomb at El-'Amarna*, vol. I, *The Objects* (Egypt Exploration Society, 1974), 96.

45 Josef Wegner, *The Sunshade Chapel of Meritaten from the House-of-Waenre of Akhenaten* (University of Pennsylvania Press, 2017).

46 Donald B. Redford, "Akhenaten: New Theories and Old Facts," *BASOR* 369 (May 2013): 9–34.

47 *Egypt: The World of the Pharaohs*, 165, fig. 31 of RT 10.11.26.3.

48 See studies linking resource abundance to authoritarianism: "High wealth inequality linked with greater support for populist leaders," *ScienceDaily,* September 30, 2019, www.sciencedaily.com/releases/2019/09/190930114808.htm.

49 Donald B. Redford, "The Sun-disc in Akhenaten's Program: Its Worship and Antecedents," *JARCE* 13 (1976): 47–61.

50 Donald B. Redford, "Studies on Akhenaten at Thebes, II: A Report on the Work of the Akhenaten Temple Project of the University Museum, The University of Pennsylvania, for the Year 1973–4," *JARCE* 12 (1975): 9–14.

51 Gay Robins, *Proportion and Style in Ancient Egyptian Art* (University of Texas Press, 1994).

52 Gohary, *Akhenaten's Sed-Festival;* Eric Uphill, "The Sed-Festivals of Akhenaten," *JNES* 22, no. 2 (1963): 123–27.

53 Battiscombe Gunn, "Notes on the Aten and His Names," *JEA* 9, no. 3/4 (1923): 168–76; Uphill, "The Sed-Festivals of Akhenaten," 123–27.

54 Marianne Eaton-Krauss, "Reprise: Akhenaten, Nefertiti, Amarna," *Chronique d'Égypte* 88, no. 175 (2013): 78–79.

55 Robins, *Proportion and Style in Ancient Egyptian Art.*

56 Katherine Stewart, *The Power Worshippers: Inside the Dangerous Rise of Religious Nationalism* (Bloomsbury Publishing, 2020).

57 Aldred, *Akhenaten: King of Egypt,* 92–94.

58 Norman de Garis Davies, *The Tomb of the Vizier Ramose* (Egypt Exploration Society, 1941).

59 See TT188. There is, of course, the possibility that this removal happened after the reign of Akhenaten. See Aldred, *Akhenaten: King of Egypt;* Norman de Garis Davies, "Akhenaten at Thebes," *JEA* 9, no. 3/4 (1923): 132–52.

60 Hornung, *Akhenaten and the Religion of Light.*

61 For more on the founding of Akhetaten, see Kemp, *The City of Akhenaten and Nefertiti,* 30–34.

62 Translation after Lichtheim, *Ancient Egyptian Literature,* vol. II, 49.

63 Translation after Lichtheim, *Ancient Egyptian Literature,* vol. II, 50–51.

64 Nick Buxton, *Understanding and Challenging Authoritarianism,* Workshop Report 2017 (Transnational Institute, 2017), www.tni.org/en/publication/understanding-and -challenging-authoritarianism.

65 Samuel Raphael Roberts, *The Fall of Democracy and the Rise of Authoritarianism in Venezuela* (UC Riverside: University Honors, 2020), https://escholarship.org/uc/item/5mj6j3t8.

66 Similar to the reformations made under Louis XIV and his establishment of the royal court at Versailles. Amarna itself has been characterized as more of a Versailles than a Paris. See Laboury, *Akhenaton and Ancient Egypt in the Amarna Era,* 265.

67 Heinrich Best and John Higley, eds. *The Palgrave Handbook of Political Elites* (Palgrave Macmillan, 2018), https://doi.org/10.1057/978-1-137-51904-7.

68 J J Shirley, "Crisis and Restructuring of the State," 521–606.

69 Lichtheim, *Ancient Egyptian Literature,* vol. II, 50.

70 Barry Kemp, *The City of Akhenaten and Nefertiti,* 34.

71 See Scott, *Seeing Like a State,* 73, in which he discusses standard official languages: "It was a state simplification that promised to reward those who complied with its logic and to penalize those who ignored it."

72 William J. Murnane, *Texts from the Amarna Period in Egypt* (Society of Biblical Literature, 1995), 78.

73 There is also Meryneith from Saqqara, who changed his name to "Meryre" during the Amarna period and then back again after Akhenaten's death. See Maarten J. Raven and R. van Walsem, *The Tomb of Meryneith at Saqqara* (Brepolis Publishers, 2014).

74 Emmeline Healey, "The Decorative Program of the Amarna Rock Tombs: Unique Scenes of the Egyptian Military and Police," in *Egyptology in Australia and New Zealand 2009: Proceedings of the Conference Held in Melbourne, September 4–6* (Archaeopress, 2012), 27–39.

75 The rows of these rectangular offering tables have not fully been excavated around the temple proper. However, estimates suggest that there were at least as many as 791 such tables at the Great Aten Temple alone. Barry Kemp, *The City of Akhenaten and Nefertiti*, 87–105, esp. 92.

76 For a comparison of examples, see Arnold, *The Royal Women of Amarna*.

77 Dodson and Hilton, *The Complete Royal Families of Ancient Egypt*, 147-48. My suggestion in *When Women Ruled the World: Six Queens of Egypt* (National Geographic, 2018), 199, is that Tutankhamun was a product of father-daughter incest. Also Zahi Hawass et al., "Ancestry and Pathology in King Tutankhamun's Family," *JAMA* 303, no. 7 (2010): 638–47.

78 As is seen in the Tomb of Ay (TA 25). Barry Kemp, *The City of Akhenaten and Nefertiti*, fig. 1.13.

79 Tilman Klumpp, Hugo Mialon, and Michael A. Willliams, "The Business of American Democracy: *Citizens United,* Independent Spending, and Elections," *Journal of Law and Economics* 59, no. 1 (2016): 1–43. Summary: *Citizens United* v. *Federal Election Commission* (Docket No. 08-205). Cornell Law School, www.law.cornell.edu/supct/cert/08-205.

80 For the forced labor, malnutrition, and disease, see Dabbs et al., "The Bioarchaeology of Akhenaten," 43–52; Mary Shepperson, "Did Children Build the Ancient Egyptian City of Amarna?" *Guardian*, June 6, 2017, www.theguardian.com/science/2017/jun/06/did-children-build-the-ancient-egyptian-city-of-armana-; Traci Watson, "Ancient Egyptian Cemetery Holds Proof of Hard Labor," *National Geographic News,* March 14, 2013, www.nationalgeographic.com/news/2013/3/130313-ancient-egypt-akhenaten-amarna-cemetery-archaeology-science-world. For a rebuttal against the more simplistic plague explanations of the malnourished and diseased working population, see Kathleen Kuckens, *The Children of Amarna: Disease and Famine in the Time of Akhenaten* (University of Arkansas, 2013).

81 Gretchen R. Dabbs, "Estimating the Sex of Ancient Egyptian Skeletal Remains: Methods From Tell el-Amarna," *Bioarchaeology of the Near East* 14 (2020): 1–16; Anna Stevens et al., "Tell el-Amarna, Autumn 2018 to Autumn 2019," *JEA* 106, no. 1–2 (2020): 3–15; Gretchen R. Dabbs, "Bioarchaeology of the Non-Elite North Tombs Cemetery at Amarna: A Preliminary Assessment of the Non-Elite Individuals of the North Tombs Cemetery at Tell el-Amarna, Egypt," *Bioarchaeology International* 3, no. 3 (2019): 174–86; Ann Stevens et al., "Tell el-Amarna, Autumn 2017 and Spring 2018," *JEA* 104, no. 2 (2018): 121–44; Gretchen R. Dabbs and Melissa Zabecki, "Slot-Type Fractures of the Scapula at New Kingdom Tell El-Amarna, Egypt," *International Journal of Paleopathology* 11 (December, 2015): 12–22.

82 M. E. Habicht, A. S. Bouwman, and F. J. Rühli, "Identifications of Ancient Egyptian Royal Mummies From the 18th Dynasty Reconsidered," *American Journal of Physical*

Anthropology 159 (S61, 2016): 216–31. Zahi Hawass has recently announced the discovery of a reused block found in a storeroom at Ashmunein in which Tutankhaten is referred to as "King's Son," thus raising the possibility that he was indeed named during the reign of his father. I have not seen a photograph of this discovery, however. There is also the possibility that the baby in the royal tomb is a representation of Tutankhaten/Tutankhamun. See also Dodson and Hilton, *The Complete Royal Families of Ancient Egypt,* 149–50.

83 MFA 63.260; Freed and Markowitz, *Pharaohs of the Sun,* 238, cat. no. 110.

84 Uroš MatiÐ, "'Her Striking but Cold Beauty': Gender and Violence in Depictions of Queen Nefertiti Smiting the Enemies," in *Archaeologies of Gender and Violence* (Oxbow Books, 2017), 103–21.

85 W. Raymond Johnson, "Fresh Evidence for an Akhenaten/Nefertiti Coregency: A Talatat Block from Hermopolis with a New Join," *KMT* 29, no. 1 (2018): 71–76; Cooney, *When Women Ruled the World,* 356–57, fn. 35–36.

86 William L. Moran, *The Amarna Letters* (Johns Hopkins University Press, 1992), 13–15; Diamantis Panagiotopoulos, "Keftiu in Context: Theban Tomb-Paintings as a Historical Source," *Oxford Journal of Archaeology* 20, no. 3 (2001): 276.

87 Uroš Matic, *Body and Frames of War in New Kingdom Egypt: Violent Treatment of Enemies and Prisoners* (Harrassowitz, 2019), 245–46, Amarna Letter EA 16. There are alternative translations. From the king of Assyria, Ashur-uballit: "Why are my messengers made to stand around in the open sun, so that they die of sunstroke? If there is benefit to the king in standing in the open sun, then let him stand there and die of sunstroke, and let it benefit the king. But if not, why should they die of sunstroke . . . ?" Translation by Eva von Dassow and Kyle Greenwood in Chavalas, *The Ancient Near East,* 197.

88 Lichtheim, *Ancient Egyptian Literature,* vol. II, 97.

89 Translation after Lichtheim, *Ancient Egyptian Literature,* vol. II, 97. High modernism fits Akhenaten's religious schema well. For more on the notion, see Scott, *Seeing Like a State,* 90–146.

90 Mark S. Smith, *God in Translation: Deities in Cross-Cultural Discourse in the Biblical World* (Mohr Siebeck, 2008), 70.

91 For a summary of the arguments, see James K. Hoffmeier, *Akhenaten and the Origins of Monotheism* (Oxford University Press, 2015); Jan Assmann, *From Akhenaten to Moses: Ancient Egypt and Religious Change* (American University in Cairo Press, 2014).

92 Laboury, *Akhenaton and Ancient Egypt in the Amarna Era.*

93 Great Hymn to the Aten; Lichtheim, *Ancient Egyptian Literature,* vol. II, 98.

94 Ibid., 99.

95 You can see the "Triumph of Christian Religion" on the Vatican Museums' website, www.museivaticani.va/content/museivaticani/en/collezioni/musei/stanze-di-raffaello/sala-di-costantino/trionfo-della-religione-cristiana.html.

96 For more on the tomb's decoration and the burial of Akhenaten at Amarna, see Geoffrey T. Martin, *The Rock Tombs of el-'Amarna,* pt. VII, *The Royal Tomb at el-'Amarna II. The Reliefs, Inscriptions, and Architecture,* vol. 39 (Egypt Exploration Society, 1989).

97 Barry J. Kemp and Anna Katherine Stevens, *Busy Lives at Amarna: Excavations in the Main City (Grid 12 and the House of Ranefer, N49.18),* vol. II, *The Objects* (Egypt Exploration Society, 2010).

98 Cooney, *When Women Ruled the World.* The American school of thought on the Amarna succession is dominated by James P. Allen. See his "The Amarna Succession," in *Causing His Name to Live: Studies in Egyptian Epigraphy and History in Memory of William J. Murnane* (Brill, 2009), 9–20. The British school is currently led by Reeves, *Akhenaten: Egypt's False Prophet,* but Aidan Dodson follows a different understanding of Amarna history and succession from Reeves. See Aidan Dodson, *Amarna Sunrise: Egypt from Golden Age to Age of Heresy* (The American University in Cairo Press, 2014); Aidan Dodson, *Amarna Sunset: Nefertiti, Tutankhamun, Ay, Horemheb, and the Egyptian Counter-Reformation* (The American University in Cairo Press, 2009). The French school is now headed by Laboury, *Akhenaton and Ancient Egypt in the Amarna Era,* much of which is influenced by Marc Gabolde, *D'Akhenaton à Toutânkhamon* (Université Lumière-Lyon 2, Institut d'archéologie et d'histoire de l'antiquité, 1998). There are few Egyptologists who connect Smenkhkare with Nefertiti. Nicholas Reeves is a notable exception. Most Egyptologists, including Allen, "The Amarna Succession," and Dodson, *Amarna Sunset,* see Smenkhkare and Neferneferuaten as two separate people. However, for Smenkhkare not to have been Nefertiti, there had to have been two kings with the same throne name, Ankhkheperure, as well as two different kings who shared the Great Royal Wife Meritaten. There is also a huge amount of disagreement over the order of Neferneferuaten and Smenkhkare, with Dodson assuming that Neferneferuaten *followed* Smenkhkare, not the other way around. Reeves argues that Tutankhamun was buried with objects reused from Neferneferuaten, indicating, from his perspective, that when Neferneferuaten became Smenkhkare, she abandoned her burial equipment in favor of something better—something that hasn't been seen yet because archaeologists have still not located that ruler's tomb. See Nicholas Reeves, *The Burial of Nefertiti?* (Amarna Royal Tombs Project, Valley of the Kings, Occasional Paper No. 1, 2015) and Nicholas Reeves, "Tutankhamun's Mask Reconsidered," in *Valley of the Kings Since Howard Carter: Proceedings of the Luxor Symposium November 4, 2009* (Ministry of Antiquities, 2016), 117–34.

CHAPTER 5

1 The Younger Memnon, British Museum EA19; T. G. H. James and W. V. Davies, *Egyptian Sculpture* (British Museum Publications, 1983).

2 Dodson, *Amarna Sunset,* 84–114; Dodson and Hilton, *The Complete Royal Families of Ancient Egypt,* 151.

3 See Nozomu Kawai, "Ay Versus Horemheb: The Political Situation in the Late Eighteenth Dynasty Revisited," *JEH* 3, no. 2 (2010): 261–92; Robert Hari, *Horemheb et la reine Moutnedjemet ou la fin d'une dynastie* [Horemheb and Queen Mutnedjemet or the End of a Dynasty] (La Sirène, 1965); and Geoffrey T. Martin, *The Hidden Tombs of Memphis: New Discoveries from the Time of Tutankhamun and Ramesses the Great* (Thames & Hudson, 1991). These scholars argue that Horemheb may have been a military official named Paatenemheb and could have risen through the ranks during Akhenaten's reign. Others find this doubtful, including Dodson, *Amarna Sunset,* and Jacobus van Dijk, "Horemheb and the Struggle for the Throne of Tutankhamun," *Bulletin of the Australian Centre for Egyptology* 7 (1996): 34.

4 Dodson and Hilton, *The Complete Royal Families of Ancient Egypt,* 153.

5   van Dijk, "Horemheb and the Struggle for the Throne of Tutankhamun," 29–42.

6   Eugene Cruz-Uribe, "The Father of Ramses I: OI 11456," *JNES* 37, no. 3 (1978): 237–44.

7   Dodson and Hilton, *The Complete Royal Families of Ancient Egypt,* 153.

8   K. Sethe, "Der Denkstein mit dem Datum des Jahres 400 der Ära von Tanis [The Memorial Stone with the Date of the Year 400 of the Tanis Era]," *Zeitschrift für Ägyptische Sprache und Altertumskunde* 65 (1930): 85–89.

9   Irene Forstner-Müller, "Centre and Periphery: Some Remarks on the Delta and Its Borders During the Ramesside Period," in *The Ramesside Period in Egypt: Studies into Cultural and Historical Processes of the 19th and 20th Dynasties, Proceedings of the International Symposium held in Heidelberg, 5th to 7th June 2015* (Deutsches Archäologisches Institut, Abteilung Kairo, 2018), 103–12.

10 Matthew Suriano, "Historical Geography of the Ancient Levant," in *The Oxford Handbook of the Archaeology of the Levant: c. 8000–332 BCE* (Oxford University Press, 2018).

11 Danielle Candelora, "The Eastern Delta as a Middle Ground for Hyksos Identity Negotiation," *Mitteilungen des Deutschen Archäologischen Instituts, Abteilung Kairo* 75 (2019): 77–94.

12 Labib Habachi, "Khatâ'na-Qantîr: Importance," *Annales du Service des Antiquités de l'Égypte* 52 (1954): 443–559. See also Helmut Becker et al., *Fenster in die Vergangenheit: Einblicke in die Struktur der Ramses-Stadt durch magnetische Prospektion und Grabung* [Window Into the Past: Insights Into the Structure of Ramses' City Through Magnetic Prospecting and Excavation] (Gebr. Gerstenberg, 2017).

13 Anthony Spalinger, "The Organisation of the Pharaonic Army (Old to New Kingdom)," in *Ancient Egyptian Administration,* 393–478.

14 Pierre Grandet, "The Ramesside State," in *Ancient Egyptian Administration,* 831–99.

15 Peter J. Brand, *The Monuments of Seti I: Epigraphic, Historical and Art Historical Analysis* (Brill, 2000), 162–63, figs. 42, 79–82.

16 Erik Hornung, Rolf Krauss, and David Warburton, eds., *Ancient Egyptian Chronology* (Brill, 2006).

17 W. M. Flinders Petrie et al., *The Temple of the Kings at Abydos (Sety I.)* (Bernard Quaritch, 1902).

18 Claude Vandersleyen, "La gloire de Ramsès III [The Glory of Ramses III]," *Bulletin du cercle lyonnais d'égyptologie Victor Loret* 9 (1995): 45–51; Brand, *The Monuments of Seti I,* 228–49.

19 Erik Hornung et al., *The Tomb of Pharaoh Seti I/Das Grab Sethos' I* (Artemis, 1991).

20 G. Elliot Smith, *The Royal Mummies* (Institut français d'archéologie orientale, 1912).

21 Brand, *The Monuments of Seti I.*

22 Jean Revez and Peter J. Brand, "The Notion of Prime Space in the Layout of the Column Decoration in the Great Hypostyle Hall at Karnak," *Cahiers de Karnak* 15 (2015): 308.

23 Danielle Candelora, "Defining the Hyksos: A Reevaluation of the Title *ḥḳз ḫзswt* and Its Implications for Hyksos Identity," *JARCE* 53 (2017): 203–21.

24 See, for example, Frederik Rademakers et al., "Copper for the Pharaoh: Identifying Multiple Metal Sources for Ramesses' Workshops From Bronze and Crucible Remains," *JAS* 80 (2017): 50–73; Anja Herold, *Streitwagentechnologie in der Ramses-Stadt:*

Knäufe, Knöpfe und Scheiben aus Stein [Chariot Technology in Ramses' City: Knobs, Buttons and Disks Made of Stone] (Von Zabern, 2006).

25 Ellen Morris, *Ancient Egyptian Imperialism* (Wiley, 2018).

26 Eric H. Cline, *1177 B.C.: The Year Civilization Collapsed* (Princeton University Press, 2014).

27 Van Dijk, Jacobus, "The Amarna Period and the Later New Kingdom (c. 1352–1069 B.C.)," in *The Oxford History of Ancient Egypt*, 289–290.

28 Lichtheim, *Ancient Egyptian Literature*, vol. II, 65.

29 Ibid., 62.

30 Ibid.

31 Ibid., 63.

32 Christiane Desroches Noblecourt, *Ramses II: An Illustrated Biography* (Flammarion, 2007).

33 Lindsey June McCandless, *The Makings of an Event: Encountering the Battle of Kadesh Through Time* (UC Berkeley: Dissertation, 2016), http://digitalassets.lib.berkeley.edu/etd/ucb/text/McCandless_berkeley_0028E_15912.pdf.

34 S. Langdon and Alan H. Gardiner, "The Treaty of Alliance Between Đattišili, King of the Hittites, and the Pharaoh Ramesses II of Egypt," *JEA* 6, no. 3 (1920): 179–205.

35 A. D. Touny and Steffen Wenig, *Sport in Ancient Egypt* (Edition Leipzig, 1969).

36 Alan R. Schulman, *Ceremonial Execution and Public Rewards: Some Historical Scenes on New Kingdom Private Stelae* (Universitätsverlag/ Vandenhoeck, 1988).

37 Ellen Fowles Morris, *The Architecture of Imperialism: Military Bases and the Evolution of Foreign Policy in Egypt's New Kingdom* (Brill, 2005).

38 Diamantis Panagiotopoulos, "Encountering the Foreign. (De-)Constructing Alterity in the Archaeologies of the Bronze Age Eastern Mediterranean," in *Materiality and Social Practice: Transformative Capacities of Intercultural Encounters* (Oxbow Books, 2012), 51–61.

39 Mohamed Raafat Abbas, "A Survey of the Military Role of the Sherden Warriors in the Egyptian Army During the Ramesside Period," *Égypte Nilotique et Méditerranéenne* 10 (2017): 7–23.

40 Egyptianization is a difficult topic, now receiving resistance as unidirectional; for more, see Michele R. Buzon, "Biological and Ethnic Identity in New Kingdom Nubia: A Case Study from Tombos," *Current Anthropology* 47, no. 4 (2006): 683–95; W. Paul van Pelt, "Revising Egypto-Nubian Relations in New Kingdom Lower Nubia: From Egyptianization to Cultural Entanglement," *Cambridge Archaeological Journal* 23, no.3 (2013): 523–50; C. R. Higginbotham, *Egyptianization and Elite Emulation in Ramesside Palestine: Governance and Accommodation on the Imperial Periphery* (Brill, 2000).

41 Antonio Loprieno, "Slaves," in *The Egyptians* (University of Chicago Press, 1997), 185–219; Antonio Loprieno, "Slavery and Servitude," in *UCLA Encyclopedia of Egyptology* (2012), https://escholarship.org/uc/item/8mx2073f.

42 Compare the 18th-dynasty biography of Ahmose, son of Ibana with Merneptah's 19th-dynasty Israel Stela, for instance. See Lichtheim, *Ancient Egyptian Literature*, vol. II, 12–14, 73–78.

43 Exodus 12:34-42.

44 Thomas E. Levy, Thomas Schneider, and William Propp, eds., *Israel's Exodus in Transdisciplinary Perspective* (Springer, 2015), 17–37.

45 Exodus 3:3.

46 Marjorie Fisher, *The Sons of Ramesses II* (Harrassowitz, 2001).

47 Christine Raedler, "Kopf der Schenut—politische Entscheidungsträger der Ära Ramses II [Head of Shenut—Political Decision Makers of the Ramses II Era]," in *Die Männer hinter dem König* [The Men Behind the King], 6. *Symposium zur ägyptischen Königsideologie* (Harrassowitz, 2012), 123–50.

48 Dodson and Hilton, *The Complete Royal Families of Ancient Egypt*, 158–75.

49 Bertha Porter and Rosalind Moss, *Topographical Bibliography of Ancient Egyptian Hieroglyphic Texts, Statues, Reliefs, and Paintings*, vol. I, *The Theban Necropolis*, pt. 1, *Private Tombs*, 2nd ed. (Griffith Institute, 1960), 61.

50 Inscription of Bakenkhonsu. For translation, see James Henry Breasted, *Ancient Records of Egypt*, vol. 3, (University of Chicago Press, 1906), 236–37.

51 Laetitia Gallet, "Karnak: The Temple of Amun-Ra-Who-Hears-Prayers," in *UCLA Encyclopedia of Egyptology* (2013), https://escholarship.org/uc/item/3h92j4bj.

52 Stela Hildesheim 374; Schulman, *Ceremonial Execution and Public Rewards*, fig. 23.

53 Nigel Fletcher-Jones, *Abu Simbel and the Nubian Temples* (American University in Cairo Press, 2020), 64–65.

54 Peter Brand, "Reuse and Restoration," in *UCLA Encyclopedia of Egyptology* (2010), https://escholarship.org/uc/item/2vp6065d.

55 Barbara Magen, *Steinerne Palimpseste: Zur Wiederverwendung von Statuen durch Ramses II. und seine Nachfolger* [Stone Palimpsests: On the Reuse of Statues by Ramses II and his Successors] (Harrassowitz, 2011).

56 Kenneth Griffin, "A Reinterpretation of the Use and Function of the Rekhyt Rebus in New Kingdom Temples," in *Current Research in Egyptology 2006: Proceedings of the Seventh Annual Symposium Which Took Place at the University of Oxford, April 2006* (Oxbow, 2007), 66–84.

57 The number of administrative texts produced by temples in the Ramesside period is likely evidence of this increasing importance of temple institutions. See Haring, *Divine Households*; Alan Gardiner, *Ramesside Administrative Documents* (Oxford University Press, 1948). For a Ramesside period onomasticon that describes crown, vizier, and army administration, see Pierre Grandet, "The 'Chapter on Hierarchy' in Amenope's Onomasticon (# 67–125)," in *The Ramesside Period in Egypt: Studies into Cultural and Historical Processes of the 19th and 20th Dynasties* (Walter de Gruyter, 2018), 127–37.

58 Desroches-Noblecourt, *Ramses II*, 16–221.

59 Kent R. Weeks, *KV 5: A Preliminary Report on the Excavation of the Tomb of the Sons of Rameses II in the Valley of the Kings*, vol. 2 (American University in Cairo Press, 2006).

60 Lichtheim, *Ancient Egyptian Literature*, vol. II, 77.

61 Kathlyn M. Cooney, "Changing Burial Practices at the End of the New Kingdom: Defensive Ddaptations in Tomb Commissions, Coffin Commissions, Coffin Decoration, and Mummification," *JARCE* 47 (2011): 3–44.

CHAPTER 6

1 For more on the temple of Jebel Barkal, see Timothy Kendall and El-Hassan Ahmed Mohamed, *A Visitor's Guide to the Jebel Barkal Temples* (Nubian Archaeological Development Organization, 2016), www.jebelbarkal.org/frames/VisGuide.pdf.

2 W. Raymond Johnson, "Akhenaten in Nubia," in *Ancient Nubia: African Kingdoms on the*

Nile (The American University in Cairo Press, 2012), 92–93; Kendall, "Talatat Architecture at Jebel Barkal," 2–16.

3 Marjorie M. Fisher, "The Art and Architecture of Nubia During the New Kingdom: Egypt in Nubia," in *Ancient Nubia*, 84–91, 94–107.

4 Kendall and Mohamed, *A Visitor's Guide to the Jebel Barkal Temples.*

5 Ibid.

6 John Coleman Darnell, "The Apotropaic Goddess in the Eye," *Studien zur Altägyptischen Kultur* 24 (1997): 35–48.

7 The five days added to the 360 to round out the year were believed to be a time of great peril. Anthony Spalinger, "Some Remarks on the Epagomenal Days in Ancient Egypt," *JNES* 54, no. 1 (1995): 33–47.

8 Kendall and Mohamed, *A Visitor's Guide to the Jebel Barkal Temples*; Simone Petacchi, "Some Local Aspects of the Cult of Bes in the Napatan Kingdom," *Der Antike Sudan. Mitteilungen der Sudanarchäologischen Gesellschaft zu Berlin* [Ancient Sudan. Announcements from the Sudan Archaeological Society in Berlin] 25 (2014): 205–09.

9 Timothy Kendall, "The Monument of Taharqa on Gebel Barkal," in *Neueste Feldforschungen im Sudan und in Eritrea, Akten des Symposiums vom 13. bis 14. Oktober 1999 in Berlin* [Latest Field Research in Sudan and Eritrea, Files from the Symposium from October 13-14, 1999, in Berlin] (Harrassowitz, 2004), 1–45.

10 Stuart Tyson Smith, "Revenge of the Kushites: Assimilation and Resistance in Egypt's New Kingdom Empire and Nubian Ascendancy Over Egypt," in *Empires and Diversity: On the Crossroads of Archaeology, Anthropology, and History* (Cotsen Institute of Archaeology Press at UCLA, 2013), 84–107.

11 Kendall and Mohamed, *A Visitor's Guide to the Jebel Barkal Temples.*

12 Diodorus Siculus, *Library of History Books,* vol. II, bk. III (Harvard University Press, 1933), 2–7. Also see Kendall and Mohamed, *A Visitor's Guide to the Jebel Barkal Temples.*

13 Rosemarie and Dietrich Klemm, *Gold and Gold Mining in Ancient Egypt and Nubia* (Springer, 2013).

14 Dietrich Raue, *Handbook of Ancient Nubia* (De Gruyter, 2019).

15 Tyson Smith, *Wretched Kush.*

16 W. M. Badawy et al., "Major and Trace Element Distribution in Soil and Sediments From the Egyptian Central Nile Valley," *Journal of African Earth Sciences* 131 (July 2017): 53.

17 Kevin G. Wheeler et al., "Understanding and Managing New Risks on the Nile With the Grand Ethiopian Renaissance Dam," *Nature Communications* 11, no. 5222 (2020).

18 Alexandre Alexandrovich Loktionov, "May My Nose and Ears Be Cut Off: Practical and 'Supra-practical' Aspects of Mutilation in the Egyptian New Kingdom," *Journal of the Economic and Social History of the Orient* 60, no. 3 (2017): 263–91.

19 Matić, *Body and Frames of War in New Kingdom Egypt,* 67.

20 Matić, 68; Karola Zibelius-Chen, "Zur Schmähung des toten Feindes [To Revile the Dead Enemy]," *Die Welt des Orients* 15 (1984): 87.

21 Matić, *Body and Frames of War in New Kingdom Egypt,* 65–71.

22 Ann Macy Roth, "Representing the Other: Non-Egyptians in Pharaonic Iconography," in *A Companion to Ancient Egyptian Art* (Blackwell, 2015), 155–74.

23 Zibelius-Chen, "Zur Schmähung des toten Feindes [To Revile the Dead Enemy]," 73.

24 For all of the following examples, see Matić, *Body and Frames of War in New Kingdom Egypt;* Stuart Tyson Smith, "The Nubian Experience of Egyptian Domination During the New Kingdom," in *The Oxford Handbook of Ancient Nubia* (Oxford University Press, 2021), 369–94.

25 Merneptah's burning of enemies is a response to a rebellion in Lower Nubia. This rebellion is described on several other monuments (Amada, Amarah West, Wadi es-Sebua, Aksha). See Matić, *Body and Frames of War in New Kingdom Egypt,* 100, doc. 39; Kenneth A. Kitchen, *Ramesside Inscriptions, Historical and Biographical, IV* (Blackwell, 1982), I, 8–3.7.

26 Matić, 281–82. On page 38 of the same source is a text that recounts that ears and eyes were taken from rebels in Wawat.

27 Matić, 307.

28 Emberling and Williams, eds., *The Oxford Handbook of Ancient Nubia.*

29 Kate Liszka, *We Have Come to Serve the Pharaoh,* vol. 2 (University of Pennsylvania: Dissertation, 2012).

30 Michele R. Buzon, Stuart Tyson Smith, and Antonio Simonetti, "Entanglement and the Formation of the Ancient Nubian Napatan State," *American Anthropologist* 118, no. 2 (2016): 284–300.

31 Konstantin C. Lakomy, *Der Löwe auf dem Schlachtfeld: das Grab KV 36 und die Bestattung des Maiherperi im Tal der Könige* [The Lion on the Battlefield: The Grave KV 36 and the Burial of Maiherperi in the Valley of the Kings] (Reichert, 2016).

32 Aaron M. de Souza, *The Pan-Grave Ceramic Tradition in Context* (Golden House Publications, 2019).

33 Kathlyn M. Cooney, "Reuse of Egyptian Coffins in the 21st Dynasty: Ritual Materialism in the Context of Scarcity," in *The First Vatican Coffins Conference, 19–22 June 2013. Conference Proceedings* (Gregorian Museums, Vatican, 2017), 87–98.

34 Kate Liszka, "'Medjay' (no. 188) in the Onomasticon of Amenemope," in *Millions of Jubilees: Studies in Honor of David P. Silverman,* vol. I (Conseil Suprême des Antiquités de l'Egypte, 2010), 315–31.

35 Thomas Schneider, "Foreign Egypt: Egyptology and the Concept of Cultural Appropriation," *Ägypten und Levante* 13 (2003): 155–61.

36 Robert Morkot, "From Conquered to Conqueror: The Organization of Nubia in the New Kingdom and the Kushite Administration of Egypt," in *Ancient Egyptian Administration,* 911–63.

37 The victory stela of King Piye. For translation, see Miriam Lichtheim, *Ancient Egyptian Literature,* vol. III, *The Late Period* (University of California, 1980), 66–84.

38 von Beckerath, *Handbuch der ägyptischen Königsnamen* [Handbook of the Ancient Egyptian Names of Kings], 206–07.

39 As evidenced in New Kingdom excavations at Tombos showing Nubian food and cookware within Egyptian-style tombs. Tyson Smith, *Wretched Kush,* 136–66.

40 See www.cdc.gov/coronavirus/2019-ncov/covid-data/investigations-discovery/hospitalization-death-by-race-ethnicity.html. According to the Centers for Disease Control and Prevention, the death rate as a result of COVID-19 compared with White, non-Hispanic people is 2.8 times higher for Black or African American, non-Hispanic people; 2.6 times higher for American Indian or Alaska Native,

non-Hispanic people; 2.8 times higher for Hispanic or Latino people; and 1.1 times higher for Asian, non-Hispanic people.

41 Most history books, including *The Oxford History of Ancient Egypt,* assign the 25th dynasty to the Third Intermediate Period; Van De Mieroop, *A History of Ancient Egypt.*

42 Similarly, see Henry Trocmé Aubin, *Has Racism Skewed Scholars' View of Kush? A Response to a Critique of The Rescue of Jerusalem* (self-pub., 2015).

43 Ian Morris and Walter Scheidel, *The Dynamics of Ancient Empires: State Power from Assyria to Byzantium* (Oxford University Press, 2009).

44 Mariam F. Ayad, *God's Wife, God's Servant: The God's Wife of Amun (c. 740–525 BC)* (Routledge, 2009).

45 Lichtheim, *Ancient Egyptian Literature,* vol. III, 75.

46 James M. Weinstein, "The Egyptian Empire in Palestine: A Reassessment," *BASOR* 241 (1981): 1–28.

47 Jerrold S. Cooper, "Divine Kingship in Mesopotamia: A Fleeting Phenomenon," in *Religion and Power: Divine Kingship in the Ancient World and Beyond* (Oriental Institute, University of Chicago, 2008), 261–64.

48 Katherine J. Eaton, "The Festivals of Osiris and Sokar in the Month of Khoiak: The Evidence from Nineteenth Dynasty Royal Monuments at Abydos," *Studien zur Altägyptischen Kultur* 35 (2006): 75–101.

49 Paul Frandsen, "Aspects of Kingship in Ancient Egypt," in *Religion and Power: Divine Kingship in the Ancient World and Beyond,* 47–73.

50 Roberto B. Gozzoli, "The Triumphal Stele of Piye as Sanctification of a King," *Göttinger Miszellen* 182 (2001): 59–67.

51 Lichtheim, *Ancient Egyptian Literature,* vol. III, 68.

52 See "Obama Tan Suit Controversy," https://en.wikipedia.org/wiki/Obama_tan_suit_controversy.

53 Kendall and Mohamed, *A Visitor's Guide to the Jebel Barkal Temples,* 56–60, figs. 5–8.

54 Ibid., 60–67.

55 Geoff Emberling, "Pastoral States: Toward a Comparative Archaeology of Early Kush," *Origini: Preistoria e protostoria delle civiltà antiche* 36 (2014): 125–56.

56 N. Na'Aman, "Sennacherib's Campaign to Judah and the Date of the lmlk Stamps," *Vetus Testamentum* 29, no. 1 (1979): 61–86.

57 Kawa Stela V. See Robert K. Ritner, *The Libyan Anarchy: Inscriptions From Egypt's Third Intermediate Period* (Brill, 2009), 544.

58 Ibid.

59 Ibid.

60 Ibid., 543.

61 Ibid.

62 Ibid., 531.

63 Ibid., 413–514.

64 Ibid., 544.

65 Ibid., 524–25; See also Jochem Kahl, "Archaism," *UCLA Encyclopedia of Egyptology* (2010), 2–5, figs. 1–4, https://escholarship.org/uc/item/3tn7q1pf.

66 Ritner, *The Libyan Anarchy,* 552.

67 Ibid., 537–38.
68 Lichtheim, *Ancient Egyptian Literature*, vol. I, 51. Taharqa's father started the trend, and his uncle Shabaka continued it. Shabaka even commissioned a religious text that we call the Memphite Theology, a treatise describing how the god Ptah had created civilization by perceiving his creation in his mind and then speaking it into being. The text was written in a stilted, old-fashioned Egyptian language, and was said to have been found on an old, worm-eaten papyrus rediscovered in the Memphis temple, carefully conserved and recorded for posterity.
69 Timothy Kendall, "Why Did Taharqa Build His Tomb at Nuri?" in *Between the Cataracts: Proceedings of the 11th International Conference of the Society of Nubian Studies, Warsaw University, 27 August-2 September 2006. Part One: Main Papers* (Warsaw University Press, 2008), 117–47.
70 Ritner, *The Libyan Anarchy*, 559–60.
71 Ibid., 538.
72 Ibid., 543.
73 Blyth, *Karnak: Evolution of a Temple*, 196–208.
74 Kathlyn M. Cooney, "The Edifice of Taharqa by the Sacred Lake: Ritual Function and the Role of the King," *JARCE* 37 (2000): 15–47.
75 Mariam Ayad, "On the Identity and Role of the God's Wife of Amun in Rites of Royal and Divine Dominion," *JSSEA* 34 (2007): 1–13.
76 Catherine Butler and Hallie O'Donovan, "The Eagle Has Landed: Representing the Roman Invasion of Britain in Texts for Children," in *Reading History in Children's Books* (Palgrave Macmillan, 2012), 17–47.
77 Dan'el Kahn, "Taharqa, King of Kush and the Assyrians," *JSSEA* 31 (2004): 109–28.
78 Victory stela of Esarhaddon. Daniel David Luckenbill, *Ancient Records of Assyria and Babylonia*, vol. 2 (University of Chicago Press, 1927), 227.
79 Kendall, *Between the Cataracts*, 120–21.
80 After Kendall and Mohamed, *A Visitor's Guide to the Jebel Barkal Temples*, 34.
81 Shellal stela; Miriam Lichtheim, *Ancient Egyptian Literature*, vol. III, 85.

CHAPTER 7

1 Erik Hornung, *The Egyptian Book of Gates* (Living Human Heritage Publications, 2014), 46. The text is located at the first division heading toward the second gate.
2 Ernestine Friedl, "Society and Sex Roles," in *Applying Cultural Anthropology: An Introductory Reader* (McGraw Hill, 2002).
3 Andrew Krietz, "Florida Man Kills Self, Wife and 2 Children in Apparent Murder-Suicide," *WTSP Tampa Bay News*, April 6, 2020, www.wtsp.com/article/news/local/polkcounty/haines-city-murder-suicide-mark-joseph-family-shooting/67-c6c6f4f3-cd65-42cf-a87b-229fdc7328f5.
4 "Mass Shooting at Orlando Gay Club: The Latest," *CBS News*, June 13, 2016, www.cbsnews.com/news/mass-shooting-orlando-gay-club-pulse-the-latest/.
5 "Gunman Opens Fire on Las Vegas Concert Crowd, Wounding Hundreds and Killing 58," *History.com*, October 1, 2017, www.history.com/this-day-in-history/2017-las-vegas-shooting.
6 Jason Kotowski, "Man Raped Woman at Gunpoint After She Rebuffed His Advances,

Reports Say," *KGET Bakersfield,* August 19, 2019, www.kget.com/news/crime-watch/man-raped-woman-at-gunpoint-after-she-rebuffed-his-advances-reports-say.

7 Khushbu Shah, "Ahmaud Arbery: Anger Mounts Over Killing of Black Jogger Caught on Video," *The Guardian,* May 6, 2020, www.theguardian.com/us-news/2020/may/06/ahmaud-arbery-shooting-georgia.

8 Ryan Golden, "5th Cir.: No Retaliation in Walmart's Firing of Worker Who Reported Sex Harassment," *HR Dive,* August 31, 2020, www.hrdive.com/news/5th-cir-no-retaliation-in-walmarts-firing-of-worker-who-reported-sex-har/584193.

9 Molly Rosbach, "LGBTQ Military Service Members at Higher Risk of Sexual Harassment, Assault, Stalking," *Oregon State University Newsroom,* April 21, 2020, today.oregonstate.edu/news/lgbtq-military-service-members-higher-risk-sexual-harassment-assault-stalking.

10 Alex Morris, "The Forsaken: A Rising Number of Homeless Gay Teens Are Being Cast Out by Religious Families," *Rolling Stone,* September 3, 2014, www.rollingstone.com/culture/culture-news/the-forsaken-a-rising-number-of-homeless-gay-teens-are-being-cast-out-by-religious-families-46746.

11 Meagan Flynn, "'What Trash Are You Speaking?': A San Diego Man Beat a Syrian Refugee Teen for Talking in Arabic," *Washington Post,* November 5, 2019, www.washingtonpost.com/nation/2019/11/05/san-diego-man-beats-syrian-teen-speaking-arabic.

12 Victor Williams, "Woman Killed by Husband in Warren Had Recently Left Him, Filed for Divorce, Family Says," *ClickOnDetroit,* October 12, 2020, www.clickondetroit.com/news/local/2020/10/12/woman-killed-by-husband-in-warren-had-recently-left-him-filed-for-divorce-family-says.

13 Katherine Blouin, Monica Hanna, and Sarah E. Bond, "How Academics, Egyptologists, and Even Melania Trump Benefit From Colonialist Cosplay," *Hyperallergic* (October 22, 2020), https://hyperallergic.com/595896/how-academics-egyptologists-and-even-melania-trump-benefit-from-colonialist-cosplay.

14 Charlene Spretnak, "Anatomy of a Backlash: Concerning the Work of Marija Gimbutas," *Journal of Archaeomythology* 7 (2011): 1–27.

15 See Australia, Canada, New Zealand, Spain, and Mexico with the highest ratings for women's workforce equality according to the Council on Foreign Relations, www.cfr.org/legal-barriers/country-rankings.

INDEX

as source of power and
wealth, 269–70, 272–
73
see also Piankhy, King;
Taharqa, King
Kushner, Jared, 109

L

Labor camps, 195–98
Language, 187–88, 282–83,
311, 312, 313
Levant, 136, 156, 180, 204,
237, 243–44, 263
Lewis, John, 350
Libya and Libyans, 241, 242,
263, 277, 279–80, 283,
291, 295–96
Lincoln, Abraham, 171
Louis IX, King of France,
114–15
Louis XIV, King of France,
114, 142–43, 149
Louis XVI, King of France,
143
Loyalist Instructions, 144–45
Luxor. *see* Thebes

M

Maat (goddess), 205, *insert 12*
Ma'at (order/right/truth),
36–38, 39–40, 257, 286,
288, 323
Macedonians, 317, 318
Maiherperi (royal
bodyguard), 278–79, 280
Malcolm X, 350
Manetho (priest), 55–56,
218–19
Mao Zedong, 18, 197, 248
Marcus Aurelius, Roman
Emperor, 171
Masculinity, 170–71, 194
McCloskey, Mark and
Patricia, 341

Medical Egyptology, 168
Medinet Habu, 41, 309
Memphis, 62, 105, 108, 175,
182, 213, 221, 257, 292,
296–97, 314
Menkaure, King, 94–95
Menkheperre (priest), 276
Mentuhotep II, King, 125–
26, 134
Mercenaries, 235, 236, 241,
280
Mereret (daughter of
Senwosret III), *insert 6*
Merneptah, King, 204, 263,
275–76
Meskell, Lynn, 348
Middle Egyptian language,
187, 282–83
Military
Akhenaten's campaigns,
275
Amenemhat I's
campaigns, 106–7
empowered elite in, 189,
216–18, 225–26
mercenaries, 235, 236, 241,
280
populism and, 239–40
professionalized, 136–37,
156–57
Psamtik II's campaigns,
317
Ramesside rise and, 220–
22
Ramses II's campaigns,
234–38, 243
Senwosret III's
campaigns, 136
Seti I's campaigns, 225,
233–34
Taharqa's campaigns,
299–300
technologies, 233, 276
wealth from war, 224–25,
234

Min (god), 128
Monotheism, 17, 204–9
Monthu (god), 308
Montuemhat, mayor of
Thebes, 306
Monuments. *see* Confederate
monuments; Pyramids;
Temples and statuary
programs; Tombs
Morgan, Jacques de, 146
Morsi, Mohamed, 240
Mubarak, Hosni, 240
Mugabe, Robert, 330
Mummification, 91–92, 231
Mut (goddess), 271, 284,
308, *insert 16*
Muwatalli II, King of the
Hittites, 235, 238

N

Nakhtmin (general), 216
Narmer Palette, 41, 95, 116
Nationalism, 138, 306
Ne'arin, 236
Necho, King, 316
Nefertari, Queen, 212, 249–
50, *insert 12*
Nefertiti, Queen, *insert 9,
insert 10*
as co-king, 200–201
imagery, 176–77, 192–93,
199–200
modern admiration of,
21–22
names, 186, 200, 210
rule after Akhenaten's
death, 210
wealth distribution and,
17
Neferu, Queen, 129
Neferusobek, Queen, 111,
148
Nefret (wife of Rahotep),
89
Neo-Babylonians, 317

ILLUSTRATIONS CREDITS

Cover, O. Louis Mazzatenta; 1, DEA/A. Jemolo/De Agostini via Getty Images; 2 (UP), Newton and Co/The Print Collector/Getty Images; 2 (LO), Library of Congress Prints and Photographs Division (1s21300); 3, Plate 5 from *Views in Egypt*, engraved by Thomas Milton (1743–1827) pub. by Robert Bowyer (1758–1834) 1801 (aquatint)/The Stapleton Collection/Bridgeman Images; 4, DEA/G. Dagli Orti/De Agostini via Getty Images; 5, © The Trustees of The British Museum/Art Resource, NY; 6 (UP), DeAgostini Picture Library/Getty Images; 6 (LO), Metropolitan Museum of Art (17.9.2), Gift of Edward S. Harkness, 1917; 7, Werner Otto/Alamy Stock Photo; 8, Rena Effendi/National Geographic Image Collection; 9 (UP), The Walters Art Museum, Baltimore, Maryland, Acquired by Henry Walters, 1929, Accession number 42.71; 9 (LO), Mike P Shepherd/Alamy Stock Photo; 10 (UP), bpk Bildagentur/ Aegyptisches Museum, Staatliche Museen, Berlin, Germany/Jürgen Liepe/Art Resource, NY; 10 (LO), Kenneth Garrett/National Geographic Image Collection; 11, Werner Forman Archive/Heritage Images/Alamy Stock Photo; 12 (UP), Kenneth Garrett; 12 (LO), Luisa Ricciarini/ Bridgeman Images; 13, Peter de Clercq/Alamy Stock Photo; 14, Aldo Pavan/Horizons WWP/Alamy Stock Photo; 15 (UP), Ashmolean Museum/Heritage Images/Getty Images; 15 (LO), DeAgostini/G. Dagli Orti/Getty Images; 16, Marcin Jamkowski/Adventure Pictures/Alamy Stock Photo; back cover, Mike P Shepherd/Alamy Stock Photo.

ABOUT THE AUTHOR

Kara Cooney is a professor of Egyptology at UCLA. Specializing in social history, gender studies, and economies in the ancient world, she received her Ph.D. in Egyptology from Johns Hopkins University. In 2005, she was co-curator of *Tutankhamun and the Golden Age of the Pharaohs* at the Los Angeles County Museum of Art. Cooney produced a comparative archaeology television series, titled *Out of Egypt,* which aired in 2009 on the Discovery Channel and is available online via YouTube and Amazon.

The Woman Who Would Be King: Hatshepsut's Rise to Power in Ancient Egypt, Cooney's first trade book, was released in 2014, and draws on her expert perspective of Egypt's ancient history to craft an illuminating biography of its least well-known female king.

Cooney's current research in coffin reuse, primarily focusing on the Bronze Age collapse during Egypt's 20th and 21st dynasties, is ongoing. Her research provides an up close look at the socioeconomic and political turmoil that affected even funerary and burial practices in ancient Egypt. This project has taken her around the world over the span of 10 years to study and document nearly 300 coffins in various collections, including those in Cairo, London, Paris, Turin, Berlin, Brussels, New York, Vienna, Florence, and Vatican City. Her books *Recycling for Death* and *Ancient Egyptian Society: Challenging Assumptions, Exploring Approaches* are forthcoming.